The

DISAPPOINTED

Religion in North America

CATHERINE L. ALBANESE AND STEPHEN J. STEIN, SERIES EDITORS

The
DISAPPOINTED

Millerism and Millenarianism
in the Nineteenth Century

EDITED BY
Ronald L. Numbers and Jonathan M. Butler

WITH ILLUSTRATIONS SELECTED BY JAMES R. NIX

Indiana
University
Press

BLOOMINGTON AND INDIANAPOLIS

Manufactured in the United States of America

Library of Congress Cataloging-in-Publication Data
The Disappointed: Millerism and Millenarianism in the
  Nineteenth Century.

  (Religion in North America)
  Includes index.
    1. Adventists—History—19th century.   2. Millennial-
ism—History of doctrines—19th century.   I. Numbers,
Ronald L.   I. Butler, Jonathan M.   III. Series.
BS6115.D57   1987   286.7'09'034   86-45504
ISBN 0-253-34299-6

1 2 3 4 5 91 90 89 88 87

TO

Vern Carner

FROM

His Friends

CONTENTS

Illustrations

Foreword

This collection of essays edited by Ronald L. Numbers and Jonathan M. Butler signals the coming of age of the study of the Millerites. Rising above the cultural prejudices and religious stereotypes of earlier writers in the nineteenth and twentieth centuries, the authors of these essays demonstrate the promise of the new wave of scholarship committed to understanding Millerism within the broader context of America's religious history. Collectively they lay to rest the caricature of the Millerites as white-robed fanatics awaiting the end of the world on mountaintops.

The essayists situate the prophet William Miller and his followers firmly within antebellum Protestant culture. They show the close relationship between the rise of Millerism and the other major cultural forces of the day—evangelicalism, reformism, and especially millennialism. Exploring parallels between Millerism and other millennial expressions at the time, they examine the problems the Millerites incurred by apocalyptic "time-setting" and the impact of the inevitable disappointments.

In this volume we are drawn, too, into a world in which biblical prophecy fueled convictions concerning the eternal plans of God and led to organizational activities on the temporal and human plane. The connection between Millerism and abolitionism is one evidence of the interaction between scriptural logic and social action. We gain insight into the dynamics responsible for the expansion of one man's private judgments into a popular, if not mass, movement with far-reaching religious and cultural impact. Here we also observe the millenarian link that ties the Millerite movement to the Adventist tradition of the twentieth century.

These essays have the further advantage of highlighting possibilities for additional study. Although the essayists include some of the brightest scholars at work in the field today, the editors, duly cautious, present this volume as an opening chapter in a larger undertaking. Indeed, among the topics inviting additional exploration several deserve special mention. The enigma of Miller himself remains largely unsolved. More critical work on him, on Joshua Himes his publicist, and on other leaders in the movement still needs doing. Further examination of the exegetical basis for Millerite prophetic calculations and for sociopolitical involvement by members of the movement still demands attention.

Above all, *The Disappointed* establishes that Millerism is best understood not in terms of eccentricity, pathology, deviance, or deprivation—social, economic, psychological, or religious—but as representative of the religious outlook of nineteenth-century America. As such, this volume takes its place alongside a growing body of literature that questions the adequacy of the notion of a religious mainstream surrounded by groups on the sectarian margin. Here the "marginal" Millerites are shown to be participants in the cultural center of religious life in the mid-nineteenth century.

Catherine L. Albanese
Stephen J. Stein, Series Editors

Acknowledgments

This volume grew out of a conference on "Millerism and the Millenarian Mind in 19th-Century America," held at the Cortina Inn in Killington, Vermont, May 31 to June 3, 1984, in honor of Vern Carner. That event, organized by Wayne R. Judd and Ronald L. Numbers, was sponsored by the following friends of Vern's:

Stan Aufdemberg
Harold Campbell
Barbara Carner
Duayne Christensen
Everett and Opal Dick
Ed and Ellie Distler
Wayne and Audrey Judd
Ron Maddox
Stanley and Suzanne Mills
Ron and Janet Numbers

Additional financial support came from Bruce Anderson, Joe and Pauline Carner, Virgil Carner, Dorothea Cheek, George Chen, Bill and Darlene Hemmerlin, John and Maurine Henderson, Alice Holst, Eric Tsao, and Vern and Linda Usher. To all we are deeply grateful.

The Association of Adventist Forums, through the good graces of its former president and current director of special projects, Glenn E. Coe, cosponsored the conference. We are especially indebted to Richard C. Osborn, AAF treasurer, for overseeing our financial affairs.

Planning for the conference began in 1980, at which time Edwin S. Gaustad, Jonathan Butler, and the late Ernest R. Sandeen consented to serve as project advisors, suggesting both topics and possible participants. Before his untimely death in 1982, Ernie contributed enthusiastically to the design of the conference; his absence in 1984 was deeply felt.

The quality of the conference—and of this book—was greatly enhanced by the comments and suggestions of the following invited participants:

Catherine L. Albanese, Wright State University
Roy Branson, Georgetown University
Glenn E. Coe, West Hartford, Connecticut
James West Davidson, New Haven, Connecticut
David A. Dean, Berkshire Christian College
Louis Filler, Ovid, Michigan
Edwin S. Gaustad, University of California, Riverside
Clarence C. Goen, Wesley Theological Seminary
Nathan O. Hatch, University of Notre Dame
Terry Hill, Cambridge, Massachusetts

Gary Land, Andrews University
R. Laurence Moore, Cornell University
James H. Moorhead, Princeton Theological Seminary
Rennie B. Schoepflin, Loma Linda University
Robert David Thomas, Chagrin Falls, Ohio
Timothy Weber, Denver Conservative Baptist Seminary

The final session of the conference was held in William Miller's chapel, adjacent to his home. Ross Lauterbach, secretary-treasurer of the New York Conference of Seventh-day Adventists, kindly arranged for the use of this historic building, where Ron Graybill led us in the singing of Millerite hymns. James R. Nix, of Loma Linda University Libraries, guided us to Miller's grave and to Ascension Rock, where Miller reportedly awaited the Second Coming; Nix also arranged for a display of Millerite documents and charts.

In the preparation of this volume we have benefited much from the advice of Catherine L. Albanese and Stephen J. Stein, coeditors of the *Religion in North America* series at Indiana University Press. We also wish to acknowledge the secretarial assistance provided by Carolyn Hackler and Julie Bixby of the Department of the History of Medicine, University of Wisconsin-Madison.

R.L.N.
J.M.B.

Introduction

JONATHAN M. BUTLER AND RONALD L. NUMBERS

William Miller, a nineteenth-century farmer and Baptist layman from Low Hampton, New York, has been called "the most famous millenarian in American history."[1] On the basis of the biblical prophecy found in Daniel 8:14— "Unto two thousand and three hundred days; then shall the sanctuary be cleansed"—he calculated that Christ would return to earth "about the year 1843," 2,300 years after Artaxerxes of Persia issued a decree to rebuild Jerusalem. By the early 1830s, he was circuit-riding small-town New England with an illustrated series of lectures, and within a decade he was preaching in the major cities of the Northeast and leading the most popular millenarian movement America has seen.

Following a series of failed prophecies in 1843 and 1844, which culminated in the Great Disappointment of October 22, 1844, the movement collapsed, splintering into three main factions. The largest body, which included Miller and other prominent leaders, admitted their incorrect chronology but continued to expect the imminent end of the world; they later took the name Advent Christians. A much smaller group, sometimes called the "spiritualizers," insisted that the Second Advent had actually occurred—in a spiritual sense—on October 22, but within a short time many of these ex-Millerites had joined other religious movements such as the Shakers. A third faction, the future Seventh-day Adventists, rationalized that Christ had entered the "most holy place" of a "heavenly sanctuary" on October 22 and that he would soon return to the earth.

Add to the above sketch of Millerism and its aftermath the obligatory references to ascension robes, insanity, and suicide, and you approximate a summary of popular and even scholarly knowledge of the movement. Much of the credit (or blame) for perpetuating the negative image of Millerites as religious fanatics goes to Clara Endicott Sears, whose fascinating but uncritical collection of reminiscences, *Days of Delusion: A Strange Bit of History* (1924), titillated readers with stories of white gowns and broken minds.[2]

Such accounts prompted Francis D. Nichol, a Seventh-day Adventist minister, to issue a laboriously researched but partisan reply on the occasion of the hundredth anniversary of the Great Disappointment. In *The Midnight Cry: A Defense of the Character and Conduct of William Miller and the Millerites, Who Mistakenly Believed that the Second Coming of Christ Would Take Place in the Year 1844*, Nichol self-consciously eschewed the detached style of the historian for the special pleading of a defense attorney. His great concern with refuting allegations of ascension robes and insanity apparently stemmed from a fear that some readers might conclude that all believers in the Second Advent—including those living in the twentieth century—were "at least mildly deranged."[3] Despite Nichol's overtly apologetical stance, his argument swayed many professional historians, including Whitney R. Cross, whose classic, *The Burned-over District* (1950), canonized Nichol's findings.[4]

Another self-made Adventist historian and hagiographer, LeRoy Edwin Froom, conveyed a large though astigmatic vision of the millenarian tradition in his monumental four-volume survey of *The Prophetic Faith of Our Fathers* (1954), the last volume of which devoted nearly a thousand pages to the Millerite movement and the theological context in which it arose.[5] Although he provided a useful catalog of millennial dogmatics down through the centuries, his determination to connect a pristine apostolic faith to the rise of Seventh-day Adventism by way of a single, unbroken chain hampered his historical judgment.

The sheer bulk of Nichol's and Froom's evidence tended to obscure a less defensive historical tradition within the Adventist community. As early as 1874 Isaac C. Wellcome, an Advent Christian, had included a relatively dispassionate account of the Millerites in his *History of the Second Advent Message and Mission, Doctrine and People,* and in 1930 a young Seventh-day Adventist historian, Everett N. Dick, had written his Ph.D. dissertation at the University of Wisconsin on "The Adventist Crisis of 1843–1844," the first such study by a trained historian.[6] However, because of Dick's candor in treating the Millerites, Nichol and Froom exercised their ecclesiastical authority over him as a new instructor at a small Adventist college in Nebraska and suppressed publication of his manuscript.[7] Although Dick went on to become a prolific and respected historian of the American frontier, his dissertation remained unpublished, and Seventh-day Adventists framed the official version of their past as if his work did not exist. Significantly, neither Nichol nor Froom deigned to mention Dick's thesis in their extensive bibliographies.

Only lately has the study of Millerism achieved its historiographical "ascension" from the more earthbound denominational histories of the apologists. This is particularly surprising in view of the efflorescence of scholarship on American millenarianism in the 1970s, which transformed our understanding of millenarians much as studies in the 1930s had recast the image of the Puritans. As a consequence, historians, comparative religionists, social scientists, and literary critics came to find in millenarians less a marginal impulse toward eccentricity and pathology than a sustained and pervasive drive toward cultural revitalization and reform. In fact, the millennial myth in American life has proven so resilient and malleable that some scholars have moved it from the periphery to the center of the nation's self-understanding.[8] Yet these advances in our appreciation of American millenarianism have only rarely been tested in the historical laboratory of Millerism, leaving this mass movement of national and international proportions less familiar to most students of millenarianism than the cargo cults of Melanesia.

The modest awakening of scholarly interest in Millerism in recent years has resulted in part from the work of Advent Christians and Seventh-day Adventists who have gone on for advanced training in history and mined the Millerite experience for research topics. The most influential of these studies, David T. Arthur's "'Come out of Babylon': A Study of Millerite Separatism and Denominationalism, 1840–1865" (1970), produced several instructive articles on Millerism.[9] Beyond the Adventist circle, David L. Rowe in 1974 completed a doctoral dissertation at the University of Virginia, subsequently published as *Thunder and Trumpets: Millerites and Dissenting Religion in Upstate New York, 1800–1850* (1985), which showed how Millerites drew on contemporary revivalism, millennialism, and pietism to create a mass movement; and Ruth Alden Doan, in a dissertation on "The Miller Heresy, Millennialism and American Culture" (1984), for the first time systematically explored the consequences of Millerism for American evangelicalism.[10] The Millerites have also received sympathetic treatment in such recent studies of American religious and cultural history as Ernest R. Sandeen's *The Roots of Fundamentalism: British and American Millenarianism, 1800–1930* (1970), J. F. C. Harrison's *The Second Coming: Popular Millenarianism, 1780–1850* (1979), R. Laurence Moore's *Religious Outsiders and the Making of Americans* (1986), and Michael Barkun's *Crucible of the Millennium: The Burned-over District in the 1840s* (1986).[11]

The 1984 conference on "Millerism and the Millenarian Mind in 19th-Century America," from which this volume resulted, formally marked a new direction in Millerite studies, because for the first time it brought together both Adventist and non-Adventist scholars interested in critically evaluating the Millerite experience and its place in American history. Although this modest volume of essays cannot bring to bear on Millerism all the methodological questions of current millenarian studies, anymore than it can provide a comprehensive narrative of the movement, it informs both enterprises.

The initial wave of contemporary scholarship on millenarianism tended to stress the disinherited or disenfranchised status of millenarians or to emphasize the pathologic or deviant aspects of the millenarian mind.[12] Although both viewpoints have been either refuted or greatly refined by later millenarian scholars, they remain relevant to Millerite studies, where they have enjoyed a long and persistent history.

As early as 1927, the sociologist Reuben E. Harkness characterized Millerites as "poor and oppressed" and linked their revival to the Panic of 1837. In 1974 Ernest R. Sandeen suggested (but later rejected) the notion that the Millerites and other millenarians were only relatively deprived; though often prosperous and socially respected, they felt anxious and insecure in a rapidly changing world.[13] In Chapter 1 of this volume, David L. Rowe employs a careful demographic analysis of Millerites in upstate New York, along with New England, the area of greatest strength, to show that they were neither materially nor politically deprived. Although earlier revolutionary apocalyptists of Britain and Europe had seemed scandalous because of their social marginality, Rowe indicates the degree to which the Millerites differed sociologically from their ideological ancestors.

The issue of psychopathology dates back to the 1840s, when Millerites and their critics argued heatedly over the relationship between the Advent message and insanity. Sears and Nichol continued the debate in the twentieth century, with Sears emphasizing Millerite deviance and Nichol insisting that Millerism had not caused a single case of insanity.[14] In Chapter 6 Ronald L. Numbers, a medical historian, and Janet S. Numbers, a clinical psychologist, relegate the question of causation to secondary status. Although their detailed examination of nineteenth-century asylum records indicates that the Millerite excitement sometimes attracted the mentally unstable and on rare occasions caused the emotionally vulnerable to crack under the strain, they redirect attention to the question of why so many contemporaries believed that Millerism caused insanity.

If the study of Millerism includes the dispossessed or disturbed on the margins of society, it does not confine itself there. For, as Rowe argues in Chapter 1, most Millerites were indistinguishable from their neighbors. Their movement comprised a cross section of Yankee society from a geographical and cultural zone that flowed from New England across upstate New York and on past the Western Reserve of Ohio to Michigan.[15] They were neither as odd and heretical as their enemies accused them of being nor as distinctive as the Millerites themselves claimed to be. As Ruth Alden Doan shows in Chapter 7, on the "Miller heresy," they shared the contemporary cultural ethos more than they spurned it. In her discussion of the Millerite relationship to the broader evangelical culture, she indicates the degree to which the Adventists sought to conserve an orthodoxy that evangelicals were squandering. Thus, for historians, the fluidity of the early Republic renders the categories of "marginality" and "mainstream" as arbitrary and inadequate as the colonial American experience does those of "sect" and "church."

The antebellum American longing for millennial happiness proliferated numerous crusades to reform society and encouraged experiments aimed at perfecting this world, or at least a small part of it. The remarkable continuities between the Millerites and contemporary reformers further blur the distinction that once prevailed in millenarian studies between pessimistic, catastrophic, and quietist premillennialists and optimistic, progressive, and reformist post-millennialists.[16] For why was it that so many Millerite leaders came from the ranks of the abolitionists and the temperance and health reformers? And if their espousal of Adventism meant an abandonment of reform, which it sometimes did, to what extent did Millerites and social reformers continue to share a common ideology and sociology? In short, what does a study of Millerism reveal about the reform spirit of the era? These and other questions are informed by Ronald Graybill's case study of the abolitionist-Millerite connection (Chapter 8) and by Louis Billington's discussion of Millerite reform activities in Great Britain (Chapter 4).

If a study of Millerism casts light on the spirit of reform, it illuminates several of the new religious movements as well. Various forms of reciprocity developed between the Millerites and three groups explored in this volume: the Oneida perfectionists, the Shakers, and the Seventh-day Adventists, each of whom realized a distinctive version of the American millennial dream. Competing movements commonly used the Millerites as a foil, but in Chapter 9 Michael Barkun uncovers the fact that the leader of the Oneida community, John Humphrey Noyes, found them to be not only a challenge to his eschatological system but a threat to his personal identity as a prophet-founder. Millerite-Shaker relations, however, proved cordial. In Chapter 10 Lawrence Foster finds that a number of former Millerites overcame the disappointment of 1844 by joining the Shaker fold and drawing, at least for a time, upon the Shakers' theological and social resources. One of the smallest and obscurest of Millerite scions found still another solution to its disillusionment in forming Seventh-day Adventism. In his discussion of this metamorphosis, Jonathan M. Butler in Chapter 11 reveals how one ephemeral millenarian cause produced a durable and successful sect.

In their influential psychosocial study of failed prophecies Leon Festinger, Henry W. Riecken, and Stanley Schachter argued that the "disconfirmation of October 22 brought about the collapse of Millerism," finally shattering all hope and destroying faith.[17] However, Adventism's afterlife among both the Shakers and the Seventh-day Adventists calls this interpretation into question. As the anthropologist Kenelm Burridge has argued, although the promised Parousia never materializes for millenarians, they often form a meaningful millenarian culture that avoids a sense of failed prophecy.[18] Foster's essay explores the deep emotional and intellectual dynamics that underpin millenarian movements and drive them to succeed despite the specific disconfirmation of prophecy, while Butler's Seventh-day Adventist "success story" digs beneath the cognitive surface to the social and cultural aspects of Adventism's survival. In this case the millenarians moved from charisma to order, spirit to structure—but in doing so their millenarianism was transformed into something else and therefore did not succeed as millenarianism. In Chapter 5 Eric Anderson offers further evidence of the malleability of the millenarian mind in his examination of the first Millerite experiment in prophetic time-setting: the prediction that Turkey would fall and probation for the wicked would end on August 11, 1840. The apparent disconfirmation not only failed to discourage the faithful but established a pattern for dealing with future disappointments in a nonfalsifiable way.

Although biographical studies offer an excellent means of exploring the Millerite experience and the psychology of dealing with disappointment, few such works exist. In fact, the only useful biography of William Miller is Sylvester Bliss's *Memoirs of William Miller, Generally Known as a Lecturer on the Prophecies, and the Second Coming of Christ*, a life-and-letters account that appeared over a century ago.[19] To help fill this void, we have included in an appendix three autobiographical recollections of the Millerite disappointment: by Luther Boutelle, a Millerite lecturer from Massachusetts who became a

leader of the Advent Christians; by Hiram Edson, a New York farmer who
joined the sabbatarian group of ex-Millerites; and by Henry B. Bear, an obscure
Millerite from Pennsylvania who joined the Shakers.[20]

In addition, two essays in this volume adopt a biographical approach:
Wayne R. Judd's sketch of Miller as a "disappointed prophet" (Chapter 2) and
David Arthur's portrait of Joshua V. Himes (Chapter 3), whose skill as an
organizer and publisher rescued Miller from obscurity. Using his considerable
talents as a propagandist, Himes launched what Nathan O. Hatch has called
"an unprecedented media blitz," circulating millions of copies of books, pamphlets, periodicals, and tracts. "The irony of Millerism," notes Hatch, "is that it
used the very latest communication techniques to champion a message of cosmic
intervention utterly opposed to cultural trends of the nineteenth century."[21]
After the Great Disappointment Himes briefly continued his crusade in Great
Britain, where, Louis Billington points out in Chapter 4, he hoped success
abroad would rekindle interest back home in the United States.

The significance of Millerism transcends the merely historical: its millenarian vision reflects a recurring quest that lies at the very heart of the human
experience. "To dream a dream and make it come true; to realize the shape of
what can be seen only in the mind's eye; to feel compelled to bring about the
seemingly impossible—these are the prerogatives of man," writes Burridge.
"Whether as fool, fraud, saint, respectable bourgeois, farmer or tycoon, the pain
of the millennium belongs only to man. It is why he is man, why, when the time
comes, he has to make a new man."[22] In the early American Republic, the
Millerite emerged as a provocative and important expression of this "new
man."

The possibilities for exploring the Millerite experience have increased
manyfold in recent years—largely through the efforts of one person, Vern
Carner, in whose honor the conference on "Millerism and the Millenarian Mind
in 19th-Century America" was originally held and to whom this book is now
dedicated. As a student at Union College in Nebraska in the early 1960s, Carner
came under the influence of Everett Dick and, like him, became enamored of
Millerite and early Adventist history. Later Carner studied church history at
Andrews University and the University of California at Riverside, where he met
Edwin S. Gaustad. While serving as an instructor in church history at Loma
Linda University in the early 1970s, he organized a path-breaking series of
lectures on the historical roots of Adventism, which were subsequently edited by
Gaustad and published under the title *The Rise of Adventism: Religion and
Society in Mid-Nineteenth-Century America* (1974). Although this volume
contains a number of notable essays, its lasting value will almost certainly derive
from the monumental 110-page bibliography of Millerite and post-Millerite
sources compiled by Carner in collaboration with Sakae Kubo and Curt Rice.[23]
Carner also put all future Millerite historians in his debt by editing for Xerox
University Microfilms a comprehensive collection of sources on "William Miller, the Millerites, and Early Adventists" (1977).

Carner's indefatigable energy and organizational drive played a central role in both the professionalization and popularization of Adventist history in the 1970s. He founded *Adventist Heritage: A Magazine of Adventist History*, now in its second decade of publication, helped to organize *Studies in Adventist History*, the first volume of which has recently appeared, and inaugurated a series of reprints of Millerite and early Adventist documents. Behind the scenes, he repeatedly provided crucial encouragement and support for students of Millerite and Adventist history, and in 1973 he assisted Ray Allen Billington in editing a *festschrift* in honor of Everett Dick.[24]

In 1975 Carner left academic life to pursue other careers, first in specialty advertising as president of Davis and Stanton Advertising in Dallas, Texas, later in the feed and cattle business in southern California and Hawaii. During these years he and his wife, Barbara, worked through the Carner Foundation to foster a number of scholarly activities, including an international conference in 1981 on "Christianity and Science: 2000 Years of Conflict and Compromise."[25] The present volume, offered as a token of appreciation by his friends, is our way of saying "Thank you, Vern Carner. You made a difference."

N O T E S

1. Ernest R. Sandeen, *The Roots of Fundamentalism: British and American Millenarianism, 1800–1930* (Chicago: University of Chicago Press, 1970), p. 50.

2. Clara Endicott Sears, *Days of Delusion: A Strange Bit of History* (Boston: Houghton Mifflin, 1924). Sears was not the first historian to draw attention to alleged Millerite fanaticism; see, e.g., John B. McMaster, *A History of the People of the United States*, 8 vols. (New York: D. Appleton, 1883–1913), 7: 134–141. Sears's influence can be seen in such works as David M. Ludlum, *Social Ferment in Vermont, 1791–1850* (New York: Columbia University Press, 1939), pp. 256–257; and Alice Felt Tyler, *Freedom's Ferment: Phases of American Social History from the Colonial Period to the Outbreak of the Civil War* (New York: Harper & Row, 1962; first published in 1944), pp. 70–78.

3. Francis D. Nichol, *The Midnight Cry: A Defense of William Miller and the Millerites* (Washington, D.C.: Review and Herald Publishing Association, 1944), p. 14. Nichol summarized his case against Millerite insanity and gown-wearing in "The Growth of the Millerite Legend," *Church History*, 1952, 21: 296–313.

4. Whitney R. Cross, *The Burned-Over District: The Social and Intellectual History of Enthusiastic Religion in Western New York, 1800–1850* (Ithaca, N.Y.: Cornell University Press, 1950), pp. 287–321, esp. 306. William Warren Sweet, *Religion in the Development of American Culture, 1765–1840* (New York: Charles Scribner's Sons, 1952), p. 307, acknowledges that Nichol had "convincingly shown that many of the stories of the excesses committed by the Millerites had little basis in fact." Cross and Sweet, as well as Nichol, overlooked Ira V. Brown's pioneering essay, "The Millerites and the Boston Press," *New England Quarterly*, 1943, 16: 592–614, which concluded that "Unquestionably many of the reports regarding Millerites were highly inaccurate" (p. 614). See also Ira V. Brown, "Watchers for the Second Coming: The Millenarian Tradition in America," *Mississippi Valley Historical Review*, 1952, 39: 441–458.

5. LeRoy Edwin Froom, *The Prophetic Faith of Our Fathers*, 4 vols. (Washington, D.C.: Review and Herald Publishing Association, 1946–54).

6. Isaac C. Wellcome, *History of the Second Advent Message and Mission, Doctrine and People* (Yarmouth, Maine: I. C. Wellcome, 1874); Everett N. Dick, "The Adventist Crisis of 1843–1844" (Ph.D. dissertation, University of Wisconsin, 1930). For an updated summary of Dick's study, see Everett N. Dick, "The Millerite Movement, 1830–1845," in *Adventism in America: A History*, ed. Gary Land (Grand Rapids, Mich.: William B. Eerdmans, 1986), pp. 1–35.

7. Everett Dick discussed these events with Jonathan Butler in the course of several conversations in 1974–75.

8. For recent reviews of the literature, see Leonard I. Sweet, "Millennialism in America: Recent Studies," *Theological Studies*, 1979, 40: 510–531; and Hillel Schwartz, "The End of the Beginning: Millenarian Studies, 1969–1975," *Religious Studies Review*, July 1976, 2: 1–15.

9. David T. Arthur, "'Come out of Babylon': A Study of Millerite Separatism and Denominationalism, 1840–1865" (Ph.D. dissertation, University of Rochester, 1970); David T. Arthur, "Millerism," in *The Rise of Adventism: Religion and Society in Mid-Nineteenth-Century America*, ed. Edwin S. Gaustad (New York: Harper and Row, 1974), pp. 154–172; David T. Arthur, "After the Great Disappointment: To Albany and Beyond," *Adventist Heritage*, January, 1974, 1: 5–10, 58. For regional studies of Millerism, see N. Gordon Thomas, "The Second Coming in the Third New England: The Millerite Impulse in Michigan, 1830–60" (Ph.D. dissertation, Michigan State University, 1967); N. Gordon Thomas, "The Millerite Movement in Ohio," *Ohio History*, 1972, 81: 95–107; and Robert W. Olson, "Southern Baptists' Reactions to Millerism" (Th.D. dissertation, Southwestern Baptist Theological Seminary, 1972). For less dispassionate studies focusing on the ways in which Advent Christians and Seventh-day Adventists interpreted the Millerite experience, see David Arnold Dean, "Echoes of the Midnight Cry: The Millerite Heritage in the Apologetics of the Advent Christian Denomination, 1860–1960" (Th.D. dissertation, Westminster Theological Seminary, 1976); P. Gerard Damsteegt, *Foundations of the Seventh-day Adventist Message and Mission* (Grand Rapids, Mich: William B. Eerdmans, 1977), based on a Doctor of Theology dissertation submitted to the Free University of Amsterdam; Ingemar Lindén, *The Last Trump: An Historico-Genetical Study of Some Important Chapters in the Making and Development of the Seventh-day Adventist Church* (Frankfurt-am-Main: Peter Lang, 1978); and Clyde E. Hewitt, *Midnight and Morning: An Account of the Adventist Awakening and the Founding of the Advent Christian Denomination, 1831–1860* (Charlotte, N.C.: Venture Books, 1983).

10. David L. Rowe, *Thunder and Trumpets: Millerites and Dissenting Religion in Upstate New York, 1800–1850* (Chico, Calif.: Scholars Press, 1985); Ruth Alden Doan, "The Miller Heresy, Millennialism and American Culture" (Ph.D. dissertation, University of North Carolina at Chapel Hill, 1984). Rowe also published three articles based on his dissertation: "Elon Galusha and the Millerite Movement," *Foundations: A Baptist Journal of History and Theology*, 1975, 18: 252–260; "Comets and Eclipses: The Millerites, Nature, and the Apocalypse," *Adventist Heritage*, Winter, 1976, 3: 10–19; and "A New Perspective on the Burned-Over District: The Millerites in Upstate New York," *Church History*, 1978, 47: 408–420. For a study of seven Adventist bodies that grew out of Millerism, see Raymond J. Bean, "The Influence of William Miller in the History of American Christianity" (Th.D. dissertation, Boston University, 1949); and for Millerism abroad, see Hugh I. B. Dunton, "The Millerite Adventists and Other Millenarian Groups in Great Britain, 1830–1860" (Ph.D. dissertation, University of London, 1984).

11. Sandeen, *Roots of Fundamentalism*, pp. 42–58; J. F. C. Harrison, *The Second Coming: Popular Millenarianism, 1780–1850* (New Brunswick, N.J.: Rutgers Univer-

sity Press, 1979), pp. 192–203; R. Laurence Moore, *Religious Outsiders and the Making of Americans* (New York: Oxford University Press, 1986), pp. 131–136; Michael Barkun, *Crucible of the Millennium: The Burned-Over District in the 1840s* (Syracuse, N.Y.: Syracuse University Press, 1986). See also Nathan O. Hatch, "Millennialism and Popular Religion in the Early Republic," in *The Evangelical Tradition in America*, ed. Leonard I. Sweet (Macon, Ga.: Mercer University Press, 1984), pp. 113–130; Gary Scharnhorst, "Images of the Millerites in American Literature," *American Quarterly*, 1980, 32: 19–36; and Donal Ward, "Religious Enthusiasm in Vermont, 1761–1847" (Ph.D. dissertation, University of Notre Dame, 1980), which includes a discussion of the Millerite excitement.

12. For influential socioeconomic interpretations, see, e.g., Peter Worsley, *The Trumpet Shall Sound* (London: MacGibbon and Kee, 1957); Vittorio Lanternari, *The Religions of the Oppressed: A Study of Modern Messianic Cults*, trans. Lisa Sergio (New York: Alfred A. Knopf, 1963); Eric Hobsbawm, *Primitive Rebels: Studies in Archaic Forms of Social Movement in the 19th and 20th Centuries* (New York: W. W. Norton, 1965; originally published in 1959); and Christopher Hill, *Antichrist in Seventeenth-Century England* (London: Oxford University Press, 1971). See Norman Cohn, *Pursuit of the Millennium* (London: Secker & Warburg, 1957), for a much-cited sociopsychological view.

13. Reuben E. Harkness, "Social Origins of the Millerite Movement" (Ph.D. dissertation, University of Chicago, 1927); Ernest R. Sandeen, "Millennialism," in *The Rise of Adventism*, pp. 104–118, esp. 116–117; Ernest R. Sandeen, "The 'Little Tradition' and the Form of Modern Millenarianism," *Annual Review of the Social Sciences of Religion*, 1980, 4: 165–181, esp. 169. Whitney R. Cross, in *The Burned-Over District*, pp. 317–320, also connected the rise of Millerism with economic depression, a view endorsed by Richard Carwardine, *Trans-Atlantic Revivalism: Popular Evengelicalism in Britain and America, 1790–1865* (Westport, Conn.: Greenwood Press, 1978), pp. 54–55.

14. Sears, *Days of Delusion*, passim; Nichol, *Midnight Cry*, p. 367. For an early study of institutionalized Millerites, see Simon Stone, "The Miller Delusion: A Comparative Study in Mass Psychology," *American Journal of Psychiatry*, 1934, 91: 593–623.

15. In her study of "The Miller Heresy," p. 27, Ruth Alden Doan shows that 84.1 percent of a total of 615 correspondents to *Signs of the Times* and *The Advent Herald* lived in New England and New York, with 3.7 percent coming from the Middle Atlantic states south of New York, 10.6 percent from the Midwest, and 1.6 percent from the South. New York claimed the highest number of correspondents with 131; Vermont was second with 107.

16. For recent scholarship that challenges these stereotypes, see James West Davidson, *The Logic of Millennial Thought: Eighteenth-Century New England* (New Haven: Yale University Press, 1978); Nathan O. Hatch, *The Sacred Cause of Liberty: Republican Thought and the Millennium in Revolutionary New England* (New Haven: Yale University Press, 1978); James H. Moorehead, *American Apocalypse: Yankee Protestants and the Civil War, 1860–1869* (New Haven: Yale University Press, 1978); Timothy P. Weber, *Living in the Shadow of the Second Coming: American Premillennialism, 1875–1925* (New York: Oxford University Press, 1979); and Stephen J. Stein, ed., *The Works of Jonathan Edwards*, vol. 5: *Apocalyptic Writings* (New Haven: Yale University Press, 1977). On the dominant postmillennialism of the nineteenth century, see James H. Moorehead, "Between Progress and Apocalypse: A Reassessment of Millennialism in American Religious Thought, 1800–1880," *Journal of American History*, 1984, 71: 524–542.

17. Leon Festinger, Henry W. Riecken, and Stanley Schachter, *When Prophecy Fails: A Social and Psychological Study of a Modern Group that Predicted the Destruction of the World* (New York: Harper & Row, 1964; first published in 1956), pp. 12–23, esp.

22. See also Bryan Wilson, *Magic and the Millennium: A Sociological Study of Religious Movements of Protest Among Tribal and Third-World Peoples* (New York: Harper & Row, 1973), pp. 500–502, who argues that all millenarian movements fail and that finally they do not "make sense," even to those caught up in them for a time.

18. Kenelm Burridge, *New Heaven, New Earth: A Study of Millenarian Activities* (New York: Schocken Books, 1969), pp. 105–116.

19. Sylvester Bliss, *Memoirs of William Miller, Generally Known as a Lecturer on the Prophecies, and the Second Coming of Christ* (Boston: J. V. Himes, 1853). Harold A. Larrabee provides a convenient sketch of Miller's life in "The Trumpeter of Doomsday," *American Heritage*, April, 1964, *15*: 35–37, 95–100. On Himes, see David T. Arthur, "Joshua V. Himes and the Cause of Adventism, 1839–1845" (M.A. thesis, University of Chicago, 1961).

20. Bear's recollection was discovered by Lawrence Foster.

21. Nathan O. Hatch, "Spreading the Millerite Message," unpublished paper presented to the conference on "Millerism and the Millenarian Mind in 19th-Century America," Killington, Vermont, June 1, 1984.

22. Burridge, *New Heaven, New Earth*, p. 3.

23. Vern Carner, Sakae Kubo, and Curt Rice, "Bibliographical Essay," in *Rise of Adventism*, pp. 207–317.

24. Ray Allen Billington, ed., with the assistance of Vern Carner, *Peoples of the Plains and Mountains: Essays in The History of the West Dedicated to Everett Dick* (Westport, Conn.: Greenwood Press, 1973).

25. The conference proceedings were published under the title *God and Nature: Historical Essays on the Encounter between Christianity and Science*, ed. David C. Lindberg and Ronald L. Numbers (Berkeley and Los Angeles: University of California Press, 1986).

The

DISAPPOINTED

ONE

Millerites

A Shadow Portrait

DAVID L. ROWE

WHO WERE THE MILLERITES? No question about the movement is as difficult to answer, despite the fact that definitions of Millerism have always been readily at hand. To scoffers, contemporary and modern, the Millerites were naïve fools, dupes, or crooks, while to hagiographers they were pilgrims conveying divine Truth, martyrs in the cause of advancing Christ's kingdom. Neither set of clichés can satisfy the objective observer. If Millerites generally were strange or insane, then how do we explain the fact that thousands of people from Maine to Michigan attached themselves to the movement? Did a significant number of Americans take leave of their senses at the same time? Or perhaps they truly were messengers of divine truth, but such a contention is not susceptible to the kind of scientific verification social scientists require. One would think that a collective biography of Millerites would help us better to define the nature and character of the movement. Strangely enough, once we begin focusing our critical faculties on Millerism, seeking its true identity lying somewhere between naïveté and sainthood, its image blurs, until it is obvious that we are viewing not the movement's reality but only the shadow it casts on the cultural and religious life of early nineteenth-century America.

For reasons that will soon become clear,[1] we will never be able to say who the Millerites collectively were. But we *can* trace the movement's shadow by delineating the nature and character of individual Millerites, and this will allow us to do three things. First, such a study will give us clues about the nature and character of Millerism generally. Second, it will allow us to assess the relationship between Millerism and the culture from which it emerged: Just how different were the Millerites? Third, it will enable us to test the way we study millenarian groups, in other words, the quality of the scholarly enterprise itself.

PROBLEMS OF DEFINITION

From 1831, when William Miller first lectured on the approaching end of the world, to 1844, when Millerism reached its denouement, thousands of Americans watched expectantly for the Second Coming of Christ. The estimated number of Millerites has varied from 10,000 to over one million.[2] We will never know the exact number, but the wide distribution of Millerism across the Northeast and Midwest, from Maine to Michigan and beyond, marks Millerism's distinctive quality. Unlike other innovative religious groups of the day which are best defined as sects or cults—for example, the Mormons, Shakers, Oneidans, Antimission Baptists, Wesleyan Methodists—Millerism was a mass movement. Antisectarian through most of its life, the movement lacked the impulse toward separatism that impelled the other groups. Millerites for the most part stayed within their churches until 1844, when come-outerism did produce separated, self-consciously Millerite meetings. Even then, not all Millerites withdrew from their churches, and Miller himself advised against it. Furthermore, Miller's message was so orthodox that the movement achieved a comprehensiveness that sociologists of religion usually ascribe to formal churches. It appealed to people from all walks of secular life and from all the evangelical sects that comprised the bulk of church members in that day. Comprehensiveness also was a product of Millerism's truly modern professional methods of propagation: newspapers, itinerant speakers, and professional organizers, both lay and religious. Truly, Millerism was the religious analog of the Whigs' successful professionalization of American politics. Together, the message and methods allowed Millerism to reach an audience the size of which other, more sectarian, innovative groups could only dream.

But in this very comprehensiveness lay an essential dilemma, both for the Millerites and for us. It guaranteed that the movement would be diverse, even contradictory. Appealing to *all* sorts of people, it attracted all *sorts* of people. This was a sign of success, of course, but it also brought conflicting ideas and personalities into the movement. Millerites disagreed over the fate awaiting the damned: annihilationists preaching the obliteration of their souls and Miller preaching the second resurrection unto eternal damnation. Others fought heatedly over whether the "carnal" Jews would physically return to Palestine and convert to Christianity before the Second Coming of Christ or, as Miller preached, Christians themselves symbolically represented spiritualized Judaism. These squabbles forced Millerite leaders to choose between religious liberty and enforced conformity. Miller himself urged toleration of theological differences among his followers, and although Joshua V. Himes, Millerism's manager and chief promoter, tried in various ways to achieve consensus on belief and action, the Adventist movement's antinomianism militated against it. Thus contemporary commentators and modern scholars have noted the problem of defining exactly who was a Millerite. Wrote one of the movement's critics, "Here we find *Annihilationists*, who unite with Universalists in denying that there is any hell for the punishment of the wicked; *Arians*, *Socinians*, etc. etc. and yet united on this one point [Millerism] they are all brethren, hale fellows well met."[3]

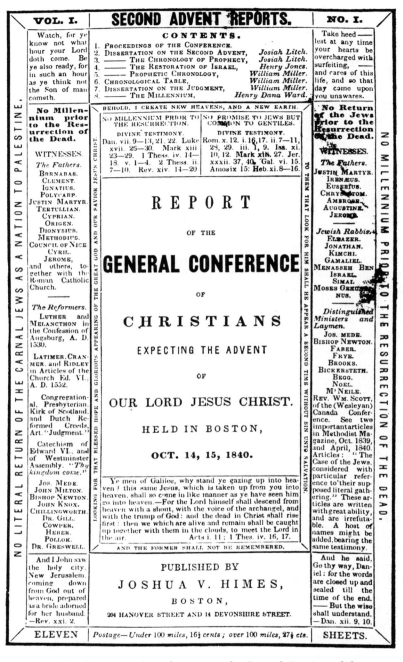

| VOL. I. | SECOND ADVENT REPORTS. | NO. I. |

Watch, for ye know not what hour your Lord doth come. Be ye also ready, for in such an hour as ye think not the Son of man cometh.

Take heed —— lest at any time your hearts be overcharged with surfeiting, and cares of this life, and so that day come upon you unawares.

CONTENTS.

No Millennium prior to the Resurrection of the Dead.

NO LITERAL RETURN OF THE CARNAL JEWS AS A NATION TO PALESTINE.

WITNESSES.

The Fathers.
BARNABAS.
CLEMENT.
IGNATIUS.
POLYCARP.
JUSTIN MARTYR.
TERTULLIAN.
CYPRIAN.
ORIGEN.
DIONYSIUS.
METHODIUS.
COUNCIL OF NICE.
CYRIL.
JEROME,
and others, together with the Roman Catholic Church.

The Reformers.
LUTHER and MELANCTHON in the Confession of Augsburg, A. D. 1530.

LATIMER, CRANMER, and RIDLEY in Articles of the Church Ed. VI., A. D. 1552.

Congregational, Presbyterian, Kirk of Scotland, and Dutch Reformed Creeds, Art. "Judgment."

Catechism of Edward VI., and of Westminster Assembly. *"Thy kingdom come."*

JOS. MEDE.
JOHN MILTON.
BISHOP NEWTON.
JOHN KNOX.
CHILLINGWORTH.
DR. GILL.
COWPER.
HEBER.
POLLOK.
DR. GRESWELL.

BEHOLD, I CREATE NEW HEAVENS, AND A NEW EARTH.

THE GREAT GOD AND OUR SAVIOR JESUS CHRIST.

LOOKING FOR THAT BLESSED HOPE AND GLORIOUS APPEARING OF

NO MILLENNIUM PRIOR TO THE RESURRECTION.

DIVINE TESTIMONY.
Dan. vii. 9—13, 21, 22. Luke xvii. 25—30. Mark xiii 23—29. 1 Thess. iv. 14—18. v. 1—4. 2 Thess. ii. 7—10. Rev. xiv. 14—20

NO PROMISE TO JEWS BUT COMMON TO GENTILES.

DIVINE TESTIMONY.
Rom. x. 12. i. 16,17. ii. 7—11, 28, 29. iii. 1, 9. Isa. xi. 10, 12. Mark xiv. 27. Jer. xxxii. 37, 40. Gal. vi. 15. Amos ix 15: Heb. xi. 8—16.

REPORT

OF THE

GENERAL CONFERENCE

OF

CHRISTIANS

EXPECTING THE ADVENT

OF

OUR LORD JESUS CHRIST.

HELD IN BOSTON,

OCT. 14, 15, 1840.

Ye men of Galilee, why stand ye gazing up into heaven ? this same Jesus, which is taken up from you into heaven, shall so come in like manner as ye have seen him go into heaven.—For the Lord himself shall descend from heaven with a shout, with the voice of the archangel, and with the trump of God: and the dead in Christ shall rise first : then we which are alive and remain shall be caught up together with them in the clouds, to meet the Lord in the air. Acts i. 11 ; 1 Thess. iv. 16, 17.

AND THE FORMER SHALL NOT BE REMEMBERED.

TO THEM THAT LOOK FOR HIM SHALL HE APPEAR A SECOND TIME WITHOUT SIN UNTO SALVATION.

No Return of the Jews prior to the Resurrection of the Dead.

NO MILLENNIUM PRIOR TO THE RESURRECTION OF THE DEAD.

WITNESSES.

The Fathers.
JUSTIN MARTYR.
IRENÆUS.
EUSEBIUS.
CHRYSOSTOM.
AMBROSE.
AUGUSTINE.
JEROME.

Jewish Rabbis.
ELEAZER.
JONATHAN.
KIMCHI.
GAMALIEL.
MENASSEH BEN ISRAEL.
SIMAL.
MOSES GERUNUS.

Distinguished Ministers and Laymen.
JOS. MEDE.
BISHOP NEWTON.
FABER.
FRYE.
BROOKS.
BICKERSTETH.
BEGG.
NOEL.
M'NEILE.
REV. WM. SCOTT, of the (Wesleyan) Canada Conference. See two important articles in Methodist Magazine, Oct. 1839, and April, 1840. Articles : " The Case of the Jews, considered with particular reference to their supposed literal gathering." These articles are written with great ability, and are irrefutable. A host of names might be added, bearing the same testimony.

And I John saw the holy city, New Jerusalem coming down from God out of heaven, prepared as a bride adorned for her husband. —Rev. xxi. 2.

And he said, Go thy way, Daniel : for the words are closed up and sealed till the time of the end. —— But the wise shall understand. —Dan. xii. 9, 10.

PUBLISHED BY

JOSHUA V. HIMES,

BOSTON,

204 HANOVER STREET AND 14 DEVONSHIRE STREET.

| ELEVEN | Postage—*Under* 100 *miles*, 16½ *cents ; over* 100 *miles*, 27¼ *cts.* | SHEETS. |

2. The first general conference on the Second Coming of the Lord Jesus Christ was held in Boston in October 14–15, 1840, in Joshua V. Himes's Chardon Street Chapel. Although the conference was not called to establish a new organization, participants laid plans for future conferences to coordinate the Adventist movement. Courtesy James R. Nix.

Both then and now, the problem of defining Millerism, even in the face of such confusing variegation, seemed simple. "[T]he only feature of [Millerism] which has given it any degree of currency in the community," wrote the *Christian Review*, "is the single article, that the second coming of Christ, to judge the world, was to take place in the year 1843."⁴ But even this cannot serve. Although Miller preached a set year for the Apocalypse and Parousia, many in the movement did not, including important leaders like Henry Dana Ward, who actually preached against the setting of a date even as imprecise as a year. Occasionally Millerite conferences adopted resolutions averring faith in the approach of the Advent, while rejecting acceptance of the set time as dogma. Some Millerites—Joseph Marsh, Elon Galusha—accepted the date reluctantly at best, and even Miller himself had to be browbeaten into endorsing S. S. Snow's prediction of a specific day, October 22, 1844. Can we say, then, that only those who accepted the concept of revealed time were Millerites and thus exclude many of the movement's most ardent leaders? Clearly not.

A second reason one cannot define Millerites solely with reference to expressed belief is that many orthodox Christians accepted Miller's tenets and used millenarian-like rhetoric without ever joining the Adventist movement. Millerism's conscious pietism and evangelicalism and its profitable recourse to the popular revivalism of the day as its principal vehicle of propagation not only encouraged commitment to Adventism; it also "interested" many professing Christians who found the Millerites' beliefs and rhetoric familiar and comfortable but who would have been shocked had anyone called them Millerites. One case in point was Judah L. Richmond, a Baptist preacher in Chautauqua County, New York, and brother-in-law of Lydia M. Richmond, a prominent Millerite preacher. Richmond remained unconvinced "that this world will perish this . . . year [1843]," but he confided in his diary that "the time is not far distant when that momentous event will take place." He expressed many of the same hostilities to materialism and secularization of the church that impelled many Adventists, and he exclaimed in good millenarian rhetoric, "Come, Lord Jesus, come quickly." But he also criticized the Millerites for predicting a time and refused to preach the imminent return of Christ from the pulpit. Similarly, Lavinia Rose of South Cortland, New York, wrote letters to her aunt in the 1830s full of Millerite-like rhetoric. "The night cometh when no man can work," she said. "I expect if we live, to visit you before the year closes, but hope not to boast of tomorrow. It seems as if the stream of time runs more swiftly than formerly. I feel the importance of having our work done, our lamps trimmed and burning."⁵ Yet, the "pearl of great price" for which she yearned so ardently would come not with the Second Coming of Christ but with her death and personal judgment. Despite the rhetorical appearances, she was not a Millerite.

How then can we define Millerites if not by belief? There is a gauge we can use—public action. Those who not only believed Miller's message but acted on behalf of that belief clearly belong in the Millerite movement. Action may have taken any number of forms, writing letters of support to the editors of the Adventist journals, contributing money publicly to the cause, preaching the message, assisting with Adventist prayer meetings or conferences, or simply writing a letter to Miller, Himes, or other of the movement's leaders expressing confidence in them. The point is, once someone not only came to believe in the imminent Apocalypse but acted on behalf of that belief specifically in support of the Millerite movement, we can logically consider that person to have been a Millerite. Furthermore, because such action was public, we can often identify the person by name and even by place of residence (from letters to editors, for example).

Microcosmic studies of Millerism are helpful in identifying these committed Adventists. The area I have studied in depth (so far the only region to receive demographic attention) was upstate New York, where 353 persons were sufficiently committed to Millerism to leave behind lasting testimony identifying them as committed and involved Millerites.[6] These people represent the leadership of Adventism in that region, leaving us with the question of how representative they were of Millerites in New York State and of how representative Millerism in New York was of the movement across the Northeast. Whitney Cross believed the movement had its greatest support in the so-called "burned-over district," and while it requires other regional studies to prove or disprove that contention, there is evidence he was correct.[7] The largest number of letters to Miller in the William Miller Collection at Aurora College were from New York State, the focus of the movement's intense evangelization in 1843 and 1844. These 353 definable Millerites thus give us a starting point for tracing the movement's shadow.

They allow us, for example, to speculate on the numerical size of the movement. For each of these identifiable Millerites, how many others go undetected? If they represent the committed leadership, how many followed? There are some tantalizing clues. The William Miller Papers at Aurora College contain many letters with multiple signers, in effect petitions asking Miller to preach. One such petition from the Adventist band in Perry, New York, a group that had separated from the Lockport Baptist Church under the inspiration of Elon Galusha, contained 60 names. Galusha's name was the only one of the 60 that appears in other Millerite sources. So in this case, at least, had the petition never been written Galusha would effectively have represented 59 other Adventists. Similarly, in Lewiston the Millerite band contained at least 42, in Ithaca at least 26, in Providence, Rhode Island, at least 43, in Newark, New Jersey, at least 36. From smaller communities came letters with only 5 or 6 signatures.[8] In each case, the leader's name is likely to have recurred in other sources while the followers' names are not. So the average ratio between the names of leaders and followers would be about 1:23. Given about 200 identified leaders of the movement in upstate New York, we can suspect the presence there of at least 4,600 followers.

Using a second measure, we know that in upstate New York alone Millerism reached over 280 communities, and in at least 200 of these there were Millerite meetings (consisting of from 5 to 60 believers) by October 1844. If the average size of these meetings was 25 members, then we can estimate that there

3. Woodcut of William Miller preaching at a camp meeting in Newark, New Jersey. From the *New York Herald*, November 13, 1842.

4. Woodcut of the Great Tent used by Millerite preachers. From the *New York Herald*, November 14, 1842.

were at least 5,000 committed Millerites in this region alone. When we consider as yet unsubstantiated rumors that entire Baptist congregations in Ithaca and Oswego "went over to Millerism," it seems likely this estimate is conservative. Also, many Millerite lecturers were itinerants, so their names would represent believers in more than one community, though how many is impossible to say.

Francis D. Nichol estimated in *The Midnight Cry* that there were at least 50,000 Millerites, a figure he considered to be conservative. If there were, using equally conservative estimates, at least 5,000 Millerites in New York State alone, and if roughly one out of five Millerites lived in New York, then the total number of Millerites would not have been under 25,000—and may well have approached Nichol's figure.

WHO WERE THEY?

Identifying 353 New York Millerites by name gives us an opportunity to compile a collective biography of the Millerite movement, at least in upstate New York. But here we face a second problem—the difficulty of finding evidence. A few Millerites—Miller himself, Joseph Bates, Jane Marsh Parker (daughter of the editor of the *Voice of Truth* published in Rochester, New York), Lydia Fassett, and others—have left behind extensive memoirs, from which to a large extent has come our current understanding of what kinds of people the Millerites were. The manuscript U.S. census conveys considerable information, more in 1850 than in 1840. Regardless of which census we use, the information is four to six years removed from the height of the movement (1844–1845), and only 17 percent of our identifiable Millerites show up in the 1850 Federal census. Whether in the interim between the Great Disappointment and 1850 the other 83 percent moved (under enormous ostracism?) or died is unclear.[9] There was an 1845 State census, but the manuscripts have virtually disappeared. For whatever reason, firsthand evidence from memoirs, letters, diaries, biographies, archival sources, and public documents is available for only 116 of our 353 clearly identifiable and definable Millerites.

But while this limits our ability to define Millerism with precision, the information we have allows us to place considerable credence in the Millerites' own claims that they sought, and reached, the broadest possible audience. We read that their halls were filled "with people of all sorts, including Judges, Doctors, Lawyers, and 'common people,'" with "all sorts, high and low, black and white, and I suppose some bond and some free."[10] These 116 Adventists, indeed, came from every walk of life. The largest number, twenty-two, made their living at farming, while seven were engaged in commerce, two were industrialists, four were professionals, sixteen were engaged in craft production from the making of wagons to stonecutting, three were laborers, one was a clerk, and nine were wives. Most significant of all, fifty-two or 45 percent of our Adventists identified themselves as ministers. (This figure includes only people who defined themselves specifically as ordained or licensed clergymen and excludes those who defined themselves only as Adventist lecturers.) Of these,

THE TRUE MIDNIGHT CRY.

BEHOLD, THE BRIDEGROOM COMETH; GO YE OUT TO MEET HIM.

Vol. I.   Edited by S. S. Snow, and published by E. Hale. Jr. Haverhill, Ms. Aug. 22, 1844.   No. I.

Our blessed Lord and Master has promised that he will come again and receive his people to himself; that where he is, they may be also. The place where he and they are to dwell forever, is the New Jerusalem, that holy city, which God hath prepared for them, and which is to come down from God out of heaven, and that New Earth, wherein dwelleth righteousness.

Concerning the *time* of that coming, he says, in Mark xiii. 32, " But of that day and hour knoweth no man, no, not the angels which are in heaven, neither the Son, but the Father." It is thought by many, that this passage proves that men are never to know the time. But if it prove this, it likewise proves that the Son of God himself is never to know the time: for the passage declares precisely the same concerning him, that it does concerning angels and men. But can any person believe that our glorious Lord, to whom all power in heaven and earth is given, is, and will remain ignorant of the time until the very moment that he comes to judge the world? If not, then certainly this text can never prove that men may not be made to understand the time. An old English version of the passage reads, " But that day and hour no man maketh known neither the angels which are in heaven, neither the Son, but the Father." This is the correct reading according to several of the ablest critics of the age. The word *know* is used here in the same sense as it is by Paul in 1 Cor. ii. 2. Paul well understood many other things besides Christ and him crucified, but he determined to *make known* nothing else among them. So in the passage first quoted, it is declared that none but God the Father maketh known the day and hour, that is, the *definite time* of the second coming of his Son. And this necessarily implies that God makes the time known. The Old Testament contains the testimony of the Father concerning his Son, and concerning the *time* of both his first and second comings. Therefore the time is to be understood. See Dan. xii. 10, " Many shall be purified, and made white, and tried; but the wicked shall do wickedly; and none of the wicked shall understand; but the wise shall understand." Rom. xv. 4, " For whatsoever things were written aforetime were written for our learning, that we through patience and comfort of the Scriptures might have hope." It is by the teaching of his word, as we are led therein by the Holy Spirit, that we are to understand the time of the coming of our GLORIOUS KING. As further proof of this, see Dan. ix. 25, " Know therefore and understand, that from the going forth of the commandment, to restore and build Jerusalem, unto the Messiah, the Prince, shall be seven weeks, and threescore and two weeks." Mark i. 14, 15, " Now after that John was put in prison, Jesus came into Galilee, preaching the gospel of the Kingdom of God, and saying the *time* is fulfilled." Luke xix. 43, 44, " For the day shall come upon thee that thine enemies shall cast a trench about thee, and compass thee round and keep thee in on every side, and shall lay thee even with the ground, and thy children within thee, and they shall not leave in thee one stone upon another; because thou knewest not the time of thy visitation." 1 Pet. i. 9–11, " Searching what, or what manner of time the spirit of Christ, which was in them, did signify, when it testified beforehand the sufferings of Christ, and the glory that should follow." Isa. xl. 1–5; Acts xvii. 30, 31, " He hath appointed a day in the which he will judge the world in righteousness." Ecc. iii. 17, " God shall judge the righteous and the wicked; for there is a time there for every purpose and for every work." Ecc. viii. 5–7, " Whoso keepeth the commandment shall feel no evil thing; and a wise man's heart discerneth both time and judgment." Jer. viii. 6–9, " I hearkened and heard, but they spoke not aright; no man repented him of his wickedness, saying, what have I done? every one turned to his course as the horse rusheth into the battle. Yea, the stork in the heaven knoweth her appointed times; and the turtle, and crane, and the swallow, observe the time of their coming; but my people know not the judgment of the Lord. How do ye say, we are wise, and the law of the Lord is with us? Lo certainly in vain made he it; the pen of the scribes is in vain. The wise men are ashamed, they are dismayed and taken; lo, they have rejected the word of the Lord; and what wisdom is in them? Hosea ix. 7–9, " The days of visitation are come, the days of recompense are come; Israel shall know it. The prophet is a fool, the spiritual man is mad." Rom. xiii. 11–14, " And that knowing the time, that now it is high time to awake out of sleep.

THE SIX THOUSAND YEARS. The period of time allotted for this world, in its present state, is 6000 years, at the termination of which commences the great millennial Sabbath, spoken of in Rev. xx, and which will be ushered in by the personal appearing of Christ and the first Resurrection; see Isa. xlvi. 9, 10; Gen. ii. 1–3; Heb. iv. 4–9; Isa. xi. 10; 2 Pet. iii. 8. According to Usher's chronology, which is commonly received, the Christian Era commenced in the year of the world 4004; but Usher has lost in the time of the judges 153 years. From the division of the Land of Canaan to the beginning of Samuel's administration, he gives but 295 years; whereas Paul, in Acts xiii. 20, gives us " about the space of 450." From the book of Judges we obtain 430 years, and Josephus gives us 18 more for the elders and anarchy, before any judge ruled; this added to 430 make 448 which

5. The first page of Samuel S. Snow's *The True Midnight Cry*, in which he presented his arguments for expecting the Lord to return on October 22, 1844. Courtesy Andrews University Heritage Room.

thirty-three were Baptists, many of whom made their living as farmers (as did Miller himself, a licensed Baptist preacher) or in some other occupation. The presence of so many preachers among the 116 Millerites (compared to less than .5 percent in the general population of New York) shows that this is not a random sample. Obviously, 45 percent of all Millerites were not preachers. Elsewhere I have defined Millerism essentially as a quest for spiritual renewal in the face of formalizing pietism, so it comes as no surprise to find so many preachers in our list of leaders. The preachers' predominant presence has the effect of skewing our impression of other occupational groups in the movement. Farmers, for instance, account for 19 percent of identified New York Adventists, but they formed 35 percent of the population of New York State.

It is clear, too, that while Baptists accounted for 63 percent of identified preachers among the Millerites, this skews the role of the Baptist Church in the movement. Baptists did form the largest denominational group in New York Millerism, and in this regard the movement there may have differed from Millerism in other parts of the country. Everett N. Dick, in his 1930 doctoral dissertation "The Adventist Crisis of 1843–1844," reported that of one hundred seventy-four Adventist lecturers nationwide whose religious affiliation was certain, 44.3 percent were Methodists, 27 percent were Baptists, 9 percent were Congregationalists, 8 percent were Christianites (members of Christian churches or the Christian Connexion), and 7 percent were Presbyterians, with the Dutch Reformed, Episcopal, and Lutheran churches and the Quakers occasionally present.[11] The New York sample shows a preponderance of Baptists and Christianites with but an occasional Methodist active as a leader. This sample may reflect the generally better availability of Baptist and Christianite sources, but it is unlikely that Methodists played a much greater role in New York Adventism than Millerite sources suggest. Since the Millerite movement occurred at the same time as the rise and separation of Wesleyan Methodists in New York State and the increasing agitation over abolition, the Methodists may have had their minds on internal theological and ecclesiological difficulties making it difficult for other issues to distract them.

If we take the ministerial bias of our sample into consideration, the census data suggest that occupationally the Adventists as a group did not significantly differ from the population as a whole. Here we have the first hint that most Millerites were like their neighbors. A second fact supports this impression. When we plot on a map the communities in upstate New York that hosted Adventist meetings, camp meetings, and lectures, we find that small towns, large cities, and rural areas were all susceptible to welcoming Millerism. Some sociologists of religion debate whether revivalism in the antebellum period was a product of the commercial or the industrial revolution, whether it could be found more readily in commercial centers or industrializing centers.[12] Eric Hobsbawm, in his study of Italian nineteenth- and twentieth-century millenarism, referred to it as an "archaic religious expression" and suggested that it resulted from a primitive rural reaction against an industrializing world.[13] Millerism does not support such a view. Simply put, the movement appeared in all sorts of communities—rural, commercial and commercializing, industrial and industrializing—with no clear affinity for any one.

Still, commercializing centers tied into the expanding regional market economy (Buffalo, Rochester, Albany) naturally served as headquarters of the movement, for here were facilities for the transportation and communication of people and ideas. Railroad and canal towns hosted large Millerite meetings and served as the movement's principal regional headquarters. Adventists consciously chose Rochester, New York, as the base of operations for the "Western Enterprise," as Himes called the evangelization of the territory west of Rome, New York, because it already was the home of a number of leading political and reform newspapers. Adventists who wanted to entice important lecturers to their town knew they could do so by emphasizing the community's "central location," from which wide influence could be spread to "the surrounding countryside."[14]

The effect of a community's progress toward commercialization and the presence of Millerism in that community leads to interesting questions about the ratio of men to women in Adventism. As with so many other questions, unfortunately our sample does not provide enough evidence on which to base a positive conclusion. Millerism occurred exactly at the point that, says Mary P. Ryan, the female associations resulting from the feminization of the churches, thanks to the Second Great Awakening, were encouraging the internalization of domestic religious values in the family.[15] Thus we find camp meeting revivalism in the 1830s and 1840s transformed into the Christian nurture, home parlor revivalism in the 1850s. We would, therefore, expect to find women prominently, if not predominantly, involved in Millerism. Because our sample consists of Millerite administrative leaders we would not expect to find women present among them in large numbers. But Millerites used revivalism as their principal method of evangelizing, so women quite naturally played roles in Adventism similar to the roles they had played in the New School revivals of the 1830s. The Adventist movement allowed, though it did not encourage, women to lecture publicly on Adventism, and Millerite sources are replete with stories of wives converting husbands both to righteousness and to Adventism in the privacy of their homes. As with other revivals, Adventist meetings were family affairs, as petitions to Miller asking him to preach indicate. But it is impossible to say yet that Millerism was essentially a female movement, nor can we yet conclude whether Millerism was the last gasp of the old camp meeting revivalism or the first cry of the new home parlor prayer meeting revivalism of the 1850s.

MILLERITES AND THE MILLENARIAN EXPERIENCE

Despite the problems of identifying committed Millerites and of discovering information about them, the material we do have reveals much about the character of the movement and those who participated in it. Thus we can speculate constructively not only about Millerism but also about the nature of millenarism. Indeed, we cannot discuss one topic without at least alluding to the other.

Students of apocalyptic movements have tried to explain millenarism in a variety of ways: sociologically, cosmologically, historically, and psychologically. Often, these scholars have suggested morphologies of millenarism that attribute these movements to such factors as yearnings for material comfort or even riches at the hands of a supernatural benefactor, for release from the oppressiveness of colonialism by a supernatural savior, or as the rebellion of one social class against displacement by another social class.[16] These scholars thus have tended to view millenarism as a religious perspective of the poor and the dispossessed.

The information we have gleaned about New York Millerites cannot prove or disprove this. But we can say that there is no evidence that Millerites were predominantly poor or even that the poor accounted for a large minority of Millerites. From time to time Millerites described themselves as "poor in the things of this world," and undoubtedly some Adventists were materially deprived and probably yearned for the comfort and ease of life in the New Jerusalem. But self-descriptions of this sort are not necessarily conclusive. For Millerites, as for some pietists, poverty was a clearer sign of salvation than wealth; as many Adventists reminded their followers, one would not wish to be found with "hoarded goods" on the last day.[17] Thus, claiming the mantle of poverty was not necessarily a sign of actual material deprivation. Rather, it set the believer apart from the corrupt—the rich, the educated, those who loved this world and not the next.

Although no evidence indicates that most Millerites were poor, some suggests that they were often comfortable and sometimes even well-off. According to the U.S. 1850 census, Clark Flint, a Millerite merchant in Attica, New York, had a personal worth of over $17,000, and Elon Galusha of $12,800. William Miller himself appears to have been worth a considerable sum when he died in 1849. John D. Miller, his son and principal heir, received the Miller farm and claimed a personal worth in 1850 of $45,000. A part of this evaluation may include John's personal property, but almost certainly its bulk consists of his inheritance from his father. Members of 16 separate families in Ithaca signed a letter in 1844 avowing their faith in Adventism. Twelve of those families appeared in the 1850 census. If we take their average worth that year and compare it with a random sample of Ithacans taken from the same census, we find that the Millerites averaged nearly $200 more in worth than the average Ithacan.[18]

Finding Millerites to be economically comfortable should come as no surprise. Paul Johnson found the same to be true of revivalists in Rochester, New York, in the 1820s and 1830s. Ronald Graybill, who undertook a collective biography of Adventists listed in a subscription account book for the *Review and Herald* dating from around 1860, found his subjects to have been "distributed in a wide spectrum of economic statuses, but favoring the upper side of that spectrum." They were "often a lot more wealthy than we had thought."[19] Nor is there any evidence among Millerites of a widespread perception of social deprivation among our Adventists. More common were concerns about being found with too much hoarded wealth when Christ returns. So if the theory that millenarism generally appeals to the socially dispossessed is true, then Millerism appears to provide a glaring exception.

The lack of identifiable social peculiarities among the Millerites forces us to question theories that reduce explanations of millenarism to single social or historical causes. Still, those who view millenarism as a product of social deprivation can salvage something from the Millerite experience. The Millerites *were* deprived, but spiritually rather than materially. Though they were not notably poor in the things of this world, as a group they certainly felt spiritually deprived—separated from God, yearning for the peace and joy of the millennium, eagerly anticipating release from the pain and troubles of this world. Furthermore, this sense of deprivation produced anger at the churches and clergy for their failure to convert the world and entice Jesus to return. The result was a real Adventist anticlerical and anti-institutional rebellion, much like millenarian revolts in other times and places.

This social radicalism has convinced many historians that Millerism was, as its contemporary detractors said, culturally aberrant, its adherents at least naïve, at most deluded or insane. Surely, there were personalities who richly colored the crusade. Michael Barton, a Shaker mystic who became a Millerite lecturer, entertained (as well as instructed?) his audiences by demonstrating his special gifts—speaking in tongues, healing the sick, prophesying the future, describing visionary tours around the world through the air—as proof of the approaching end of the world. Some Perfectionists attached to the movement practiced feet washing, advocated communalism, and attempted to raise the dead—all reported in the Millerite press. Some Millerites apparently did become insane under the spiritual pressure of anticipating the rapidly approaching Final Judgment. So if we wanted to find peculiarity in Millerism we could, for, then as now, the deviant were the ones who attracted the media's attention.

But we need to bear in mind, first, that antievangelicals leveled the same charges against revivalism in general and, second, that activities like these took place among other innovative groups. Though feet washing and similar activities were not common and many Americans would have defined them as aberrant, given the general quality of religious experimentation in that day they were probably less shocking than would have been the case in earlier decades. Third, shocking or not, while these activities took place under the aegis of Millerism, there is no evidence they were typical of Adventists. If the largest number of Millerites encouraged and rewarded such aberrant views and activities, we could reasonably describe them all as their popular reputation, then and now, would have it—strange, to say the least. But if Millerism were a mass movement, we would expect Millerites to represent accepted religious and cultural values. And that is clearly what we find. As a group the Millerites were traditional, orthodox, and even reactionary. We are accustomed to lumping them with other innovative groups of the day that offered truly new religious perspectives. For example, the Shakers combined mystical messianism with communalism; the Mormons preached a new revelation; the Oneidans combined pietism and communalism and ended up with a nearly scientific millennial expectancy. But the Millerites did none of these things, and in this fact lies the secret of their success.

Miller attracted support in part because of his rationality. He based his argument for the Second Coming on traditional methods of interpreting the Bible. He marshaled compelling historical evidence for the fulfillment of prophecy according to his hermeneutic. Instead of claiming to be a prophet or to have received a new revelation, he explained how each person could discover the "truth" he had found, thus making the secrets of revelation accessible to any believer. In this regard his views were the religious counterpart of the political antinomianism and popular democracy of the age of the common American.

Furthermore, the images and doctrines on which his message rested were orthodox Christian tenets. All churches, to one extent or another (save for the more "liberalizing" rationalists) preached the Parousia (Second Coming of Christ), Apocalypse (end of the world), and Final Judgment. Dreams of entering the New Jerusalem and the Millennium were frequent themes of preachers in all the evangelical churches as were vivid nightmares of the Last Day and the Lake of Fire awaiting unrepentant sinners.

Finally, the principal method Miller and others used to convey their message was no different from that of any other conventional evangelical—the revival. In fact, so close were the revivals of the 1820s and 1830s and Millerism connected in the public mind that many Americans could not differentiate between the two. Under the inspiration of Charles Grandison Finney, who preached that each sinner could be brought to repentance, "New School" preachers were turning to new techniques to achieve conversions. These new measures included the use of exhorters at revivals, anxious benches where penitents could receive special attention, allowing women to pray in public, and home visitations. Some local preachers viewed Adventism as nothing but Miller's particular measure for bringing sinners to repentance, and they sometimes expressed willingness to use his services while at the same time disagreeing with his views.[20]

In each of these ways—in their message, their images, and their methods—Millerites must be defined as universal rather than particular in their approach. Therefore, if we are to delineate the "typical" Millerite and at the same time to suggest why Millerism erupted when it did, we need to look not at the social structure of the movement, which differed little from that of the general population, but at the cultural structure of the movement. For more than anything else Millerism was born of and shaped by a coherent set of cultural religious values.

The first consistent quality of Millerism was its Yankeeness. Whitney Cross described the burned-over district as a product of Yankee culture, and Millerism in upstate New York bears him out.[21] Millerism spread uniformly throughout the region—except in the single area of the state where non-Yankees predominated, the Pennsylvania Triangle of counties in the Southern Tier whose settlers came north through the Susquehanna and Delaware valleys rather than west from New England. There alone Millerism gained no foothold. Furthermore, the regions settled by New Englanders, and New England itself, showed the strongest support for Millerism. The movement was strongest in New England, upstate New York, Ohio, northern Illinois and Indiana, and Michigan (the "third New England").

As part of this Yankee culture came a pietism deeply rooted in Calvinism. Miller himself was a Calvinist Baptist. Millerism gained support from its affinity for the more Arminian New School evangelicalism, but the tenets of pietism—individual competence to discover truth through grace, reliance on the revealed word of God, God's capacity to provide direct revelation—bridged the theological gap between orthodox and New School evangelicals in the movement. As previously noted, theological differences among Millerites were rife, but their pietist dream of union with God, a dream that Adventists preached would soon be realized, constituted the true heart and soul of their crusade. While theology divided Millerites, this religious cultural perspective united them.

The particular Yankee quality of this perspective provided the motivation to public action that other more quiescent pietist groups lacked. And it was precisely this active quality that defined who was a committed Millerite and who was not. Nowhere is this clearer than in Millerite dissidence, their attack on the churches, and the decision of many Adventists to withdraw from them. Long before the Millerite movement, New England Protestants achieved a well-earned reputation for innovation, dissidence, and separatism.[22] In fact, the sectarianism characteristic of upstate New Yorkers from 1820 to 1850 may well have been but a continuation of this Yankee proclivity for antinomianism, expressed in different cultural terms. There are too many links between the two periods to believe otherwise. Miller's own roots in the heart of the first "burned-over district," western Vermont, where he lived for eight years after marrying, and his support in the second "burned-over district," upstate New York, is just one case in point. Joseph Smith's experience in founding the Mormon Church shows similar connections between the cultural life of Vermont and upstate New York. So although not all Millerites condemned the churches and withdrew from them, those who did were evincing a certain Yankee cultural consistency.

All three qualities—"Yankeeness," pietism, and commitment to action—characterized other groups, of course. It is only when we combine them with the Millerite movement's traditional message and methods that we come to understand both its unique character among the sectarian movements of the day and its ability to achieve mass support. Since none of these characteristics were associated with any specific social class, it is not surprising that the movement was socially comprehensive. The full explanation of Miller's success must also consider regional cultural influences, widespread antagonism toward the professionalizing (formalizing) evangelical churches, and purely personal motivations. But the coincidence of popular religious imagery and values and Millerite imagery and values helps to explain Millerism's broad appeal.

This is not to say that all Millerites were rational, sane, and moderate. To be sure, anyone wishing to find those who were crazy, naïve, or even crooked would find more than one example of each. Millerism's comprehensiveness would guarantee that even these parts of the general population would be represented. But it would be erroneous to describe the movement generally in these terms. Millerites are not fascinating because they were so different from everyone else but because they were so like their neighbors. Once we get beyond the reductionist impulse to view all millenarist movements as solely or even predominantly social protest, we can look at how more fundamental concerns about evangelical church structure and yearning for spiritual renewal shaped this, America's most significant millenarian expression.

NOTES

1. My conclusions throughout this essay derive from research undertaken for and incorporated in *Thunder and Trumpets: The Millerites and Dissenting Religion in Upstate New York, 1800–1850* (Chico, Calif.: Scholars Press, 1985). A more detailed demographic description of Millerism and more pointed discussion of difficulties in researching the movement appear there.

2. Whitney R. Cross, *The Burned-over District: The Social and Intellectual History of Enthusiastic Religion in Upstate New York, 1800–1850* (Ithaca, N.Y.: Cornell University Press, 1950), p. 287. Cross cites the work of two other writers, Clara Endicott Sears, *Days of Delusion: A Strange Bit of History* (Boston: Houghton Mifflin, 1924), p. 244, and Francis D. Nichol, *The Midnight Cry: A Defense of William Miller and the Millerites* (Washington, D.C.: Review and Herald, 1944), p. 204. In neither case, however, did they mention the figure one million as the upper limit for the movement, so it may be Cross's own estimate. Miller himself estimated the size of the movement to be about 50,000 in *Apology and Defense* (Boston: Joshua V. Himes, 1845), p. 22.

3. (New York State) *Baptist Advocate*, July 4, 1843.

4. *Christian Review*, December, 1844, 599.

5. Judah L. Richmond, Diary, 1844, microfilm of the original at the University of North Carolina; Lavinia Rose to Elizabeth Abell, March 13, 1836, August 7, 1842, Abell Family Papers, Local and Regional History Collection, Cornell University.

6. Nondemographic regional studies include N. Gordon Thomas, "The Second Coming in the Third New England (The Millennial Impulse in Michigan, 1830–1860)" (Ph.D. dissertation, Michigan State University, 1967); and "The Millerite Movement in Ohio," *Ohio History*, Spring 1972, *81*: 95–107. Everett N. Dick assessed the denominational composition of Millerism on a national, but not regional, level as well as available information permitted in "The Adventist Crisis of 1843–1844" (Ph.D. dissertation, University of Wisconsin, 1930), pp. 232–234.

7. Cross, *Burned-over District*, p. 288.

8. Elon Galusha et al., to William Miller, Lockport, N.Y., October 22, 1843; William M. Collins et al. to Miller, Lewiston, N.Y., November 21, 1843; Henry B. Squires et al. to Miller, Ithaca, N.Y., December 27, 1843; N. Hervey et al. to Miller,

Providence, R.I., March 8, 1844; L. D. Fleming et al., to Miller, Newark, N.J., February 18, 1844; William Miller Papers, Second Advent Collection, Aurora College, Aurora, Illinois.

9. There is an entire literature devoted to assessing possible bias in census figures, all discussed specifically in terms of Adventism by Ronald Graybill, "Millenarians and Money: Adventist Wealth and Adventist Beliefs," *Spectrum*, August 1979, *10*: 31–40.

10. E. Jacobs, Syracuse, N.Y., *The Midnight Cry*, November 6, 1843; H. V. Teal, *The Midnight Cry*, June 15, 1843.

11. Dick, "Adventist Crisis," p. 232–233.

12. See particularly Paul E. Johnson, *A Shopkeeper's Millennium: Society and Revivals in Rochester, New York, 1815–1837* (New York: Hill and Wang, 1983), and Mary P. Ryan, *Cradle of the Middle Class: The Family in Oneida County, New York, 1790–1865* (Cambridge: Cambridge University Press, 1981).

13. Eric J. Hobsbawm, *Primitive Rebels: Studies in Archaic Forms of Social Movement in the 19th and 20th Centuries* (New York: W. W. Norton, 1959).

14. Hugh Bremner, *The Midnight Cry*, December 21, 1842.

15. Ryan, *Cradle of the Middle Class*, pp. 105–144.

16. The pioneering study is Peter Worsley, *The Trumpet Shall Sound: A Study of Cargo Cults in Melanesia* (London: MacGibbon and Kee, 1957). For a listing of sociological analyses of millenarism, see A. J. F. Kobben, "Prophetic Movements as an Expression of Social Protest," *International Archives of Ethnography*, 1960, *49*, part 1:117–161.

17. Millerites also emphasized the salutary value of contributing to the Millerite movement, thus cleansing oneself of materialism's corrupting influence.

18. The sample consisted of a random 10 percent computation of the entire census of Ithaca based on a selection of every tenth household.

19. Graybill, "Millenarians and Money," p. 32.

20. See particularly Emerson Andrews to Miller, March 20, 1838, and an unidentified, undated letter to Miller, Miller Papers.

21. Cross, *Burned-over District*, pp. 288ff.

22. Stephen Marini, *Radical Sects of Revolutionary New England* (Cambridge: Cambridge University Press, 1982).

TWO

William Miller

Disappointed Prophet

WAYNE R. JUDD

WHEN WILLIAM MILLER preached that the world would end with Christ's second coming in 1843, he spoke to a society whose optimistic belief in progress was matched by anxiety over the accompanying threat to traditional Yankee values. During these transitional years from Enlightenment to Romanticism, from Federalism to Jacksonianism, Americans who indulged in laissez-faire capitalism required assurances that the yeoman republic was still intact. It was an age, wrote Marvin Meyers, of "grinding uncertainties" and "shocking changes."[1]

From the ranks of the Jacksonians came the self-made farmer-preacher who provided certainty for those facing culture shock. By use of charts based on Bible prophecy, William Miller guided many who were navigating from an old order into a new one. Miller introduced a precisely defined cataclysm that promised to transcend both the old and the new orders, and thousands of Americans gladly heard his radical message. It is in the context of his era's paradoxical combination of assurances and insecurity that the personal story of Miller's own hopes and disappointments unfolded. But before proceeding further in this volume with interpretations of Miller and his movement, it is necessary to sketch a narrative of the disappointed prophet's life and career.

Born in Pittsfield, Massachusetts, February 15, 1782, Miller moved with his parents to Low Hampton, New York, when he was a small child. The eldest of sixteen children, his was the classic story of poverty, uncommon zeal to learn to read, and the necessity of diligence at farming to assure survival. His pious mother taught him to read, but his thirst for knowledge could not be satisfied by the few books he was able to secure.

In 1803, he married Lucy Smith and moved to Poultney, Vermont. Miller's love for the Poultney library reduced farming to the distraction it would be to him for the rest of his life. Shortly after his marriage, Miller read his way into deism, a commitment he maintained from 1804 to 1816. During this period of time he studied the writings of Voltaire, Hume, Paine, and Ethan Allen.[2] He claimed that he had not rejected God, though he forsook the Bible and Baptist piety.

"While I was a Deist, I believed in a God, but I could not, as I thought, believe that the *Bible* was the *word of God*."[3] He was offended not only by the contradictions and inconsistencies of the Bible, but also by the "history of blood, tyranny, and oppression; in which the common people were the greatest sufferers." He believed religion to be a "system of *craft* rather than *truth*." Young Miller was deeply offended by a God who would inspire a book that could not be understood, then punish man for not understanding it.[4]

As with his study of the Bible during this period, Miller's pursuit of human history disappointed him. "The more I read, the more dreadfully corrupt did the character of man appear. I could discern no bright spot in the history of the past."[5] Disappointed by God and man, he nevertheless refused to give up his quest for meaning. Although "distrustful of all men," he entered the Vermont militia, hoping to "find one bright spot at least in the human character, as a star of hope: *a love of country*—PATRIOTISM."[6]

From the battlefield during the War of 1812, Miller wrote his wife, Lucy, an apocalyptic description of the battle of Plattsburgh.

> Yesterday was a day of great joy. We have conquered! . . . The British had thrown up a number of batteries on all sides of us. The next minute the cannon began playing—spitting their fire in every quarter. What a scene! All was dreadful!— nothing but roaring and groaning, for about six or eight hours. I cannot describe to you our situation. . . . My God! what a slaughter on all sides!—out of 300 on board of one ship, 24 only remained unhurt! I cannot describe to you the general joy. . . . How grand, how noble, and yet how awful![7]

Captain Miller was unable to explain the stunning American victories in natural terms. "Many occurrences served to weaken my confidence in the correctness of deistical principles. . . . It seemed to me that the Supreme Being must have watched over the interests of this country in an especial manner, and delivered us from the hands of our enemies." Miller concluded that the defeat of 15,000 British by 5,500 Americans at Plattsburgh was "the work of a mightier power than man."[8]

Improbable victories dealt a hard blow to Miller's deism. But war made another, more significant, mark on him. Accompanying the glories of war were the horrors of death. War taught Miller that life in Poultney required far less fidelity than death on the battlefield.

Death had haunted Miller since childhood. "In my youth, between the years of seven and ten, I was often concerned about the welfare of my soul, particularly in relation to its future destiny."[9] Even in 1812, before joining the militia, Miller rejected deism's "denial of a future existence." He asserted,

"Rather than to embrace such a view, I should prefer the heaven and hell of the Scriptures, and take my chance respecting them."[10]

Sobered by death, and still unfulfilled, Miller left military life after two years to seek peace at home. Domestic life, however, soon became "monotonous," and Miller looked for "more active employment."[11]

During this critical period, Miller almost completely abandoned his idealism.

> It appeared to me that there was nothing good on earth. Those things in which I expected to find some solid good had deceived me. I began to think man was no more than a brute, and the idea of hereafter was a dream; annihilation was a cold and chilling thought; and accountability was sure destruction to all. The heavens were as brass over my head, and the earth as iron under my feet. ETERNITY! *What was it? And death, why was it?*"[12]

In this anxious state, which lasted for several months, Miller turned toward his mother's faith.[13] He began to attend church each week with Baptist friends and relatives in Low Hampton. He dismissed the implications of his willingness to read prepared sermons on those Sundays when no minister was present on the basis that he could not endure the way the deacons read the sermons.[14] Persisting in his commitment to deism, he had not yet accepted Christianity as a balm for his troubled spirit. But his association with the Baptists and his volunteer pulpit work exerted an influence, given Miller's troubled state of mind.

Attempting one Sunday to read a sermon on the duties of parents, Miller became choked with unexpected emotion. Unable to continue, he sat down. He chronicled the transition that followed soon after:

> Suddenly the character of a Saviour was vividly impressed upon my mind. It seemed that there might be a Being so good and compassionate as to himself atone for our transgressions, and thereby save us from suffering the penalty of sin. I immediately felt how lovely such a Being must be; and imagined that I could cast myself into the arms of, and trust in the mercy of, such an One.[15]

Although his lifelong question had been answered, his faith remained incomplete. Miller addressed the dilemma of proving the existence of the Being to whom he had surrendered himself. In order to do this, it was necessary for him to authenticate the source of information that revealed the Saviour. Making the Bible the new center of his life, he exclaimed, "I found everything revealed that my heart could desire, and a remedy for every disease of the soul. I lost all taste for other reading, and applied my heart to get wisdom from God."[16] He found that the Bible was perfectly adapted to his needs. "I saw Jesus as a friend, and my only help, and the Word of God as the *perfect rule* of duty."[17] His deist associates now assaulted him with familiar arguments. Somewhat intimidated by their taunts, Miller declared, "Give me time, and I will harmonize all those apparent contradictions to my own satisfaction, or I will be a Deist still."[18]

Miller's course was established. He would never again entertain doubts about the Bible, or about God. He was less certain about himself and his conversion, however. Years later, with more than a little self-disgust, he doubted his conversion. "I have many doubts whether I was ever born of Christ," he wrote, "and I confess, my Br., I have so much Pharisee about me that I abhor myself."[19] He longed to enjoy the same objective certainty in his personal faith that he had found in Bible chronology. "I wish I could know my adoption as strong, as I believe my calculation is right. But alas, my corrupt, my wicked heart looks so little like Christ."[20]

He determined to make his election certain before pursuing his calling. Already disappointed in his efforts to locate life's meaning through the mediation of learned men, he would take no chances this time. He recalled, "I laid by all commentaries, former views and prepossessions, and determined to read and try to understand for myself."[21] Miller's claim is also an admission. He did have commentaries to "lay by," after all, and his writings indicate he had spent many hours poring over them. Indeed, after his prophecy of the Second Coming had failed, he confessed, "I was misled in my calculations; not by the words of God, nor by the established principles of interpretation I adopted, but by the authorities which I followed in history and chronology."[22]

During two years of study, Miller concluded that the prophecies of the Bible were always literally fulfilled, and that God had provided rules for interpreting figures and metaphors. To his great satisfaction, he learned "that the Bible contained a system of revealed truths, so clearly and simply given that the 'wayfaring man, though a fool,' need not err therein."[23] Miller identified fourteen rules of interpretation. He listed these in a two-column chart, with "rules" in the left column and "proofs" in the right column. The Bible proof texts were simply listed as references, without text or summary included. The rules themselves reveal much about Miller and the Millerite movement:

1. Every word must have its proper bearing on the subject presented in the Bible.
2. All scripture is necessary, and may be understood by a diligent application and study.
3. Nothing revealed in the scripture can or will be hid from those who ask in faith, not wavering.
4. To understand doctrine, bring all the scriptures together on the subject you wish to know; then let every word have its proper influence, and if you can form your theory without a contradiction, you cannot be in an error.
5. Scripture must be its own expositor, since it is a rule of itself. If I depend on a teacher to expound it to me, and he should guess at its meaning, or desire to have it so on account of his sectarian creed, or to be thought wise, then his *guessing, desire, creed* or *wisdom* is my rule, not the Bible.
6. God has revealed things to come, by visions, in figures and parables, and in this way the same things are oftentime revealed again and again, by different visions, or in different figures, and parables. If you wish to understand them, you must combine them all in one.
7. Visions are always mentioned as such.
8. Figures always have a figurative meaning, and are used much in prophecy, to represent future things, times and events; such as *mountains*, meaning *govern-*

ments; *beasts*, meaning *kingdoms*; *waters*, meaning *people*; *lamp*, meaning *Word of God*; *day*, meaning *year*.

9. Parables are used as comparisons to illustrate subjects, and must be explained in the same way as figures by the subject and Bible.

10. Figures sometimes have two or more different significations, as day is used in a figurative sense to represent three different periods of time. . . . If you put on the right construction it will harmonize with the Bible and make good sense, otherwise it will not.

11. How to know when a word is used figuratively. If it makes good sense as it stands, and does no violence to the simple laws of nature, then it must be understood literally, if not, figuratively.

12. To learn the true meaning of figures, trace your figurative word through your Bible, and where you find it explained, put it on your figure, and if it makes good sense you need look no further, if not, look again.

13. To know whether we have the true historical event for the fulfillment of a prophecy. If you find every word of the prophecy (after the figures are understood) is literally fulfilled, then you may know that your history is the true event. But if one word lacks a fulfillment, then you must look for another event, or wait its future development. For God takes care that history and prophecy doth agree, so that the true believing children of God may never be ashamed.

14. The most important rule of all is, that you must have *faith*. It must be a faith that requires a sacrifice, and, if tried would give up the dearest object on earth, the world and all its desires, character, living, occupation, friends, home, comforts, and worldly honors.[24]

These rules, with their appeal to the comon man and their "good sense" logic, were well-fitted for Jacksonian America. Miller's application of the rules resulted in a quasi-system that was thoroughly orthodox, with one notable exception:

I found, in going through with the Bible, the end of all things was clearly and emphatically predicted, both as to time and manner. I believed; and immediately the duty to publish this doctrine, that the world might believe and get ready to meet the Judge and Bridegroom at his coming, was impressed upon my mind.[25]

To understand the meaning of William Miller's life and the lives of those who were called Millerites, it is critical to remember the great, overriding touchstone of their existence. For them there was no future. Miller had settled the question of ultimacy. The world was coming to an end in 1843. It was this reality that made the Millerite movement one of the most dramatic expressions of revivalism in nineteenth-century America.

Despite his "duty to publish," Miller delayed spreading the urgent message for over twelve years. Initially, he excused himself from the task on the basis that he was not a minister. But that excuse faded as the years passed, and the professional ministry still had not responded. Miller's persistent denial of the prophetic office throughout his life suggests that during these silent years of waiting his fear of public rejection was somewhat larger than his concern to warn the world. It might have been otherwise if his efforts among neighbors and

6. The manuscript of William Miller's first published account
of his views on the Second Coming, which appeared as a series
of articles in the *Vermont Telegraph* that began on May 15,
1832. Courtesy Aurora University Library.

local ministers had produced better responses. But Miller exclaimed, "To my
astonishment, I found very few who listened with any interest. Occasionally,
one would see the force of the evidence; but the great majority passed it by as an
idle tale." He expressed disappointment that he could not find "any who would
declare this doctrine, as I felt it should be, for the comfort of saints, and as a
warning to sinners."[26]

But it was not only the unwilling others that concerned Miller. However
great the evidence might be, he still had doubts of his own. For example, he
found texts in the Bible that did not support setting a date for the end of the
world. Matthew 24:36, "Of that day and hour knoweth no man," especially
troubled Miller. However, he dismissed its warning on the basis that its context
declared the end was near; "consequently, that text could not teach that we
could know nothing of the time of that event."[27]

I tried to excuse myself to the Lord for not going and proclaiming it to the world. I
told the Lord that I was not used to public speaking, that I had not the necessary
qualifications to gain the attention of the audience, that I was very diffident and

feared to go before the world, that they would "not believe me nor hearken to my voice," that I was "slow of speech, and of a slow tongue." But I could get no relief.[28]

Finally, he could resist no more. After receiving the strong impression, "Go and tell it to the world," one Saturday morning, Miller wrestled with God:

The impression was so sudden, and came with such force, that I settled down into my chair, saying, "I can't go, Lord." "Why not?" seemed to be the response; and then all my excuses came up—my want of ability, &c.; but my distress became so great, I entered into a solemn covenant with God, that, if he would open the way, I would go and perform my duty to the world. "What do you mean by opening the way?" seemed to come to me. "Why," said I, "if I should have an invitation to speak publicly in any place, I will go and tell them what I find in the Bible about the Lord's coming." Instantly all my burden was gone, and I rejoiced that I should not probably be thus called upon; for I had never had such an invitation.[29]

But Miller scarcely had a chance to rise from his chair before his nephew from Dresden came into the room and asked him to preach the next day. "I rebelled at once against the Lord, and determined not to go," Miller declared, but the mystic voice instantly chided, "Will you make a covenant with God, and break it so soon?" Miller finally agreed to keep covenant.[30]

One-and-one-half years after he consented to his calling, however, Miller still remained in Low Hampton. His correspondence with his friend Truman Hendryx reflected his personal frustration. "We have no preacher as yet," wrote Miller, "except the old *man* with his *concordance*. And he is so shunned with his cold, dull, lifeless performance, that I have strong doubts whether he will attempt again." He disdained his perceived deficiencies. "I wish I had the tongue of an Apollos, and the mental powers of a Paul: what a field might I not explore; and what powerful arguments might be brought to prove the authenticity of the Scriptures!"[31]

By the time he began to preach, Miller was 50 years old. Too old, he thought, to initiate a movement. He described himself as weak, wicked, ignorant, feeble, disobedient, dull, dry, stammering, cold, lifeless, proud, impatient, and unworthy. He called himself a "worm," an "old dry stick," and a "poor feeble creature."[32] Such conventional prophetic rhetoric reflected genuine self-doubt, but it also conveyed Miller's positive sense of destiny. The magnitude of his mission demanded a very high standard of character and performance. His stated self-expectations, however frustrating, were expressions of a man who believed he had found his place in history.

The power and election of God were Miller's answers to his unworthiness. After a successful series of lectures in Lansingburgh, New York, he shared his new insight with Hendryx:

It astonished me, and I can only account for it by supposing that God is supporting the *old man*, weak, wicked, imperfect and ignorant as he is, to confound the wise and mighty, and bring to nought things that are. . . . Infidels, Deists, Universalists,

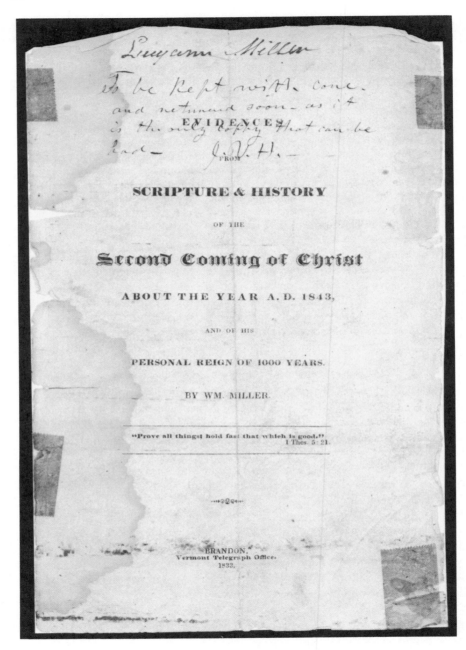

7. The cover of William Miller's first pamphlet on the Second
Coming, which contained 64 pages and appeared in 1833.
Courtesy Aurora University Library.

8. On September 12, 1833, the Baptist church in Hampton, New York, of which William Miller was a member, issued him a ministerial license to preach. Courtesy Review and Herald Publishing Association.

Sectarians: All, all are chained to their seats, in perfect silence, for hours, yes days, to hear the *Old Stammering Man*. . . . Oh, my Br., it makes me feel like a worm, a poor feeble creature. For it is God only that could produce such an effect on such audiences. Yet it gives me confidence.[33]

Weak, wicked or ignorant though he may have declared himself to be, Miller also knew there was power in his message. "I have been into a number of towns in Vermont. Some old, hardened rebels have been brought to plead for mercy, even before my course of lectures was finished."[34] Success forced him to add the fear of pride to his other inadequacies. "Oh! Br. Hendryx, this is marvelous in our eyes that he should take such an old dry stick as I am, and bring down the proud and haughty infidel." But he pleaded with his friend, "Pray for me, my Br. that I may be kept humble, for I am exceeding jealous of my proud heart."[35] Success also compounded Miller's anxieties by increasing public expectations. "The world do not know how weak I am. They think more, much more, of the old man than I think of him."[36] In fact, when Miller wrote these

9. Beginning in October 1834, William Miller kept a diary or "Text Book" in which he recorded his speaking engagements and the texts he used. Courtesy Aurora University Library.

words in 1838, "the world" had not yet discovered him as it would through the agency of Joshua V. Himes, who was arrested by Miller's message a year later.

Whatever Miller's self-perceptions, he almost certainly would have remained an obscure figure, traveling the backroads of New England, had it not been for the determination of Joshua V. Himes to bring the Millerite message to Boston and other cities. Himes expressed amazement that the message had been muted. "If Christ is to come in a few years, as you believe, no time should be lost in giving the church and world warning, in thunder-tones, to arouse them to prepare." Miller heartily agreed, but still demurred, "I know it, I know it, Br. Himes, but what can an old farmer do?"[37]

Miller's relationship to Himes reveals that he did not resent Himes's assertive role in the movement. In view of Miller's expressed reluctance to take the lead role in spreading the message, the ambitious Himes was a welcome convert. There is no reason to doubt Miller's expressed personal inadequacies, even when allowing for considerable exaggeration. Nor is it necessary to question the urgency he assigned to the warning message. His dilemma was real, and Himes rescued Miller and Millerism from obscurity. Until his death in 1849, Miller regarded Himes as one of his dearest friends.[38]

Joshua V. Himes gave the movement and its founder a public identity. But there remained much in the movement that frustrated William Miller. The world was unresponsive. He faced endless vilification in press and pulpit. His health was constantly breaking down. He was rejected by his own church. And finally he watched a growing come-outer spirit among his followers that resulted in the formation of a new sect.

Miller was never able to comprehend why the people of New England did not heed his warning cry, since it was so clearly supported by Scripture. Historian Everett Dick commented, "William Miller never had any other idea than that the churches would receive his explanation of the Scriptures gladly and rejoice with him in expecting their Saviour soon in the clouds of heaven to take His faithful children home."[39] Instead, Miller developed a reputation as a false prophet. As late as December 28, 1845, Miller received a letter which began, "I believe I never saw you but your name has been familiar as the old fanatic, the false prophet, the world burner, &c. &c."[40] In a letter to a "sister" on his fifty-ninth birthday, Miller regretted that he was called to be a pilgrim "through this dark, unfeeling and unfriendly world."[41] Even among his neighbors Miller felt the chill. To his eldest son, who tended the Miller farm, he wrote, "I do not suppose many of my neighbors care anything for me: yet I do feel for, and love them all."[42] Miller's earlier hopes of a positive response from the world were thwarted, and he became more pessimistic. The broad, inclusive tolerance of Miller and his early followers gradually shifted to a "remnant," reductionist soteriology. And even though persecution itself was a recognizable sign of the end, Miller could not celebrate its fulfillments. After nine years of proclamation, he catalogued his opposition in an address "To the Believers in the Second Advent Near, Scattered Abroad."

THE DISAPPOINTED

10. The first issue of *The Midnight Cry*, edited by Joshua V. Himes, began with a "Memoir of William Miller." Courtesy Andrews University Heritage Room.

I was alone; "no man stood with me" for a number of years. I had to contend against the prepossessions and prejudices of the entire christian community; the systems, talents, as also the superior education of the clergy; the religious press, and the political also, throughout the country; the institutions of learning, both literary and theological; the unbelief of the church; and, in short, the whole world were against me.[43]

In the same address he declared, "They have reported that I was insane, and had been in a mad-house seven years; if they had said a mad world fifty-seven years, I must have plead guilty to the charge."[44]

Critics said that to go hear William Miller was even worse than going to the theater.[45] Dartmouth emphatically refused to provide financial aid to students who embraced Miller's views.[46] Millerism was dubbed "a new edition of Mormonism."[47] A critical correspondent told Miller that he and Joseph Smith were "two kings speaking lies at one table."[48]

Miller was more concerned, however, about the unresponsive clergy. The abundant invitations to speak in churches throughout New England did not convince Miller that the clergy were supportive. In a messianic prayer, he asked questions for which he already had answers. "And yet how few of the professed ministers of Christ will believe? Oh my God why am I left alone? And why my father will men reject thy Word which all acknowledge is truth? Because they are too proud to be humble, too worldly to study, too blind to see and too hard to believe. Come then Lord Jesus for vain is the help of man."[49] He resented the fact that without believing the new doctrine themselves, the clergy found its revival value irresistible. He complained that the ministers "like to have me preach, and build up their churches; and there it ends. . . . I have been looking for help—I want help."[50]

Miller acknowledged that there were a few honest ministers, but he found the majority to be corrupt. These he described with prophetic wrath: they were bigoted, they loved large salaries and prestige, they "put off" the second coming of Christ in order to get personal gain. They were "dumb dogs," "ravening wolves," "Wise-heads," and "wiseacres."[51] They loved to be called "reverend," and to have titles attached to their names.[52] But ultimately, God would deal with these "priestly dandies," who had their "consciences cased in corsetts of steel."[53] One anonymous writer gently counseled Miller to be less severe. The writer suggested that Miller stop calling the clergy liars, since this "is not the best way." The Christian brother cautiously disclaimed, "There is no design in this to dictate to you." Nevertheless, he told Miller that his aggression "does turn away the minds of some from your teaching," and counseled him to use the "might of meekness" instead.[54] There is no indication that Miller accepted this friendly advice.

In his more serene moments, Miller simply awaited God's vindication. "The scoffers now will scoff, and say, 'Where is the promise of his coming.' But I must let them scoff, God will take care of me, his truth, and scoffers too."[55]

Another way in which Miller responded to criticism appears almost contradictory to his severe personality. Not unwilling to smile occasionally en route to the kingdom, Miller illustrated a sermon by employing a humorous dialogue between "Guest" and "Host" at an inn overlooking the construction site of Noah's ark.

> *Guest.* What great building is that in yonder field, on that eminence?
>
> *Host.* That is called "Noah's Ark."
>
> *Guest.* But what use is he going to put it to? It seems to be built for sailing. Surely the old man does not expect to sail on dry land.
>
> *Host.* Yes; you are right. The old man says the world is coming to an end (Gen. 6:13), and he has prepared an ark to save himself and family; for all flesh will be destroyed by water, as he says.
>
> *Guest.* But how does he know this?
>
> *Host.* He says God told him.
>
> *Guest.* What kind of a man is he? He must be a great fanatic, I am thinking.
>
> *Host.* Why, yes; we think he is crazy a little; but you cannot discover it in anything else but his building that great ark, and neglecting his farm and other worldly matters. But what he has lost I have gained.
>
> *Guest.* A farmer, say you?—a farmer! Why did not God tell some of our 'mighty men, which are men of renown'? (Gen. 6:4) A farmer, too! There is no truth in it. But do any believe him?
>
> *Host.* Believe him! No. We have other things to attend to, and cannot spend time to hear the old farmer.

But Miller's humor concluded with a rebuke: "Ye scoffers, take warning; cease your reviling, your newspaper squibs, your bombast. . . . And you, my dear reader, prepare! for lo!—

> 'He comes, he comes, the Judge severe;
> The seventh trumpet speaks him near.'"[56]

Miller admitted that he had not aged well. The demand of his successes and failures had been too great. "I have preached about 4,500 lectures in about twelve years, to at least 500,000 different people. I have broken my constitution and lost my health; and for what? That if possible I might be the means of saving some."[57] In December 1842, he wrote, "I find that, as I grow old, I grow more peevish, and cannot bear so much contradiction. Therefore I am called uncharitable and severe. No matter; this frail life will soon be over." He would wait to face the scoffer in the "Supreme Court of the Universe. . . . The World and Clergy vs. Miller."[58]

By appealing to a divine tribunal, Miller was better able to cope with the disappointments he sustained from the world and the clergy. More difficult to endure was the growing sectarian spirit of his followers. Unlike other groups in the nineteenth century, his was not a "true church" movement. He consistently advised converts to return to their churches, never favoring "any one denomination."[59] He had no wish to divide the churches. He did not view himself as theologically aberrant, but rather as one who preached plain Bible

11. A sketch of William Miller by an artist for the *New York Herald*. From the *New York Herald*, November 12, 1842.

truth that should have been acceptable to all churches. Sectarianism was the enemy of the message. The sectarian mind, he thought, was selfish, bigoted, prejudiced, and intolerant. To be viewed as a sectarian leader would hinder access to the populace, and thus prevent the speedy spread of the vital warning. Besides, the message of the Second Coming of Christ strongly implied the end of competing religious bodies. In 1822, almost ten years before Miller gave his first lecture, he wrote, "I believe that before Christ comes in his glory, all sectarian principles will be shaken."[60] He even dreamed that there would be no sects in heaven.[61]

Little wonder, then, that he was saddened when his own people moved strongly in a sectarian direction. Six weeks after the Great Disappointment, Miller wrote, "For years after I began to proclaim this blessed truth of Christ at the door, I never, if possible to avoid it, even alluded to sectarian principles." But if Miller was able to remain ecumenical in his outlook, despite persecution and rejection, his people were not. Deeply sorrowful, he continued,

But we have recently, my brethren, been guilty of raising up a sect of our own; for the very things which our fathers did, when they became sects, we have been doing. We have, like them, cried Babylon! Babylon! Babylon! against *all but Adventists*. We have proclaimed and discussed, "pro et con," many sectarian dogmas, which have nothing to do with our message. May God forgive us![62]

He expected too much. He could not so roundly condemn the ministers of other churches, and still expect his followers to enjoy good denominational relations. He also failed to account for the social cohesion the blessed hope of Christ's coming brought to believers. Furthermore, the excitement of Miller's message reduced the appeal of traditional church services for many people. This inadvertent come-outerism is illustrated by a letter Miller received from a woman who had heard him preach. "The night after you finished at the Museum, I went to the church of which I was a member, and never was there since. I came completely Out."[63] Another individual went a step further: "I hope, too, that provision will be made, if not done already, that in all the Advent congregations . . . those who *cannot* abide in the churches . . . may have a place to flee to."[64] The

12. In May 1844, William Miller penned these lines of verse expressing his disappointment that Christ had not come in the spring, as once expected. Courtesy Review and Herald Publishing Association.

message of hope was too strong, the bond of persecution and fellowship too great, for Miller to sustain his nonsectarian dream.

Miller's lifelong search for certainty had culminated in his confirmation that the Bible was absolutely trustworthy. After his initial two years of study, he found Scripture more reasonable than deism. "The Bible was now to me a new book. It was indeed a feast of reason; all that was dark, mystical or obscure, to me, in its teachings, had been dissipated from my mind before the clear light that now dawned from its sacred pages." Although he began his study "with no expectations of finding the time of the Saviour's coming," he rejoiced that "the evidence struck me with such force that I could not resist my convictions."[65] He was further gratified when he discovered that his emerging hermeneutic, with numerous fulfilled prophecies based on the day-year principle of interpretation, was impenetrable to refutation. It seemed reasonable to assume that if every Bible prophecy had been fulfilled precisely on schedule, so would the promise of the Second Coming of Christ.

Ultimately, Miller's prophecy failed. And when the divine appointment was not kept, Miller faced an obvious crisis of faith. He would not concede, however, that either the Bible or his method of interpreting it had failed him. He believed he had been misled by Bible scholars and historians. The populace had also disappointed him: "But, above all things else, I was deceived in the number and character of those who, without study, argument, or reason, rejected the . . . glorious news of the coming Saviour."[66]

But neither the misguided learned nor the faithless populace could sway Miller. Hermeneutically, he stood firm: "On the passing of my published time, I frankly acknowledged my disappointment in reference to the exact period; but my faith was unchanged in any essential feature."[67] He declared that if he were to live his life over again, he would pursue the same course. "My belief is unshaken in the correctness of the conclusions I have arrived at and maintained during the last twenty years. I see no reason to question the evidence on which rest the fundamental principles of our faith."[68]

Yet the dissonance of the delay could not be ignored. Miller rationalized, "In the evening [October 21, 1844] I told some of my brethren Christ would not come on the morrow." When his waiting friends asked for an explanation of this contradiction, Miller referred to the New Testament prediction that the Second Coming would be "in an hour they think not."[69] He refused to bear responsibility for deception. "No one can honestly say that he has been deceived by me. My advice has always been for each to study the evidence of his faith for himself."[70] He speculated that God may have designed the delay so that people would turn to the Bible to study further and be reconciled to God. After all, to have erred in the precise date did not reduce the advent urgency. Every passing day was one day nearer the end. On November 10, 1844, Miller safely revised the date and finally overcame all possibility of disappointment. "I have fixed my mind upon another time, and here I mean to stand until God gives me more light.—And that is *Today*, TODAY, and TODAY, until He comes."[71]

N O T E S

1. Marvin Meyers, *The Jacksonian Persuasion* (Stanford: Stanford University Press, 1957), pp. 1–10.

2. Joshua V. Himes, ed., *Miller's Works*, 3 vols. (Boston: Joshua V. Himes, 1842), 1:8. Hereafter cited as *Miller's Works*.

3. *Miller's Works*, 1:9.

4. Ibid.

5. Ibid., p. 10.

6. *The Midnight Cry*, November 17, 1842.

7. Quoted in Sylvester Bliss, *Memoirs of William Miller* (Boston: Joshua V. Himes, 1845), p. 4.

8. William Miller, *Apology and Defence* (Boston: Joshua V. Himes, 1845), p. 4.

9. *Miller's Works*, 1:9.

10. *Advent Herald*, August 13, 1845.

11. *Miller's Works*, 1:10.

12. Ibid.

13. *Miller's Works*, 1:11.

14. Bliss, *Memoirs of William Miller*, pp. 64, 65.

15. Miller, *Apology and Defence*, p. 5.

16. *Miller's Works*, 1:11.

17. Ibid.

18. Miller, *Apology and Defence*, pp. 5, 6.

19. Letter of May 14, 1835, from William Miller to Joseph Atwood. This and subsequent letters cited are from the Miller Papers in the Jenks Memorial Collection of Adventual Materials, Aurora University Library, Aurora, Illinois.

20. Letter of October 23, 1834, from William Miller to Truman Hendryx.

21. *Miller's Works*, 1:11.

22. *Advent Herald*, September 9, 1846.

23. *Miller's Works*, 1:11, 12.

24. Ibid., pp. 20–21.

25. *Miller's Works*, 1:12. Miller, of course, was not unique in his prophetic interpretations. See David L. Rowe, "Thunder and Trumpets: The Millerite Movement and Apocalyptic Thought" (Ph.D. dissertation, University of Virginia, 1974), pp. 37–39.

26. *Advent Herald*, August 13, 1845.

27. Bliss, *Memoirs of William Miller*, p. 83.

28. *Advent Herald*, August 13, 1845.

29. Miller, *Apology and Defence*, pp. 17, 18.

30. Ibid.

31. Letter of April 10, 1833, from William Miller to Truman Hendryx.

32. Examples can be found in letters written to Miller's friend Truman Hendryx dated February 8, April 10, and September 16, 1833.

33. Letter of July 21, 1836, from William Miller to Truman Hendryx.

34. Bliss, *Memoirs of William Miller*, p. 118.

35. Letter of March 6, 1835, from William Miller to Truman Hendryx.

36. Letter of November 17, 1838, from William Miller to his son, William S. Miller.

37. Bliss, *Memoirs of William Miller*, p. 140.

38. Himes was with Miller when he died. See Bliss, *Memoirs of William Miller*, pp. 82, 83, for Miller's deathbed story.

39. Everett N. Dick, "The Adventist Crisis of 1843–1844" (Ph.D. dissertation, University of Wisconsin, 1930), p. 29.

40. Letter of December 28, 1845, from Calvin Bateman to William Miller.

41. Letter of February 15, 1841, from William Miller to C. S. Kilton.

42. Letter of March 9, 1840, from William Miller to his son, William S. Miller.

43. *Miller's Works*, 1:55.

44. Ibid., p. 57.

45. *The Midnight Cry*, November 21, 1842.

46. Isaac C. Wellcome, *The History of the Second Advent Message* (Yarmouth, Maine: I. C. Wellcome, 1874), p. 203.

47. *Signs of the Times*, October 5, 1842.

48. Letter of February 9, 1844, from Margaret L. Bishop to William Miller.

49. Letter of February 21, 1837, from William Miller to Truman Hendryx.

50. Bliss, *Memoirs of William Miller*, p. 140.

51. *Miller's Works*, 1:58, 124, 167–170.

52. *Miller's Works*, 2:72, 73, 132, 278.

53. Letter of December 23, 1836, from William Miller to Truman Hendryx.

54. Letter of December 17, 1842, from "A Friend" to William Miller.

55. Letter of April 5, 1844, from William Miller to Br. Galusha.

56. Bliss, *Memoirs of William Miller*, pp. 210–212.

57. *Signs of the Times*, January 31, 1844.

58. Letter of December 7, 1842, from William Miller to Joshua V. Himes.

59. *Advent Herald*, August 13, 1845.

60. Quoted in Bliss, *Memoirs of William Miller*, p. 79.

61. *Review and Herald Extra*, "Dream of William Miller," p. 15.

62. Letter of December 3, 1844, from William Miller to the *Advent Herald*.

63. Letter of December 29, 1844, from Rebecca T. Marshall to William Miller.

64. Letter of November 7, 1844, from Genshem P. Cox to William Miller, Josiah Litch, and J. V. Himes.

65. Bliss, *Memoirs of William Miller*, pp. 76, 77.

66. *Advent Herald*, September 9, 1846.

67. *Advent Herald*, August 13, 1845.

68. Letter of May 12, 1849, from William Miller to the Advent Conference at Boston.

69. Letter of December 13, 1855, from William Miller to J. O. Orr.

70. Letter of November 29, 1844, from William Miller to T. E. Jones.

71. *The Midnight Cry*, December 5, 1844.

THREE

Joshua V. Himes and the Cause of Adventism

DAVID T. ARTHUR

JOSHUA V. HIMES was a man of great energy, strong humanitarian convictions, and, most of all, action. Although not an original thinker, he avidly collected the thoughts of others and put them to use. He sought to reform both individuals and society—to create a new world of righteousness. He rose to prominence first as a church builder, then as an antislavery leader and colleague of William Lloyd Garrison. He was also active in the temperance, women's rights, Christian Union, and peace and nonresistance movements. It was Millerism, however, that provided Himes the ultimate opportunity. In Millerism he discerned God's plan for humankind and the world; it promised the fulfillment of the reformer's humanitarian goals. In a short time he became Millerism's most visible advocate and the principal target of its opponents. For a few years he was a national figure, a representative type of both the self-made man and humanitarian reformer in the age of Jackson.

William Miller once remarked that Himes did more than any other ten persons to arouse the world to the Advent message of warning and hope, and, in fact, the widespread attention that Miller received resulted largely from Himes's efforts. Himes took Miller out of rural and small-town America and introduced him to the major cities. He established strategic outposts and staffed them with efficient workers. He founded newspapers in most of the nation's leading cities and issued millions of copies of books, periodicals, pamphlets, tracts, hymnbooks, and visual aids. He convened conferences and camp meetings to promote the cause and recruited other men of ability to assist in the work. He established Second Advent Book Depots in cities across the country and printed illustrated charts, some of huge size, depicting various biblical images and events and showing the successive prophetic periods leading to the end of the world in 1843. As a speaker Himes could arouse people and stir them into action. In the early 1840s he preached in nearly all the states north of the Mason-Dixon line, averaging one speaking engagement a day. He commissioned the construction of a "great tent" and traveled with it into areas where adequate accommodations were unavailable. Arguably most important, Himes raised and administered the funds that sustained Millerism nationwide. Although assisted by others, he provided the initiative, coordination, and overall leadership for the movement. He made Miller's name a household word; without Himes, Miller might have remained simply another obscure figure predicting the end of the world.

IN SEARCH OF A CAUSE

Joshua V. Himes was born in Wickford, Rhode Island, on May 19, 1805. His father was a well-known West India merchant, and both parents were prominent members of St. Paul's Episcopal Church. Stukeley and Elizabeth Vaughan Himes intended that Joshua, the eldest of their seven children, should be educated for the Episcopal ministry. Toward this end the Himeses planned for Joshua to attend Brown University. These plans were dashed when the father's business failed because of a dishonest associate. Joshua's formal education thus ended at thirteen years of age. Four years later he was bound as an apprentice to a cabinet maker in New Bedford, Massachusetts, his father having decided that he should learn a trade. Here he remained until he was twenty-one.[1]

In New Bedford Himes at first attended Unitarian Church services with his master. Not finding these to his liking and there being no Episcopal Church in town, he decided to unite with the First Christian Church. The Christian Church, or Christian Connection, as it was usually known, believed that sectarian names and human creeds should be abandoned and advocated freedom in religious thought and fellowship. The Bible served as the only rule of faith and duty, and matters of doctrine were left to private judgment. "Here," wrote Himes, "I found the open Bible and liberty of thought, and made good use of both."[2]

It was a custom in the Christian Church to "speak in meeting" as a confirmation of salvation. At the age of nineteen, "with a heart burning with zeal for his Master," Himes began "to tell the story of the cross and to urge men to repent." Noting that he had a gift for public speaking, some church members concluded that he had "a call to preach." The result, Himes wrote, was that "I soon became an exhorter and license was given me to improve my gift." While serving out his apprenticeship as a cabinet maker, he spent some time once or twice a week doing missionary work in destitute neighborhoods. At the conclusion of his apprenticeship he was commissioned a missionary of the Conference of Christian Churches at no pay, and he resolved "to enter into business for my support and preach what I could." In 1826 he married Mary Thompson Handy, who was to bear nine sons. The following year he was ordained a minister.[3]

Leaving New Bedford in 1828, "not with misgivings or lack of energy, but with a determination that he was bound to win," Himes went to Plymouth, where he preached in schoolhouses, rooms or wherever he could get a hearing. A revival followed, a new church was organized, and a chapel built. In the following year he repeated the process in Fall River, where he gathered a church of 125 members—and enhanced his growing reputation as a church builder.[4] At this time the Christian Church in Boston, then near dissolution, invited the twenty-five-year-old Himes to become their pastor. According to a contemporary description, "His hair was then very dark. . . . His eyes, very black and sharp, glistened as though an ardent zeal was burning within him. His face was round and ruddy. His dress was always neat and clean, and his entire manner and bearing were those of a very honest, sincere, earnest young man."[5] Within two years Himes was filling the Boston chapel every Sunday.

One person wrote that "Himes was by nature a reformer of men and things. He always wished evils done away with and the present condition of mankind improved. He was also radical and an enthusiast by temperament. Whatever work he undertook he entered into with a whole heart. He never faced both ways."[6] Boston, the reform center of the nation, provided an ideal environment for such a man. He soon became a temperance lecturer and, with two other men, established a school where boys could receive an education and learn a trade, while working to pay their tuition. Conscious of his lack of higher education, he sought to improve himself by reading, occasionally borrowing books from such prominent Unitarians as William Ellery Channing and Henry Ware.[7]

The antislavery movement, however, engaged Himes most completely, and he was among the earliest supporters of William Lloyd Garrison, who became a lifelong friend. Himes was elected to the board of the Massachusetts Anti-Slavery Society and served as president of the Young Men's Anti-Slavery Society. His wife, Mary, joined the Women's Anti-Slavery Society. Himes gave "special emphasis to the anti-slavery movement and made speeches upon every occasion, facing mobs, defying them to do their worst and pouring hot shot into their ranks in his peculiar and emphatic style of denunciation of the nation's disgrace and burning shame."[8]

Himes also participated in the movements for women's rights and world peace, going so far as to join Garrison in organizing the Non-Resistance Society. In addition, he became an agent for the works and periodicals of Alexander Campbell, leader of the Disciples of Christ. As he would do later for Miller, Himes introduced Campbell to a Boston audience, in 1836. One Campbellite quoted Himes as saying "you cannot succeed with that doctrine *yet* in New England," but that did not prevent Himes from assisting Campbell.[9] Such activities proved too disturbing for the more conservative members of his Boston church, who asked him to step down as their minister. Along with the more radical members Himes formed the Second Christian Church. Their Chardon Street Chapel subsequently became the meeting place of many of the reform groups of the day.

Applied Christianity, Himes believed, provided the solution to the evils of society. One observer of Himes during these years reported that he seemed to be engrossed with the question of success. Himes, he wrote, "*wanted faith in the success* of the apostolic gospel."[10] He believed that Christians must participate in causes designed to further the establishment of the kingdom of God. In each of the various reform movements Himes found something of that success for which he yearned, but progress was slow, internal strife common, and society reluctant to change. He had not yet found the cause that would bring ultimate success.

THE MILLERITE CAUSE

Himes first met William Miller at a conference of Christian ministers held in Exeter, New Hampshire, in 1839. He invited Miller to Boston for a series of lectures in December. Miller's preaching and Himes's vigorous promotion produced results. Miller wrote to his son: "I am now in this place lecturing, twice a day, to large audiences. Many, very many, go away unable to gain admittance. Many, I am informed, are under serious convictions."[11] One such person was Himes, who now found himself "in a new position. I could not believe or preach as I had done. Light on this subject was blazing on my conscience day and night." At the close of Miller's lectures Himes asked him:

> "Do you really believe this doctrine?"
> He replied, "Certainly I do, or I would not preach it."
> "What are you doing to spread or diffuse it through the world?"
> "I have done, and am doing, all I can."
> "Well, the whole thing is kept in a corner yet. There is but little knowledge on the subject, after all you have done. If Christ is to come in a few years, as you believe, no time should be lost in giving the Church and the world warning, in thundertones, to arouse them to prepare."
> "I know, I know it, Bro. Himes," said he; "but what can an old farmer do? I was never used to public speaking: I stand quite alone; and, though I have labored much, and seen many converted to God and the truth, yet *no one*, as yet, seems to enter into the *object* and *spirit of my mission*, so as to render me much aid. They like to have me preach and build up their churches; and there it ends, with most of the ministers, as yet. I have been looking for help,—I want help."[12]

Himes was not yet convinced that the world would end in 1843, but the possibility stirred him to action. Miller's message promised not merely a better world, but a new world wherein would dwell peace and righteousness. If Miller were correct, Himes had found the cause that promised ultimate success—and time was short.

Having undertaken to help Miller, Himes moved quickly. In the spring of 1840 Himes issued the inaugural number of *Signs of the Times*, the first Millerite newspaper, which within seven months had one thousand subscribers. The printing firm of Dow and Jackson, long associated with Garrison, served as publisher for the first year, with Himes acting as editor and agent free of charge. Thereafter Himes became both publisher and editor. Miller noted that "an entire new era in the spread of information on the peculiar points of my belief" had begun.[13] The stated object of the paper was a "full and free discussion of the

13. Portrait of Joshua V. Himes from about the 1840s.

merits of the question" of the Second Advent. Echoing the principles of his church, Himes stated that writers must not attempt to gain mastery, but rather present the truth fairly, leaving readers to judge for themselves. During its first two years the *Signs* published diverse and opposing opinions on the nature and time of Christ's Second Advent.[14] Himes also began to edit *The Second Advent*, a periodical in pamphlet form, and prepared a new edition of Miller's lectures.

With the publication of the *Signs of the Times*, invitations for personal appearances began to overwhelm Miller. Meanwhile, Himes was planning a general conference for the purpose of "edifying and unifying" the growing number of Adventists. He issued a call for a conference to be held in Chardon Street Chapel in October 1840 to "discuss the whole subject faithfully and fairly" and to "accomplish much in the rapid, general, and powerful spread of 'the everlasting gospel of the kingdom at hand,' that the way of the Lord may be speedily prepared, whatever may be the precise period of his coming."[15] In a statement that revealed his current position, Himes wrote:

We live in a time of extraordinary changes in Commerce, and Arts, Politics and Religion. The elements of this world are heaving and teeming with improvements, inventions, and innovations. All the world *is looking* for far greater changes and multitudes are expecting a long period of peace, safety, and blessedness for themselves and their children, to the end of many generations. But the faithful believer in Jesus looks only for the Lord, and for the glory, and for the restitution of all things, which will attend his coming.[16]

The conference was a success, although Miller was prevented from attending by illness. In a report to the public, conference leaders stated that their object was to revive the ancient faith in the kingdom of heaven at hand. Adventists had no wish to "distract the churches," or to found a new sect, but simply wanted to express their convictions.[17] In response to Himes's urgent appeal, money was raised to publish the conference report and distribute it nationwide. Later he wrote to readers of the *Signs*:

Our work is before us. Are we sincere in our faith of the *near approach* of the Lord Messiah? If we are, we shall never want for the means to accomplish the above work. Brethren, you have only to devote a *little* of your Lord's silver and gold, that he has given you, to accomplish this work. The politicians of this age have spent *millions of silver and gold* to elevate a *man*, to the presidency of these United States! Shall we not pour out our treasures, to give the slumbering church and world, the news of the approach and reign of our Eternal King? Have the daughters of Columbia, by their indefatigable efforts in a few month's time raised $25,000, to finish a monument of everlasting granite reared upon the top of Bunker Hill, to perpetuate deeds of murder and the violation of God's everlasting law! And the daughters of Zion not give their attention, time, and money to send forth the tidings of the speedy establishment of the glorious and everlasting kingdom of God upon Mount Zion? The money will not be wanting.[18]

By the end of 1840 the cause of Adventism was doing so well that Himes began planning for its extension worldwide. Success would be a sign that God was in the movement.[19]

Despite his growing involvement in Millerism, Himes did not at once sever his connections with other reform movements. On the contrary, he continued to serve as a member of the executive committee of the Non-Resistance Society, counselor of the Massachusetts Anti-Slavery Society, traveling lecturer for the temperance cause, and participant in the Christian Union movement. Not yet convinced that Miller's time calculation was correct, Himes remained active in these other pursuits until mid-1842, when the definite-time message began to acquire greater urgency and more intense commitment. Nonetheless he was already becoming somewhat disenchanted with these reform movements. He disliked the growing opposition of abolitionists and nonresistance men to church and state, and was disturbed by the lack of faith in revivals among Unitarians and others, which led him to doubt the prospects of these causes. Meanwhile the Second Coming of Christ to earth to make all things new promised complete success. By the end of 1840 Himes had accepted the idea of Christ's imminent return and abandoned both his belief in the conversion of the world before the millennium and what he called his "former Unitarian views."[20]

One observer thought Himes had grown more conservative, noting that "Hitherto he had been ranked among the most radical of radicals."[21] But despite his changing theological views, Himes remained committed to reform. During the conventions of the Friends of Universal Reform held in Chardon Street Chapel, attended by Garrison, Bronson Alcott, Theodore Parker, Maria W. Chapman, James Russell Lowell, and Ralph Waldo Emerson, among others, Himes had spoken out against "those who are 'always pulling down Babylon, but know not how to lay a single brick in building the walls of Jerusalem.'"[22] Frustrated, he called for action—and results. For Himes, the impending end of the world required intense activity on a grand scale. The world must be warned. "Our cause is of God; he will sustain us," he wrote. "He will raise up friends, and multiply homes and faithful patrons, who will see to it, that an enterprise so vitally connected with the interests of his glorious kingdom at hand, shall not wane or fall, till our work is done."[23] Through Adventism, Himes set out to build the walls of Jerusalem. To Miller he wrote: "What we do must be done quickly."[24]

THE CAUSE BECOMES A MASS MOVEMENT

By the end of 1840 Himes had emerged as the principal promoter, manager, and financier of the Millerite cause. For the next eighteen months he increased his activity, until by the end of that time it had largely replaced his other involvements and he had accepted fully Miller's time calculation. Himes and Miller had developed a close personal relationship. When Miller could not attend conferences, which was frequently the case because of illness, Himes read his messages. Theirs was a relationship of mutual respect and trust. Himes generally deferred to Miller in matters relating to the message, and Miller to Himes in matters of promotion and administration. In time this relationship and Himes's prominence aroused the envy of jealous rivals, but this problem did not become serious until after the Great Disappointment, especially after Miller's death. Despite his energetic, sometimes flamboyant, leadership, Himes seems not to have consciously striven for personal position. His place emerged as a by-product of his commitment to a cause larger than himself. Those who knew him best spoke of his unassuming nature, especially in his earlier years.[25]

During the eighteen months between January 1841 and June 1842 the Adventist cause took definite shape as Millerite lecturers and publications spread the Millerite message. On January 15, 1841, Himes announced that fifty thousand copies of the *Signs* had been distributed, eight thousand gratuitously.[26]

Josiah Litch and Sylvester Bliss joined Himes as coeditors, and agents were appointed to obtain new subscriptions. The need for money was great, and Himes's personal financial position was suffering because of the need to secure substitute preachers during his frequent absences from Boston and the fact that he received no pay for his work with Miller. At this point Himes decided that the profit made from publications could be better employed in promoting the cause than in enriching Dow and Jackson. He therefore proposed himself as publisher. At first Dow and Jackson refused to relinquish their position, but under pressure they relented. As Moses Dow later wrote, "the two principles of *hope* and *fear*, being brought to bear on our mind, we finally consented to the proposition."[27] Their hope derived from Himes's promise that Dow and Jackson would receive the printing business plus a $100 bonus. Their fear stemmed from Himes's hint that unless they accepted his offer he might find it necessary to withdraw his influence from the *Signs* and start another paper. On February 25, 1841, Himes assumed full control of the *Signs* and other Millerite publications.

Books, pamphlets, and tracts flowed from the press. Himes himself compiled a book of Miller's views together with a memoir of his life. *The Second Advent* was enlarged with new numbers, and reading rooms were established in several cities. A new series of *Second Advent Tracts* was begun, and Himes and Litch compiled the first collection of Second Advent hymns and songs. From June 1841 to June 1842 fifteen or sixteen general conferences were held in various eastern locations, and Himes attended all but two or three. Himes usually served as one of the conference secretaries, opening each conference, reading the call, explaining the object and purpose of the meeting, and supervising the election of officers. When key lecturers could not be present, Himes would read their letters and addresses for them, but he was chiefly concerned with conference business—resolutions calling for increased activity, the raising of funds, and the appointment of committees to carry out conference suggestions. He seems to have had the final word at most conferences, using these opportunities to exhort Adventists to work still harder.

At the sixteenth general conference, held in May 1842 in Boston, three important decisions were made. The first concerned stronger advocacy of definite time. Some opposed this, but they were in a dwindling minority. The conference declared that definite time should occupy a more prominent position in Millerite lectures and writings: "Believing as we do, that God has revealed, not only the manner, but also the time of Christ's Second Advent, your committee are fully of the opinion that the time has now come when the conference should distinctly avow this sentiment to the world, and urge it with double diligence upon *all* men."[28] Pressure on Miller to be more specific about the time of the Advent had increased, and by year's end he had settled on the year from March 21, 1843, to March 21, 1844, using the Hebrew calendar.

The second decision was to publish a prophetic chart, prepared by Charles Fitch and Apollos Hale, for the purpose of illustrating the ending of prophetic time in 1843. The third important decision was to hold a series of camp meetings

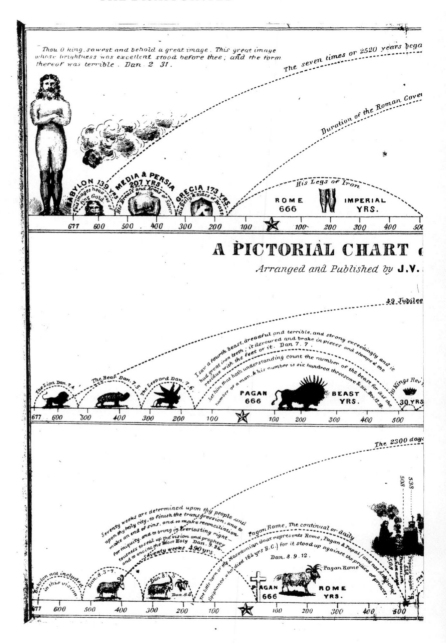

14. This small (7½ × 10 inches), hand-colored prophetic chart, published by Joshua V. Himes, was printed on half of one side of a large sheet of paper, the remainder of which could be used for writing letters. Courtesy Loma Linda University Heritage Room.

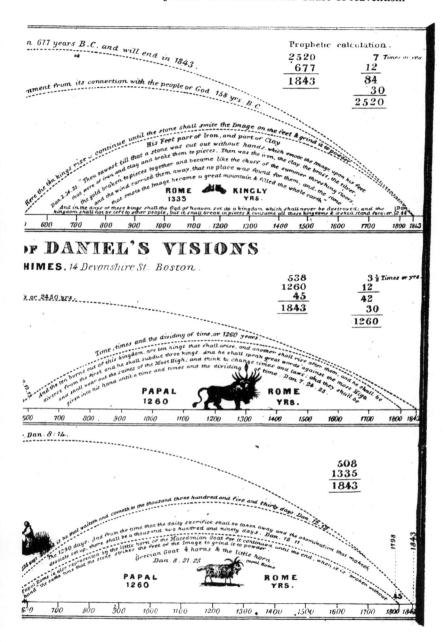

n 677 years B.C. and will end in 1843.

nment from its connection with the people of God 158 yrs. B.C

Prophetic calculation.

2520	7 Times or yrs.
677	12
1843	84
	30
	2520

Here the ten kings rise or continue until the stone shall smite the Image on the feet & grind it to powder

His Feet part of Iron, and part of Clay

Dan. 2. 34. 35. "Thou sawest till that a stone was cut out without hands, which smote the Image upon his feet that were of iron and clay and brake them to pieces. Then was the iron, the clay, the brass, the silver and the gold broken to pieces together and became like the chaff of the summer threshing floors; and the wind carried them away, that no place was found for them: and the stone that smote the Image became a great mountain & filled the whole earth —

ROME 1335   KINGLY YRS.

And in the days of these kings shall the God of heaven set up a kingdom which shall never be destroyed; and the kingdom shall not be left to other people, but it shall break in pieces & consume all these kingdoms & it shall stand forever. Dan. 2. 44.

600 700 800 900 1000 1100 1200 1300 1400 1500 1600 1700 1800 1843

⸱F DANIEL'S VISIONS

HIMES, 14 Devonshire St. Boston.

⸱ or 2450 yrs.

538	3½ Times or yrs.
1260	12
45	42
1843	30
	1260

Time, times and the dividing of time, or 1260 years

And the ten horns out of this kingdom, are ten kings that shall arise, and another shall rise after them, and he shall be diverse from the first and he shall subdue three kings. And he shall speak great words against the most High, and shall wear out the saints of the Most High; and think to change times and laws; and they shall be given into his hand until a time and times and the dividing of time. Dan. 7. 24. 25.

PAPAL 1260   ROME YRS.

600 700 800 900 1000 1100 1200 1300 1400 1500 1600 1700 1800 1843

⸱ Dan. 8. 14.

508
1335
1843

is he that waiteth and cometh to the thousand, three hundred and five and thirty days. Dan. 12. 12.

The 1290 days. And from the time that the daily sacrifice shall be taken away and the abomination that maketh desolate set up, there shall be a thousand and two hundred and ninety days. Dan. 12. 11.

1335 days

Papal Rome is also represented by the little horn of the Macedonian Goat for it continued until the end; when it is broken without hand the same time that the stone strikes the feet of the Image to grind it to powder. Grecian Goat 4 horns & the little horn papal Rome Dan. 8. 21. 25.

PAPAL 1260   ROME YRS.

1198   1843

45

600 700 800 900 1000 1100 1200 1300 1400 1500 1600 1700 1800 1843

to spread the midnight cry more effectively. With this action a new evangelistic era was begun. Although conferences continued to be held, they were soon overshadowed by camp meetings and tent meetings.

In the January 15, 1842, issue of the *Signs*, Himes claimed fifty thousand readers, although subscribers represented only one-tenth that number. In addition, sixty thousand books, pamphlets, and tracts were in circulation. Himes estimated that from 300 to 400 ministers were engaged in spreading the midnight cry, although some still did not favor setting a definite time. The very success of the movement seemed cause to work harder, for surely God was in the movement; thus Himes announced that beginning with the next volume the *Signs* would become a weekly paper.[29]

At a camp meeting in East Kingston, New Hampshire, in the early summer of 1842 Millerite leaders authorized the construction of a "great tent" to seat from 3,000 to 5,000 persons. Himes quickly implemented the decision by hiring a tentmaker and raising the necessary funds. While waiting for the tent to be constructed, he announced an important personal decision:

> The time has come for me to say something respecting myself and my respected colleagues, in connection with the cause we advocate. During the last three years I have given my special attention to the subject of Christ's second coming in the clouds of heaven, as being near at hand. I am fully persuaded of the truth of the theory respecting it, as advocated in this paper. I will say here once for all, that I am *confirmed in the doctrine of Christ's personal descent to this earth to destroy the wicked, and glorify the righteous some time in the year* 1843.[30]

Although Himes was convinced of the accuracy of Miller's calculation and the soundness of Miller's reasoning, he admitted that errors in human chronology were possible and that Adventists might be mistaken about the exact time of Christ's return.

From the end of July to mid-November Himes and the great tent traveled the Northeast, creating excitement wherever they went. With a seating capacity of approximately 4,000, the tent was reportedly the largest of its kind ever seen in America—a most effective promotional device. People came out of curiosity and stayed to listen to the Millerite message.

During the winter of 1842–1843, while in New York City for a series of lectures by Miller, Himes launched a second newspaper, *The Midnight Cry*, and secured Nathaniel Southard as editor. In commencing this new work, Himes emphasized the importance of the Advent cause:

> Our work is one of unutterable magnitude. It is a mission and an enterprise, unlike in some respects, anything that has ever awakened the energies of man. It is not a subserviency to human institutions. It is not a conflict on a political arena. It is not the operation of a distinct religious sect. But it is an *alarm*, and a Cry, uttered by those who, from among all Protestant sects, as Watchmen standing upon the walls of the moral world, believe the World's Crisis Is Come—and who, under the

influence of this faith, are united in proclaiming to the world, "Behold the Bridegroom cometh, go ye out to meet him!" It is an enterprise that swallows up all the petty peculiarities of sectarianism, and unites us upon an elevation so far above those mercenary undulations, that they are utterly lost to our view below.[31]

The Midnight Cry, with a weekly circulation of 10,000 copies, enjoyed great success. Early in 1843 Himes started still another newspaper, the *Philadelphia Alarm*, which Josiah Litch, leader of the Philadelphia Adventists, continued to publish until the Great Disappointment.

As the movement prospered, its critics increasingly heaped ridicule and abuse on Himes and other Millerite leaders. The Universalist *Trumpet* argued that Miller had become prominent only because Himes had used him for his own gain: "Joshua is very much in need of converts; and he is in hopes to get a good batch out of Miller's oven. We are afraid some of them will not be more than half baked."[32] Himes was also accused of preying on the ignorance and fears of people in order to turn a personal profit. The press duly reported his new clothing as well as the safe he purchased. Greatly exaggerated accounts appeared of offerings and donations and of the prices charged for publications. The *Olive Branch*, a particularly abusive Methodist publication, charged that: "Elder Himes is a man with a mind in a nut shell, extremely weak in every point of light. . . . He is fat as an Alderman and lives like a Prince."[33] On another occasion it concluded that "Robespierre scarcely was a greater scourge to mankind."[34] The Boston *Investigator*, published by religious skeptics, described Himes as "the prophet's right hand man, his shield and fortress, helmet and buckler. With the most commendable gravity, he strenuously urges the friends of *the cause*—that is, all who are in favor of a general blow up in 1843—to patronize his publications!" As a former mechanic, the editors continued, Himes "was more honorably employed . . . than he ever has been since, according to our standard of usefulness; still, we believe him strictly honest in his teachings, notwithstanding his superstition, and in the main a very good kind of man, which is more than we dare say of many Christians who abuse him."[35]

According to critics, Millerism itself was a major source of social evils, leading to divorce and the breakup of families, inducing poverty and misery, creating madness, and inciting to murder. Himes's reacted to all this in various ways. Sometimes he reasoned, sometimes he roared, sometimes he mocked, and sometimes he despaired. On one occasion he and his fellow editors wrote:

It is not surprising that an unwonted intensity of feeling should, to some extent, pervade those portions of the community who believe the present order of things in this world will cease before the current year shall have completed its course. Nor is it matter of wonder that this intensity of feeling should occasionally manifest itself in seeming extravagances, since extravagant manifestations of highly excited religious feeling are by no means uncommon; and should the zealous preaching of the doctrine occasionally result in insanity, as has been so often alleged, even this effect is not new, nor is it peculiar to Mr. Miller's exposition of the Scriptures as the official documents from our public institutions for the insane abundantly testify.[36]

In responding to charges of speculation, Himes resorted to sarcasm: "We have devoted one year's indefatigable effort to get up, and establish the 'Signs of the Times.' Our accusers could not be hired to do the service that we have performed for $500. And yet we have not realized *one penny*. This is our speculation. Terrible, very terrible!"[37] On another occasion, in late 1843, Himes wrote bitterly: "I am now satisfied that we have nothing of truth or justice to expect from the scorners of our hope. They are filled with indignation, and all means which they can use to injure our feelings, or reputation, or influence, will be used with the greatest advantage."[38] Criticism, however, never discouraged Himes for long—perhaps because he recognized the publicity value of even the most vicious attacks.

In February 1843 Himes returned to Boston. The new Hebrew year was about to commence, which prompted Himes to write:

> In view of all that has now transpired, and the increased knowledge, that time, observation, study, prayer, and the spirit have taught us, we can most sincerely affirm, that our faith in the glorious Advent of the blessed savior this year, is steadfast and unwavering, having become strengthened and enlarged by the experience of the past, the unequivocal indication of the present, and the joyous foretaste and blissful anticipations which the Lord gives us of the future.[39]

He urged all ministers to awake from their slumbers and prepare their flocks for the day of judgment, all professed Christians to trim their lamps and put oil in their vessels and go to meet the Bridegroom, and all disbelievers to "Escape for thy life, tarry not, hesitate not. 'PREPARE TO MEET THY GOD.'"[40]

THE LAST YEAR OF TIME

Spring 1843 marked the beginning of the last year of time, and Himes planned accordingly. The three general conferences held in May recommended expanding the cause into the West and South as well as into Canada and England. During the next few months Himes extended the field of operations until he had agents and book depots in cities from Boston to St. Louis and from Montreal to Louisville. At Himes's request the Boston conference conducted a thorough examination of his activities and finances. The committees that investigated found everything to be in order and declared the reports that Himes had enriched himself and misused funds to be false. Donations had been used as the donors directed, they reported, and profits had been turned back into the cause.[41]

With the coming of summer he once again set out with the great tent. Going to western New York, he stopped in Rochester, where the tent collapsed during a severe wind- and rainstorm, possibly aided by vandals. The citizens of Rochester paid to have the tent repaired, which left it somewhat smaller.[42] Himes believed that "the west" was the most important field of labor. Lack of funds, however, threatened his tour. In a typical appeal he wrote: "Thus far I have sustained it with my only remaining available means. I have not only done *what* I could but *all* I could. Our other missions have been aided; this needs it. Shall I have help [?] I leave it with God to direct; and the stewards of his goods to do their duty."[43]

While George Storrs raised the tent in Buffalo, Himes returned to Boston by way of Canada and eastern New York, preaching along the way. Next he visited New York City, where *Midnight Cry* editor Nathaniel Southard was ill. Then Himes rejoined Storrs, who was moving the tent to Cincinnati. There the two established *The Western Midnight Cry*. Himes then went on to lecture in Louisville and southern Indiana for several days. Returning briefly to Cincinnati, he left for Boston by way of Philadelphia and New York City. Although these travels had been arduous, his survey of the field had left him optimistic: "The virgins are truly waking up in every part of the country. The saints are 'lifting up their heads and looking up.' The scoffers are raging and 'foaming out their own shame.' But the Lord is at the door."[44]

Himes had reason to be pleased. Although Miller had been seriously ill and unable to leave his home for months, the cause had prospered. Fanaticism had arisen in some places, but Himes was relieved that there were "so few excesses and extravagances among us." He warned Adventists against those "who have more of pretension to sanctity and purity, than reality," and against following their example of "living in idleness, neglecting themselves, and those dependent upon them for support." Such persons had "become a burden to the honest and industrious portion of the community." "From *such*," he advised, "let all second advent believers 'turn away!' "[45] Fortunately for Himes, the majority of Adventists were sober, hard-working, pious people. "Good order," wrote Joseph Marsh of Himes, "reigns in every department over which he presides."[46]

At a conference in New York City early in 1844 Himes called for taking the message to the poor of the city "for whom no man seems to care." These, he said, must be hunted out and comforted with the promise of the new heaven and new earth, which would soon be theirs. "At the same time," he continued, we must "do all that we can to relieve their pressing temporal wants."[47] Apart from revealing the humanitarian side of Himes, this comment indicates that the poor and the destitute did not form a significant part of the Millerite constituency. According to Himes, Miller's message appealed most readily to the working class, with professional people forming a smaller, secondary group. From Cincinnati Himes had written to Bliss that "here, as elsewhere, the 'common people hear us gladly.' "[48]

Himes had long dreamed of holding a Second Advent revival in the nation's capital. "Caesar's household" was the heart and center of temporal government, and he felt that it must be reached before time ran out. In late February Miller, Himes, and Litch descended upon Washington, preaching in two locations and printing 10,000 copies of a newspaper, *The Southern Midnight Cry.* "Our meetings," wrote Himes, "have had a powerful influence here, and we trust much good will have been accomplished. . . . It is a solemn time."[49]

The three men then moved on to Baltimore, taking *The Southern Midnight Cry* with them. From there Miller and Himes traveled to Philadelphia, Newark, and New York City. On March 14, with one week of allotted time remaining, each man returned to his home to await the "day for which all other days were made—a day in the scenes of which we must all take a part."[50] As the end approached, Himes issued a series of thirty-six single-sheet tracts titled "Words of Warning." Altogether he supervised the distribution of five million copies of Millerite publications. Himes believed truly that he had done all he could to arouse the world.

The setting of an exact time for Christ's return did not play the all-important role, at least among leaders such as Himes, that some have imagined. In mid-1842 Himes wrote, "If we are mistaken in the *time*, what harm can result to the church or world?" He continued:

> *As far as prophecy*, in connection with history, presents evidence that may point to any particular time, it is our duty to consider it faithfully, but we have no right to be dogmatical respecting it; and we should consider how fallible we are, and how liable we are to be deceived. We should therefore so live that we may be prepared for the *earliest* appearing of our Lord; and yet also so manage our affairs in connection with the business of life, that we may occupy till he come.[51]

Nevertheless, when the end of March 1844 arrived and the Savior had not appeared, disappointment spread through the ranks. When Himes admitted that the predicted time had passed, Miller commended him. Said Himes: "We have no desire to extend the time, as others have predicted we should do. We have no desire to avoid or defer the crisis; and we freely say to all men that we expected our Savior before the present time."[52] Miller wrote: "*I confess my error*, and acknowledge *my disappointment*; yet I still believe that the day of the Lord is near, even at the door; and I exhort you, my brethren, to be watchful, and not let that day come upon you unawares."[53] Many Adventists agreed with Himes that "It is not safe, therefore, for us to defer in our minds the event for an hour, but to live in constant expectation, and readiness to meet our Judge."[54]

For Himes, waiting did not mean idleness. He urged Millerites to labor to the end. The midnight cry must still be proclaimed—through lectures, conferences, and the distribution of literature. "We must work with more zeal, decision, and perseverance, than ever,"[55] he proclaimed. He resumed his travels, visiting congregations in New England and eastern New York. In May he held conferences in New Hampshire, Boston, New York City, and Philadelphia, emphasizing that God had been in the Adventist cause and that God was still in the movement, and that God would be with them until the end.[56]

THE TRUE MIDNIGHT CRY AND THE GREAT DISAPPOINTMENT

Following the spring conferences, Himes spent the remaining weeks in June attending conferences and camp meetings. He reported seasons of comfort and refreshing, but wrote that "there was but little impression made upon the wicked. The word took hold of them, but seemed not to melt or break the heart, as in former times."[57] A few Adventists abandoned their general routine of business, "performing only so much labor as was necessary for their present wants, and devoting the rest of their time to duties of philanthropy and religion." But most "continued in their usual employments, curtailing only so much as not to have 'the heart overcharged with surfeiting and care of this life.'"[58] Fanaticism continued to be a problem in places, despite warnings from Millerite leaders to place no confidence in "impressions, and dreams and private revelations, so called, as independent sources of information."[59]

During the summer of 1844 Himes continued to expand the publishing ministry. He even initiated two new periodicals: the *Advent Shield and Review*, a quarterly devoted to long articles on theological subjects, and the *Advent Message to the Daughters of Zion*, edited by Clorinda Minor and Emily Clemons and directed to women.

From July through September Himes traveled extensively. After an eastern tour he joined Miller for a trip through Canada and upstate New York, then went to Cleveland, Akron, and Cincinnati. During this time Himes changed his mind on the question of Adventists separating from their churches. Previously, Himes and Miller had opposed leaving the churches unless forced out. Other leaders, such as Charles Fitch and Joseph Marsh, had advocated separation on principle. Facing growing opposition, Himes declared that Adventists could no longer remain in fellowship with those who oppressed them. If churches continued to treat the Advent doctrine lightly, Adventists should withdraw.[60]

While Miller and Himes were in the West, Samuel S. Snow, a heretofore obscure Millerite preacher, was stirring up great excitement in the East by preaching that Christ would return on the tenth day of the seventh month of the Hebrew calendar, the Day of Atonement—October 22, 1844. Snow believed that he had found an error in William Hale's chronology on which Miller's original calculation had been based. Snow's was thus the true midnight cry. At first none of the established leaders, who opposed all attempts to set future dates, accepted Snow's view. Snow's followers complained that Miller, Himes, and Litch considered themselves above receiving light from a lesser person. Snow's message, however, caught fire at the summer camp meetings, especially among eastern Adventists. In August Himes conceded that Snow's message should be examined.[61] By the end of September Himes was writing to Miller that although the new date "was not yet clear to my mind," he found that "the fruits are glorious. . . . It has done away all Fanaticism, and brought those who were given to extravagance into sober discreet state of mind. '43 never made so great, and good an impression as this has done upon all that have come under its influence. . . . With this view of the matter, I dare not oppose it, although I do not yet get the light as to the month + day."[62]

On October 2 Himes called off an announced trip to Europe because "the recent remarkable movement among the Advent brethren on the *time*, and the great work which God is doing for his people, certainly gives a new indication of the near approach of the glorious Bridegroom."[63] On October 6 he announced to an audience at the Boston Tabernacle his conversion to the "true midnight cry," and three days later he joined with fellow *Advent Herald* editors, Sylvester Bliss and Apollos Hale, in announcing: "We are shut up to this faith, and shall, by the grace of God, look for the event, and act accordingly."[64] David Rowe, in *Thunder and Trumpets*, concludes that regarding this new movement "Himes was more interested in its effects than in its correctness."[65] This judgment is well-founded. Although at the very end Himes could state that he was "shut up to this faith," his reasoning was based on the success of the movement rather than on biblical evidence. For him the results bore witness to the truth.

In the October 16 issue of the *Herald* Himes announced the cessation of publication:

> As the date of the present number of the Herald is our last day of publication before the tenth day of the seventh month, we shall make no provision for issuing a paper for the week following. And as we are shut up to this faith—by the sounding of this cry at midnight, during the tarrying of the vision, when we had all slumbered and slept . . .—we feel called upon to suspend our labors and await the result.[66]

During the final ten days before October 22 most Adventists suspended secular business and gave themselves over to the work of preparing for their Master's return. It was a time, said Himes, "both electrifying and solemn."[67] Excitement and expectation reached a higher pitch than at any point earlier in the movement. The leaders—Miller, Himes, and others—found themselves swept along by forces they could not control and could not explain, except by attributing them to God.

Eight days after the Great Disappointment of October 22 Himes addressed readers of *The Advent Herald*:

> God has brought us through a most trying ordeal. We have been enabled to stand under the full expectation of meeting our Savior and King. We have seen and felt our own nothingness—we have found the grace of God sufficient to sustain us, even at such a time. While we have been abased before God, and have fled to his mercy and grace through Jesus Christ, our hearts have been inspired with a tender sympathy for each other; and farther, while the unbelieving world have treated us with contempt and scorn, and even violence, we have been enabled to endure this also, with uncomplaining patience.[68]

To Himes, Miller wrote: "I have been waiting and looking for the blessed hope, and in expectation of realizing the glorious things which God has spoken to Zion. Yes, and although I have been twice disappointed, I am not yet cast down or discouraged. God has been with me in Spirit, and has comforted me."[69] In an "Address to the Public," published on November 13, Himes confessed having been wrong: "We admit that it is proved that we do not yet know the definite time; but we have seen no evidence yet, to disprove that it is at the very door, and that it cannot be long delayed."[70] He argued against setting future dates, saying

THE ADVENT HERALD,

AND SIGNS OF THE TIMES REPORTER.

BEHO'LD! THE BRIDEGROOM COMETH!! GO YE OUT TO MEET HIM!!!

VOL. VIII. NO. 11. | Boston, Wednesday, October 16, 1844. | WHOLE NO. 181.

THE ADVENT HERALD

☞ As the date of the present number of the Herald is our last day of publication before the tenth day of the seventh month, we shall make no provision for issuing a paper for the week following. And as we are shut up to this faith,—by the sounding of this cry at midnight, during the tarrying of the vision, when we had all slumbered and slept, and at the very point when all the periods, according to our chronology and date of their commencement, terminate—we feel called upon to suspend our labors and await the result. Behold, the Bridegroom cometh; go ye out to meet him! is the cry that is being sounded in our ears; and may we all, with our lamps trimmed and burning, be prepared for His glorious appearing.   J. V. HIMES.

Oct. 8.

Second Edition.

Bro. Litch on the seventh Month.

DEAR BRO. HIMES:—I wish to say to my dear brethren and sisters who are looking for the coming of the Lord on the tenth day of the seventh month, but especially to those who have hesitated on the question—that the strong objections which have existed in my mind against it, are passed away, and I am now convinced that types, together with the signs of the times, are sufficient authority for believing in the Lord's coming at that time; and henceforth I shall look to that day with the expectation of beholding the King in his beauty. I bless the name of the Lord, for sending this midnight cry to arouse me, to go out to meet the Bridegroom. May the Lord make us meet for the inheritance of the saints.   J. LITCH.

Boston, Oct. 11, 1844.

Letter to N. N. Whiting.

AND TO EVERY ONE WHO READETH.

ON THE TIME—THE DAY—OF THE ADVENT.

The knowledge of the day is in accordance with analogous cases, the Flood and the deliverance from Egypt—indicated by the fulfillment of the seventy weeks.—Paul's argument in the Epistle to the Hebrews, shows that the unfulfilled type points to a distinct part of the work of Christ, the author and finisher of our faith—that work to be performed at his second appearing—the type points to the tenth day of the seventh month.

DEAR BROTHER:—I am informed that you still doubt that we are ever to understand anything more definite about the time of the coming of the Son of Man, than can be obtained from the prophetic periods of Daniel; and as I have till within a very few days, stood in the same position, allow me to call your attention to the considerations which have induced me to take a different one, viz: that it was intended by the great Author and Finisher of our faith, that we should know the time—the day —in which the second advent is to take place.

1. It is in accordance with other cases, to which we are repeatedly referred as analogous, that the definite time—the day, should be ultimately known. "As it was in the days of Noah, even thus shall I be in the day when the Son of Man is revealed."—In that case the time, in years, was made known "a hundred and twenty years" before the event. And during that time "the long-suffering of God

waited, while the ark was a preparing." But when that period drew to a close, the day was pointed out. "And the Lord said unto Noah, Come thou and all thy house into the ark : for thee have I seen righteous before me in this generation : for yet seven days, and I will cause it to rain upon the earth forty days and forty nights : and every living substance that I have made will I destroy from off the face of the earth. And Noah did according unto all that the Lord commanded him. And it came to pass after seven days, (Margin, in the seventh day) that the waters of the flood were upon the earth." Here the particular time—the day—was unknown till the event was at the door; then it was made known, and so the event took place.

So also, in the deliverance from Egypt, the time, as to the year, was predicted to be 430 years from one point, 400 from another, before the event. Moses evidently understood it, for we are told that "when the time of the promise drew nigh, which God had sworn unto Abraham"—"Moses was born," and when he was "forty years old" he visited the Israelites—"for he supposed his brethren would have understood how that God, by his hand, would deliver them : but they understood not." Forty years after that, God appeared to him to prepare him for his mission. But nothing was said of the day, till the contest between God and idols—the rights of man and oppression—had continued, down to the last miracle, and the last plague, in the month in which the promise was fulfilled. Then a new revelation was made upon the time :—

"And the Lord spake unto Moses and Aaron in the land of Egypt, saying, This month shall be unto you the beginning of months : it shall be the first month of the year to you. Speak ye unto all the congregation of Israel, saying, In the tenth day of this month they shall take to them every man a lamb, according to the house of their fathers, a lamb for a house : and ye shall keep it up until the fourteenth day of the same month : and the whole assembly of the congregation of Israel shall kill it in the evening. And they shall take of the blood, and strike it on the two side-posts, and on the upper door-post of the houses wherein they shall eat it : and they shall eat the flesh in that night, roast with fire, and unleavened bread ; and with bitter herbs they shall eat it.

And thus shall ye eat it ; with your loins girded, your shoes on your feet, and your staff in your hand : and ye shall eat it in haste ; it is the Lord's passover : for I will pass through the land of Egypt this night, and will smite all the first-born in the land of Egypt, both man and beast : and against all the gods of Egypt I will execute judgment : I am the Lord.

And the blood shall be to you for a token upon the houses where ye are : and when I see the blood I will pass over you, and the plague shall not be upon you to destroy you, when I smite the land of Egypt.

Thus did all the children of Israel ; as the Lord commanded Moses and Aaron so did they. And it came to pass the self-same day, that the Lord did bring the children of Israel out of the land of Egypt by their armies."—Ex. xii.

In these two analogous cases, expressly pointed out, as such, the day was ultimately made known. God required faith in the day, and, singular as must have been the spectacle exhibited to an unbelieving world, God honored the faith of his servants, which they evidenced by performing what he required.

And why should we not expect a similar designation of the time, in reference to the Advent, the end of man's probationary state. You will not contend that there is anything in the word of God which forbids it. But if the day is made known, it must be done by a new revelation from God, or by his di-

recting his people to some portion of the revelation we already have, which is adapted and designed to give that information.

A new revelation we have no reason to expect. And if that knowledge of the time is found in the word of God, must it not be in the types which point to months and days?

2. We have allowed that the fulfillment of the seventy weeks sealed or made sure, the remainder of the vision, from which they were cut off. It illustrated the manner of time expressed. Now nothing was said by Daniel of the month or day, when Messiah should be cut off. He gave the year only; but when Christ came, and entered upon his work, and the malice of his enemies plotted his death, for a considerable length of time we are told, that they could not effect it, because "his hour was not yet come." But when the day of his crucifixion arrived, we are told that "when Jesus knew that his hour was come," he ate the last supper with his disciples, washed their feet, and repaired to the garden to prepare for the painful scene before him.

Here let us ask—how was the more definite time —"the hour" designated? Not by the seventy weeks, but by the types, the passover. And if this was one of the "things" which was "written" by Moses concerning him, has not the Father thus intimated to us, that by the types, He designed to "make known" the day when the Son of Man is to be revealed? And should we not receive the evidence from this source as sufficient, if it harmonizes with that from other forms of prophecy? Nay, is it not the only evidence which the nature of the case admits of? Shall we, then, be "slow of heart to believe all that the prophets have spoken?" It would seem from Isaiah (viii. 16—20) that the law as well as the testimony of the Lord, was to be shut up till his "disciples should look for him;" and as it was left "to the time of the end for the Father" to make known "the times and seasons" of the prophets, which he had "reserved in his own power," should we not expect, that he would also unseal the law, so far as it refers to these times and seasons, before the times run out?

In the case of the prophetic periods of Daniel, as soon as their bearing upon the end was pointed on it, it was so obvious, that no man has been able to gainsay it, without showing his ignorance or disregard of the 'truth'; and the truth has so far triumphed by observing the prophet's maxim : "To the law and to the testimony : if they speak not according to this word, it is because there is no light in them." We may expect it will be the same in the case of the types, as to their bearing upon the time of the Advent.

If one who has stood on both sides of the question may be allowed to decide, it is even so!

3. If such a bearing of the types may be found in the word of God, we should expect it would be found in the epistle of Paul to the Hebrews ; for nothing is more evident than that his design, in this epistle, was to show the relation of former dispensations to the Christian dispensation.

He begins by shewing that the word spoken by the Apostle and High Priest of our profession, Christ Jesus, was from the same God, who had spoken of old unto the fathers by the prophets;—"God, who at sundry times, and in divers manners, spake in times past unto the fathers by the prophets, hath in these last days spoken unto us by His Son."—Heb. i. 1, 2.

He shows that the former dispensations were incomplete of themselves, and that they looked forward to that of Christ ; and, as the interpreter of the Infinite Mind, which had spoken in all the former communications of divine truth, he puts his finger upon those communications, and then points out their application to the future—to the person,

---

15. In the October 16, 1844, issue of *The Advent Herald and Signs of the Times Reporter*, Joshua V. Himes announced that this would be the last number published before the anticipated Second Coming of Christ. Courtesy Loma Linda University Heritage Room.

that the only safety for Adventists lay in continually watching. He urged them to hold fast and keep the love of God in their hearts—to commit all to God, confide in one another, love one another, and be patient. "We cannot doubt that God has brought us into our present position, and he will deliver us. Be not in haste, nor over anxious to learn what is to come!"[71]

Himes could not explain why Christ had not come. The very success of the late movement had led him to believe it was of God. "It was entirely unanticipated by ourselves, and equally uncontrolled," he wrote.[72] Despite his disappointment, he expressed continuing confidence "that God has been in it, and that He has wise ends respecting it. He has wrought a great, a glorious work in the hearts of his children; and it will not be in vain. He has prepared his people for some great end; just what it may prove to be, is not now manifest: but the Advent must be at the door."[73] Hope remained, but the old confidence was gone.

While disappointment afflicted Himes within, critics assailed him from without. They accused him of dishonesty, of speculating on the fears of the community, of disturbing the peace, of duping unsuspecting persons and obtaining large sums of money from them under false pretenses, of soliciting money for public purposes and appropriating it to private uses. Reports circulated that he had absconded to Canada, Texas, or England, that he was liable to arrest under warrants issued, or that he had already been arrested and was in jail. One report had him dead by suicide. Others claimed that he had accumulated great wealth in land and investments and that he had sold vast quantities of jewelry. One wag suggested that possibly he had ascended to heaven, taking his loot with him.[74] Shortly after the Great Disappointment Himes struck out at his accusers:

> It is no time for us to defend ourself now, against the thousand rumors that are rife in the community. We have been a close observer of all the movements and doings in the enemy's camp, but as yet we have not seen a *single truth*. —Lies! Lies!! Lies!!! in any amount. But the truth remains to be told at the judgment, where I will meet my accusers, and the doom that awaits us both.[75]

The abuse reached a climax when a writer for the Boston *Post* called the Adventist leaders unprincipled men, perfectly conscious of the absurdity of their opinions and reckless of the injury they caused. In his reply Himes expressed confidence that the *Post* would not knowingly have published such falsehoods and asked it to make amends by publishing a lengthy defense prepared by himself and Sylvester Bliss. This the *Post* did. In his defense Himes stated his willingness for a complete investigation at the hands of any proper or interested person. He asked all those who had business dealings with him to make their records public. He opened his office books to a public investigation. He asked anyone who had been defrauded by him to make it known, promising fourfold restoration. "If I possess any thing which is not consecrated to the advent cause," he concluded, "the public shall be welcome to it."[76]

Regarding stories generally circulating about the "fruits of Millerism"—insanity, suicides, breaking up of families, poverty, and other distresses—Himes claimed to know "from personal observation and an extensive correspondence, that they are, most of them, unfounded; and those which have any semblance of truth, are greatly distorted and exaggerated."[77] He admitted that there had been cases of extravagance, but reminded readers that he had protested against such behavior. While conceding that many Adventists had left their secular callings, he pointed out that he had always warned against it and had advised all to fulfill their obligations. He reported that arrangements had been made in various towns and cities for the relief of poverty and distress that might have been caused by the late movement. Sylvester Bliss continued the defense of Himes, using letters he had solicited from parties supposedly injured by Himes to refute specific charges brought against him. In conclusion Himes declared: "I thus throw open my heart to the severest scrutiny, and shrink from no investigation, before any tribunal, human or divine."[78]

Following the lead of the Boston *Post*, other newspapers published Himes's defense. The Boston *Bee* stated: "We hold it to be even-handed justice to allow every man to speak in his defence, and even Elder Himes should not be condemned unheard."[79] The Boston *Daily Mail* declared: "It is but justice to say that he most effectually disarms his enemies, and nails their slanders to the counter. . . . We have never given countenance to any of the insinuations against the personal honesty of Mr. Himes. We have known him for years, and have ever considered him an honest and upright, though a deluded man."[80] The Philadelphia *Pennsylvanian*, the *Mercantile Journal*, and the New England *Puritan* joined in publishing the defense, as did the *Liberator*, edited by Himes's old friend Garrison. While believing Millerism to be a pernicious and monstrous delusion of Christianity, Garrison called the charges against Himes "gross calumnies, set afloat in the community for an evil purpose."[81] Although a few of the more hostile religious papers continued their attacks for a time—the Methodist *Olive Branch* called down "thunderbolts red with uncommon wrath" upon the heads of Himes and other "authors of the Miller mania"—by the middle of November Himes was able to write that the tone of the press toward himself and Adventists generally had greatly improved. He thanked the papers that had published his defense for their justice.[82]

Despite the unrest in his own mind and the cries of his accusers, Himes set out almost immediately after the Great Disappointment to visit Adventist bands in various parts of the country. He corresponded with groups he could not see personally. Regarding Adventists who had left their occupations and were in want, he wrote in *The Midnight Cry*: "I wish to have immediate provision made for the comforts and wants of all such persons, and families, by the advent brethren."[83] He did not want Adventists dependent upon the charity of public organizations or religious institutions that had been unsympathetic in the past. "We hope no application will be made to such for aid in this work of charity," he declared. Believing this was a matter for the Adventist family to handle, he urged that committees be set up in every city and town to receive contributions and to distribute goods to those in need. "Some among us still have this world's goods," he wrote, "and can render present aid to the destitute. I doubt not all will do their duty."[84]

Throughout his travels Himes urged the Advent people to face up to their disappointment and make provision for their temporal wants. Those who had left their occupations were advised to return to work. This was not easy advice for some to accept. James White, later one of the founders of the Seventh-day Adventist Church, wrote that "When Elder Himes visited Portland, Maine, a few days after the passing of the time, and stated that the brethren should prepare for another cold winter, my feelings were almost uncontrollable. I left the place of meeting and wept like a child."[85] Such people looked elsewhere for leadership.

After traveling over New England, eastern New York, and Pennsylvania, Himes on January 6, 1845, reported that he was back in Boston, "much worn down, but otherwise in safety and health."[86] During his recent labors he had found some who had given up their faith in the Second Advent, but he reported that many were standing fast in the faith of the near approach of Christ. "The brethren say everywhere that the 'Herald,' and the 'Cry,' and the cause *must* be sustained. The question is settled. . . . Be of good courage. All hands are coming to the work."[87] He was eager to start working again, but knew that times were different. The Disappointment had convinced him that Adventists should never again advocate an exact time, but should continue to look for Christ at any time. "Let us, dear brethren, once more arise in the greatness of our faith and might, and gird on our armor for the conflict in this last crisis," he wrote. "God is still with us, and will go before the army of the faithful, and lead them on to victory and the Crown."[88]

As he penned these words, J. V. Himes was nearing his fortieth birthday. More than half a century of life and work lay before him. Until 1876 he served consecutively two of the Adventist bodies that emerged from Millerism: the Evangelical Adventists and the Advent Christians. Returning to the Episcopal Church, he was ordained in 1878 and spent his last sixteen years serving two Episcopal missions in South Dakota, building congregations and constructing churches with his own hands. He died in 1895 at the age of ninety, having asked to be buried in a hillside cemetery in Sioux Falls "because he wanted to be on the top of a hill when Gabriel blows his trumpet."[89]

NOTES

1. *Union County Courier*, May 24, 1895, p. 3.
2. Ibid.
3. Ibid.
4. Ibid.
5. John Gale, "A Brief Recollection of Rev. J. V. Himes," *Advent Christian Times*, February 6, 1872, p. 220.
6. *Union County Courier*, August 1, 1895, p. 5.
7. J. V. Himes, "An Apology," *The Advent Christian Quarterly*, July 1869, 1:5.
8. *Union County Courier*, May 24, 1895, p. 3.
9. Gale, "A Brief Recollection," p. 220.
10. Ibid.

11. Sylvester Bliss, *Memoirs of William Miller, Generally Known as a Lecturer on the Prophecies, and the Second Coming of Christ* (Boston: J. V. Himes, 1853), p. 139.

12. Ibid., p. 140.

13. William Miller, "Apology and Defence," in *Advent Tracts*, ed. J. V. Himes, 2 vols. (Boston: J. V. Himes, n.d.), 2: 21.

14. *Signs of the Times*, April 15, 1840, p. 16.

15. Ibid., September 15, 1840, p. 92.

16. Ibid., September 1, 1840, p. 84.

17. *First Report of the General Conference of Christians Expecting the Advent of Our Lord Jesus Christ, Held in Boston, October 14, 15, 1840* (Boston: J. V. Himes, 1841), pp. 20–21.

18. *Signs of the Times*, November 1, 1840, p. 113.

19. Ibid., September 1, 1840, p. 84.

20. *The Advent Herald*, March 9, 1861, p. 75.

21. *Liberator*, December 4, 1840, p. 194.

22. Ibid.

23. *Signs of the Times*, August 2, 1841, p. 68.

24. Ms. letter from Himes to Miller, June 26, 1841. Orrin Roe Jenks Memorial Collection of Adventual Materials, Aurora College, Aurora, Illinois.

25. [Wendell Phillips Garrison and Francis Jackson Garrison], *William Lloyd Garrison, 1805–1879: The Story of His Life told by His Children*, 4 vols. (New York: The Century Company, 1885–1889), *3:17–18*; Gale, "A Brief Recollection," p. 220.

26. *Signs of the Times*, January 15, 1841, p. 157.

27. *Trial of Elder J. V. Himes Before the Chardon Street Church, Together with A Vindication of the Course taken by Prof. J. P. Weethee and Elder George Needham Relative to the Late Difficulties* (Boston: Published by Order of the Church, 1850), p. 72.

28. *Signs of the Times*, June 1, 1842, p. 69.

29. Ibid., January 15, 1842, p. 160.

30. Ibid., August 3, 1842, p. 140.

31. *The Midnight Cry*, November 17, 1842, p. 2.

32. Quoted in *Signs of the Times*, May 1, 1840, p. 23.

33. Quoted in *The Midnight Cry*, December 5, 1842, p. 1.

34. Quoted in *The Advent Herald*, August 21, 1844, p. 23.

35. Quoted in *Signs of the Times*, August 1, 1840, p. 72.

36. Ibid., March 22, 1843, p. 17.

37. Ibid., May 15, 1841, p. 28.

38. Ibid., December 13, 1843, p. 141.

39. Ibid., March 8, 1843, p. 4.

40. *The Midnight Cry*, December 9, 1842, p. 2.

41. *Signs of the Times*, July 5, 1843, pp. 143–144.

42. *The Midnight Cry*, July 20, 1843, p. 174; *Signs of the Times*, July 5, 1843, p. 144; ibid., July 12, 1843 p. 152.

43. *The Midnight Cry*, July 20, 1843, p. 173.

44. *Signs of the Times*, November 15, 1843, p. 112.

45. Ibid., October 4, 1843, p. 56; October 18, 1843, p. 68.

46. Ibid., January 3, 1844, p. 166.

47. *The Midnight Cry*, February 15, 1844, p. 233.

48. *Signs of the Times*, October 4, 1843, p. 56.

49. *The Midnight Cry*, March 7, 1844, p. 257.

50. *Signs of the Times*, November 9, 1842, p. 60.

51. Ibid., August 3, 1842, p. 141.

52. *The Advent Herald*, April 3, 1844, p. 68.

53. Bliss, *Memoirs of William Miller*, p. 256.

54. *The Advent Herald*, April 10, 1844, p. 80.

55. Ibid.

56. Ibid., May 22, 1844, p. 124.

57. *The Midnight Cry*, July 18, 1844, p. 5.

58. *The Advent Herald*, July 17, 1844, p. 188.

59. Ibid., June 5, 1844, p. 141.

60. Ibid., August 21, 1844, p. 20.

61. Ibid., p. 21.

62. Quoted in David L. Rowe, *Thunder and Trumpets: Millerites and Dissenting Religion in Upstate New York, 1800–1850* (Chico, Calif.: Scholars Press, 1985), p. 135.

63. *The Advent Herald*, October 2, 1844, p. 68.

64. Ibid., October 9, 1844, p. 80.

65. Rowe, *Thunder and Trumpets*, p. 135.

66. *The Advent Herald*, October 16, 1844, p. 81.

67. Ibid.

68. Ibid., October 30, 1844, p. 81.

69. Ibid., November 27, 1844, pp. 127–128.

70. Ibid., November 13, 1844, p. 108.

71. Ibid., October 30, 1844, p. 96.

72. Ibid., October 30, 1844, p. 93; November 20, 1844, p. 116.

73. Ibid., November 6, 1844, p. 102.

74. *Liberator*, November 15, 1844, p. 184.

75. *The Advent Herald*, October 30, 1844, p. 94.

76. Ibid.

77. Ibid.

78. Ibid.

79. Quoted in *The Advent Herald*, November 6, 1844, p. 104.

80. Quoted, ibid., November 13, 1844, p. 105.

81. Ibid., November 27, 1844, p. 123.

82. Ibid., December 18, 1844, p. 152.

83. *The Midnight Cry*, October 31, 1844, p. 140.

84. Ibid.

85. James White, *Life Incidents, in Connection with the Great Advent Movement, as Illustrated by the Three Angels of Revelation XIV* (Battle Creek: Seventh-day Adventist Publishing Association, 1868), p. 182.

86. *The Advent Herald*, January 15, 1845, p. 181.

87. Ibid., January 8, 1845, p. 176.

88. *Morning Watch*, February 13, 1845, p. 56.

89. Clara Endicott Sears, *Days of Delusion: A Strange Bit of History* (Boston: Houghton Mifflin, 1924), pp. 255–256.

FOUR

The Millerite Adventists in Great Britain, 1840–1850

LOUIS BILLINGTON

THERE IS SOME EVIDENCE that William Miller's exegesis was being studied in Great Britain before he had achieved more than a local reputation in the United States. British "students of prophecy" and millennial sects like the Irvingites, the Southcottians, and the offshoots of British Israelitism took an interest in Miller as offering a new and controversial interpretation of difficult prophetic passages. Miller reciprocated their interest, encouraging his followers to study all writers on prophecy and publishing long extracts from British authors in his journals.[1] The British followers of the American preacher Alexander Campbell, founder of the Disciples of Christ, were also soon aware of Miller and his message. Campbell himself was looking for the millennium and called his principal magazine the *Millennial Harbinger*, but he refused to consider an exact date and did all that he could to dissuade his American and British followers from accepting Miller's interpretation of prophecy. However, the Campbellite congregations were among Miller's earliest British readers and they provided some of his most loyal followers.[2] In Liverpool, Bristol, and other ports there is evidence that local Millerite pioneers borrowed copies of Miller's works and Adventist magazines from visiting American sea captains and merchants.[3] In Liverpool, for example, a local dockmaster, Joseph Curry, borrowed Millerite material and was converted. He became a correspondent of American Adventist magazines and imported Millerite literature from the United States. He had long been interested in millennial doctrines and sometimes attended the church of Hugh McNeile, the Anglican minister famous as a writer on prophecy.[4] Himes and Miller spent nearly a thousand dollars supplying literature to inquirers from Great Britain and to the Millerite preachers who went to work there.[5]

Between 1839 and 1844, as the Millerite movement grew rapidly in the United States and Canada, converts were made among immigrants from Britain

16. "Last Day Tokens" illustrating events preceding the Second Coming of Christ. From a reprinted edition of S. S. Brewer, *The Last Day Tokens: Nos. 1, 2, 3* (Yarmouth, Me.: I. C. Wellcome, 1874). Courtesy Aurora University Library.

and others with close British connections, and with the fervor of the converted these were soon writing, to their families and friends, of the hope of Christ's Second Advent. Letters, magazines and books were sent explaining the Millerite message and refuting stories of fanaticism, which began to be reprinted, from American sources, in the British religious and secular press.[6] This hostile publicity itself was a means of first acquainting some British Millerites with the news of Christ's impending return. They then went on to perceive the truth of the message by reading Millerite literature and listening to Millerite preachers. One important source of information for prospective British converts was the *Voice of Elijah*, a Millerite magazine published by Robert Hutchinson at Sherbrooke, Quebec, and sent to many readers in Great Britain. Hutchinson was a former Wesleyan Methodist missionary to Canada who had been converted to Adventism. He used his magazine to justify his conversion to his British friends and former colleagues in the Methodist ministry. He also tried to refute anti-Millerite stories such as accounts of hopeful Adventists gathering in high places wearing ascension robes, which appeared in the British as well as the American press. The *Voice of Elijah* produced a number of important converts to Millerism, including Edmund Micklewood, who became a leader in Nottingham and Plymouth.[7]

From about 1841, Millerite preachers began to appear in Britain. Many were fairly recent emigrants to the United States and they usually returned to the district from which they had emigrated. These pioneers were enthusiasts filled with the hope of the Lord's early return, and some of the later and more effective Millerite leaders complained of their individualism and ignorance. Individual preachers could preach of the impending Advent, but they lacked the determination and ability to organize congregations among the converted: "We want a centre of action in this country. . . . No effectual good can be accomplished without union."[8] During the exciting months of 1843 and 1844, however, even many better-educated and responsible Millerite preachers found it difficult to concentrate on organization or even correspondence, in view of the expected Second Advent, and this enthusiastic phase was carried over into 1845 in Britain, where the Second Coming was looked for during that year: "I have had a strong desire for more than twelve months past to send a few lines to you, to inform you of the prospects of the Second Advent cause in England, but I have been prevented by the strong expectation of seeing the Lord and meeting his people in his blessed and everlasting kingdom."[9]

The Millerite preachers in Britain received some financial support from the United States, but after 1844 the American movement itself lacked resources. Therefore the preachers in Britain relied upon their own funds, the charity of British converts, and the income from the sale of literature. These sources were often inadequate and the preachers were very poor; they operated in such obscurity that it is often difficult to trace their activities, even during the period 1842–1844, the years of greatest enthusiasm. William Barker, who was active in Britain between the summer of 1843 and the early months of 1845, provides a good example of the methods and difficulties encountered by these early Millerite evangelists in proclaiming the Second Advent:

I have been lecturing in the streets and commons . . . and I trust some good has been done, but to hire places to lecture in I have not had the means. . . . I intend, God willing, should the vision tarry, to sound the cry indoor and out as the way may be open this winter in London. It is now about fourteen months since I left New York for my native land; I have lectured at most of the large towns in the South of England, and likewise in Norfolk, Suffolk and the Isle of Wight. I have lectured in chapels among different denominations and given hundreds of lectures to large and attentive congregations. . . . I feel much obliged to you for sending us publications to assist us in publishing the glad tidings of the kingdom. . . . I have never taken up a collection to pay my expenses. I have sometimes met with friends that have assisted me, but generally the English people are not so liberal as they are in America, besides thousands can hardly get their daily bread. The poor in England are miserably poor. I see them every day in the streets of London, destitute of clothing and in a state of destitution. . . . This makes me cry Come Lord Jesus and come quickly. . . .[10]

By street preaching and lectures, through camp meetings and the distribution of literature, the Millerite preachers reached thousands in the years between 1842 and 1846. To attract attention and to assist them in explaining the prophetic books, they used large charts with illustrations of the Book of Daniel.

17. *The Voice of Elijah*, published in Sherbrooke, Canada East, circulated in Great Britain as well as in Canada. Courtesy Aurora University Library.

"I preach about the streets with my chart hoisted on a pole."[11] In time, British converts joined in the missionary work, leaving the preachers from the United States and Canada to move farther afield.[12] There is much evidence that the British Millerites were less disappointed than their American counterparts when the Lord failed to appear in October 1844, and staked their hopes on a Second Advent in October 1845, although they had to contend with much adverse publicity in the press stemming from the débâcle in the United States:

> The Advent doctrine is chiefly the talk in this country now—newspapers often contain sketches about the people in America, especially Mr. Miller. Many reports have been circulated in this country in reference to him; some say that he is in prison—some say he has denied his doctrine and altered his calculations. . . . Thousands are now looking for the Coming of the Lord and believe it is at hand.[13]

In Liverpool, Joseph Curry preached in the streets wherever he could attract a congregation. He received some assistance from American Millerites passing through the city and gradually collected a group of believers. In some places during 1844 and 1845 many who accepted Miller's doctrines remained in their own denominations; this was particularly true of the Baptists and of some Methodists. Emphasis was placed upon the preaching of the Lord's expected return rather than the organization of a new sect. London and East Anglia were the scenes of the work of William Barker and Robert Winter, as well as more transient preachers. They established a tract depot in London, and during 1844 reported favorably on their progress: "Our London mission is doing well. . . . One thousand have embraced this doctrine in Norfolk of late." A Congregationalist home missionary working among the lower classes in the county reported Barker and Winter holding many open air services, visiting house to house and selling books and papers announcing that "Christ is about to descend."[14]

In the North Midlands, the most fruitful seeds were sown by Charles Dealtry, who was probably the ablest Millerite to preach in Britain before the arrival of Joshua Himes in 1846. Dealtry arrived in Britain about the close of 1843, and conducted a brief mission in the Nottingham area before moving to the West Country. In Nottingham, Millerite doctrines were accepted by some members of the local Campbellite congregation. Although the leading British Campbellite, James Wallis, a Nottingham draper, worked hard to destroy Millerite influence, some Campbellites persisted in encouraging the Millerite preachers, and there were local divisions and the formation of separate Millerite groups in Nottingham and neighboring towns. An important Millerite center for some years was New Radford, a working-class suburb of Nottingham, where a Millerite chapel was established. The leader at New Radford, for more than a year, in 1844–1845, was Edmund Micklewood. Micklewood's conversion was influenced by the fact that he was dissatisfied with the rigid structure and authoritarian leadership of the Wesleyan Methodists, of which body he was a member.[15] The Millerites later claimed that no denomination in England was more opposed to Adventism than the Methodists and that Methodist local preachers with Adventist sympathies were silenced.[16] Micklewood tried to reach his fellow Methodists, as well as the wider public, by publishing a magazine, *The Midnight Cry*, between August and December 1844, reprinting much material from the New York journal of the same name. He was helped in this work by the Millerite group in Leeds, whose leader owned a small printing works. The paper eventually failed for lack of funds.[17] In the North Midlands and the North, the Millerite preachers encountered much indifference and some ridicule but there seems to have been less active opposition than in the South and West. By 1844 Millerite preachers had penetrated most areas of Britain and believed that thousands were looking for the Second Advent. A nucleus of small congregations had also been established which became more important later.

During 1844 Charles Dealtry rented a former Methodist chapel in Guinea Street, Bristol, where he held a series of stirring meetings proclaiming the Lord's early return. As in a number of towns, a short-lived magazine was published and between 200 and 300 converts were baptized. A congregation was organized, and supplied with preachers by local converts and traveling evengelists. Dealtry was ridiculed and abused in the local press, and efforts were made to drive him from the city.[18] When he and William Burgess, another preacher who had previously been active in Bedford and elsewhere, arranged a series of meetings in the West Country in 1845, they received similar treatment. In Exeter they distributed tracts and placarded the city with challenges to the clergy to meet them and discuss the prophecies of Daniel. Although Dealtry lectured in a black silk gown with black bands and was dignified and moderate in the presentation of his material, the local press aroused the public against the "fanatics," their meetings were disrupted and they were forced to leave the city. Converts were nevertheless made and looked hopefully for the end of time on 10 October 1845.[19] In Plymouth and Devonport they received a slightly more favorable hearing and obtained considerable publicity in the local press. Tracts were distributed and some progress made in spreading the message in Devon and Cornwall. Dealtry gave public lectures, while Burgess often preached in the streets. The cost of this West Country mission was largely met by a small group of more wealthy supporters in Bristol, Tiverton, and Plymouth.[20]

During these months the Millerite preachers emphasized the impending Second Advent, and in their letters stressed the numbers who had heard the message, rather than the development of separate Millerite congregations. They looked anxiously for the Lord's return on 10 October 1845 and suffered the same shock and disappointment as their American colleagues the previous year, when the "vision tarried." Himes had already warned the British Millerites of the dangers of setting a specific date for the Second Advent, but the British movement was still gaining ground when the disappointment occurred in the United States, and its leaders easily convinced themselves that all that was needed was a simple revision of their chronology. When the disappointment took place, Himes repeated his warning against too exact a chronology: "We are warranted in proclaiming it [the Second Advent] nigh, even at the door, but further than this, with our present knowledge we may not go. We sincerely sympathize with our brethren in their disappointment."[21] This shock and disappointment affected even the most enthusiastic preachers, like Dealtry and Burgess, for a time. They gradually recovered their faith, but many, who had perhaps only half believed the message, failed to do so. From Liverpool, Joseph Curry reported that many professed believers had fallen away, although others were already looking hopefully to 1846.[22] In that year there were only four Millerite preachers active in Britain, their work being made much more difficult by the ridicule and skepticism which everywhere followed the failure of the earlier prophecy. Repeated calls were made to the United States for a full-scale Millerite mission to Britain, headed by Himes or another American leader of comparable stature.[23]

THE MILLERITES AND BRITISH SECTARIANISM

By the close of 1845 Himes began to appreciate the way in which a successful British mission might restore interest in the American Adventist movement if it was widely reported in the Adventist press. An appeal fund to finance a British mission was organized and a plan of operations published in the *Advent Herald*. The mission was finally approved at the Advent Conference in New York in May 1846, and Himes, Robert Hutchinson, and F. G. Brown sailed for Britain at the beginning of June.[24] Himes and Brown remained in Britain until the end of October 1846 and Hutchinson until early the following year. During that time they preached in all parts of Britain, visited the scattered Millerite congregations, and published eleven issues of the *European Advent Herald*, which was made up of material from the American Adventist press. Although many British Millerites remained hopeful of the Lord's early return, the movement was in the process of forming a sect.[25] In the West Country, where Micklewood had joined Dealtry and Burgess, Himes was impressed by the progress that had been made, even though numbers had fallen off after the disappointment of 1845. In Plymouth a congregation of between 200 and 300 had been gathered, and more than 500 people attended a reception in his honor. Despite local opposition, Himes's lectures were well attended and the Millerite congregation which had been hiring the Central Hall for their services considered building their own chapel.[26] In Exeter, Tiverton, and Truro there were also congregations. In Exeter the "Free Chapel" had been hired, and Burgess lectured regularly and distributed literature. The Truro congregation consisted of a small, previously independent, congregation which had been converted to Millerism, while in Tiverton there were a few brethren, who found it impossible to hire a hall and met in private houses.

Elsewhere the pattern was much the same. The largest Millerite congregations, usually estimated at between 200 and 300 during 1846, acquired permanent premises. This was the case at New Radford, at Uckfield in Sussex (where a congregation of 207 had built a chapel which could seat many more), at Liverpool, and in London, where there were at least two Millerite groups, the largest being in Finsbury.[27] Other fairly stable congregations of between fifty and a hundred members would hire a hall from week to week. This was the case at Derby, Bristol, Lincoln, and a few other towns, but some of these congregations soon declined and met in private houses, only hiring a hall for special occasions. In Birmingham, Sheffield, Leeds, and many small towns and villages, meetings were usually held in members' homes; the average size of these congregations was usually less than forty. When they increased beyond that size they usually hired a hall, at least for a time, although it is difficult to establish how frequently this happened.[28] During 1846 a Millerite preacher, a native of Londonderry, returned from the United States and established a few small congregations in Northern Ireland which were later visited by Himes, but little progress was made.[29]

Robert Hutchinson had more success in Scotland, where there was much interest in millenarianism among the Bible-reading Scots, but the established denominations were experienced in religious controversy and exerted strong pressure against the Millerites. Hutchinson preached every day during an eight-week mission in the autumn of 1846, dramatizing his work by publicly baptizing his converts by immersion in local streams. His greatest success was among the Campbellites, and in Hawick he recruited a congregation of about thirty from the Campbellite church.[30] Where independent Millerite congregations had been established by separation from the Campbellites, they often remained linked with the latter body. At New Radford the Millerite congregation was sometimes assisted by the junior minister of the Nottingham Campbellites, although James Wallis remained hostile; and in Derby the officiating Millerite elders "were deeply tinged with the views of Alexander Campbell." The same was true at Lincoln and in Scotland.[31] The Millerites, like the Baptists and the Campbellites, practiced adult baptism by immersion as a condition of membership. Their services were simple, with a weekly celebration of the Lord's Supper, as befitted a body of "Primitive Christians." Each congregation was autonomous and was governed by elders chosen from the members.[32] In 1846 many churches were still served, at least occasionally, by traveling preachers from the United States and Canada, but the usual practice was for some of the elders to preach and officiate in turn. Even large congregations like New Radford, Derby, or Liverpool had no regular pastor.[33] The Millerites attached no special importance to the pastoral office, although they supported some full-time preachers. In the West Country, where the Plymouth congregation had the longest history, Micklewood ceased to work as an itinerant preacher and became the pastor at Plymouth, although he continued to visit other Millerite congregations as long as these existed. Micklewood was one of the few Millerite preachers to be styled "Reverend," although that title was used by Himes and some Americans who had been regular ministers of other denominations before accepting the Advent faith.[34]

Besides their close links with the Campbellites, the Millerites also had some contacts with other millennial sects such as the Irvingites, the Plymouth Brethren, and a number of Southcottian and British Israelite groups. They also had much discussion with the individual Anglican and Nonconformist "students of prophecy." Many of these were post-millennialists and held other interpretations that the Millerites fiercely resisted. These independent millennialists saw no reason to disturb their established positions and reputations within the Anglican or Nonconformist bodies by accepting Miller's chronology or transforming their bookish preoccupation into a living faith. The Millerites were deeply disappointed that so many well-known British "students of prophecy" seemed "formal and lifeless" in their millennialism.[35]

Many of the small sects like the Plymouth Brethren with whom the Millerites came into contact seemed narrowly exclusive, and vigorously defended the peculiar interpretations of Scripture which gave them identity and purpose. All such controversies rested upon a literal interpretation of the prophetic passages of the Bible, which makes much of the literature repetitious and tedious to read.[36] Among the more extreme chiliastic movements, the Millerites were fascinated by the Princeites, the followers of the former Anglican minister Henry Prince, who was then preaching the imminent return of Christ. Prince's career was followed in the Millerite press, and his later experiments in "spiritual wifery" at the "Abode of Love," in Somerset, would not have surprised Miller and Himes, some of whose own followers went off into similar extremes after the disappointment of 1844. Their great contemporary American advocate of his own version of the Millennium, John Humphrey Noyes, conducted similar experiments.[37] The Millerites also showed some interest in the tiny Seventh Day Baptist sect, whose strict literalism led them to worship on Saturday, the Sabbath. The larger American branch of the Seventh Day Baptists was to influence the American Millerites and to assist in their transformation into Seventh-day Adventists. James A. Begg, one of the leading British Seventh Day Baptists, owned a bookstore in Glasgow, where he sold American Adventist literature and entertained Millerite preachers.[38] Begg was also acquainted with some Southcottians, whose literature and activities intrigued every Millerite preacher who came across them.[39]

The Millerites met with many types of opposition. The majority of British Christians, including Evangelicals with millenarian sympathies, rejected their fervent version of Adventism and their practice of adult baptism by immersion: "Our brethren meet with almost as much opposition in the advocacy of baptism, as of the Advent. Hence they spend much time and labour in their oral and printed discourses in defence of it."[40] Both the larger denominations and small sects also disliked what they considered to be attempts at proselytizing by the Millerites among their members, and the more socially accepted denominations were delighted when the Millerites clashed with other "Fanatics." In Exeter, for example, Anglicans and Nonconformists were delighted to see the Millerite meetings disrupted by the followers of a local "prophet," Robert Stark. Stark was minister of Salem Chapel, Torquay, and was well known as a writer on prophecy and as a contributor to a local Adventist magazine. Stark and his followers argued that the Second Advent had already taken place at the destruction of Jerusalem, and they frequently clashed with the Millerites. In Exeter the local leader of the Starkites was a wine merchant who encouraged his followers among the tradesmen of the town to attend the chapel that the Millerites had hired and to interrupt the proceedings.[41] Earlier, the Millerites had been driven from Exeter by a campaign of abuse in the local press. Efforts were made to break up their meetings and to prevent their organizing a congregation. Similar opposition was encountered in other West Country towns, and the local newspapers generally published satirical and scurrilous material about Miller and his "prophets." However, there seem to have been few cases of physical opposition outside the South-West. More anonymous activity seems to have been easier in London, the Midlands, and the North.[42] Everywhere, the Millerites faced denunciation as "Latter Day Saints," and accusations of preaching for profit and charging high fees for baptism. In Exeter they offered to donate any profits from their meetings to the local hospital, but this offer only provoked satirical comments about their "generosity" in view of their belief that the world was about to end.[43] In many places they were refused the hire of halls, and tradesmen refused to print and distribute handbills, sometimes of their own volition but more usually under pressure from local religious leaders or prominent citizens. On occasion the Millerite preachers were refused food and lodgings in public houses, and in the South-West, at least, they were brought before the magistrates for preaching in the streets. As late as August 1846 Burgess was denounced as a "Latter Day Saint" in Tiverton, and prosecuted for creating a public nuisance by preaching in the streets; he was fined four shillings with ten shillings costs, or one month's imprisonment with hard labor. At first, he refused to pay and was led off to jail, where he reconsidered and agreed to pay the fine. In the small community of Tiverton, Anglicans and Nonconformists opposed every effort of the Millerites to gain a foothold in the town.[44]

BRITISH MILLERITES AND SOCIAL REFORM

Although the Millerites believed that sin would continue in the world as long as time existed, they did not feel free to tolerate or ignore evil until the Lord returned. It was their duty to prepare the way by exposing and protesting against every form of iniquity which they saw around them, and the American Adventists were abolitionists, temperance reformers, and opponents of capital punishment and the use of tobacco. Many were typical universal reformers of the period, and remained active in the work of creating the millennium while looking for the Lord's return.[45]

Himes and other Millerite preachers sometimes lectured on the American antislavery movement in Britain, and thus avoided the usual British criticism of American revivalists and preachers, that they were silent on the slavery question. Himes recognized the difficulty that the British attitude created: "There is nothing more sinks our country in the minds of Britons than the existence of slavery among us; it seems almost the only barrier to full and permanent fraternal feeling between the two nations." Himes sympathized with those British and American abolitionists who were working for the rejection of all friendly cooperation in religious, benevolent, or reform affairs between Britain and America, when it was not associated with the radical antislavery movement. "No Union with Slaveholders" was the rallying cry and Himes played his part with William Lloyd Garrison, Frederick Douglass, and Henry C. Wright in publicizing this position during 1846. He attended the inaugural meeting of the short-lived Anti-Slavery League, and sympathized with the efforts that were made to raise the question of American slavery and color prejudice at the World's Temperance Convention in London.[46] Himes played a more important role in the meeting of the Evangelical Alliance, which opened at the Freemasons' Hall on 19 August 1846. The idea of a Protestant Union was popular with some Evangelical leaders in Britain and the United States. Some of the American delegates to the conference were shocked to see the Millerite Adventists represented and attacked Himes as a fanatical extremist. But the British organizers were reluctant to distinguish between the respectability of the various American denominations as long as they accepted the general Evangelical principles on which the conference was based, and Himes received some support from delegates with millenarian sympathies. His part in the conference was reserved for the last session, when he was the only American to join John Howard Hinton—a Baptist minister and abolitionist who had opened his pulpit to the Millerite preachers—in sponsoring a resolution which disqualified slaveholders from being members of the Evangelical Alliance. After much discussion it was decided to form separate Alliances for Britain and the United States with their own rules of admission. Himes was praised by the Garrisonian abolitionists for preventing a union with slaveholders, although he was attacked by the Evangelical press in the United States and by some British Evangelicals, who claimed to be sound abolitionists but disliked his association with the "infidel" Garrison. For Himes, the incident was most useful in gaining publicity for the Advent faith.[47]

Looking at British social and political problems, Himes sympathized with the work of such middle-class reformers as George Thompson, whom he had known in the United States, Henry Vincent in his post-Chartist phase, and the leaders of the Anti-Corn Law League. The impending Advent made him focus little on long-term programs, but his concept of the ideal society was essentially the same as that of many American and British middle-class reformers of this period. His objectives were cheap, efficient, and limited government, elected by universal male suffrage which would be exercised by a temperate and educated people; religious freedom and equality with all churches on equal terms and without the expense of an Establishment; and universal free trade which would promote prosperity and international peace.[48] It is difficult to decide how many British Millerites sympathized with Himes's wider range of reform interests, but it is clear that they accepted the moral and social values which he advocated and which became part of the ideology of the sect. In many respects, these were the "puritan" values of contemporary Evangelicalism, but they were held more rigidly and applied more rigorously to a wider range of social relationships. Himes was appalled by intemperance and licentiousness, which he saw as the prevailing sins of the day, especially in great cities:

Statuary and paintings which fill so many public galleries and carry so many of their fascinating products to almost every fireside cannot fail to awaken the first impure thoughts and then lustful desires. Parents take their young sons and blushing daughters to studios and galleries of art where modesty ought to be shocked. . . . Is it not a fact that in every civilized land, licentiousness prevails in proportion as the arts of painting and sculpture have been carried to their highest pitch of refinement? Are not France and Germany illustrations of this remark?[49]

The Millerites insisted on sobriety, order, and decorum at their own social gatherings, and although some of them were suspicious of total abstinence—it being thought unbiblical—they constantly stressed the need for temperance. Himes was shocked by the poverty and degradation of the mass of the British people during the "hungry forties," and he frequently contrasted it with the pomp and luxury of the privileged. Windsor Castle, "Eaton College," and Oxford University represented an old and decayed order that Himes was anxious to see swept away.[50] Alexander Campbell reacted in much the same way when he visited Britain in 1847.[51] In part, this was the reaction of the "democratic" American traveling in "aristocratic" Britain, but it was given greater meaning and intensity by a constant hope of the Second Advent, when the Lord's faithful followers would be rewarded. Even when the chiliastic fervor of 1844–1845 subsided, the scattered Millerite congregations found purpose and hope in their frequent meetings on Sundays and during the week. The frequency of these meetings also enabled them to examine collectively their experience and to shield them from too much contact with the wider world, except for the necessary contacts of work. The group had a set of religious beliefs that converts were expected to accept, in a ceremony which symbolized their purification from the world, and membership in the group carried with it the acceptance of a code of behavior which often assisted them in their wider social roles.

THE DECLINE OF MILLERITE ADVENTISM IN BRITAIN

Probably no more than 2,000 or 3,000 converts joined the British Millerites during the years of greatest success between 1842 and 1846, although thousands more heard the Advent message and may have believed for a time.[52] The majority of those who joined Millerite congregations seems to have had some previous religious affiliation with the Baptists, Methodists, or one of the small millennial or extreme literalist sects. The Millerites frequently stressed the poverty of their members and the limitations placed upon their work by lack of funds, and there is obviously some truth in these statements. The American movement also was in financial difficulties and found it very difficult to find the modest $1,207 to pay for Himes's mission in 1846. The Millerites themselves qualified the statement that most of their congregations were poor with the recognition that "some of the families have a sufficiency of this world's goods."[53] What the movement lacked was men who were rich and influential. Charles Stoodley of Tiverton was described as a gentleman of means, but he had recently lost part of his fortune, and although he gave £50 to finance the *European Advent Herald*, and similar sums to maintain the preachers, his wealth was very limited.[54] A family named Tanner, which appears to have devoted itself to full-time evangelism during 1844–1845, spent at least £300 in reprinting and distributing American Adventist literature, but these are the only examples of largess that I can find.[55] Like the Campbellites, with whom they were so closely associated, each Millerite congregation seems to have possessed at least one wealthier member, although usually with very limited funds to spare. At New Radford the leading members were a lace dealer and the superintendent of the goods depot at Nottingham station; in Liverpool, Joseph Curry was a dockmaster, and in Leeds one member owned a small printing works. Advertisements in both Millerite and Campbellite literature seeking work for unemployed "brothers" suggest that some members were ironmongers, grocers, and other shopkeepers. The rest of each congregation seems most likely to have been made up of skilled artisans.[56]

When Robert Hutchinson returned to Canada in the spring of 1847 the British Millerites lost their last leader and evangelist with more than local influence. Charles Stoodley offered to bear the cost of bringing Hutchinson's family from Canada, but the latter believed that there was more scope for his work outside Britain.[57] The dependence of the British congregations upon foreign leadership and the importance attached to visiting evangelists can be seen in the disappointment which followed Himes's inability to accept repeated calls for a second British mission. There is some evidence that the British converts who had been swept into the movement by the chiliastic fervor of the American preachers failed to develop sufficient missionary spirit to enlarge and maintain the sect. Because of their congregational polity they were isolated, and they failed to evolve an effective system of central leadership and control. There were only very irregular and short-lived Millerite magazines, although other small sects like the Campbellites maintained at least one regular publication. The Millerites' strict biblical literalism and their constant need to re-examine prophecy resulted in a number of controversies and schisms. Such divisions are a mark of this type of sect and occurred at this time among the Plymouth Brethren, the Campbellites, and the Southcottians. The frequent disappointments which followed the failure of prophecy discouraged many, and those who continued to look to an exact date were merely postponing the inevitable shock. "The dear brethren are steadfast and are persuaded that our redemption is at hand."[58] It has been suggested that in less democratic and pluralistic societies sects are more likely to be pushed into a search for isolation, and certainly, compared with their American counterparts, many British Millerite groups seem to have developed very quickly into closed circles of extreme literalists, united by their devotion to the study of prophecy, and almost afraid to undertake further evangelistic work in case it weakened their beliefs or invited opposition. As early as May 1847, J. W. Bonham of New York found the Bristol Millerites meeting in private houses or in a small hired room. They had been discouraged by opposition and ridicule and by the desertion of many members after repeated disappointments.

A congregation of between 200 and 300 had shrunk to less than fifty, and these had failed to hold a public meeting for more than a year. In Exeter, Burgess was forced to give up the chapel he had hired because "the cause had gone down," and although things were better in Plymouth, Micklewood was aware that a fresh impulse was needed if the congregation was not to become static.[59]

The Plymouth congregation gradually succeeded in winning acceptance in the city; Micklewood was recognized as a minister and the Second Advent Chapel listed among the smaller Nonconformist bodies. Elsewhere many congregations dwindled away or merged with other sects. Alexander Campbell's visit to Britain in 1847 helped to revitalize some of his British followers, and Campbellite publications between 1847 and 1851 noted the return of Millerite Adventists who had broken away during earlier years. In London a Campbellite preacher reported the reception into membership of a brother who had been "a member of the Adventist Church as long as it continued," while in Brighton the Campbellites received some members originally baptized by the Millerite preachers. Alexander Campbell continued to condemn Miller's views, but it is clear that there were some fervent premillennialists among the British Campbellite congregations.[60] These millenarians provided support for John Thomas, the founder of the Christadelphians, when he visited Britain from the United States in 1848. Thomas himself was a former Campbellite and had introductions to Campbellite congregations in Britain. As a result of his visit the Campbellites were divided and declined in numbers to less than 2,000. "Doctrines most fearfully antagonistic to each other divide our congregations among themselves."[61] Some of the remaining Millerite congregations also welcomed Thomas and fell under his influence. He preached at New Radford, and was introduced to Millerite groups at Derby, Lincoln, Birmingham, Plymouth, and in other towns, but if some of these joined the nascent Christadelphians to form a new movement, this remained very small down to the 1860s, when the Christadelphians began to gain ground.[62] The religious census of 1851 reveals the existence of five millenarian congregations and more than 100 which rejected "sectarian" names and called themselves "Christians," "Christ's Disciples," "Primitive Christians," "Free Gospel Christians," and similar names. Some Millerite groups, as well as Campbellites and other literalist sects, must be found among these congregations.[63]

The British Millerite movement shows that the premillennial fervor which swept parts of the United States during the early 1840s was not without its impact in Britain. The movement throws light on the nature and mechanics of the contacts between British and American religious groups below the level of the major denominations and religious societies. The response of the British press and the larger denominations was, on the whole, as hostile as that of their American counterparts; indeed the British press made even less effort than the American to understand the Millerite ideology and generally confused them with the Mormons. Primitive Methodists who lost members to the Millerites in many parts of the country later depicted the Adventists as comic examples of the extreme literalist preacher.[64] After the great shocks of 1844 and 1845, the

Millerites were transformed from a chiliastic movement into a sect, and as such they lacked a sufficiently distinctive ideology and set of social values to distinguish them from other millenarian and extreme literalist sects in Britain. At the other extreme, for example, the Wroeites practiced circumcision, wore long beards and followed certain Old Testament dietetic rules as symbols of their identity, while the Mormons added to a unique doctrine the prospect of material advancement in the United States.[65] The social code and system of beliefs of the British Millerites was very similar to that of the Campbellites, or for that matter the Plymouth Brethren, whom they admired.[66] In Britain the antagonism of the Established Church and the large and respectable denominations may have contributed to the more rapid transformation of the British Millerite congregations into narrow exclusive groups than was the case in the United States, where the Adventists were better placed to win acceptance from the wider community as merely another sect, and where it seems likely that the members were less financially restricted; but it is obviously difficult to evaluate the social pressures exerted against Millerism in different communities. In both countries the wider society was opposed to a fervent millennialism, but more tolerant of the closed literalist sect as such, although the Americans seem to have been driven less rapidly in that direction. Himes was an important religious leader in the United States and brought some prestige to his obscure followers in Britain, while his role at the World's Temperance Convention and the Evangelical Alliance showed him as a useful ally of Garrisonian abolitionism. It is difficult to determine the exact relationship between the Millerite movement and political, economic, and social conditions during the 1840s, although periods of rapid social change and unrest often result in the proliferation of sects. Thousands of those who heard the Millerite message were very poor and may have been swept up for a time by the chiliastic fervor of the preachers and the hope of their message, and although it seems clear that the Millerites as a sect were not composed of the least privileged, some members may have been precariously close to the bottom of the social abyss. The Millerite preachers themselves certainly interpreted the poverty, disease, and famine of the mid-forties as "signs of the times" heralding the Lord's return.[67]

NOTES

An earlier version of this essay appeared under the same title in the *Journal of American Studies*, 1967, 1: 191–212, and is reprinted here with the permission of the publisher, Cambridge University Press.

1. *Advent Herald and Signs of the Times Reporter* (Boston), May 28, 1845. Henceforth cited as *Advent Herald. The Time of the End or Prophetic Witness; Recognising the Israelitish Origin of the English Nation and Advocating the Pre-Millennial Coming of our Lord* . . . (London), no. 4, January 1845. See also Hugh I. B. Dunton, "The Millerite Adventists and Other Millenarian Groups in Great Britain, 1830–1860" (Ph.D. thesis,

University of London, 1984), pp. 102ff. Dr. Dunton's thesis is the most comprehensive account of British Millerism but as he acknowledges, p. 355, it has not "overthrown" the account presented here.

2. *Christian Messenger and Reformer* (Nottingham), 1843, 7: 127ff., 204–205. See also Louis Billington, "The Churches of Christ in Britain: A Study in Nineteenth-Century Sectarianism," *Journal of Religious History*, 1974, 8: 24–25.

3. *Advent Herald*, January 29, 1845, and February 10, 1847.

4. Ibid., January 29, and March 26, 1845.

5. Ibid., November 26, 1845, and February 4, 1846.

6. Ibid., January 29, and April 9, 1845. For adverse reports about the Millerites in magazines of opposite principles, see the *Evangelical Magazine* (London), December 1844, p. 690, and the *Movement and Anti-Persecution Gazette* (London), April 20, and July 20, 1844.

7. F. D. Nichol, *The Midnight Cry: A Defence of William Miller and the Millerites* (Washington, D.C.: Review and Herald Publishing Association, 1944), p. 527; I. C. Wellcome, *History of the Second Advent Message* (Yarmouth, Maine: I. C. Wellcome, 1874), pp. 338–339; *Advent Herald*, April 9, 1845, and March 17, 1847; Dunton, "The Millerite Adventists," pp. 117–118.

8. *Advent Herald*, February 4, 1846.

9. Ibid., November 26, 1845.

10. Ibid., March 5, 1845.

11. *The Midnight Cry* (New York), May 18, 1843, and January 4, 1844.

12. *Advent Herald*, November 26, 1845.

13. *The Midnight Cry* (New York), January 4, 1844.

14. *Advent Herald*, January 29, and March 26, 1845; *The Midnight Cry* (New York), January 4, 1844; *The Christian Witness* (London), March 1, 1844.

15. *Christian Messenger and Reformer* (Nottingham), June 1844, 8: 294ff.; *Gospel Banner* (London), June 1848; *Advent Herald*, March 17, 1847. The *Christian Messenger and Reformer* was a Campbellite publication controlled by Wallis, while the *Gospel Banner* was also Campbellite but more sympathetic toward Millerism. See also Billington, "The Churches of Christ," pp. 25–26.

16. *Advent Herald*, January 6, 1847; Dunton, "The Millerite Adventists," pp. 117–118.

17. *Christian Messenger and Reformer* (Nottingham), August 1844, 8: 414; *Advent Herald*, April 23, and November 26, 1845.

18. *Advent Herald*, November 26, 1845; *Felix Farley's Bristol Journal*, November 2, 1844; *Christian Messenger and Reformer* (Nottingham), December 1844, 8.

19. *Advent Herald*, April 8, 1846; *Western Times* (Exeter), issues for September and October 1845; R. S. Lambert, *The Cobbett of the West: A Study of Thomas Latimer* (London: Nicholson and Watson, 1939), p. 127. See also Dunton, "The Millerite Adventists," pp. 115–117.

20. *Advent Herald*, November 26, 1845, and February 4, 1846. The *Advent Herald*, April 8, 1846, reprinted a large quantity of material from West Country papers for and against the Millerites; much of it, of course, was against.

21. *Advent Herald*, November 26, 1845.

22. Ibid., January 7, February 4, and March 4, 1846.

23. Ibid.

24. Ibid., June 3 and 10, 1846; Dunton, "The Millerite Adventists," pp. 132–134.

25. This is based on the *Advent Herald* for the months of Himes's visit. *The European Advent Herald* and all short-lived Adventist magazines are very difficult to trace even in American Adventist libraries, which have the largest holdings. For the problem see Dunton, "The Millerite Adventists," pp. 171–191.

26. *Advent Herald*, August 12 and 19, 1846; and the *Christian Messenger and Family*

Magazine (London), August 1846, pp. 366–368. This was the successor to the *Christian Messenger and Reformer*. *Advent Herald*, August 5, 1846, and March 17, 1847.

27. *Advent Herald*, April 8, August 26, and November 18, 1846, and March 10, 1847. See also F. and J. White, *History, Directory, and Gazetteer of Nottingham* (Sheffield, 1844), p. 516.

28. This is based on scattered information in the *Advent Herald* for the months of Himes's visit.

29. *Advent Herald*, September 16, 1846, and January 20, 1847. Dunton, "The Millerite Adventists," pp. 169–70, lists congregations with chapels and towns with known groups of believers. It enlarges but does not alter the interpretation presented in the last two paragraphs.

30. *Advent Herald*, November 18, 1846–April 24, 1847.

31. Ibid., November 18, 1846, and December 30, 1846.

32. Not all the converts to Millerism were happy with their methods of baptism, and Micklewood, Dealtry, and other leaders were accused of keeping too closely to Campbellite practice. See *Christian Messenger and Family Magazine*, November 1846, pp. 529–530.

33. *Advent Herald*, November 18, and December 30, 1846.

34. By 1850 Micklewood was styled "Reverend" in William White's *History, Gazetteer, and Directory of Devonshire* (Sheffield, 1850), p. 668.

35. *Advent Herald*, January 13, 1847; Dunton, "The Millerite Adventists," pp. 192–232.

36. *Advent Herald*, February 4, and August 19, 1846.

37. For Prince, see Charles Mander, *The Reverend Prince and His Abode of Love* (East Ardsley: E. P. Publishing Ltd., 1976); and for Noyes, see Robert David Thomas, *The Man Who Would Be Perfect: John Humphrey Noyes and the Utopian Impulse* (Philadelphia: University of Pennsylvania Press, 1979). For similar activities among the Millerites, see Wellcome, *Second Advent Message*, pp. 357–394; and *Advent Herald*, April 8, 1846.

38. *Advent Herald*, October 14, 1846. For Begg, see J. E. Lee Gamble and Charles H. Green, "The Sabbath in the British Isles," in *Seventh Day Baptists in Europe and America: A Series of Historical Papers*, 2 vols. (Plainsfield, New Jersey, 1910), 1:67.

39. Himes made a study of the Southcottian movement in London and published a report in *Advent Herald*, September 23, 1846. He visited their church and examined their books and manuscripts, which he thought contained "pretty good sentiments," although he found it difficult to follow their method of interpretation. Letters were later received from a rival Southcottian group based in Ashton-under-Lyme who claimed to be the only true followers of Joanna Southcott and to have a membership of "40,000." These were the Christian Israelites or Wroeites, followers of the prophet John Wroe, who was not without his supporters in the United States. For the Southcottian movements generally, see G. R. Balleine, *Past Finding Out* (London: S.P.C.K., 1956); and for John Wroe, see *Divine Communications and Prophecies given to John Wroe, . . . Also an Account of His Life . . .* (Wakefield, 1834), and W. H. Armytage, *Heavens Below: Utopian Experiments in England 1560–1960* (London: Routledge & Kegan Paul, 1961), pp. 274–276.

40. *Advent Herald*, August 12, 1846.

41. Ibid., August 26, 1846; and *Plymouth, Devonport and Stonehouse Herald*, June 6, 1846. For Stark, see Miss Stark, *A Divinely Commissioned Ministry . . . with a Memoir of the Author* (London, 1858), and *Biblical Inquirer* (Exeter), March 1844–January 1846.

42. A reading of local newspapers in the Midlands has produced fewer hostile comments about the Millerites than in the South-West, and some editors reprinted West Country material while ignoring local Millerite activity. See, for example, *Leicester Chronicle*, October 12, 1844 and September 27, 1845.

43. *Advent Herald*, April 8, and August 5, 1846; and *Western Times* issues for September and October 1846.

44. *Advent Herald*, August 12, and November 25, 1846; and *Plymouth, Devonport and Stonehouse Herald*, August 29, 1846.

45. *Advent Herald*, April 16, and July 22, 1846.

46. Ibid., September 23, and October 14, 1846.

47. Ibid., September 30, and November 4, 1846; *Abstract of the Proceedings and Final Resolutions of the Conference of the Evangelical Alliance Held in Freemasons' Hall, London on 19 August and Following Days* (London, 1846); L. Billington, "Some Connections Between British and American Reform Movements, 1830–60" (M.A. thesis, Bristol University, 1966), pp. 198–201.

48. This is based on much scattered material in the *Advent Herald* for 1846.

49. *Advent Herald*, September 16, 1846.

50. Ibid., September 9, 1846.

51. See Campbell's own account in the *Millennial Harbinger* (Bethany, Va.), August 1847–August 1848.

52. This is based on the numbers for different congregations given in the *Advent Herald* during the years 1845–1847. Dunton, "The Millerite Adventists," pp. 167–170, arrived at similar figures.

53. The details of the cost of Himes's mission are in the *Advent Herald* for June 3 and 10, 1846, and the quotation is from the issue for September 2, 1846.

54. *Advent Herald*, August 5, 1846. Dunton, "The Millerite Adventists," p. 236.

55. *Advent Herald*, November 26, 1845.

56. This is based on the *Advent Herald*, the *Christian Messenger*, and the *Gospel Banner* cited above. See also a letter from the New Radford congregation in Robert Roberts, *Dr. Thomas, His Life and Work* (Birmingham, 1884), pp. 251–253, and the short-lived Campbellite magazine, the *Bible Advocate and Precursor of Unity* (London), May 1849. See Billington, "The Churches of Christ," pp. 30–31 for a detailed analysis of the British Campbellites' social composition, and Dunton, "The Millerite Adventists," pp. 233ff.

57. *Advent Herald*, May 1, 1847.

58. Ibid.; Dunton, "The Millerite Adventists," pp. 188–191.

59. *Advent Herald*, July 3, 1847; and see also E. Micklewood, *Key to the Chronological Arrangement of the Apocalypse* (London, 1847); R. Hutchinson, *The Kingdom of God* (London, 1847); and H. Jones, *Modern Phenomena of the Heavens, reprinted . . . with a Sermon on the Signs of the Times by W. C. Burgess* (Exeter, 1847). The question of the relationship between the wider society and the nature of the sects within it is discussed in Bryan Wilson, "An Analysis of Sect Development," *American Sociological Review*, 1959, 24:3–15. When the American Campbellites sent a mission to Great Britain after the Civil War, its leaders were alarmed by the excessive narrowness of the British Campbellite congregations compared with their American counterparts. See John T. Brown, ed., *The Churches of Christ: A Historical, Biographical and Pictorial History . . .* (Louisville: J. P. Morton & Co., 1904), pp. 130ff.

60. *Bible Advocate*, April and May 1848; *Gospel Banner*, March 1848.

61. *Gospel Banner* for 1848, and issue for September 1851. See also Roberts, *Dr. Thomas*, pp. 250–280, and *Herald of the Kingdom and Age to Come* (Richmond, Va.) 1: 157–161 and passim, which contains Thomas's letters from Britain.

62. Roberts, *Dr. Thomas*, pp. 250ff.; *Gospel Banner*, August 1851; *Millennial Harbinger*, March 1853.

63. Census of Great Britain, 1851: *Religious Worship England and Wales: Report and Tables* (London, 1853), pp. cxiii-cxiv. Dunton, "The Millerite Adventists," pp. 334–345, has brought together more scattered material on the Millerites after 1850 but does not significantly differ from this account.

64. Dunton, "The Millerite Adventists," p. 157; *The Messenger of Mercy and Old Methodist Revivalist* (London), 1844, no. 15, 126; George Shaw, *The Twistings and Twinings of Mr. Timothy Turnabout* (London, 1874), p. 100.

65. Some Campbellites did use their American connections to emigrate. See *Gospel Banner*, February 1848, May and August 1849, and March 1851.

66. David King, a British Campbellite leader in the 1850s, hated "costly entertainment, dancing, novel reading, concerts, bagatelle and other trifling games," and thought the church-going public excessively worldly. *Millennial Harbinger*, February 1855.

67. *Advent Herald*, January 7, and November 18, 1846. For another view of the connection between millenarianism and the working class, see E. P. Thompson, *The Making of the English Working Class* (London: Gollancz, 1963), pp. 116–129, 382–389, 799ff.

FIVE

The Millerite Use of Prophecy

A Case Study of a "Striking Fulfilment"

ERIC ANDERSON

And the four angels were loosed, which were
prepared for an hour, and a day, and a month,
and a year, for to slay the third part of men.
Revelation 9:15

WILLIAM MILLER AND HIS followers began their schooling in failed prophecy
long before the morning of October 23, 1844. Indeed, the history of the
American "second advent awakening" is a history of recurring disappointment
as well as a "blessed hope."

It is possible to count a dozen or more lesser disappointments before and
after 1844 as Millerism (like Jonah's gourd) rapidly grew and then withered.
Before the "Great Disappointment," enthusiastic Adventists calculated other
dates for the Second Coming, including February 10, February 15, and April 14,
1843, as well as the 1843 autumnal equinox, and March 21, 1844. After 1844
increasingly obscure "timists" found that Bible prophecy pointed to the
Parousia in 1847 or 1851 or 1866 or 1873.[1]

The first Millerite experiment in prophetic time-setting, which occurred in
1840, set a pattern for all the rest. On August 11, 1840, many Adventists,
including Miller himself, expected two dramatic end-time events: the fall of
Turkey and the close of God's "probation" for the unregenerate world. Immediately after August 11, Adventists were on the defensive, embarrassed as
their critics triumphed. As one Millerite leader confessed, "it was for a few
weeks a time of trial to many." Then new information convinced them that
Turkey really had fallen, after all, and August 11, 1840, became "one of the
main proofs of their system." An Adventist pamphleteer remembered later,
"The events of August 11th, 1840, was to the Advent movement what the power

of steam is to the machinery of the railroad locomotive."[2] The apparent accuracy of the Turkish prediction revitalized the power of the idea that the "door of mercy" was on the verge of shutting forever. In future crises Adventists would, remembering this experience, have strong incentive to persevere in the face of preliminary disappointment, and ever after they fell easily into talk of last chances, tests, and shut doors.

Historians sometimes fancy themselves simple myth-killers, discoverers of original, primary, reliable evidence which destroys legends and polemical distortions. In the story of August 11, 1840, however, the myth can illuminate the history, helping us understand the Millerites and their view of history and prophecy. It may be useful, therefore, to proceed in reverse order, beginning with later Adventist interpretations and working back to the more reliable contemporary documents.

LOUGHBOROUGH'S VERSION

The most influential retelling of the "fall of Turkey" was written decades afterwards by Seventh-day Adventist minister John N. Loughborough. In two

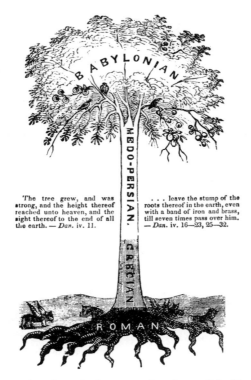

The tree grew, and was strong, and the height thereof reached unto heaven, and the sight thereof to the end of all the earth. — *Dan.* iv. 11.

... leave the stump of the roots thereof in the earth, even with a band of iron and brass, till seven times pass over him. — *Dan.* iv. 16—23, 25—32.

18. A woodcut from the June 15, 1840, issue of the *Signs of the Times* illustrating the prophecies of Daniel 4:10–32. Courtesy Loma Linda University Heritage Room.

historical works (published in 1892 and 1905), Loughborough presented a version of events which most subsequent writers have followed. It is a story in which there is no hint of disappointment.

Loughborough began his account with a review of the prophecies of Revelation 8–10. The prophet described, in these chapters, seven angels ("who stand before God") successively blowing seven trumpets, each trumpet blast accompanied by dramatic symbolic actions. In keeping with Millerite "historicist" practice, Loughborough tied each symbol to specific historical events. "The first four trumpets," he declared, "met their fulfilment in the wars of the Goths, Vandals, Huns, etc., which divided Western Rome into ten parts or kingdoms." (Somehow this prosaic summary drains the power from verses which speak of "hail and fire mingled with blood," a mountain cast into the sea, a great star named Wormwood falling from heaven to poison a third part of the waters, and an angel smiting the sun, moon, and stars.) The fifth and sixth trumpets Loughborough applied to the Ottoman Turks—an interpretation with roots reaching back to the sixteenth century.[3]

The symbols of the fifth trumpet—billowing smoke, stinging locusts, and the angel of the bottomless pit—represented (according to Loughborough) the 150-year period during which Turks "tormented" the Eastern empire, from July 27, 1299, to July 27, 1449. When the sixth trumpet sounds (Rev. 9:13), four angels "which are bound in the great river Euphrates" are loosed. These angels, according to the Apocalypse, "were prepared for an hour, and a day, and a month, and a year, for to slay the third part of men," a statement taken by Loughborough (and the Millerites before him) to refer to the specific period of time after 1449 in which the Ottoman empire controlled former Byzantine territory.[4]

The key figure in the Millerite interpretation of the sixth trumpet was Josiah Litch, a "well-known" Methodist minister in New England "who embraced the truth set forth by William Miller" in 1838, at the age of 29. According to Loughborough, Litch then published a study of the seven trumpets in which "he took the unqualified position that the sixth trumpet would cease to sound on the 11th of August, 1840, and that that would demonstrate to the world that a *day* in symbolic prophecy represents a *year* of literal time." (The key to all Millerite prophetic interpretation was the assumption that the prophetic "days" employed in Daniel and Revelation were really years. The theory, which usually cited Numbers 14:34 and Ezekiel 4:6 as proof of a "year-day principle," can be traced as far back as Joachim of Fiore. In the case of Revelation 9:15, the calculation was that the hour, day, month, and year of the prophecy meant 391 years and 15 days.)[5]

"Some of the brethren," reported Loughborough, "even those who believed with him on this point, trembled with fear of the result, if it should not come to pass' as he said."

This did not however, daunt him, but he went forward to do all in his power to give publicity to his views on the Turkish question. Public journals spread abroad the claim he had made on the subject. Infidel clubs discussed the question in their meetings, and said, "Here is a man who ventures something, and if this matter comes out as he says, it will establish his claim without a doubt that a day in prophecy symbolizes a year, and that twenty-three hundred days is so many years, and that they will terminate in 1844."[6]

Loughborough asserted that when the day came Turkey showed that its independence was gone by accepting the "dictation" of the European powers in the Sultan's quarrel with the Pasha of Egypt.

This striking fulfilment of the prophecy had a tremendous effect upon the public mind. It intensified the interest of the people to hear upon the subject of fulfilled and fulfilling prophecy. Dr. Litch said that within a few months after August 11, 1840, he had received letters from more than one thousand prominent infidels, some of them leaders in infidel clubs, in which they stated that they had given up the battle against the Bible, and accepted it as God's revelation to man. Some of these were fully converted to God, and a number of them became able speakers in the great second advent movement.[7]

Such is the legend of August 11, 1840. Loughborough's version of history underlines the Millerites' self-understanding as thoroughly rational students of a complicated prophetic code, men who were willing to subject their theories to tests which would satisfy objective, honest skeptics.

Loughborough made no mention of the post-1844 evolution of Litch's prophetic interpretation. The fact is, a reader would never surmise from Litch's later writings that August 11, 1840, had ever been central to his understanding of eschatology. In 1867 he published a rejection of the prophetic day-literal year formula as a general principle of hermeneutics. Noting that the standard proof texts were unrelated to the issue of prophecy, he concluded that the 2,300 days were literal days. "The burden of proof . . . that some other rule has been given rests on those who maintain the year-day theory, not on those who reject the theory," he added. Litch offered a specific commentary on the sixth trumpet in an 1873 work entitled *A Complete Harmony of Daniel and the Apocalypse*. No longer did he read deep, secret meanings in Revelation 9:15: "The exact hour for [the angels] to be loosed was fixed. They were prepared *unto* an hour, day, month, and year. That is, the exact time for their loosing was fixed, to a year, a month, a day, and an hour; it is not an exact period during which they should act."[8]

AWKWARD DETAILS

Neither the oblivion to which Litch eventually condemned August 11, 1840, nor the triumph Loughborough bestowed upon the day accurately reflects the actual events relating to Litch's prophecy. Contemporary accounts preserve certain awkward details about this paradoxical day, helping to explain the mentality of the Millerite movement.

19. On March 2, 1843, Horace Greeley published a special issue of the *New-York Tribune* devoted to William Miller's prophetic interpretations and a refutation of them. Courtesy Loma Linda University Heritage Room.

JOHN'S VISIONS.

"TO SHOW CHRIST'S SERVANTS THINGS WHICH MUST SHORTLY COME TO PASS."

8. "He shall be broken without hand." *Second Rome.* (See ch. 2.) "Broken by the stone cut out *without hands.*"

9. Rome was the *only* power which could be referred to, for it was the only "EXCEEDING GREAT" power which succeeded the four kingdoms, and fulfilled all parts of the description. *Finally.* As Medo-Persia and Grecia succeed each other in this vision, just as they had been seen *once before*, it is absurd to suppose that the power which follows them in this vision is a *different power* from the one which *once before* had been seen *succeeding them.*

We turn now to Rev xii and xiii where we find other waymarks set up on the stream of time by other

PROPHETIC SYMBOLS.

In the book of Revelation we have the fourth kingdom of Daniel's visions brought to view again under different figures. The three preceding kingdoms have ere all passed away. John commences with Rome in its PAGAN state.—See Rev. 12 : 3, 4. "And there appeared another wonder in heaven, and behold, a great red dragon, having seven heads and ten horns, and seven crowns upon his heads. And his tail drew the third part of the stars of heaven, and did cast them to the earth."

PAGAN ROME.

The dragon, in his various modification, is the great agent and master spirit directing all the beasts, described in Daniel and John's prophecies. The seven heads denote the seven forms of government in the Roman Empire, one of which was "not yet" when John wrote.

"And the dragon [Pagan Rome] stood before the woman [the Church] to devour the child [Christ] as soon as it was born." See Matt 2 : 1—13, 16. "Arise, take the young child and his mother and flee into Egypt, for Herod will seek the young child to DESTROY HIM."

PAPAL ROME. REV. 13.

1 And I stood upon the sand of the sea, and saw a beast rise up out of the sea, having *seven* heads and *ten* horns, and upon his horns *ten* crowns, and upon his heads the name of BLASPHEMY.

2 And the beast which I saw, was like unto a leopard and his feet were as the feet of a bear, and his mouth as the mouth of a lion and the dragon [Pagan Rome] gave him [Papacy] his power, his seat, and great authority.

This beast combines all the *three* preceding empires—body like *a leopard*, feet like *a bear*, and mouth like a *lion*.

THE TWO HORNED BEAST FROM THE EARTH.

"And I beheld another beast coming out of the earth and he had two horns like a lamb, and he spake as a dragon. And he exerciseth all the power of the first beast before him, and causeth the earth and them which dwell therein to worship the first beast, whose deadly wound was healed." Rev 13 : 11, 12.

This evidently refers to the infidel French government under Bonaparte, which came up out of the earth [the ten kingdoms,] and had two horns [France and Italy.] By comparing the history of Bonaparte with the prophecy there will be seen a most striking fulfilment.

PROPHETIC PERIODS.

The first great question respecting the visions of Daniel and John, is: Do they extend to the time of Christ's second coming to judgment?

For an answer, read Daniel 2, 7, 8, and 12. The image representing all earthly kingdoms, is dashed in pieces; or, which is the same thing, the beast representing the fourth kingdom, is given to the burning flame—and then, Christ's everlasting kingdom is set up. In Daniel 8: 19, the angel said, "I will make thee know what shall be in the last end of the indignation," and "at the time of the END shall be the vision." In Daniel 12 : 2, 3, he winds up his discourse by describing the resurrection, and says the words are shut up till the *time* of THE END. Then Christ himself gives a new series of prophetic days, and tells Daniel he shall stand in his lot [or RISE UP in his lot, as Luther's German Bible reads] at the end of the days. Now let us consider the periods and the waymarks.

The great prophetical period of the Apocalypse is 1260 years, the semi-circle of the full-orbed period of the Gentiles, 2520 years. Like the "seven times," the "three times and a half" has its germination and maturity. At the middle point of the "seven times" we find the Edict of Justinian, granting the Pope civil power, A. D. 538.

"Time, times, and a half," or 1260 years, the kings of the earth were to scatter the people of God; and "time, times, and a half," they were to be trodden down by Papal rule. See Daniel 7: 25, and 12: 7. These two periods put together, make just 2520 years.

The scattering commenced in Babylon B. C. 677, and continued by kingly power to A. D. 538, making in all to that time, 1215 years.

In the year A.D 538 began the papal oppression, and it was continued for 1260 years, bringing us down to 1798, just accomplishing the time of papal rule, when the Pope was taken captive by General Berthier. Now remember that 45 years of the scattering of God's people by kingly power, remained to be accomplished in A. D 538, when papacy took the power. Since the Pope lost his civil power, that prerogative has fallen back to the kings of the earth, which they began to exercise in A. D 1798. The remaining 45 years from 1798, will be accomplished in 1843. And when he shall have accomplished to *scatter the power* of the holy people, then all these things shall be finished. Daniel 12: 7.

All the wonders of Daniel's vision were to be finished at the end of 2300 days, or years. Daniel 8: 14, and 12: 7. This period commenced at the going forth of the commandment to restore and build Jerusalem, which was given by Artaxerxes 457 years before the birth of Christ. Ezra 7: 11—13. Now if we add 1843 to 457, we have the 2300 years just completed this year. Gabriel, in explaining the vision of 2300 days of Ch. 8 : 14, says Ch 9 : 24, seventy weeks are determined (cut off) upon thy people, i. e. 70 weeks or 490 years of the 2300. Then at verse 25, he tells Daniel when to commence, viz at the decree as above. At the end of the 490 years, Messiah was to be cut off, or crucified. This time was fulfilled to a day.

Again we are told that the saints, or God's people, were to be given into the hands of papacy, and should be oppressed a time, times, and an half, or 1260 years; and that the dominion of the beast or papacy should then be taken away. Daniel 7. 25, 26. The Pope began his oppressive reign by the authority of Justinian the Greek Emperor, A D. 538. See Gibbon's Rome, vol. 3, p. 87. Just 1260 years from that time, viz. A. D. 1798, the Pope was taken prisoner by Berthier, one of Bonaparte's Generals, and led into captivity, where he died the following year, since which time Popery has never regained its civil power.

Again we are told, Dan 12: 11, that from the time that the daily [*sacrifice* is not in the original] shall be taken away to set up the abomination that maketh desolate, [see margin] there shall be 1290 days or years. That is, from the time the daily pagan abominations shall be taken away, to open the way for the setting up of papacy, to the fall of papacy, shall be 1290 years. This was done A. D. 508. See Gibbon, vol. 3. pp. 262 and 263, just 30 years before the Bishop of Rome began to exercise his authority by the law of Justinian. This ended also in 1798. At verse 12 it is said, "Blessed is he that waiteth and cometh to the 1335 days," or years. Then Daniel was to stand in his lot, i. e. in the resurrection. Now if we add to A. D. 508, the 1335, where will it bring us? TO 1843!!

THE THREE WOE TRUMPETS.

The seven trumpets cover part of the time marked in Daniel. After the four had been sounded, an angel flying through the midst of heaven said, with a loud voice,

"WOE! WOE!! WOE!!! to the inhabiters of the earth, by reason of the other voices of the trumpet of the three angels which are yet to sound." Rev 8 : 13.

And the fifth angel sounded, and I saw a star fall from heaven to the earth, and to him was given the key of the bottomless pit. . . . And there came out locusts upon the earth. . . . And the shape of the locusts were like horses prepared for battle. . . . And their power was to hurt men five months, [150 prophetic days.] See Rev. 9 : 1—11. This star was undoubtedly the Arabian Impostor Mahomet: a fallen star being a false teacher.

FIFTH TRUMPET.

The fifth trumpet commenced July 27, 1299, when Othman, the founder of the Turkish empire, made his first attack on the Greeks. When the fifth angel ceased, it was said, "One woe is past, and behold there come two woes more hereafter."

"And the sixth angel sounded, and I heard a voice saying to the sixth angel, Loose the four angels which are bound at the great river Euphrates. And the four angels were loosed which were prepared for an hour and a day and a month and a year to slay the third part of men." [or to blot out from among the nations the Greek division of the Roman Empire.]

SIXTH TRUMPET.

The sixth trumpet commenced July 27, 1449, when the 150 years ended, and continued,

One day, that is,	1 prophetic day,	1 year
One month,	30 prophetic days,	30 years
1 year 12 months, 360	" "	360 "
And one hour,	1-24th of a prophetic day,	15 days

This period ended August 11, 1840, WHEN THE OTTOMAN SUPREMACY CEASED. Thus the Lord has most plainly showed us that we are living in the days of the voice of the seventh angel!

SEVENTH TRUMPET.

And the seventh angel sounded, and there were voices in heaven saying: "The kingdoms of this world are become *THE KINGDOM* of our Lord, and of his Christ; and he shall reign forever and ever."

This sound of the last trump, at which the dead will rise, (1 Cor. 15 : 52,) and BE JUDGED, (Rev. 11 : 18,) we now expect to hear. Reader, slight not the Lord's warnings. Improve the present moment. PREPARE TO MEET THY GOD.

9

Litch was not unusual, of course, in finding Islamic powers in Revelation, nor in predicting the fall of the Ottoman Turks—just as Miller himself was not unique in preaching the Second Coming or expecting some great change about the middle of the nineteenth century. Each man was remarkable for his predictive precision and for carrying common assumptions to extremes.

Litch saved his greatest precision, it is true, until after the event. Writing in 1838, Litch predicted that Turkish power (under the sixth trumpet) would be overthrown "in A.D. 1840, some time in the month of August." "The prophecy," declared Litch, "is the most remarkable and definite, (even descending to the days) of any in the Bible, relating to these great events."[9]

The fall of Turkey would be followed by even more dramatic events. Litch quoted Revelation 10:7: "But in the days of the voice of the seventh angel, when he shall begin to sound, the mystery of God should be finished, as he hath declared to his servants the prophets." He interpreted these words to mean "there shall be no more season of mercy" for the great mystery of "salvation by faith shall be ended."[10] In other words, God would cease saving sinners.

"Some time in the month of August" became a specific date—August 11, 1840—only a few days before the projected event. Writing in the August 1 issue of Joshua V. Himes's *Signs of the Times*, Litch noted that the "public mind" was deeply interested in the developments around Constantinople, a state of affairs that he connected to "Brother Miller's lectures" (and "other works on the same subject"), as well as the general impression prevailing "among all classes and in all countries" that "we are on the point of some great revolution, both in the political and moral world." As in 1838, Litch calculated the beginning of Ottoman power from July 27, 1299, using as his authority Edward Gibbon's *Decline and Fall of the Roman Empire*. Assuming that the fifth trumpet covered exactly 150 years and that the period of the sixth trumpet began immediately afterward, he argued that "the Ottoman power in Constantinople may be expected to be broken" on the eleventh of August, 1840.[11]

Litch made his prediction with a great deal of tentativeness, a fact that both his critics and admirers were to overlook. "There is no *positive* evidence," he admitted, "that the first period [i.e., corresponding to the fifth trumpet] was exactly to a day fulfilled; nor yet that the second period began, to a day, where the first closed." He was open to the possibility of some "variation in the conclusion," though not as much as a year's margin of error. Litch prepared a careful fallback position in case he was wrong: "But what, it is asked, will be the effect in your own mind, if it does not come out according to the above calculation? Will not your confidence in your theory be shaken? I reply, not [at] all." Nothing in his statement suggested that he was making the fulfillment of his August 11 prediction a test of the year/day connection—or of the Millerite theory of prophecy in general. "The prophecy in hand is an issolated [*sic*] one; and a failure in the calculation does not necessarily affect any other calculation. . . . Let no man, therefore, triumph, even if there should be an error of a few months in our calculation on this prophesy [*sic*]." Litch also carefully qualified his earlier statement on the closing of the "season of mercy."

The question is often asked, Do you believe with Mr. Miller that the day of grace will close in the month of August? To this, I reply, It is impossible for me to tell what will come in the month of August. If the foregoing calculations are correct, . . . we shall be brought to a point where there is no certainty that the day of grace will be continued for one hour.[12]

EXPLAINING EMBARRASSMENT

When the month of August passed with no evidence either that Turkey had fallen or probation closed, Adventist spokesmen took several months to explain away the embarrassment. "The opponents of Mr. Miller are making themselves merry in the supposed failure of what they are pleased *falsely* to call 'Mr. Miller's prediction,' relative to the day of grace," commented the *Signs of the Times* in September. The truth was, said the *Signs*, that Miller never said that the day of grace would close on the eleventh of August *"without qualification. He always spoke of it as a matter of opinion. . . ."*[13]

Dependent on slow-moving ships for news from the East, Litch waited until November to explain that the prophecy on Turkey had in fact been fulfilled. "The world have, since the 11th of August, had a strong disposition to triumph, as though they were past all danger . . . ," he wrote. "But what will they say now?" As Litch read the news, a general war was likely which would destroy Turkey. The great powers of Europe had tried to end the conflict between the Sultan of Turkey and his rebellious vassal, Mehemet Ali, Pasha of Egypt. On August 15, 1840, Litch noted with great interest, Mehemet Ali had rejected the four European Powers' ultimatum, thus assuring war—and the doom of the Ottoman empire. "It is a very striking fulfilment of the calculation; for that decision was but four days after the 11th of August, the period fixed for the termination of the prophecy. The like singular accuracy in the fulfilment of a prophetic period cannot be found in history. Will men lay it to heart?" (An editorial note explained that the fulfillment could not have been more precise, since four days were only 16 prophetic minutes!)[14]

By early 1841, it was clear that a general war was not in the offing, and Litch shifted ground again. Now he argued that the fulfillment had occurred exactly on August 11 and that the "fall" of Turkey consisted of "a voluntary surrender of Turkish supremacy in Constantinople, to Christian Influence"—just as, by his reckoning, the Byzantine empire fell in 1449 (not 1453) when the last emperor secured Turkish assent to his accession to the throne. According to Litch, the intervention of England, Russia, Austria, and Prussia meant the end of Ottoman independence, and the moment the European powers' ultimatum to Mehemet Ali was delivered into his hands, the Ottoman ruler lost all control of events. He was now a puppet "of the great christian powers of Europe." Litch asked, "When then was the question put officially within the power of Mehemet Ali?" The answer, he found by consulting the *London Morning Chronicle* of September 18, 1840, was August 11! He concluded: "I am now entirely satisfied that on the 11th of August, 1840, *The Ottoman power according to previous calculation* DEPARTED TO RETURN NO MORE."[15]

The argument for August 11, 1840, reached its full elaboration in 1842 in Litch's *Prophetic Expositions: or A Connected View of the Testimony of the Prophets Concerning the Kingdom of God and the Time of Its Establishment.* Again citing the *London Morning Chronicle*, Litch found another event of August 11, 1840, which was evidence "that Ottoman supremacy died, or was dead, that day." The new proof was a diplomatic note sent to the Sultan by the ambassadors of the four European powers in response to his question about their specific plans in the contingency that Mehemet Ali defied their ultimatum. The response, according to the London newspaper report, simply stated "that provision has been made, and there is no necessity for the Divan alarming itself about any contingency that may afterward arise."

"Where was the Sultan's independence that day?" asked Litch. "GONE. Who had the supremacy of the Ottoman empire in their hands? *The great powers.*"[16]

Another Millerite publication recapitulated the Eastern events in terms that made compelling sense to the touchy nationalistic sensibilities of nineteenth-century Americans. "Imagine an ambitious politician at the southwest part of the Union," an adventurer who leads the section into rebellion against the central government, wrote *The Midnight Cry*:

> Our President is reduced to such an extremity that he is compelled to accept the intervention of friendly powers. They, by their ambassadors at Washington, agree upon terms to be offered to the bold rebel. . . . The President agrees to those terms, with the further humiliating proviso that, if they are not accepted by the rebel, the friendly powers may take the matter into their own hands. After the messenger has left Washington, the President sends to the ambassadors of the friendly powers to know what is to be done, if the successful rebel refuses even this offer. The ambassadors answer, WE WILL TAKE CARE OF THAT! Would not every one feel that the independence of this country had departed?[17]

IGNORING EVIDENCE

Although Loughborough attributed a powerful impact to Litch's prophecy, Litch himself complained that people were ignoring his evidence. In fact, it is difficult to imagine a more thorough contradiction of Loughborough's version of events than Litch's summary in 1842:

> There are few persons, in New England at least, whose minds were not arrested and turned to the 11th of August; and vast multitudes were ready to say, ay, did say, If this event takes place according to the calculation, at the time specified, we will believe the doctrine of the *advent near*. But how is it with them now? Why, just as it was with the old Jews in the days of Christ; when he was every day performing the most stupendous miracles in their sight, they said to him, "Master, we would see a sign of thee." So now: men desire a sign from heaven. But let them be assured, they can never have a more convincing one than this. . . .

Another Millerite author complained: "The events fully confirmed the exposition, but instead of waking up the world, they were overlooked, or denied."[18]

One person deeply impressed by Litch's arguments was the abolitionist Angelina Grimké Weld. Early in 1843 she wrote to her husband that she had been studying the fifth and sixth trumpets. "It does seem to me," she wrote, "the fulfilling of the period of an hour, a day, a month, and a year—391 years and 15 days from the rise to the fall of the Ottoman Empire—is the most startling and convincing evidence that the end of all things is at hand, of any thing I have seen." Less startled was the Millerite critic Reverend O. E. Daggett, who wrote: ". . . they say the Turkish power was to be broken in the summer of A.D. 1840, and for the result they refer to the interference of the Allied Powers, at that time, in the political affairs of Turkey." But Turkey did not "fall" in 1840, argued Dagget, any more than France permanently lost its independence when "the same Allied Powers" deposed Napoleon. James Hazen, a Massachusetts clergyman who denounced Millerism as *A False Alarm*, noted that Miller's followers "triumphantly" pointed to Turkey's fall, August 11, 1840. But the facts were, he said, that European intervention had kept Turkey from falling. The argument that in accepting European aid Turkey fell was "ridiculous," Hazen wrote. "Do these men know no better than to believe this story themselves?"[19]

As a partisan caught up in polemical fervor, Hazen perhaps missed the full import of his question. Litch did indeed believe what he said, a fact that tells us a good deal about this obscure episode and the Millerite movement it stimulated.

Millerites (and some of their later apologists) liked to describe their approach to prophecy as rational, systematic, scientific (though they did not use the word), and based on unshakable confidence in the accuracy of the Bible. The "fall of Turkey" prediction suggests a more complex picture.

Litch's prediction rested entirely on a single date in the writings of a cultured despiser of religion, Edward Gibbon. To believe Litch's theory, in other words, one had to accept the accuracy of this historian and this particular fact, as well as the accuracy of the Bible. In actual practice, the Millerite interpretation of prophecy strayed from the ideal of letting the Bible interpret itself. (Perhaps the reliance on Gibbon is apposite, for more than they realized, Millerites built on an Enlightenment foundation, especially in matters relating to pre-modern history and pre-Reformation Christianity.)

During this period of his life, Litch never allowed events to be the test of his theory. If Mehemet Ali overthrew the Sultan, or if the Sultan maintained his throne with outside help, the prophecy was still "fulfilled." If general war broke out, or if it did not, the prophecy was still "fulfilled." Whether probation closed on August 11, 1840, or appeared to continue after that date, the fall of Turkey was still a sign that the door of mercy would close "quickly." In short, the hypothesis was simply not "falsifiable."

THE ESSENCE OF THE MOVEMENT

The "fall of Turkey" reminds us, if reminder is needed, that we must not overemphasize the *calculating* aspect of Millerism. They wanted the world to believe—and wished so to believe themselves—that their numerology was really

mathematics open for the "honest-hearted" to see. Yet in moments of disappointment they admitted otherwise.

Writing in the delicate interlude between the major disappointment of
March 21, 1844, and the onset of the climactic "seventh-month movement,"
Josiah Litch explained the essence of the movement: "The doctrine does not
consist in merely tracing prophetic periods, though that is an important part of
the work." The Millerites believed, he wrote, that the "whole prophetic history
of the world" provided "indubitable evidence" that the world had "approached
a crisis." Therefore, "no disappointment respecting a definite point of time can
move them, or drive them from their position, relative to the speedy coming of
the Lord."[20]

Though its advocates were sober men, Millerism represented a sensational-
ized variant of a long Christian tradition emphasizing Jesus' promise to return.
Within the movement a few voices spoke for the more cautious kind of Adventism, at least until fervent enthusiasm silenced them. The most distinguished,
perhaps, was Harvard-trained Episcopal minister Henry Dana Ward. His eloquent dissent against time-setting, published in December 1841, suggests a
direction Millerites might have taken, a road which many did in fact take after
1844. His comments are in sharp contrast to the hermeneutic employed by
Litch, Miller, and the majority.

Because God has wisely concealed the time of the Second Coming, Ward
wrote, "men of soundest learning and piety, in all ages of the church, . . . have
looked and waited for the coming of the Lord in their age." Men have been
alarmed by comets, earthquakes, falling stars, and "lights in the North." Emi-
nent men "in this age" have "foretold by the prophets many things which should
come to pass, respecting or growing out of the French Revolution and the fall of
the Ottoman Porte, which things they have lived with us to prove mistaken in
the time. To all such the word is spoken: 'It is not for you to know the times or
the seasons, which the Father has put in his own power.'"

Ward pointed to the story of Jonah as a warning to all time-setters. "And
now, if the years expire in which the Lord is understood by many to have said he
will do by this world, as by Nineveh, within our day. . . , the gracious God and
merciful, knows how to keep his word, and yet disappoint his prophet; *how to
prolong the day of grace*, and the time of the world; and, also how to keep his
word, and yet to shorten the days."[21]

Some historians have argued that the presence of Ward in the Millerite
movement is proof of the movement's tolerance and an indication that Millerism "must have been something larger than this one teaching on *time*." But after
his dissent against time-setting, Ward lost his influence among Millerites and
was "seldom heard from again."[22]

The experience of Ward suggests, in fact, the centrality of time-setting for
Millerism. As Millerism became an organized mass movement, with its own
publications, exchequer, and "general conferences," the "time question held
center stage in the thinking of the Millerites and their opponents." Millerism, at

its zenith (1842–1844), could not tolerate Ward's point of view within its ranks.[23]

For a long time historians have been sedulously taming Miller and his movement. From Francis Nichol and LeRoy Froom to Whitney Cross and David Rowe, they have emphasized the ways in which Millerites resembled non-Millerites, picturing Millerism as the logical extension of views held by a majority of Americans in the 1840s. One recent scholar even declared: "Miller's specific calendar prediction was rather incidental to his message."[24]

In all this, there is a danger of missing the "scandal" of Millerism. Historians should not carry the search for antecedents and results so far that there is nothing unexpected, shocking, or infuriating about this ephemeral movement called Millerism. Froom made Miller into a fiery comet with a 1000-year tail, insisting that almost every millenarian from apostolic times to the nineteenth century was a necessary forerunner of the New York farmer-preacher. But that is not the way Miller's contemporaries saw it. They were scandalized by the novelty of Miller's teaching, and especially his time-setting.

It may not be a coincidence that the most numerous and influential group to emerge from Millerism has been the Seventh-day Adventists. Unlike most ex-Millerites and their children, Seventh-day Adventists have continued officially to support the validity of October 22, 1844, as the key to Daniel and Revelation. Long after August 11, 1840, has been forgotten by other Christians, Seventh-day Adventists have the word of their prophet, Ellen G. White, affirming that August 11 represented a "remarkable fulfillment of prophecy." When Turkey "accepted the protection of the allied powers of Europe," according to Mrs. White, Litch's 1838 prediction was "exactly fulfilled."[25]

In short, those who were determined to preserve October 22, 1844, as a theological milestone could point to August 11, 1840. The Millerite interpretation of prophecy had been vindicated in illusory failure and temporary disappointment.

NOTES

1. Josiah Litch, "The Rise and Progress of Adventism," *Advent Shield and Review*, May 1844, pp. 73–80, lists the various disappointment days of 1843–1844, excluding, of course, the Great Disappointment. An interesting example of post-1844 time setting is Hiram Edson, *The Time of the End: Its Beginning, Progressive Events, and Final Termination* (Auburn, N.Y.: 1849), a work which predicts the Second Coming "before 1850 passes" (p. 13). For "timists" after 1844, see Isaac C. Wellcome, *History of the Second Advent Message and Mission, Doctrine and People* (Yarmouth, Maine: I. C. Wellcome, 1874), pp. 482–488.

2. James A. Hazen, *The False Alarm: A Discourse Delivered in the Congregational Church, South Wilbraham, Sabbath Evening, June 12, 1842* (Springfield, Mass.: Wood & Rupp, Printers, 1842), pp. 7–9; Litch, "Rise and Progress," p. 59; Edson, *The Time of the End*, p. 8.

3. J. N. Loughborough, *The Great Second Advent Movement: Its Rise and Progress* (Washington, D. C.: Review and Herald Publishing Association, 1905), pp. 128–129. *The Great Second Advent Movement* gives a somewhat fuller account of Litch's prediction than Loughborough's *Rise and Progress of the Seventh-day Adventists With Tokens of God's Hand in the Movement and a Brief Sketch of the Advent Cause From 1831 to 1844* (Battle Creek, Mich.: General Conference Association of the Seventh-day Adventists, 1892).

For earlier applications of the sixth trumpet to the Turks, see LeRoy E. Froom, *The Prophetic Faith of Our Fathers: The Historical Development of Prophetic Interpretation*, 4 vols. (Washington, D.C.: Review and Herald, 1946–1954), 2: 530–531, 785–786, passim; Bryan W. Ball, *A Great Expectation: Eschatological Thought in English Protestantism to 1660* (Leiden: E. J. Brill, 1975), pp. 144–45.

4. Loughborough, *Great Second Advent Movement*, pp. 128–29. Miller himself established the basic outline of this interpretation by connecting the fifth and sixth trumpets in immediate chronological sequence and applying both to the Ottoman Turks. He first expected the fall of Turkey, on the basis of his first calculations, in 1839. *Seventh-day Adventist Bible Commentary*, rev. ed., 10 vols. (Washington, D.C.: Review and Herald, 1980), 7: 794–795.

5. Froom, *Prophetic Faith*, 4: 528–529; Loughborough, *Great Second Advent Movement*, pp. 129–30. On the year-day link, see "year-day principle" in *Seventh-day Adventist Encyclopedia*, rev. ed. (Washington, D. C.: Review and Herald, 1976), p. 1623; Froom, *Prophetic Faith*, 1: 700–701; 712–716.

6. Loughborough, *Great Second Advent Movement*, pp. 130–132.

7. Ibid., pp. 130–132. The most recent officially supported history of Seventh-day Adventism uncritically repeats Loughborough's account. R. W. Schwarz, *Light Bearers to the Remnant* (Mountain View, Calif.: Pacific Press, 1979), p. 34.

8. Litch, *Prophetic Significance of Eastern and European Movements: Being a Plain, Literal, and Grammatical Construction of the Last Five Chapters of Daniel, Applied to Passing Events: Showing Conclusively That a Syrian Prince, Not Napoleon III, Is the Antichrist of the Last Days* (Boston: Author, 1867), pp. 15–16; Litch, *A Complete Harmony of Daniel and the Apocalypse* (Philadelphia: Claxton, Remsen & Haffelfinger, 1873), p. 170.

9. Litch, *The Probability of the Second Coming of Christ About A.D. 1843* (Boston: David H. Ela, 1838), pp. 157–158.

10. Ibid., pp. 158–159.

11. Litch, "Fall of the Ottoman Power in Constantinople," and "Events to Succeed the Second Woe," *Signs of the Times*, August 1, 1840, p. 70. Gibbon wrote: "It was on the twenty-seventh of July, in the year twelve hundred and ninety-nine of the Christian era, that Othman first invaded the territory of Nicodemia; and the singular accuracy of the date seems to disclose some foresight of the rapid and destructive growth of the monster." *The History of the Decline and Fall of the Roman Empire*, vol. VII (London: Methuen, 1914), p. 25.

12. *Signs of the Times*, August 1, 1840.

13. *Signs of the Times*, September 15, 1840, p. 92.

14. *Signs of the Times*, November 1, 1840, pp. 117–118. Litch later recalled: "As the spring opened, and the summer came, the entire community were excited, and expectation on tiptoe, in reference to the 11th of August and its anticipated events, the fall of the Ottoman empire, &c, &c. Many were the predictions that when the day should have passed by, as it certainly would do, without the event being realized, that then the spell would be broken, and Adventism would die." "Rise and Progress," p. 59.

15. Litch, "The Eleventh of August, 1840. Fall of the Ottoman Empire," *Signs of the Times*, February 1, 1841, pp. 168–169.

16. Litch, *Prophetic Expositions: or A Connected View of the Testimony of the*

Prophets Concerning the Kingdom of God and the Time of the Establishment, 2 vols. (Boston: J. V. Himes, 1842), 2: 189–198.

17. *The Midnight Cry*, November 25, 1842, quoted in *Signs of the Times*, May 31, 1843.

18. Litch, *Prophetic Expositions*, 2: 200; *The Midnight Cry* quoted in *The Western Midnight Cry*, January 20, 1844, p. 45.

19. Angelina Grimké Weld to Theodore Weld, February 2, 1843, in the Weld-Grimké Papers. (I am indebted to Ronald Graybill for this reference.) *Signs of the Times*, February 1, 1843; Hazen, *The False Alarm*, pp. 7–9.

20. Litch, "Rise and Progress," p. 80.

21. *Signs of the Times*, December 1, 1841, pp. 135–36.

22. F. D. Nichol, *The Midnight Cry: A Defense of William Miller and the Millerites* (Washington, D. C.: Review and Herald, 1944), p. 95; Everett N. Dick, "The Adventist Crisis of 1843–1844" (Ph.D. dissertation, University of Wisconsin, 1930), p. 44; David T. Arthur, "Millerism," in Edwin Gaustad, ed., *The Rise of Adventism: Religion and Society in Mid-Nineteenth-Century America* (New York: Harper & Row, 1974), p. 161.

23. Arthur, "Millerism," pp. 158–162.

24. Jonathan Butler, "When Prophecy Fails: The Validity of Apocalypticism," *Spectrum*, September, 1976, 8:9.

25. Ellen G. White, *The Great Controversy Between Christ and Satan: The Conflict of the Ages in the Christian Dispensation* (Mountain View, Calif.: Pacific Press, 1911), pp. 334–335.

SIX

Millerism and Madness:

A Study of "Religious Insanity" in Nineteenth-Century America

RONALD L. NUMBERS AND JANET S. NUMBERS

THE RELATIONSHIP BETWEEN Millerism and madness has stirred passionate debate since the early 1840s, when, according to one Millerite magazine, insanity emerged as the "touchstone" representing everything critics thought wrong with the movement.[1] For several years the popular and religious press reveled in recounting the lurid, sometimes fictional, details of Millerites gone amuck, while physicians responsible for treating the nation's insane decried the sudden influx of patients suffering from this latest "delusion." Rumors and refutations of insanity appeared as standard fare in Millerite publications, as outraged and embarrassed leaders fought to protect their movement's good name.

Their efforts were scarcely helped by the numerous spirit-filled enthusiasts and fanatics who attached themselves to the cause, prompting the decorous William Miller to protest that some meetings sounded "more like Babel, than a solemn assembly," and moving Joshua V. Himes, the movement's chief organizer and publisher, to complain at one point of being mired in "mesmerism seven feet deep."[2] The obvious affinity between enthusiasm and insanity—described by George Man Burrows, the British expert on mental disorders, as "often too indistinct to define which is one and which the other"—undoubtedly contributed to the Millerites' tarnished reputation for sobriety and sanity.[3]

The historiographical debate over Millerism and madness has centered on two books, Clara Endicott Sears's popular *Days of Delusion* (1924) and Francis D. Nichol's scholarly *The Midnight Cry* (1944), works so dissimilar in tone and content that a reader might wonder whether the two authors are describing the same people. Sears, though far from hostile to the Millerites, entertained readers with such stories as that of Ben Whitcomb, the mad Millerite of Stow, Mas-

20. This anti-Millerite broadside of October 1844 depicts the ascension of the Boston tabernacle. William Miller is shown seated on a prophetic chart, and Joshua V. Himes is standing below surrounded by bags of money and being held by a fork-tailed devil. Courtesy Review and Herald Publishing Association.

sachusetts, who galloped through the countryside excitedly waving a prophetic chart.[4] Whatever acclaim Sears's book enjoyed among scholars ended in 1944, when Nichol, a Seventh-day Adventist minister and amateur historian, brought out *The Midnight Cry*, an apologetical masterpiece, appropriately subtitled "A Defense of William Miller and the Millerites," which included two chapters and an appendix refuting charges of Millerite insanity. For Nichol, the basic question was: "Did Millerism Cause Insanity, Suicide, and Murder?" By marshaling evidence skewed geographically, chronologically, and epidemiologically, he was able to answer with an unequivocal "No." His argument rested in large part on the case histories of reputed Millerites committed to four asylums in New England during the years from 1842 to 1844, by which time "the subject was no longer a new topic of interest." Using historical sleight of hand, he first eliminated from consideration "all cases where insanity is in the family or where the patient himself has recurring attacks," thus at one stroke reducing the number of problem patients to 39—an "insignificant" figure, he claimed, which began "to melt rapidly under case history scrutiny." Indeed it did. By the end of his performance he had ruled out every instance of "so-called Millerism-induced insanity" and reached the conclusion "that Millerism was not really the cause of *anyone's* insanity."[5]

Despite Nichol's frank admission that his was not "an objective history of Millerism," his skillful polemics and copious citations generally persuaded American historians to desist from describing the Millerites as mad.[6] Now and then a mild demurrer was heard,[7] but to a generation increasingly skeptical about the appropriateness of labeling people insane and troubled by flagrant abuses of psychiatry to silence dissidents, Nichol's arguments retained an intuitive appeal.[8]

In this chapter, instead of simply asking whether Millerism caused insanity, we address the question: Why did so many contemporaries, including some Millerites, *believe* that Millerism caused insanity? In search of an answer we explore both the medical and ideological contexts in which such charges were discussed and examine the issue from the perspectives of both the psychiatric and Millerite communities. To resolve the dispute over whether Millerites were institutionalized because of their deviant beliefs or because they were truly ill—even by present-day standards—we also analyze the case histories of nearly one hundred hospitalized patients whose afflictions were attributed to Millerism or who were identified as Millerites.

RELIGIOUS INSANITY

It is impossible to understand the phenomenon of "Millerite insanity" without reference to the climate of opinion in which it arose. Since antiquity excessive religious enthusiasm had sometimes been regarded as a species of madness, but it was not until the seventeenth century that it acquired definition as a distinct disease. In 1621 in *The Anatomy of Melancholy* the Anglican vicar Robert Burton coined the term "religious melancholy" to describe the often intense religious experiences of Puritans and other sectarians. As the medical historian George Rosen observed in a pioneering essay on religious enthusiasm, "it is quite likely that the sectarian ranks included individuals whose mental and emotional balance was at the least precarious," but it seems equally probable, as Michael MacDonald has recently argued, that the "ruling elite" at times used the concept of religious insanity to discredit socially disruptive religious dissidents such as the Puritans.[9]

With the rise of Methodism in the eighteenth century, talk of religious insanity in the English-speaking world shifted from the Puritans to the even more enthusiastic followers of John Wesley. Under the influence of Wesley's preaching, anxious listeners would sometimes drop "as dead," experience temporary blindness, tremble violently, tear their clothes, or groan and shout loudly. Wesley himself reported numerous cases of insanity associated with his ministry, and between 1772 and 1795 the Hospital of St. Mary of Bethlehem in London (better known as Bedlam) admitted 90 patients alleged to be suffering from "religion and Methodism." By the middle of the eighteenth century, writes MacDonald, "the idea that religious zeal was a mental disease had become a ruling-class shibboleth," widely acknowledged by both medical and lay opinion.[10] By the nineteenth century medical authorities commonly used the term "religious insanity" to connote an etiologically distinct mental disease.[11]

In the first major American work devoted to the subject of insanity, *Medical Inquiries and Observations upon the Diseases of the Mind* (1812), Benjamin Rush, arguably the most influential physician in the United States in the early nineteenth century, noted that 10 percent of the 50 "maniacs" then residing in the Pennsylvania Hospital owed their misfortune to "erroneous opinions in religion," especially ones that burdened the pious with unbearable guilt. Writing years before the advent of Millerism, he expressed particular concern about the baleful effects that often accompanied "researches into the meaning of certain prophesies in the Old and New Testaments," noting that madness associated with such activity arose "most frequently from an attempt to fix the precise time in which those prophesies were to be fulfilled, or from a disappointment in that time, after it had passed."[12]

The wave of revivals that passed over the United States in the early nineteenth century, characterized by protracted meetings that involved days of nearly constant preaching and praying, seemed only to confirm the connection between religious enthusiasm and insanity. The evangelist Charles Finney, for example, who rose to prominence in the mid-1820s, sometimes reduced whole congregations to wailing and writhing, ostensible manifestations of the Holy Spirit. When, on occasion, the excitement and fear generated by his sermons pushed a poor soul over the brink of sanity, Finney blamed the victim, saying that he had "made himself deranged by resisting" the Spirit. Such goings on naturally attracted the attention of physicians who cared for the insane—and prompted one of them, Amariah Brigham, to write a controversial book on religion and mental health, in which he attributed the "outward signs" associated with revivals to overstimulation of the nervous system rather than to the *"special outpouring of the Spirit of God."* In New England and New York alone, for the period 1815 to 1825, he knew of more than 90 instances where "religious melancholy" had led to suicide and an additional 30 cases where it had resulted in attempted murder.[13] The implication that clergymen could not distinguish between "the ravings of the insane or semi-insane and the operations of the Holy Spirit" did not go unchallenged. As Frederick A. Packard explained in the *Princeton Review*, "An enthusiast preaching wildly would at once pass among us for an insane man, and his influence would extend but little if at all beyond those who are predisposed to the same class of mental aberrations or already under their power."[14]

The religious revivals of the early nineteenth century coincided with—and indirectly encouraged—a boom in asylum building that saw the opening of approximately two dozen new asylums in America between 1810 and 1850. The annual reports of these institutions, which customarily included statistical tables listing the supposed causes of insanity, provided apparent scientific confirmation of the connection between religious excitement and mental illness. When the New Hampshire Asylum for the Insane opened in 1842, the first patient to enter its doors was a Millerite, and 21 of the first 76 admissions to that institution were thought to have resulted from religious excitement, more than twice as many cases as assigned to ill health, the second leading cause. When the Utica State Lunatic Asylum opened the next year, it, too, listed "religious anxiety" as the number one cause of insanity.[15] A recent analysis of patients admitted to the Hartford Retreat for the Insane during its first twenty years, 1824–1843, reveals that "twenty-two percent involved cases of religious insanity directly linked to evangelism"—and that admissions for religious insanity corresponded strikingly with outbursts of revival activity in Connecticut.[16]

The 1840s seem to have been particularly conducive to the production of religion-related insanity, if the experiences of the McLean Asylum for the Insane at Boston (opened 1818) and the State Lunatic Hospital at Worcester, Massachusetts (opened 1833), were typical. As the following figures show,[17] the number of religiously insane patients in the decades before the Civil War reached a peak in the 1840s:

	1820–1829	1830–1839	1840–1849	1850–1859
McLean	9	19	48	30
Worcester	—	75	161	81

In both theory and practice, mid-nineteenth-century physicians commonly attributed each case of insanity to two causes: predisposing and exciting. The former, such as inherited tendencies and poor physical health, made one vulnerable to mental illness, but did not directly cause it. The latter, which allegedly precipitated abnormal behavior, could involve anything from excessive study, disappointed love, and physical abuse to Mesmerism, Mormonism, Swedenborgianism, Fourierism, Grahamism, and, of course, Millerism—all of which appeared as exciting causes of insanity in the reports of American asylums during the 1830s and 1840s.[18]

Because asylum physicians usually relied on information supplied by a patient's friends or relatives to ascertain the exciting cause of a breakdown, most of them readily conceded the possibility of error and the likelihood of confusing cause with effect, especially when religion was involved. "In such cases," wrote the superintendent of the Western Lunatic Asylum in Staunton, Virginia, "the brain has no doubt frequently been acting morbidly for some time, without its being discovered, and at length when influenced by religious feeling, its manifestations upon this subject indicate mental disorder—this the *effect*, is hastily seized upon and assigned as the *cause* of the malady."[19] There also existed the danger, pointed out by the English physician Burrows, that those treating the insane might "impugn opinions, merely because they differed from their own."[20]

Some superintendents, such as Luther V. Bell of the McLean Asylum, held the so-called "*statistics*" of insanity in such low esteem they refused to append the expected tables of supposed causes to their annual reports.[21] But even the most skeptical among them—including William H. Stokes of the Mount Hope Institution in Baltimore, who claimed never to have "succeeded in tracing any one case unequivocally and directly" to the influence of religious hopes and fears—stopped short of denying that religious anxiety, acting as "a whip of scorpions lacerating and torturing to the utmost limit of endurance," as Isaac Ray described it, could, and did, derange persons predisposed to insanity.[22] Thus most superintendents continued to compile their tables—while at the same time warning against placing too much confidence in them.

MILLERITE INSANITY

In the early 1840s, as Millerite enthusiasm approached its zenith, asylum superintendents in the Northeast began reacting with alarm to the influx of patients seemingly deranged by "the Miller excitement." Samuel B. Woodward, superintendent of the Worcester State Lunatic Hospital and soon to become the first president of the Association of Medical Superintendents of American Institutions for the Insane (the present-day American Psychiatric Association), noted in his annual report for 1843 that nearly 7 percent of all admissions during the previous year—and over half of all cases resulting from religious causes (15 of 28)—could be charged to Millerism. He believed that in the other asylums of New England Millerites constituted an even larger percentage of the patient population. Although he regarded it as unusual for a "popular religious error" to have "produced so much excitement in the community and rendered so many insane," he professed to understand why so many minds were unsettled by Millerism: "the subject is momentous, the time fixed for the final consummation of all things so near at hand, and the truth of all sustained by unerring mathematics." At Worcester the Millerite cases fell into two categories: the true believers so "full of ecstacy" [*sic*] that some refused even to eat and drink, and the unconverted who feared that Miller's prophecy might be correct, "who have distracted their minds by puzzling over it, thinking about it, and dreading its approach, who have sunk into deep and hapless melancholy."[23]

Amariah Brigham, the distinguished head of the Utica State Lunatic Asylum in upstate New York and, as previously mentioned, author of a book on religion and insanity, also addressed the Millerite problem in 1843 in his annual report—and devoted an entire article to the subject in the first volume of the American *Journal of Insanity*, which he founded and edited. In Brigham's opinion, the insidious effects of Millerism stemmed less from its peculiar teachings than from its tendency to deprive "excitable and nervous persons" of needed sleep while they attended protracted meetings. To illustrate his point, he related the history of one of his own patients:

S. H. attended from idle curiosity a religious meeting, and heard for the first time the doctrine of the immediate destruction of the world. His attention was awakened and he attended similar meetings several evenings in succession; commenced studying the bible on the subject; passed several nights in the investigation; had but little or no sleep for above a week; then had contests with devils; determined not to eat until the end of the world, and became decidedly deranged.

Brigham acknowledged that "for the most part" Millerites were "sincere and pious people." However, he believed that their teachings threatened the mental health not only of the present population but of generations yet to come, who, because of their ancestors' errors, would enter the world predisposed to insanity. Such prospects prompted him to rank Millerism above even yellow fever and cholera as a threat to the public's health.[24]

Despite a wealth of sources linking Millerism to insanity, it is impossible to estimate with any confidence the number of Americans who suffered mental breakdowns as a result of the Millerite excitement. Many persons who experienced only temporary derangement undoubtedly remained outside of institutions and thus off the asylums' registration books. As one historian of religious insanity in the early nineteenth century has recently observed, "the evidence from church records, published accounts, and private archives indicates that 'religious failures,' the obsessed men and women broken down by the burdens of scrupulous conscience, generally lived out their lives in quiet desperation within the sphere of the private family."[25] Besides, as even the popular press occasionally recognized (and as we shall see below), it was notoriously difficult to isolate the contribution of Millerism to any one person's mental illness.[26]

Even if we limit ourselves to institutionalized "Millerites," their numbers can be estimated only in the crudest fashion. Several superintendents refused to assign supposed causes of insanity; others subsumed "Millerism" under the categories "religious excitement" or "popular errors," especially in the early 1840s, before "Millerism" reached epidemic proportions, and after 1850, by which time Millerite enthusiasm had subsided. Nevertheless, from the annual reports of some two dozen asylums, the clinical records of three institutions, and miscellaneous secondary sources, we have sketched a tentative demographic profile.[27]

During the middle third of the nineteenth century, American asylums admitted no fewer than 170 patients for causes related to Millerism. Of this number, about 70 percent entered institutions in New England; over 20 percent went to asylums in New York, especially the state hospital in Utica, which apparently treated the largest number of Millerites in the country; the remaining 10 percent were scattered throughout a region stretching south to Virginia and west to Indiana. Asylums in major cities, even in New England and New York, seem to have admitted proportionally fewer Millerites than those located in smaller towns and rural areas. For example, the Boston Lunatic Hospital, which served a predominantly foreign-born and presumably Catholic clientele, reported only three or four cases related to Millerism; the Bloomingdale Asylum in

New York City treated only one. Pliny Earle, physician to the latter institution, commented in 1848 that the "exciting doctrines of Miller, the self-styled prophet of the immediate destruction of the world, gained but little hold of the public mind in this vicinity."[28]

Chronologically, the admission of Millerite-related cases followed no predictable pattern, except for the obvious clustering of admissions in the 1840s. If the records of "Millerites" admitted to the New Hampshire Asylum for the Insane, founded in 1842, and the Utica State Lunatic Asylum, opened in 1843, are in any way typical,[29] the disappointments of 1844 seem to have had little effect on hospital censuses:

	'42	'43	'44	'45	'46	'47	'48	'49	'50
N.H.	7	6	1	2	2	2	2	0	2
Utica	—	7	6	6	11	3	3	2	5

Patients identified as Millerites continued to straggle into asylums well into the 1850s—and even into the early 1860s. The state asylum in New Hampshire, for example, admitted four Millerite cases between January 1854 and May 1855 and one as late as 1862. Among the first patients to enter the new Taunton State Lunatic Hospital in Massachusetts, which opened in 1854, were three Millerites, including one described as "an old and nearly hopeless" case, who presented "the sad spectacle of a promising man blasted in mind and prospects by a foolish and wicked delusion."[30]

By the late 1840s Millerism had come to occupy a prominent place in the literature of American psychiatry as the very stereotype of epidemic "religious insanity." Far after the disintegration of the Millerite movement asylum superintendents and students of insanity continued to draw lessons from the Millerite experience, and as late as 1858 Dorothea L. Dix cited the unfortunate victims of the "Millerite delusions" in her appeals to provide better care for the insane.[31]

CASE HISTORIES

To clarify the alleged relationship between Millerism and insanity, and to check the possibility that Millerites may have been institutionalized merely because of their deviant beliefs, we examined the clinical records of 98 "Millerite" patients (56 men, 42 women) from three asylums: the New Hampshire Asylum for the Insane, the Worcester State Lunatic Hospital in Massachusetts, and the New York State Lunatic Asylum at Utica.[32] (See Table 1.) In 93 of these cases Millerism was listed as an exciting cause of insanity; the remaining five patients were merely identified in their histories as being Millerites. Not surprisingly, this exercise only partially dissipated the cloud of confusion obscuring the Millerite-insanity issue. Eleven of the patients in question, for instance, supposedly lost their reason through a multiplicity of exciting causes, which linked Millerism with such diverse influences as animal magnetism, loss of property, pecuniary embarrassment, and ill health. Three other patients (Case Nos. 401, 466, and

TABLE I
Millerite-Related Insanity in Three Asylums
(Readmissions Not Included)

	Utica	New Hampshire	Worcester
1842	a	8	*
1843	8	13	*
1844	10	2	*
1845	6	2	o
1846	2	3	5
1847	4	2	2
1848	4	3	o
1849	4	o	o
1850	3	3	1
1851	*	o	1
1852	*	o	2
1853	*	o	o
1854	*	1	1
1855	*	1	3
1856	*	o	1
1857	*	1	o
1858	*	o	o
1859	*	o	o
1860	*	1	o
1861	*	1	*
Total	41	41	16

(a) The Utica asylum opened in 1843.
(*) Records for these years were not used.

1823), whom we did not include in our sample, were judged by the superintendent at Utica to have become insane because of their intense opposition to Millerism.

Nevertheless, our examination of these case histories did answer a number of questions. Contrary to our early expectations, it confirmed what admissions data from the New Hampshire and Utica asylums also indicated, namely, that the disappointments of 1844 rarely precipitated mental breakdowns. In fact, only one of the 98 case histories identifies disappointment over the failure of Christ to appear in 1844 as a precipitating cause of derangement. In 1847 the New Hampshire Asylum admitted a woman (Case No. 476) who had been disturbed for the past three years, supposedly because of the "excitement produced by Millerism." According to her history,

She confidently looked forward to a set time when the crisis was to take place according to prophecy and that time having passed and her expectations not being realized disappointment and melancholy ensued. This state continued with some variation until six weeks ago, when there was a change for the worse. Now refuses to eat, and is very much emaciated and debilitated in consequence. . . . [Her skin] has now a very cadaverous aspect. Appears to be conscious of her situation but too much debilitated to say much or help herself.

Our analysis of the case histories also allows us to say with reasonable certainty that asylum physicians rarely, if ever, diagnosed a patient insane merely because of his or her Millerite beliefs; in virtually every case pathological behavior was the deciding factor. Perhaps the most convincing evidence that physicians commonly distinguished between heterodox and pathological beliefs comes from the records of the five patients identified as Millerites but for whom Millerism was not listed as an exciting cause. One of them, a "noisy" young woman (Case No. 49) admitted to the New Hampshire Asylum in 1843, was described as having been excited by Millerism for two weeks; she walked around the hospital "swinging and spatting [i.e., slapping] her hands, singing loud the Miller songs." Yet in spite of her enthusiasm for Millerism, the admitting physician attributed her insanity to a bout of "nervous fever" two years earlier. In 1848 the Utica asylum admitted the disturbed wife (Case No. 1699) of "an intemperate dissolute man"; although she constantly talked about Millerism, the "neglect and bad conduct of husband" was recorded as the supposed cause of her breakdown. Another Utica patient (Case No. 2545), admitted in 1850, was said to dwell "much on religion. Inclined to be a Millerite. Thinks this generation is only 4 years & 16 days old, etc." An excitable man, he had considered "blowing up [his] son-in-law's house to make a passage to China where he would find gold." Despite this background, the admitting physician thought his illness had been brought on by the "pressure of business and loss of property," not Millerism. Such cases suggest that asylum physicians did not indiscriminately blame Millerism for every case of insanity associated with the Advent movement.

Further evidence of their objectivity comes from five additional case histories, which show that they did not always accept the testimony of friends and relatives that Millerism was the culprit. One of these histories (Case No. 353) describes a mother of three children, the youngest being only four months old, who was brought to the Utica asylum in 1844. Although Millerism had reportedly driven her insane, a skeptical doctor noted: "Supposed cause Millerism, it is said, but probably puerperal." A second of these histories (Case No. 1397) tells of a man "deranged about 18 months" who entered Utica in 1847. Because he had been attending Millerite meetings since the time of his breakdown, his neighbors attributed his insanity to Millerism. However, given the patient's history—he had previously been insane and his acceptance of Miller's teachings was in doubt—the doctor thought it impossible to isolate the cause of insanity. Thus, in spite of his conviction that Millerites were "fanatics," he concluded that the supposed cause of insanity was "unknown."

As a further test to determine whether asylum superintendents were labeling otherwise normal people insane primarily because of their odd beliefs or whether they were diagnosing truly disturbed persons, we analyzed the 98

"Millerite" cases by mental disease. Although the clinical records are often not as extensive as we might like (they vary in length from a few sentences to over a page), they usually indicate the supposed cause of insanity, the duration of the illness before admission, any previous episode of insanity or history of mental illness in the family, aggressive and suicidal tendencies, and the patient's symptoms and behavior, including sleeping, eating, and evacuating habits. Most records also contain brief monthly treatment notes, indicating any change in symptoms and behavior, as well as data regarding the patient's age, marital status, occupation, religion, dates of admission, discharge, and subsequent admissions. On the basis of this information, we have, wherever possible, rediagnosed the patients using present-day criteria—fully realizing that even today the diagnosis of mental illness remains an uncertain art and that relying on sketchy records written over a century ago, long before the advent of modern classificatory systems, is not without hazards.

Almost all of the institutionalized Millerites in our sample displayed significant symptoms of mental disorder. Table 2 lists the probable diagnoses, with the cases divided into chronic and acute (the latter involving symptoms of no more than six months' duration at the time of admission, a hospitalization of less than six months, and no prior or subsequent history of insanity). In 21 cases there was insufficient evidence upon which to base even a probable diagnosis,

TABLE 2

Diagnoses of Millerite Patients and Estimated Chronicity

Psychotic Disorders		Number of Cases
Affective Psychoses (Mania and Manic Depression)	28	
Schizoaffective Psychoses	15	
Schizophrenia	19	
TOTAL		62
Nonpsychotic Disorders		
Major Depression (without psychotic features)	10	
Postpartum Depression	2	
Dementia	3	
TOTAL		15
Undetermined		21
GRAND TOTAL		98

Probable Chronic Disorders	69
Probable Acute Disorders	18
Undetermined	11
GRAND TOTAL	98

although for 15 of these there was enough information to determine chronicity. The table shows that a large majority of the diagnosable Millerite patients (80.5%) were psychotic: manic-depressive with psychotic features, schizophrenic, or schizoaffective. The remainder (19.5%) suffered from such nonpsychotic disorders as depression or dementia without psychotic features.

The largest number of diagnosable Millerite patients displayed symptoms suggestive of manic-depressive or schizoaffective psychoses: alternating periods of depression and agitated excitement, sleeplessness, delusions, hallucinations, and grandiosity. For example, a Millerite (Case No. 2657) admitted to Utica in 1843 (and again in 1850) was described as experiencing mood cycles that swung suddenly from "quietude . . . to excitement and rage." He thought himself to be "a Saint . . . commanded to destroy all sinners, that the more he destroys the greater Saint he shall be, & the greater enjoyment he shall have." Another Utica patient (Case No. 665) displayed psychotic grandiosity, imagining himself to be "*every inch a King*." During his manic periods he talked repeatedly of "being the Law, Prince, King, etc. etc." A Millerite patient (Case No. 540) in New Hampshire had hallucinations in which she saw and heard devils, whom she suspected of hiding in her bed. Three months after her admission she was described as remaining "entirely naked" and using "up a blanket in a short time, fighting the devil out of her room."

Two Millerite patients at Utica (Case Nos. 552 and 1803) reportedly spent money recklessly or gave away their possessions—behavior that might, under different circumstances, be construed as symptomatic of mania. However, since such actions could be perfectly logical if one believed in the imminent end of the world, we did not consider them in these instances to be indicative of mental disorder. But even after eliminating such behavior from consideration, we found ample evidence to warrant tentative diagnoses of mania in the one case and schizoaffective psychosis in the other.

Nineteen (24.7%) of our diagnosable patients seem to have been victims of schizophrenia, a disease manifested by such symptoms as paranoid delusions, hallucinations (particularly auditory ones), delusional fantasies concerning their bodies, incoherent or bizarre speech, and catatonia. Typical of those who suffered from paranoid delusions was a man (Case No. 8) admitted to the New Hampshire Asylum in 1842 (and twice thereafter), whose record contained the following description:

> For several months he spent much of his time in attending meetings and examining the Bible to prove the Second Advent doctrines. He became suspicious of his friends and family and jealous. He assaulted his father with a stick of wood and injured him severely. . . . Four men brought him to the asylum. He looked anxious and when opposed furious. Eyes wide open and staring, breathing hurriedly and was agitated. Said he was Jesus Christ. . . . At times he was frightened and cried out in great alarm "you are going to kill me."

Another New Hampshire patient (Case No. 137), admitted in 1843, displayed classic manifestations of bodily delusions and auditory hallucinations:

[December 1843] Attended Miller meetings and along in April last the neighbors thought he was not right in his mind for he went about the neighborhood praying in families. About this time while going to a neighbor's early in the morning he turned around and saw a great and burning light in the heavens and at the same time a voice said "your religion is good for nothing." He says he was stunned for a few minutes but kept going on about his business at the same time. He says a grunting kind of noise came upon him which he keeps up especially when thinking upon religion. . . . [February 1844] When the light appeared to him a stammering or "a voice" as he calls it came upon him. He now says that "the voice" relieves the pain in his bowels. . . . [March 1844] It was revealed to him by seeing "the light" and hearing the voice say "your religion is good for nothing" that he had turned away the day of grace and that the Lord had cast him off.

Although he did not improve during his three-month stay at the asylum, his friends, ignoring the advice of the asylum physician, took him home.

The combination of delusions and incoherent speech so often found among schizophrenics appears in the case history of a Utica woman (Case No. 538), admitted in November 1844: "Eats irregularly, feels things are poisoning. . . . August 1845. No change. Talks ramblingly & often spells out sentences. Charges others with murdering children etc." Finally, a Worcester patient (Case No. 4001), admitted in June 1852, illustrates the muteness and physical rigidity characteristic of catatonic schizophrenics:

This woman sat stupid not speaking for two days or so and took no notice of anything. Refused food and took drink reluctantly. . . . [August 1852] She remains in a silent, stupid state, scarcely speaking a word and taking no notice of anyone, sitting with her eyes fixed or closed. . . . [January 1853] No change in this woman. She sits or stands as mute as a statue all the day long except when pushed to the dining room or to her sleeping room. Seldom speaks a word. . . . [April 1853] She continues as stupid and silent as ever. Standing or sitting in a fixed posture without a movement of her body or change of countenance like "Patience on a monument."

Twelve (15.6%) of the diagnosable patients—described in their case histories as melancholy, despondent, gloomy, and in most cases suicidal but not delusional—seem to warrant a diagnosis of nonpsychotic depression. Representative of this group was a New Hampshire woman (Case No. 59) hospitalized in 1843 after some troubling contacts with Millerism:

Has been subject to depression of spirits especially whenever there has been any religious awakening in her vicinity and now in consequence of a revival in her neighborhood has been greatly depressed for eight weeks and insane two weeks. She started for the water to drown herself a few days ago. She says it is because she has no hope.

Three patients (3.9%)—forgetful, confused, incontinent, unable to answer questions satisfactorily, and prone to wander aimlessly or to perform repetitive movements—were almost certainly demented. The physician at Worcester described one of these Millerites (Case No. 2483), admitted in July 1846, as being in a very absent and confused state. Takes no notice of what is going on about him. Stands for hours with his head out of the window and forgets himself so much as to wet his clothes. . . . [November 1846] Is not able to converse in the least. . . . [December 1847] The same. No mind. Sits all day looking at his fingers or feeling his hair. Talks to himself in a kind of mixed up unintelligible gibberish. . . . [January 1851] He is in his usual good health of body and dull demented state of mind. Walks his corner a step or two and turns and walks a step or two all the while repeating lowly words from a revival hymn.

Even if we rule out the likelihood that asylum physicians routinely confused excessive religiosity with madness, we are still left with the nagging question of what causative role, if any, Millerism played in the cases we have found. Millerism certainly seems only incidental to the pathology of the three demented patients, since dementia is an organic disease. But what of the other patients? Were they psychologically fragile persons traumatized by their experience with Millerism? Or were they, perhaps, mentally unstable persons for whom the exciting doctrines of Miller merely served as a magnet?

Since chronic mental illness generally stems from biochemical, genetic, or early environmental conditions, it seems unlikely that Millerism constituted a significant etiological factor in the majority of our patient sample, 69 of whom were chronically mentally ill—although their encounters with Adventism may have triggered a particular psychotic episode or given a distinctive coloration to their symptoms. For example, one Millerite (Case No. 1263) who entered Utica in 1847 kept demanding a "rocking chair and a white robe trimmed off with flowers"—an unmistakable allusion to the much-disputed ascension robes allegedly worn by Millerites in expectation of their imminent journey to heaven.

Although Millerites seem to have been no more prone to mental illness than their neighbors, their movement—not surprisingly—attracted some marginally and poorly functioning persons to its fringes, Americans who might have gravitated toward any religious fad. In fact, at least two of our patients quickly deserted Millerism for spiritualism; one of them, a woman (Case No. 1789) admitted to the New Hamsphire Asylum in 1860, was described as being "always inclined to radicalism. First carried away by Birchard's [sic] preaching. Next Millerism. Last spiritualism."[33] Another patient (Case No. 58), admitted to the New Hampshire Asylum for the Insane in 1843 after having "suddenly taken crazy" following attendance at Millerite meetings, was readmitted in 1864 because of spiritualism.

Only in 18 cases involving acute, short-term episodes might Millerism have been a contributing cause of mental disease. The intense emotional excitement of the movement, the inner conflict and confusion induced by dashed hopes and hellish fears, the loss of community as the Millerite movement disintegrated, and the exhausting toll of body and mind taken by prolonged exposure to noise, fasting, or sleep deprivation—the factor identified by Amariah Brigham as the greatest source of breakdowns among Millerites—might well have caused the emotionally vulnerable to crack under the strain. The rapidity with which the 18 acutely ill Millerites resumed normal functioning upon being removed from an overstimulating environment to an asylum, where they could better regulate their lives and regain balance and perspective, suggests that their former involvement with Millerism may indeed have aggravated, if not precipitated, their emotional problems.

We believe it is significant that none of these patients seems to have needed further hospitalization in any of the three asylums during the twenty-year period for which records were examined, and we know that at least some of them resumed normal, productive lives. For example, a female patient (no case number) who entered the Utica asylum on February 18, 1843, suffering from severe depression after hearing the Advent message recovered sufficiently after only three months to begin working as an attendant at the institution. She held that position for over forty years, and was regarded as "one of the most efficient attendants in the house." Another depressed Millerite woman (no case number) arrived at Utica on June 14, 1843, believing that she was "lost for eternity [and had] committed the unpardonable sin" and threatening to kill herself "by cutting her throat." A month after her admission, she was able to leave the hospital, having been cured by "morphine and sleep." A third Millerite (Case No. 98), admitted to the New Hampshire Asylum in a state of acute agitation and confusion—he insisted on calling the superintendent "Brother Himes"—was released two months later "happy and rational." At discharge the attending physician noted that "there is but little fear to be apprehended of his becoming insane again unless he joins some religious excitement." Such persons, it seems fair to say, might never have seen the inside of an asylum had they not heard "the midnight cry."

THE MILLERITE VIEW

In a recent book on popular millenarianism, including Millerism, the British historian J. F. C. Harrison urged historians to spend less time "worrying whether millenarians were mad or sane" and more time exploring "how they perceived themselves and their needs." Millenarians, he suggested, "did not accept the culturally dominant conception of reality, but inhabited a distinctive world of their own. In this (largely traditional) world, madness was explained in terms of supernatural intervention, not as due to natural psycho-medical causes."[34] A study of Millerite attitudes toward insanity shows this assessment to be only partially true. Although Miller's followers did commonly explain the various manifestations of religious enthusiasm (e.g., visions, hallucinations, and fainting fits) in terms of divine or diabolical influence, to a surprising degree they adopted the prevailing medical model of insanity, even in cases involving religion.

For the most part, Millerites viewed the alleged insanity in their midst as a public-relations, rather than a medical or humanitarian, problem. Thus, although they did not flatly deny its presence, they minimized its incidence. As Joshua V. Himes put it, reports of insanity, suicide, and other supposed "fruits of Millerism" were "most of them, unfounded; and, those which have any semblance of truth, are greatly distorted and exaggerated."[35]

Himes, on the one hand, regarded the allegations of Millerite insanity as validating the righteousness of his cause and demonstrating the "want of good argument and scriptural reasons to meet us." He took comfort from the fact that the devil always opposes "the truth" and that infidels had long claimed that gospel preaching "makes people *crazy*."[36] On the other hand, he greatly resented the seemingly universal tendency among critics to attribute every crime and calamity to Millerism. Thus when one newspaper in 1841 implied that "the Miller humbug" had driven a crazed man to murder his wife and children to save them from the impending end of the world, the *Signs of the Times*, which Himes coedited, responded sarcastically with a piece headed "Is There Any Evil in the Land, and Miller Not Done It?" "This sagacious editor ought to have known, that no murders, or any dreadful evils could take place without Mr. Miller's aid," wrote the editors of the *Signs*, adding that no doubt the recent failure of the United States bank was also "a legitimate fruit of the Miller humbug." In a similar vein, the *Signs* ended a report on widespread insanity abroad with the quip: "What is the cause of insanity in Europe? It surely cannot be Millerism."[37]

Although the Millerite press regarded one minister's claim that William Miller himself was "probably mad, and ought to be put under the care of Dr. Woodward, at the State Lunatic Hospital" as too ludicrous to warrant a refutation, Millerite editors went to great lengths to refute other charges of insanity, sometimes securing and printing affidavits showing that the person involved was not a Millerite, that the Advent doctrine had not precipitated the breakdown, or that the wrong person had been identified.[38] On one occasion a delegation of Millerite brethren called on the superintendent of the New York City Lunatic Asylum at Blackwell's Island to check a rumor that eleven Millerites had recently been admitted. The correct number, they learned from the superintendent, was only four. Further investigation revealed that one of the four was a Baptist partially insane before he read a Second Advent paper; the second was an Episcopalian with a history of insanity who had never attended a Millerite meeting; the third was a chronically insane person whose connection with Millerism could not be determined; the fourth, the only undisputed Millerite, had lost his mind as a result of "domestic affliction," not religious excitement. In such manner was the cause vindicated.[39]

At times Millerite leaders took the offensive and invited critics to submit "*proof* that the preaching of the immediate coming of Christ has been signalized in any place, as a cause of insanity"—fully knowing that, given the uncertain state of medical knowledge about the etiology of insanity, no evidence, not even the testimony of attending physicians, would suffice.[40] Mere presence in an asylum for the insane was also insufficient, because as the editors of the *Signs* pointed out in an article titled "The Doctrine of the Advent Not a Cause of Insanity," virtually anyone could be committed for any reason:

It should be remembered that to be found within an Asylum of the Insane, is no proof of insanity. Friends have only to report a friend insane, and get the opinion of a physician to that effect, and they have power *vi et armis* to incarcerate them according to their own pleasure in any insane hospital and for any length of time they please.

Only a difference of opinion is often called insanity, and when ones [*sic*] opinions are so obnoxious, as is a belief in the immediate coming of Christ, to those who do not love his appearing . . . it is not strange that they should be regarded as beside themselves, and that their friends should take this method to get rid of the annoyance which the fear of the truth will necessarily produce on an unwilling conscience. When we consider how the doctrine is hated by the friends of many, it is surprising that so few have been denounced by them as insane.

Although Millerite leaders rarely complained about their followers being committed to mental institutions, the editors on this occasion went on to relate "an anecdote" about a man who, upon converting to Adventism, was denounced by his friends as insane and tricked into entering an asylum. "Could the tales of misery that individuals have suffered under a *suspicion* of insanity, be told, it would reveal many a scene of wrong and suffering that would cause humanity to shudder."[41]

In view of the Millerites' strict demands for proof—and their concern about the image of their movement—it is little wonder that, to our knowledge, no Millerite paper ever confirmed an instance in which a believer had become deranged for any reason connected with Millerism. In fact, Millerite writers repeatedly implied just the opposite. "We have become extensively acquainted with the operations of the Advent cause, particularly in the New England and middle States," wrote one Millerite leader, "and we have never fallen in with a *single case* of insanity, which even our enemies, when their candor has been appealed to, in view of all the facts in the case, could attribute to a belief in the Advent doctrine."[42]

But despite the numerous attempts by the Millerites to show that their message did not cause insanity, a considerable body of evidence indicates that they, like asylum superintendents and other physicians, believed that an intimate relationship existed between mental health and religious belief, even Millerism. Of course, whenever possible, they stressed the positive aspects of believing in the Advent doctrine, which according to the editors of the *Signs* "seems wonderfully adapted to restore to sanity the monomania [*sic*], &c, by its glorious promises and hopes." Relying on hearsay testimony they would never have allowed as evidence that Millerism *caused* insanity, they readily published accounts of how Millerism *cured* insanity. As illustrative of an "instance of recovery from insanity, by the preaching of the immediate coming of Christ," the *Signs* printed a letter from a man certifying that his insane mother, formerly a patient at the private asylum in Pepperell, Massachusetts, had been "fully restored to her reason" by having the prospect of Christ's return kept constantly on her mind. In another case, a man "so deranged as to render it necessary to keep him constantly lashed to the floor" had supposedly regained his sanity by reading Millerite papers, attending meetings, and finally embracing the Advent cause.[43]

Millerites also liked to contrast their own relatively benign teachings with the "*terror*" preached by their evangelical critics. "[W]hen they can produce *one* made insane by us," charged Himes, "*many* might be produced who have become insane by their terrific descriptions of the judgment!"[44] Ellen Harmon White, who converted to Millerism as a youth and later led the schismatic movement that resulted in the Seventh-day Adventist Church, graphically described the terror to which Himes alluded. Her autobiographical writings reveal how as a teenager she suffered intense anxiety about her chances for salvation. While listening to sermons describing hell, her "imagination would be so wrought upon that the perspiration would start, and it was difficult to suppress a cry of anguish." Sometimes she spent entire nights agonizing about her spiritual condition and once slipped into "a melancholy state" for several weeks, during which "not one ray of light pierced the thick clouds of darkness around me." Her own history led her to suspect that

> many inmates of insane asylums were brought there by experiences similar to my own. Their consciences were stricken with a sense of sin, and their trembling faith dared not claim the promised pardon of God. They listened to descriptions of the orthodox hell until it seemed to curdle the very blood in their veins, and burned an impression upon the tablets of their memory. Waking or sleeping, the frightful picture was ever before them, until reality became lost in imagination, and they saw only the wreathing flames of a fabulous hell, and heard only the shrieking of the doomed. Reason became dethroned, and the brain was filled with the wild phantasy of a terrible dream.[45]

If the Advent message did cause insanity, Millerites wanted to believe that it resulted not from anticipating the Second Coming of Christ, but from failing to prepare for that event. To corroborate this view, the *Signs* quoted the superintendent of the New Hampshire Asylum as saying that "*No one, as far I have seen, of those who truly believed in the speedy coming of Christ, has been made sad or melancholy.* Some patients who have been disturbed and perplexed by these startling theories, and yet have doubts and fears of their reality, come to us sad and desponding."[46]

According to Ellen White, the uncertainty and turmoil that followed the Great Disappointment of October 22, 1844, proved particularly unsettling to some minds. Years later she recalled that

> after the passing of the time in 1844, fanaticism in various forms arose. . . . I went into their meetings. There was much excitement, with noise and confusion. . . . Some appeared to be in vision, and fell to the floor. . . . As the result of fanatical movements such as I have described, persons in no way responsible for them have in some cases lost their reason. They could not harmonize the scenes of excitement and

tumult with their own past precious experience; they were pressed beyond measure to receive the message of error; it was represented to them that unless they did they would be lost; and as the result their mind was unbalanced, and some became insane.[47]

How much this account paralleled her own experience, we cannot be sure. We do know, however, that during this same period *she* had visions and fell to the floor and became so mentally distraught that for two weeks her "mind wandered," an episode she described as her "extreme sickness"—and which her enemies used in an attempt to discredit her ministry.[48]

Recollections such as White's reinforce the suspicion that Millerite leaders in their public statements deliberately underplayed the incidence of madness among their motley group of followers. Such accounts also provide persuasive evidence of the extent to which even Millerites themselves adopted the prevailing view that undue religious excitement might be harmful to a person's mental health.

THE END OF AN ERA

In the 1850s, as admissions of Millerites dwindled, asylum superintendents began noting with alarm that spiritualism was playing the same role in the 1850s that Millerism had played in the previous decade. " 'Millerism,' in its day, sent many victims to most of our hospitals," noted Thomas S. Kirkbride of the Pennsylvania Hospital for the Insane in a typical statement, "and what is now called 'spiritual investigations,' is a not less prolific cause of the disease."[49] In the 1870s psychiatrists shifted their concern again, this time to the evangelistic campaigns of Dwight L. Moody and Ira Sankey, whose emphasis on "conviction of sin" and "a sense of divine wrath" seemed to be upsetting "the mental equilibrium of many a youth, at least temporarily."[50] The now-obscure Adventists attracted little attention in the psychiatric literature, except in connection with one particularly gruesome incident that occurred in the late 1870s, when an Adventist man in Massachusetts, believing himself to be the archangel Michael, received a vision in which God instructed him, in the manner of Abraham, to sacrifice his child. Confident that this was only a test of faith, and that death would be only temporary, he plunged a knife into his daughter's heart, killing her instantly. The case presented "such blended features of rational and irrational conduct" that it moved the editor of the *Alienist and Neurologist* to suggest that it might represent some "new form of mental disease."[51]

Meanwhile, skepticism regarding the usefulness of identifying the supposed causes of insanity, such as religious excitement, continued to grow. As early as 1863 Isaac Ray, described by one historian as "probably the most influential nineteenth-century American psychiatrist" and a person long suspicious of the value of statistical tables of causes, noted that "the proportion of cases attributed, in our hospital reports, to 'Causes unknown,' has been steadily rising from zero to half or more of the whole number," thus destroying, "at a blow, a great deal of fancied knowledge."[52] That same year John P. Gray, who had succeeded Brigham as superintendent of the Utica asylum and as editor of the *American Journal of Insanity*, noted an apparent "decrease of religious anxiety, as an attributed cause of insanity," owing, he thought, to "the steady progress of medical knowledge," which was beginning to emphasize the organic, rather than moral, causes of mental illness. His own opinion, undoubtedly still a minority view, was that "religious anxiety is rarely, if ever, a cause of insanity."[53]

Despite such sentiments, many American psychiatrists continued to subscribe to the notion that religious excitement produced insanity. A survey of about sixty American asylums in 1876 revealed that religious excitement was thought to be the probable exciting cause of insanity for 5.79 percent of all patients; it ranked among the top four or five causes in a list of more than 30.[54] Statistics from the Pennsylvania Hospital for the Insane giving the average number of admissions per year attributed to religious excitement suggest that significant change may not have come until the 1880s. For the years 1841–1849, the average number of yearly admissions was 6.8; for 1850–1859, it was 6.6; for 1860–1869, 4.5; for 1870–1878, 6.4; and for 1879–1885, 2.1. After the death of long-time Superintendent Kirkbride in 1883, religious excitement disappeared entirely from lists of supposed causes at the Pennsylvania Hospital, and his successors attributed only one new case to religion during the late 1880s.[55] This pattern lends credence to Barbara Sicherman's observation that "The older view that religious revivals themselves caused insanity had generally declined by 1880."[56] However, some asylums continued for years to list religious excitement among the alleged causes of insanity, and well into the twentieth century psychiatric texts commonly mentioned religious excitement as a possible, but overrated, cause of mental illness.[57]

Contemporary explanations for the decline of religious insanity varied widely. We have already noted that Ray attributed it to a growing agnosticism about the etiology of insanity, and Gray thought it resulted from increased knowledge about the somatic origins of mental disorders. Other writers credited the decline to the secularization of the modern mind, which dwelled less and less on religious subjects, while Theodore W. Fisher, a Boston psychiatrist, attributed it to changing theological fashions. "The number of persons actually made insane by religious excitement has probably diminished with the gradual softening of the rigors of orthodox belief," he wrote in 1877. "Those nowadays who, 'like Sir Harry Vane, have caught gleams of the beatific vision or awaked screaming from dreams of everlasting fire,' are apt to be accounted insane and treated accordingly."[58] At any rate, with the appearance of new nosological systems toward the end of the century, psychiatric authorities tended increasingly to view religious agitation as a *symptom* of dementia praecox (schizophrenia) or some other disease, and the term "religious insanity" slowly disappeared from the vocabulary of medicine.[59]

N O T E S

A slightly different version of this chapter appeared in the *Bulletin of the Menninger Clinic*, 1985, *49*: 289–320, and is reprinted with the kind permission of the editor, Paul W. Pruyser.

In preparing this paper, we benefited greatly from the generosity and courtesy of numerous persons, whose help we would like to acknowledge: Ellen Dwyer, who shared her microfilm copies of the casebooks of the New York State Lunatic Asylum at Utica and her knowledge of the literature of the period; Barbara G. Rosenkrantz, who provided us with a computer printout of demographic data regarding "religious enthusiasm" at the McLean and Worcester asylums and invited us to use her office while examining the Worcester records; Stephen N. Harnish, M.D., Assistant Superintendent of the New Hampshire Hospital, and Frank C. Mevers, State Archivist of New Hampshire, who allowed us to use the records of the New Hampshire Asylum for the Insane; Richard Wolfe, curator of rare books at the Countway Library of Medicine, Harvard University, who arranged for us to use the records of the Worcester asylum and permitted free access to the Countway's unparalleled collection of annual reports from American asylums; the staffs of the National Library of Medicine and the Library of the College of Physicians of Philadelphia, who furnished us with additional annual reports; Kathy Holtgraver, Phil Shoemaker, and Sue Voegele, who assisted us in our search of nineteenth-century literature; Teresa Hill, Peter McCandless, Michael MacDonald, Todd Savitt, and Ronald F. White, who directed our attention to—and sometimes provided—sources we might otherwise have overlooked; and Loren J. Chapman, Teresa Hill, Lawrence J. Friedman, and the members of the Mid-America Psychological Study Group, who suggested ways to improve our manuscript. To all we are grateful.

1. "Insanity," *The Midnight Cry*, 1843, 4: 21.

2. *A Brief History of William Miller: The Great Pioneer in Adventual Faith* (Washington: Review and Herald Publishing Association, 1915), p. 251; Joshua V. Himes, quoted in [James White], "The Gifts of the Gospel Church," *Advent Review and Sabbath Herald*, 1851, 1: 69. The late historian Whitney R. Cross, who cautiously discounted rumors of Millerite insanity, speculated that for a time after October 1844 fanatics may have been in the majority; *The Burned-Over District: The Social and Intellectual History of Enthusiastic Religion in Western New York, 1800–1850* (New York: Harper & Row, 1965 [copyright 1950]), p. 314.

3. George Man Burrows, *Commentaries on the Causes, Forms, Symptoms, and Treatment, Moral and Medical, of Insanity* (London, 1828), p. 33. See also Charles F. Folsom, "Cases of Insanity and of Fanaticism," *Boston Medical and Surgical Journal*, 1880, *102*: 271.

4. Clara Endicott Sears, *Days of Delusion: A Strange Bit of History* (Boston: Houghton Mifflin, 1924), esp. pp. 204–214. See also two other early discussions of Millerite insanity: Everett N. Dick, "The Adventist Crisis of 1843–1844" (Ph.D. dissertation, University of Wisconsin, 1930); and Simon Stone, "The Miller Delusion: A Comparative Study in Mass Psychology," *American Journal of Psychiatry*, 1934, *91*: 593–623.

5. Francis D. Nichol, *The Midnight Cry: A Defense of William Miller and the Millerites* (Washington: Review and Herald Publishing Association, 1944), pp. 337–369, 488–495; emphasis added.

6. Ibid., p. 13. For examples of Nichol's influence, see, e.g., Cross, *Burned-over District*, p. 306; Ira V. Brown, "Watchers for the Second Coming: The Millenarian Tradition in America," *Mississippi Valley Historical Review*, 1952, *39*: 454–455; and William Warren Sweet, *Religion in the Development of American Culture, 1765–1840* (New York: Charles Scribner's Sons, 1952), pp. 306–311.

7. See, e.g., David Leslie Rowe, "Thunder and Trumpets: The Millerite Movement and Apocalyptic Thought in Upstate New York, 1800–1845" (Ph.D. dissertation, University of Virginia, 1974), pp. 201–205; and Ronald L. Numbers, *Prophetess of Health: A Study of Ellen G. White* (New York: Harper & Row, 1976), pp. 12, 214.

8. See, however, the recent study by Julius H. Rubin, "Mental Illness in Early Nineteenth Century New England and the Beginnings of Institutional Psychiatry as Revealed in a Sociological Study of the Hartford Retreat, 1824–1843" (Ph.D. dissertation, New School for Social Research, 1979), which argues that Millerism and other revivalistic activities caused numerous Americans to experience "social-psychological torment, guilt, and mental breakdowns" (p. 22).

9. George Rosen, "Enthusiasm," *Bulletin of the History of Medicine*, 1968, 42: 393–421, quotation on p. 417; Michael MacDonald, "Insanity and the Realities of History in Early Modern England," *Psychological Medicine*, 1981, 11: 11–25; Michael MacDonald, "Religion, Social Change, and Psychological Healing in England, 1600–1800," in *The Church and Healing*, ed. W. J. Sheils, vol. 19 of *Studies in Church History* (Oxford: Basil Blackwell, 1982), pp. 101–125. See also Michael MacDonald, *Mystical Bedlam: Madness, Anxiety, and Healing in Seventeenth-Century England* (Cambridge: Cambridge University Press, 1981); John F. Sena, "Melancholic Madness and the Puritans," *Harvard Theological Review*, 1973, 66: 293–309; and Vieda Skultans, *English Madness: Ideas on Insanity, 1580–1890* (London: Routledge & Kegan Paul, 1979), pp. 22–25.

10. MacDonald, "Religion, Social Change, and Psychological Healing," pp. 120, 124; Sydney G. Dimond, *The Psychology of the Methodist Revival: An Empirical & Descriptive Study* (Oxford: Oxford University Press, 1926).

11. See, e.g., Nathaniel Bingham, *Observations on the Religious Delusions of Insane Persons* (London, 1841), pp. 117–123.

12. Benjamin Rush, *Medical Inquiries and Observations upon the Diseases of the Mind* (Philadelphia, 1812), pp. 36–37, 44–47.

13. Amariah Brigham, *Observations on the Influence of Religion upon the Health and Physical Welfare of Mankind* (Boston, 1835), pp. 260, 284–285, 291, 312. Regarding Finney's revivals, see William G. McLoughlin, Jr., *Modern Revivalism: Charles Grandison Finney to Billy Graham* (New York: Ronald Press, 1959), pp. 27–29, 90–93; and Rubin, "Mental Illness in Early Nineteenth Century New England," pp. 81–82. In the early 1840s medical journals carried reports of an epidemic of religious enthusiasm in Sweden, which may have been tangentially related to the Millerite movement; see C. V. Sonden, "Memoir on an Epidemic of Religious Ecstasy Which Prevailed in Sweden in 1841 and 1842," *Dublin Journal of Medical Science*, 1843, 24: 226–237; and J. N. Loughborough, *The Great Second Advent Movement: Its Rise and Progress* (Washington: Review and Herald Publishing Association, 1909), first published in 1905.

14. [Frederick A. Packard], "The Relations of Religion to What Are Called Diseases of the Mind," *Princeton Review*, 1850, 22: 1–41. After reading Packard's essay, the editor of the *American Journal of Insanity*, 1851, 7: 286–287, suggested substituting the term "ir-religious insanity" for religious insanity. For a general discussion of religion and insanity in the early nineteenth century, see Norman Dain, *Concepts of Insanity in the United States, 1789–1865* (New Brunswick, N.J.: Rutgers University Press, 1964), pp. 183–193.

15. *Annual Report*, New Hampshire Asylum for the Insane, 1843; *Annual Report*, New York State Lunatic Asylum at Utica, 1843. (Hereafter, *Annual Report* will be abbreviated as *AR*.) On the growth of asylums, see Gerald N. Grob, *Mental Institutions in America: Social Policy to 1875* (New York: The Free Press, 1973).

16. Rubin, "Mental Illness in Early Nineteenth Century New England," pp. 46, 59–60.

17. These figures are based on data for the two asylums provided by Barbara G.

Rosenkrantz, who has coded the records of these institutions preserved in the Countway Library of Medicine, Harvard University. During the first eight years of operation at Worcester, 1833–1840, the percentage of cases assigned to religious causes varied from a low of 4.7 (1840) to a high of 9.0 (1838); AR, State Lunatic Hospital at Worcester, 1840, p. 61. The little comparative evidence we have found suggests that American asylums tended to admit—or diagnose—a slightly higher percentage of religion-related cases than did British institutions; see, e.g., the figures for ten U.S. and nine British asylums, ibid., 1843, pp. 50–51.

18. "Masturbation (and vegetable diet)" appeared in the AR, McLean Asylum for the Insane, 1835, p. 8; "Insufficient nutrition (Grahamism)" was listed in the AR, Hartford Retreat for the Insane, 1846, p. 20.

19. AR, Western Lunatic Asylum, Staunton, Virginia, 1841, p. 23. See also, AR, Hartford Retreat for the Insane, 1846, p. 20; and AR, Ohio Lunatic Asylum, Columbus, 1842, pp. 51–52. On the statistics of insanity, see James H. Cassedy, *American Medicine and Statistical Thinking, 1800–1960* (Cambridge, Mass.: Harvard University Press, 1984), Chap. 7, "Statistics of Mind and Madness."

20. Burrows, *Commentaries*, p. 25.

21. AR, McLean Asylum for the Insane, 1843, pp. 28–29. See also the views of Isaac Ray in AR, Maine Insane Hospital, 1842, pp. 14–19.

22. AR, Mount Hope Institution, Baltimore, 1849, p. 19; AR, Butler Hospital for the Insane, 1856, p. 29. Isaac Ray's observations on religion and insanity in the AR of the Butler Hospital also appear in his book *Mental Hygiene* (Boston: Ticknor and Fields, 1863), pp. 186–190.

23. AR, State Lunatic Hospital at Worcester, 1843, pp. 52–53. See also Woodward's comments in the AR for 1844, p. 52.

24. AR, New York State Lunatic Asylum at Utica, 1843, pp. 22–23; [Amariah Brigham], "Millerism," *American Journal of Insanity*, 1844–45, 1: 249–253. For another early case history related to Millerism, see the AR, Western Lunatic Asylum, Staunton, Virginia, 1843, pp. 32–33. Some critics expressed concern about the economic cost of caring for the deranged disciples of Miller; "Scoffers Shall Arise," *Signs of the Times*, 1843, 4: 179.

25. Rubin, "Mental Illness in Early Nineteenth Century New England," p. 77.

26. See, e.g., "Millerism and Insanity," *New York Daily Tribune*, March 24, 1843.

27. We examined the following annual (or biennial) reports:

New England: Boston Lunatic Hospital, 1840–1855
Butler Hospital for the Insane, Providence, Rhode Island, 1847–1865
Maine Insane Hospital, 1840–1842, 1844–1850
McLean Asylum for the Insane, Boston, 1835–1859
New Hampshire Asylum for the Insane, 1842–1862
Retreat for the Insane at Hartford, 1830–1870
State Lunatic Hospital at Worcester, Massachusetts, 1833–1852
State Lunatic Hospital at Taunton, Massachusetts, 1854–1863
Vermont Asylum for the Insane, 1837–1862

Mid-Atlantic: Friends' Asylum for the Insane, Philadelphia, 1834–1851
Maryland Hospital for the Insane, 1843–1849
Mount Hope Hospital, Baltimore, 1843–1853
New York Hospital and Bloomingdale Asylum, 1844–1859
New York State Lunatic Asylum, Utica, 1843–1860
Pennsylvania Hospital for the Insane, 1841–1900

South:	Eastern Lunatic Asylum, Williamsburg, Virginia, 1842–1857
	Kentucky Lunatic Asylum, 1840–1849
	Lunatic Asylum of South Carolina, 1842–1860
	Lunatic Asylum of Tennessee, 1845–1849
	Lunatic, Idiot & Epileptic Asylum of the State of Georgia, 1844
	Western Lunatic Asylum, Staunton, Virginia, 1840–1863
Midwest:	Central Ohio Lunatic Asylum, 1839–1859
	Illinois State Hospital for the Insane, 1847–1862
	Indiana Hospital for the Insane, 1848, 1851, 1858–1859

We also searched the following unpublished documents: Records of the New Hampshire Asylum for the Insane (NHAI), 1842–1861, Division of Records, Management, and Archives, State of New Hampshire, Concord; Casebooks 1–8, 1843–50, New York State Lunatic Asylum, Utica (NYSLA), from microfilm copies loaned by Ellen Dwyer; and Casebooks 16–17, 19–24, 26–27, 1845–60, State Lunatic Hospital at Worcester, Mass. (SLHW), Countway Library of Medicine, Harvard University. Nichol summarizes the records of four New England asylums in *The Midnight Cry*, p. 495.

28. *AR*, Boston Lunatic Hospital, 1843, 1844, 1845; *AR*, New York Hospital and Bloomingdale Asylum, 1845; Pliny Earle, *History, Description and Statistics of the Bloomingdale Asylum for the Insane* (New York, 1848), p. 97.

29. *AR*, New Hampshire Asylum for the Insane, 1849; Records of the New Hampshire Asylum for the Insane; *AR*, New York State Lunatic Asylum at Utica, 1843–50.

30. *AR*, New Hampshire Asylum for the Insane, 1855, 1862; *AR*, State Lunatic Hospital at Taunton, 1845, 1855. The Taunton Millerites may have been transferred from the overcrowded facility at Worcester.

31. "Memorial of D. L. Dix, Praying a Grant of Land for the Relief and Support of the Indigent Curable and Incurable Insane in the United States," *Journal of Mental Science*, 1858, *4*: 131. See also, e.g., *AR*, Eastern Lunatic Asylum, Williamsburg, Virginia, 1848, p. 14; "The Nervous Epidemic Connected with the Religious Revival in Ireland," *American Journal of Insanity*, 1860, *16*: 357; *Biennial Report*, Illinois State Hospital for the Insane, Jacksonville, 1862, p. 27.

32. Because some casebooks could not be located, we were unable to include fifteen additional cases of Millerite-related insanity mentioned in the *AR* of the Worcester State Lunatic Hospital for 1843.

33. Jedediah Burchard was a flamboyant revivalist in the 1830s.

34. J. F. C. Harrison, *The Second Coming: Popular Millenarianism, 1780–1850* (New Brunswick, N.J.: Rutgers University Press, 1979), pp. 215, 218.

35. "To the Public: The Second Advent—Mr. Himes' Statement," *Advent Herald*, 1844, *8*: 100.

36. Joshua V. Himes, "Letter to Charles Fitch," *Signs of the Times*, 1843, *5*: 53.

37. "Is There Any Evil in the Land, and Miller Not Done It?" *Signs of the Times*, 1841, *2*: 40; "Foreign," ibid., 1843, *5*: 64.

38. See, e.g., "To the Public," p. 101; "Calumnies Refuted," *Advent Herald*, 1844, *8*: 123; "Case of Mr. Walker, of Belchertown," ibid., 1846, *11*: 29–30. The reference to Miller's insanity appeared in Rev. T. F. Norris, "Millerism," *Signs of the Times*, 1842, *3*: 8.

39. "Insanity," *The Midnight Cry*, 1843, *4*: 21–22.

40. Editorial statement accompanying "Letter from Rev. N. Colver," *Signs of the Times*, 1842, *4*: 110. See "Case of Mr. Walker," pp. 29–30, for an example of rejecting medical testimony.

41. "The Doctrine of the Advent Not a Cause of Insanity," *Signs of the Times*, 1843, *5*: 173.

42. "Insanity," *Advent Herald and Signs of the Times Reporter*, 1844, 7: 100.

43. "Insanity," *Signs of the Times*, 1843, 5: 69; Letter from George A. Reed in "Letter from Rev. N. Colver," p. 110; "A Fact for Our Opponents," *Signs of the Times*, 1843, 6: 111.

44. Himes, "Letter to Charles Fitch," p. 53. A similar statement, apparently by Himes, appeared in "Letter from Rev. N. Colver," p. 110.

45. *Life Sketches of Ellen G. White* (Mountain View, Calif.: Pacific Press, 1915), pp. 29–31; Ellen G. White, *Spiritual Gifts: My Christian Experience, Views and Labors* (Battle Creek, Mich.: James White, 1860), pp. 16–18; Ellen G. White, *Testimonies for the Church*, 9 vols. (Mountain View, Calif.: Pacific Press, n.d.), 1: 25–26. On Ellen White, see also Numbers, *Prophetess of Health*; and Ronald L. Numbers and Janet S. Numbers, "The Psychological World of Ellen White," *Spectrum*, August, 1983, 14: 21–31.

46. "The Doctrine of the Advent Not a Cause of Insanity," pp. 172–173. See also "Insanity from Millerism," *Signs of the Times*, 1843, 6: 72.

47. *Selected Messages from the Writings of Ellen G. White*, 2 vols. (Washington: Review and Herald Publishing Association, 1958), 2: 34–35, from a statement made in 1901.

48. White, *Spiritual Gifts*, pp. 51, 69.

49. *AR*, Pennsylvania Hospital for the Insane, 1856, p. 25. For similar statements, see also *AR*, Eastern Lunatic Asylum, Williamsburg, Virginia, 1853–1854 & 1854–1855 [1 vol.], p. 20; and *AR*, New York State Lunatic Asylum at Utica, 1858, p. 30. For discussions about the extent to which spiritualism was causing insanity, see Review of "Spiritualistic Madness," by L. S. Forbes Winslow, *American Journal of Insanity*, 1877, 33: 441–442; "Insanity and Spiritualism," ibid., pp. 593–594; and Eugene Crowell, "Spiritualism and Insanity," in *Psychic Facts: A Selection from the Writings of Various Authors on Psychical Phenomena*, ed. W. H. Harrison (London: W. H. Harrison, 1880), pp. 111–129. We are indebted to Roy DeCarvalho for this last citation.

50. Theodore W. Fisher, "Insanity and the Revival," *Boston Medical and Surgical Journal*, 1877, 97: 59–62. See also George H. Savage, "Religious Insanity and Religious Revivals: Effects of the 'Moody and Sankey Services,'" *The Lancet*, Aug. 28, 1875, pp. 303–304.

51. Charles F. Folsom, "Cases of Insanity and of Fanaticism," *Boston Medical and Surgical Journal*, 1880, 102: 265–271; [C. H. Hughes], "Editorial: New Forms and Symptomatic Phases of Insanity," *Alienist and Neurologist*, 1887, 8: 267–268.

52. *AR*, Butler Hospital for the Insane, 1863, p. 22; Grob, *Mental Institutions in America*, p. 146.

53. *AR*, New York State Lunatic Asylum at Utica, 1863, pp. 38–40. See also [John P. Gray], "Religious Insanity," *American Journal of Insanity*, 1876, 33: 126–131.

54. Fisher, "Insanity and the Revival," p. 62. The breakdown by region was: New England (4.97%), Middle States (2.78%), Southern States (7.43%), Western States (8.37%). Fisher attributed the low percentage in the Middle States to the fact that New York and Philadelphia furnished so few cases of religious insanity.

55. *AR*, Pennsylvania Hospital for the Insane, 1841–1900.

56. Barbara Sicherman, *The Quest for Mental Health in America, 1880–1917* (New York: Arno Press, 1980), p. 88.

57. See, e.g., Daniel R. Brower and Henry M. Bannister, *A Practical Manual of Insanity for the Medical Student and General Practitioner* (Philadelphia: W. B. Saunders, 1902), p. 30; and H. I. Schou, *Religion and Morbid Mental States*, trans. W. Worster (New York: Century, 1926), pp. 116–133.

58. Fisher, "Insanity and the Revival," p. 62. See also J. G. Havelock, "An Epidemic of Religious Mania Originating from a Case of Spurious Pregnancy," *Edinburgh Medical Journal*, 1894–95, 11: 261–263; and Leonardo Bianchi, *A Text-Book of Psychiatry for*

Physicians and Students, trans. James H. MacDonald (London: Bailliere, Tindall and Cox, 1906), p. 599.

59. See, e.g., T. W. Fisher, *Plain Talk about Insanity: Its Causes, Forms, Symptoms, and the Treatment of Mental Diseases* (Boston: Alexander Moore, 1872), p. 24; George H. Savage, *Insanity and Allied Neuroses: Practical and Clinical* (London: Cassell & Co., 1884), pp. 50–53; and R. von Krafft-Ebing, *Text-Book of Insanity Based on Clinical Observations for Practitioners and Students of Medicine*, trans. Charles Gilbert Chaddock (Philadelphia: F. A. Davis, 1905), p. 143.

SEVEN

Millerism and Evangelical Culture

RUTH ALDEN DOAN

CONTEMPORARIES VIEWED MILLERITES as fanatics, or lunatics, or at the very least as dreamers and nay-sayers. Many could hardly imagine that those who anticipated the breaking open of the heavens and the burning of the world bore any relation to popular orthodoxy. Yet the Millerites were the offspring of American evangelicalism. And these aberrant cousins remained just close enough to the more successful branches of the evangelical clan to irritate, anger, and even threaten. Millerites posed for contemporaries, and demonstrate to historians, an alternative that did not follow some of the major changes in American religious culture during the nineteenth century. They were not only evangelicals with a difference, however. Through the impassioned responses that they provoked, Millerites gave striking evidence of some of the very changes that they themselves resisted. They forced critics to articulate and define more closely their positions on a set of issues raised by the new adventism. In responding, articulating, and defining, the opponents of the "Miller heresy" ended up accelerating processes that they would never have willingly promoted. The Millerite excitement, then, highlighted strains within antebellum evangelicalism and contributed to a complex process whereby evangelicals helped to undermine their own position of strength.

Simply put, four foci expressed antebellum evangelicalism: new birth, Bible, mission, and millennium. The individual needed conversion, and the message of the gospel had to be spread. The end result would be a glorious age of peace and harmony under the rule—spiritual or physical—of Jesus Christ. These four foci blended into one in the revival. Individual experience took its cues from and fed into the revival, creating energies and structures that rolled out into the community and the nation in institutions, modes of organization, behavioral norms and ideals, and assumptions about the course of history. This process of spreading ramifications of the evangelical revival along with the transformation of the evangelical message in the context of the revival gave form and power to the increasingly persuasive, more general "evangelical culture" of the mid-nineteenth century. That culture struck an uneasy balance. Lip service to the power of God masked the degree to which experience and belief lent credence to the vast abilities of man. Insistence on the facticity of the Bible implied too often that facticity was becoming more important than the Bible. Hope and fear of millennial consummation became confused with technological change, republican politics, and disciplined character. Antebellum evangelicals found it difficult to reconcile appeals to the authority of earlier generations—Reformation fathers, Puritan fathers, Christian fathers of the republic—with their own experience of feverish competition, booming progress, and reeling change. Most maintained a balance in the 1830s, falling wholly neither back into an old orthodoxy nor forward into new forces and fantasies. Yet the strains inherent in maintaining that balance made for a volatile situation indeed. Each difference of opinion seemed a full-scale conspiracy, each new group a treacherous threat to virtue or stability. And Millerites appeared both new and different.

MILLERITE EVANGELICALISM

In its origins, Millerism stood well within the evangelical culture of the early nineteenth century. William Miller himself typified, in many ways, the young men of his generation. Born of a Revolutionary War veteran and a Baptist preacher's daughter in Pittsfield, Massachusetts, in 1782, he migrated to the recently settled Low Hampton, New York, with his family. Familiarity with the Bible, the influence of his mother's piety, and the occasional preaching of his grandfather left Miller with a firm grounding in evangelical religion. It was largely through the cadences of the Scriptures and the preacher that he could make sense of his world.

Miller did not immediately follow a religious vocation. In Low Hampton and in Poultney, Vermont, he became a farmer, a Mason, and a sheriff. He also became a deist, as befitted an official in the land of Ethan Allen. Now a mocker of the Baptist Bible, he took to reading history. As he remembered it later, that study only deepened his skepticism: "The more I read, the more dreadfully corrupt did the character of man appear. I could discern no bright spot in the history of the past." In the War of 1812, he sought a "bright spot" in the fulfillment of patriotic duty. Disappointed by the performance of his fellows, he could explain their success only through recourse to a Supreme Being. Although he still referred to that Being by a deistic title, he now posited a unique interest, even intervention, on the part of that Being for the new nation.[1]

When he returned from the war, Miller moved his family back to Low Hampton. There, in the lull of peace and following the dark "year without a summer," he was caught up in the blaze of revival fires that swept the northern states in 1816. His conversion was a model of evangelical transformation. First had come the youthful falling away from the faith in which he was raised. In his espousal of deism, his mockery of local preachers, and his attachment to history and patriotism, more than through the traditional sinful diversions of unconverted youth, he had acted out his alienation from evangelical Christianity. As a soldier, too, he developed the habit of "taking the name of God in vain." Bringing this last habit into the context of Low Hampton set Miller on the road to conversion. A simple profane outburst cast his adult life into sharp contrast against his childhood and threw him into a state of "despair" that continued for some months. This conviction of sin formed an important part of the classic evangelical conversion. The convert had to be convinced of his utter hopelessness, of the futility of going on without God, before he could turn to Jesus in full faith.

Finally the hoped-for break in the tension came. "God by His Holy Spirit opened my eyes," Miller would later recall, "I saw Jesus as a friend, and my only help, and the Word of God as a *perfect rule* of duty." He would put his trust in the Lord, and live his life by the Scriptures; this became possible, his statement implies, after his moment of conversion. His experience placed him directly at the core of the evangelical ethos of his day. With other seekers he found confirmation of his sense of a merciful God and a divine Christ not only in his religious experience but also in the Bible. As he had once searched books of history for an alternative to Christian understanding, he now ransacked the Bible for further evidence of the legitimacy of his new Christian commitment. And in the Scriptures he found "just such a Savior as [he] needed."

Since the Bible was clear even to a "wayfaring man" or a "fool," and since it acted as "its own expositor," the challenge was to eliminate all prior prejudices and assumptions and to allow scriptural evidence itself to point the way.[2] After two years, Miller decided where a literal reading of the Bible led. Miller's literalism allowed that some parts of the Scriptures were figurative, and the prophecies were among these. But they were not figurative in result—they would, rather, issue in a literal fulfillment. The books of Daniel and Revelation contained figures foreshadowing the return of Christ. The return itself would be no shadowy figure, but a literal return. Miller expected that return to be personal and premillennial. He also found evidence in his reading of Scripture of the Second Coming as a "continually-expected event" to be watched for until it came. Moreover, since all Scripture was "necessary," Miller applied himself to the numbers in the prophetic books as seriously as to any other part of the Bible. When he combined his arithmetic with his assumption that Christ would return personally and soon, Miller arrived at his most famous conclusion—the existing world would come to an end "about A.D. 1843."

Miller held to his conviction of Christ's impending return through the 1820s without making it the center of a new vocation. He continued to farm, became a justice of the peace, and acted the respectable citizen in Low Hampton. When he told his neighbors of his prophetic conclusions, little excitement ensued. The equanimity that met his announcement of the time was perhaps a measure of both the remaining distance from 1843 and the general acceptance of the possibility that the Bible made special mention of the days following the "democratic revolutions." Millennialism, without too much concern about the distinction between pre- and post-millennialism, formed an integral part of the evangelical, and political, ethos of the early republic.[3] Moreover, focus on the 1840s had gained popularity among interpreters of Scripture after the presumed fulfillment of certain prophecies in the French Revolution.[4] Miller fit comfortably enough into this generalized sense of anticipation.

Fed by the revival, millennial expectation in turn stoked the revival in a cycle of rising fervor during the 1820s and 1830s. Revival and millennium also gave impetus to the sense of mission shared by evangelicals. In this, too, Miller proved typical. After a revival struck Low Hampton in the late 1820s, he grew increasingly uncomfortable in his position of knowing what he thought to be a great truth but not sharing it as broadly as he might. He came to feel that God's demands pressed him toward going out to tell his fellowmen that they would witness the return of Christ before two decades had passed. He took it as a sign, therefore, when he received an invitation to speak on his doctrines and calculations in a neighboring town. Miller joined a herd of itinerants who, in the early 1830s, carried messages of salvation through temperance, education, nonresistance, and abolition, as well as through conversion.

As Miller carried his message from town to town, the convictions of a single individual became the foundation for an expanding movement. This movement did not take shape separately from the broader evangelicalism of the day, but rather drew on it and gave it renewed impetus. The experience of new birth familiar to Miller was repeated in the lives of most of his followers. Many Millerites came out of Baptist churches, and a good number also found fellowship among the Methodists, Presbyterians, and Congregationalists. In all of these denominations, the conversion experience took a central place in the individual's spiritual, and social, journey. Second, Miller's careful and literal reading of the Bible as the primary spiritual and historical authority carried over and became central to the movement that grew around him. Although the emphases of Millerite biblicism seemed idiosyncratic, they were in fact part of a general obeisance to biblical authority in evangelicalism. That authority dictated the mission responsibilities that Millerites took quite seriously. They set up an elaborate network of traveling lectures and camp meetings, often under the voluminous great tent, to carry the word to the people. Millerites' relation to the fourth point of reference of evangelicalism, the millennium, requires little explanation. If they spoke for anything, the Millerites spoke for the reality of another order which could break through and pass judgment over history at any moment.

Millerites not only fit into evangelicalism, they also played a significant role in revitalizing it. A number of ministers and laymen credited conversions to Miller, his printed lectures, or his associates. The word spread during the 1830s that Millerite lectures stirred up revivals wherever they were heard. Reports laid heavy emphasis on extreme cases, including conversions of infidels and Universalists. Miller, it seemed, had initiated a movement that could bring even the intransigent into the fold. At the same time, announcement of the impending advent gave new life to people already within the sphere of evangelical influence, pressing the young on to the moment of decision, convincing men whose mothers, wives, and daughters had already joined the ranks, and renewing fervor in communities suffering "lukewarmness," laxity, and backsliding. Converts differed in the degree to which they accepted Millerism itself. Some came to full faith in "43ism." Others were persuaded that the return of Christ would be personal, premillennial, and soon, but rejected the date. A number accepted the legitimacy of their conversions brought about by Millerism while denying specifically adventist doctrines completely.[5]

By 1843, suspicion of Millerism had grown to the point that credit for revivals was often denied the End-of-the-World men. Yet Millerite influence, credited or not, reached its peak in 1843 and 1844. The power of the Millerite message increased in tandem with its immediacy. The promise and threat of meeting the Lord at any moment brought audiences to a pitch of excitement. Fervor was matched by resources—a good number of Millerite lecturers, a centrally directed campaign of camp meetings, and a developed structure of prayer meetings, conferences, and publications stood ready to reinforce and build on successes. The result was an astounding impact that has led historians to consider the great revival wave of 1843–1844 as essentially inspired by Millerism.[6]

In many ways, the Millerites supported the broader evangelical culture of antebellum America. This raises a perplexing question: If the Millerites were, in so many ways, good evangelicals, of what heresy could they have stood accused? And, if their contributions to spreading evangelical influence were so often positive, from whence arose the negative which proved their longest lasting legacy?

MILLERITE HERESY

Millerism may have been evangelicalism with a twist, but observers of the movement found that twist peculiar indeed. Spokesmen for evangelical denominations, for religiously inspired reform, and for a Christian (evangelical) America saw much that was ridiculous, strange, and even frightening in Millerism. The primary line of attack against the new Adventists was a set of objections to "43ism"—that is, arguments against the assertion that the year 1843 would witness the Second Coming of Christ. In addition to harping on the question of the time, opponents of Millerism discovered—or imagined—both religious and social deviance in the rhetoric and behavior of Miller and his followers. The heresy under which those perceived peculiarities were subsumed might best be called "radical supernaturalism."[7] The phrase is not one that the anti-Millerites themselves used, but rather an umbrella that sums up much of what was behind a confusion of anecdotes and accusations. "Radical supernaturalism" can be defined simply as an insistence on the absolute reality of a transcendent order, but it can best be understood in this context by surveying its components as they appear in the anti-Millerite literature.

The primary argument against the Millerites was the specific dating—scandalously imminent—of Christ's return. For Millerites themselves, the date held a certain ambiguity. Miller had added up the prophetic numbers and found that the sums converged on 1843. "Father Miller" and several of his itinerant lecturers emphasized the year of the hoped-for end. At the same time, Miller often qualified his chronological precision about the end. He looked for the final day "on or before" 1843, or "about" 1843. Some of the most prominent Millerites never accepted date-setting at all. Henry Jones asserted that the "prophetic *times* and *seasons* were indefinitely foretold," yet he remained a major figure in the movement associated with "43ism" almost until its climax. N. N. Whiting maintained his connection with the movement in spite of his disavowal of the 1843 date.[8]

It was not the proclamation of "1843" alone that brought Millerites together. Well into 1842, the date stood as a symbol for a set of assumptions rather than a literal test of faith for most adherents. Those assumptions were shared by Old Father Miller and the frenetic reformer Jones, and they provided a binding common ground for the movement as a whole. Both the joyous shout "1843!" and the reasoned exposition of Millerite chronology expressed a hope and faith that a transcendent order existed which held out both promise and threat of judgment to man and his world. Miller and Jones could agree that the return of Christ would be personal and premillennial, and that it would come soon. They shared a belief that Christianity was not a set of myths about spiritual forces, but a belief in the absolute reality of Christ, the urgent demands of God, and the immediate overturning of the existing order. For most Millerites, mention of 1843 served as a reminder of a supernatural order so real as to be almost palpably, physically present.

In fact, by 1843 or 1844, Millerites increasingly took acceptance of the date—either 1843 or, later, October 22, 1844—as the defining tenet of their faith. This resulted from no conscious decision, but rather from the escalating demands of heightened fervor, an increasing number of people attracted to the movement, ironically, by attacks on Millerite date-setting, and both internal and external pressure to resolve the ambiguity surrounding the issue of the date. The greater importance placed on the date itself did not, however, eliminate the radical supernaturalism associated with the date. Although the emphasis changed, the dominant assumption of Millerism might still be summarized as a belief in a divine order outside human history which would break into the lives of men and transform the earth.

Was the heresy, then, the date or the supernaturalism behind the date? The answer, not surprisingly, is both. Some critics picked through Miller's numbers to tear down his chronology at various points. Among the 160 points in his widely read "Mistakes of Millerism," for example, the Reverend William R. Weeks included a denial that pagan Rome fell in A.D. 508—the year to which Miller added the 1335 of Daniel 12 to calculate the time of the end. Weeks was also suspicious of Miller's fusing of the 70 weeks of the ninth chapter and the 2,300 days of the eighth chapter of Daniel. Similarly, Samuel Farmer Jarvis pointed out that Miller's addition did not mesh with the analysis of that great authority on prophecy, Bishop James Ussher. If Ussher were correct in stating

George H. Witherl... Bastin

THE
SERMONS, DOCTRINES,

AND

PECULIAR VIEWS

OF

THE MILLERITES,

AS PREACHED BY

FATHER MILLER AND HIS BRETHREN,

MESSRS. HIMES, LITCH, FITCH, &c.,

IN

THE BIG TENT AT NEWARK,

November, 1842,

WHEREIN THEY ATTEMPT TO PROVE, FROM THE PROPHECIES OF SCRIPTURE, THAT

The World will be Destroyed in 1843.

ALSO,

Dr. Brownlee's Sermon,

IN REPLY TO FATHER MILLER,

WHEREIN HE ATTEMPTS TO PROVE THAT THE MILLENNIUM WILL NOT COMMENCE BEFORE 1866.

NEW YORK:

Published at the Herald Office, Northwest Corner of Fulton and Nassau Streets.

1842.

21. In November 1842, Dr. William C. Brownlee, pastor of the Collegiate Protestant Reformed Church of New York City, preached against the Millerite interpretation of prophecy. Courtesy Andrews University Heritage Room.

that the world began in 4004 B.C., and if the world were to last 6000 years, then the end could not come in 1843.[9] A favorite way of ridiculing the Millerites was to associate their anticipation with failed prophecies of the past. The *New York Evangelist*, in "Millerism in the XVIIth Century," told readers of London's Reverend Thomas Beverly, who foresaw the end of Popery and the commencement of the millennium nine years after his 1688 announcement. "Credulity of 'Millerites' in 1712" did not mention Millerites at all, but rather told of Englishman William Whiston, who in that year predicted the appearance of a comet followed by "*a total dissolution of the world by fire.*"[10] The vocal anti-Millerite Luther Dimmick set up the example of the sixteenth-century prophet of violent apocalypse Thomas Munzer as a warning of the dangers involved in seeking a precise date for the end.[11]

It was not simply the setting of a date in itself that set so many against the Millerites. The imminence and the nature of the event foretold were profoundly disquieting. Just as the Millerites saw "1843" as a symbol for a set of beliefs and assumptions, so their opponents saw the pronouncement on the year as the focus for an intertwined set of errors. Even those who professed a belief in the personal return of Christ often denounced the rapidity with which the Millerites saw that moment approaching. The largest organized group of premillennialists—besides the Millerites themselves—in antebellum America followed a line of interpretation that required the return of the Jews to Jerusalem before the Second Coming. The upshot of this approach was often to delay the final events to the point of making its adherents hardly millenarians at all.[12] There were more common objections to such a fast-approaching end, too. One writer stated that "while our commerce is stretching over every sea" few would fall for Millerism. In a similar vein, the anti-Millerite Dimmick rejected the notion that recent discoveries could have appeared for such brief use. He pointed to the steam engine and even to the printing press as innovations recent enough that so swift an interruption of their use was inconceivable.[13]

Related to Dimmick's concern was the widespread objection to the kind of event that the Millerites anticipated. Miller himself dramatized their hope:

> . . . The clouds have burst asunder. The heavens appear. The great white throne is in sight—Amazement fills the universe with awe—he comes—he comes behold the savior comes, lift up your heads ye saints he comes!—he comes!!—he comes!!!![14]

The gripping image presented Christ returning personally to reign in power over this earth. He would break into nature and cut all historical processes short, accomplishing by divine intervention what man could not achieve on his own. Opponents found such a denial of the ability of man and the meaning of history unacceptable. A writer in the *Methodist Review* put it quite simply: "*It is in accordance with the divine economy to save man by human instrumentality.*"[15] The *Oberlin Evangelist* agreed that to think "God will bring in the Millenium by a sort of miracle, and chiefly without human agency" was "a sad, dreadful mistake."[16] The experience of Finneyite revivals convinced many that "God works by means to bring his ends to pass."[17] Men working through natural and social means would serve God's ends, convert the world, improve the social order, introduce the millennium. From this perspective, Millerite supernaturalism was deserving of ridicule or worse.

In the face of growing opposition, Millerites maintained their straightforward belief. "You regret that I should be so confident of 1843," wrote one convert. "The reason I am so, is *I believe God*."[18] The Millerite system, for the believer, hung together as an inseparable whole. Affirmation of the date, or of the imminent, personal return of Christ sometime close to 1843, was the equivalent of a statement of faith in God. If one did not believe that Christ would return, physically and soon, one could also reject the first appearing of Christ on earth, the salvation of men through Jesus Christ, the other teachings of the Bible, indeed, the entire plan and providence of the Christian God.[19]

Opponents of Millerism, for their part, objected to the assumptions they read into Millerite literature about God's ways. A writer in the *Christian Reflector* proclaimed that "By no whirlwind power, by no exhibition of mere almightiness, is the conquest of the world for Christ to be achieved."[20] Another anti-Millerite asked if Jesus would now "confess that he can rule on earth only by physical force?"[21] Supernatural power was, for these Christians, not a wonderful and awe-inspiring force, but "mere almightiness," a sad last resort inadequate for a God capable of triumph through nobler means. Another column noted that a God who would come "in terror from the flaming sky" and "destroy or disturb" the world "would not be treating us as we would like to be treated."[22] Not only would a supernatural break into history be a sign of divine weakness, it would also represent the triumph of values not human in origin or orientation. Opponents of the new Adventism saw the Millerite God as Lord of a transcendent order separate from and standing in judgment over human actions and values, and they rejected the image.

Millerites turned to the Bible as the preeminent authority through which they buttressed their anticipation of an immiment end and their image of an almighty, intervening deity. As noted above, William Miller had found the Bible a source of rule for life that could, when read by its own light, open the intentions and demands of Providence to man. He continually advised others to return to the Bible, to study the Bible, to speak from the Bible, and to encourage others to center themselves on the Bible, too.[23] Miller's reliance on Scripture is revealed in his explanation of a favorite parable—the story of the wise and foolish virgins and the midnight cry:

> The Ch[urc]h[e]s through the instrumentality of Bibles are giving the world the *Lamp* (word) all may trim (read) but all do not have oil (faith) in the lamp (word) therefore to those who have no oil (faith) it can give no light, and he that hath no oil (faith) will be shut out (damned).[24]

In what was the Christian required to have faith? In the word. The parable, as the Millerites read it, referred to the necessary preparations for the return of the bridegroom, or Christ. Central to the distinction between the wise and foolish virgins—the righteous and the wicked—was the level of dedication to the word. The Adventists occasionally went so far as to equate Millerism explicitly with "Bibleism."[25]

Millerite biblicism was a fitting addition to—even extension of—supernaturalist adventism and subjection to a transcendent God. Once again the authority posited was absolute, neither created by nor subject to the will of men. Moreover, the Bible was the written expression of that powerful God, and it was no more historically determined nor mythical in intent than the deity himself.

Evangelical spokesmen became uneasy with Millerite claims of biblical authority. It was not that they denied the legitimacy of the Bible themselves—on the contrary, biblicism remained an integral component of evangelicalism. The problem was, first of all, the dramatically different conclusion that the Millerites reached. How could they, after all, be properly reading the evangelicals' Bible and still come up with visions of Christ bursting through the clouds on a particular fast-approaching day? Inseparable from this was the problem of the irritating certainty of the Millerites.[26] At a time when the seminary-trained, at least, were aware of challenges to the integrity of the Bible on a variety of fronts, the Millerites seemed most content to assert simply that they believed in an inspired Bible, including the whole Bible, and consistent within itself.

It was not in a rejection of scholarly criticism, however, so much as in their ways of integrating Bible-reading with the power of the Holy Spirit that Millerites fed ammunition to their enemies. Generally Millerites, like other evangelicals, struck a balance between faith and Scripture. As one convert confessed, he had become an Adventist "by the united influence of the Word and the Spirit."[27] One of Miller's "Rules of Interpretation" of the Bible—the one he called the "most important rule of all"—was that "you must have faith."[28] The converted Christian could read the Bible literally and find God's truth. Occasionally, however, and with increasing frequency as the movement gained momentum, a Millerite would claim a special inspiration or a special experience associated with his or her acceptance of Second Adventism. The individual who combined "the Word and the Spirit" spoke of his "conversion to the Second Advent doctrine."[29] Another correspondent put it this way: "my heart received the doctrine of the speedy coming of Christ."[30] Miller had said that Bible truths were accessible to all men. Evangelicals, along with most Millerites, believed that the converted Christian had more or less all he needed to read the Bible correctly. But now, some Millerites were not talking about doctrines discovered by a faithful individual in serious study of the Scriptures. Some Adventists received in their hearts, others were converted to, the tenet that defined their group. This smacked of a special revelation or of an experience after and above the experience of conversion. The Rochester Methodist Samuel Luckey threw in an extended attack on these points among his complaints against Millerism. To speak of an expectation of the end of the world in 1843 as the "hope within them," said Luckey, was a "wretchedly perverted use of the Scripture language." While claiming to rely on the "facts" of the Bible, Millerites also "set themselves to praying *for evidence* of the truth, and profess to *receive* it" as they would "their personal *state of grace!*" This, Luckey pronounced, revealed the Adventists' "secret infidelity respecting the truth of the Bible." Bible truth clearly showed Luckey and other evangelicals that conversion was sufficient for salvation, and if that were true then belief in "1843" could not also be necessary.[31] A correspondent to the *Signs of the Times* accused the Millerites of substituting belief in the imminent Second Coming for regeneration as the point on which salvation turned and of a "reliance upon dreams and individual revelations, and vague impressions made upon the imagination."[32] The idea that God would alter established processes of salvation by sending—and requiring—an additional shower of grace ran against the grain of evangelical orthodoxy.

If observers suspected that Millerites had to claim a special revelation to buttress their annoying certainty about biblical truth, that claim for a Second Advent experience reaffirmed opponents' objections to Millerite supernaturalism. The Millerite God appeared to be not only transcendent and all-powerful, but also inclined to muscle his way into the world, giving no notice before he broke across human history. Millerites expected Jesus Christ to appear, here and now, literally and personally. Such an image was too disruptive and too physical to fit emerging notions of God and his providence. In this context, the compelling popularity of ascension robe stories assumes new significance.

In Macedon, New York, a man "dressed himself in white, and spent the whole day, either on the woodpile, or on top of the hog-pen."[33] In Albany, one couple and one entire family "actually dressed themselves in long white robes, and with white slippers on their feet, sat all day long in patient yet confident expectation of the end of all earthly things!"[34] So ran the stories of Millerite ascension robes. Readers were treated with elaborations of the basic theme as the tales were repeated in paper after paper. A Mr. Shortridge of New Hampshire first appeared simply climbing a tree in a "long white dress," falling and breaking his neck. With more dramatic effect, another paper added that "he made one aspiring effort [to rise], but was precipitated to the ground." Before the story had run its course, the tree had become an apple tree and Mr. Shortridge had "run mad with Millerism." All delighted dismay was then cut short by the arrival of letters from Shortridge, who proclaimed himself very much alive.[35] Corrections of such legends were rare, however, and Americans through the northern United States read of Millerites dressed in white in numerous secular and religious publications.

At least as much fancy as fact went into the ascension robe stories. Yet they caught the imagination of contemporaries and became central to the popular image of Millerites. The message the tales carried was one of individuals taking the word and promises of God literally to the point of absurdity. Anyone who believed that Jesus Christ would actually descend from the clouds of heaven could also go so far as to expect a physical force to pick him up and carry him away. Anyone who would read the Bible with such insistent and precise literalism could well take the white robes of Revelation 6 and 7 not as metaphors for faith, but as actual garments. Ridicule summarized graphically the position of critics of Millerism. A transcendent God who intervened in history, a personal Christ who would return to reign physically, a literal Bible that spelled out precise and realistic details of a fantastic end of the world—these had as much to do with genuine Christianity, according to anti-Millerite propagandists, as sitting in a tree wearing a flowing white gown.

NEW EVANGELICALISM

In response to Millerism, said Silas Hawley in 1843, "Old and long-settled principles have been abandoned; . . . and new views and principles hastily adopted," even to the extent that "the opposers of this system [Millerism] find themselves in sweet and delightful fellowship" with their former adversaries. The anti-Millerites, Hawley claimed, had moved dangerously close to "Infidelity, Romanism, and Universalism."[36] These three kinds of "errorists" make strange bedfellows. In fact, their common ground may have been largely the receipt of the antipathy of their contemporaries. Moreover, it was rather extravagant to claim that Millerism, and objections to it, were at the root of major changes in the popular religious culture of the 1840s. Yet it behooves us to look more closely at what Hawley had to say. His perception hints at the function that Millerism, and the excitement of the early 1840s, served at the time and can serve for those who look back at antebellum America from the distance of a century and a half.

Millerism grew out of popular evangelicalism. Indeed, Millerism could well be said to have been an evangelical movement. But popular culture cannot be frozen, and the evangelicalism that gave force to Millerism shifted its ground even as it sent off its Adventist offshoot. The general process of change has been described by historians of American religion. Calvinism declined, the "Methodist Era" took hold, postmillennialism triumphed in the guise of faith in progress, and "secularization" accelerated apace.[37] Hawley would have agreed with much of what the historians have found, but he named the process more simply: "making the infidels."[38] Millerism set up a standard of belief at a time when evangelicals as a group hardly knew what they believed. Evangelicals had moved away from areas of agreement without recognizing what major differences had arisen. When the Millerites appeared, they presented an implicit challenge: Name the ground on which you stake your claim to orthodoxy. The Millerite excitement forced evangelical spokesmen to articulate and to strive to make coherent the new assumptions under which they had begun to work. The study of Millerism and anti-Millerism, therefore, opens up a moment when the broader changes in religious culture were broken into components and analyzed by both sides. In addition, the very act of articulating and organizing new understandings accelerated the changes that were already taking place. Hawley erred in stating that it was in response to Millerism that "the most undisputed and generally received views [had] been relinquished." Millerism was neither the sole nor the determinative influence on changes in antebellum religious culture. But it was true that Millerism forced into the open an awareness of the degree to which old views had already faded away.[39]

To return to the accusations of virtual heresy leveled against the Millerites in view of Hawley's assertion, then, is to approach the problem as one of understanding cultural change in specific forms and especially in those forms that seemed to contemporaries most worthy or needful of defense. Objections to claims about the imminent, personal return of Christ, to a powerful and distant God, and to a Bible complete and absolute in its authenticity and authority arose from a new configuration of beliefs and values.

Behind opposition to the vision of the sudden return of Christ in the clouds of heaven lay an increasing assumption that change was gradual and progressive. "The speedy ushering in of the judgment and end of the world, seems unlikely," wrote Dimmick. John Dowling looked forward to "the gradual, though certain approach of the millennium." The secular mingled with the religious in this vision of steady upward movement. A Baptist paper noted that "In this age of steam, progress is more rapid than formerly." Although evangelicals did not envision a future free of all threats, they pictured obstacles as tests to be overcome on the great and certain march forward.[40]

As important as the gradual nature of the anticipated change was the presumed locus of that change. Antebellum Christians increasingly looked for a millennium growing within the hearts of believers.[41] No imposition from outside, but an internal alteration would provide the foundation for progress. Renewed emphasis on a change of heart differed from the traditional evangelical requirement of conversion. No longer a climactic melding of individual, social, and divine demands initiated from on high, the spreading millennium of the heart grew slowly, perhaps even from a seed of divinity within the individual. In any case, it was less a gift from a powerful deity than a treasure to be nurtured.[42]

That spreading holiness of heart could not be induced by force. If gradualism was the way, then influence was the means to the introduction to the millennium. The "mere almightiness" that the *Christian Reflector* denigrated found its nobler replacement in persuasion and example, in "*moral means*" rather than "*physical means.*"[43] The new era would flourish under "the reign of argument and motive."[44]

The influence that would change human hearts would naturally result in different behavior. The popular view of holiness balanced these two sides—internal renewal and right behavior. The plan of God depended on both. The proper approach to an impending end would be no different from the judicious path to be followed with no final day in sight, according to Lydia Maria Child. She sought "purity of life and conversation, a heart at peace with all men, and diligent efforts to do all in my power to save and bless."[45] The *New York Evangelist* could agree with Child's fellow-Unitarian William Ellery Channing on this point, that God intended mankind "for effort, conflict, and progress," and call for "wisely directed . . . labor."[46] The *Christian Secretary* explicitly posed the need for reformed behavior against anticipation of the Advent:

22. John Dowling, pastor of the Pine Street Baptist Church in Providence, Rhode Island, was one of many ministers who wrote books or pamphlets against Millerism. This 18 × 24-inch broadside announces the publication of the second edition of Dowling's *Reply to Miller*. Courtesy of the American Baptist Historical Society, Rochester, N.Y.

"People would be much better employed in mending their own ways, and doing good to others, than by striving to find out the precise *time* of an event which . . . God has no where revealed in the Bible."[47] Action was posed against speculation.

Evangelicals envisioned constant activity not just in strictly religious and moral spheres. The presumed passivity of the Millerites was cast into contrast with the energetic "discharge of our various duties to our families [and] to the State" as well as to the church. Obligation extended to "far-reaching schemes of national improvement" and "judicious domestic economy." To apply old principles, "to carry them out—to translate them into action. . . . This," proclaimed one writer, "is progress."[48] Whether they emphasized religious activity, work at labor or business, or social reform, most critics of Millerism found the great process of redemption pervasively at work in the historical development of the American republic. If evangelicals would but fight personal sin and "extravagance and idleness"—including that inevitably encompassed by the system of slavery in the South—if they would promote the pursuit of "industry and economy," then the United States would be "the instrument in the hands of Divine Providence for re-modeling the visible condition of the world."[49]

These arguments broke into public view in reaction to the perceived heresies of the Millerites. Perceptions, not surprisingly, differed from the reality that Adventists pictured for themselves. Certainly, Millerites did not believe that they misconstrued the nature and intentions of God nor that they misread the Bible. More specifically, they often drew closer to their critics on questions of holiness, behavior, and reform than those opponents allowed. Adventists of later years often focused on the need for "holiness of heart." Even early in his career, Miller had urged his associates on in quest of holiness and argued that "we ought to strive to attain to perfection as much as if it was [possible]." Millerites exhibited remarkably little deviant behavior, and except at the peak of the movement posed no real threat to work or family structures. If activity in the world was what was required, the list of Adventists who continued their association with reform movements even after their acceptance of Millerism should have given their contemporaries pause.[50] The kinship between his followers and the new evangelicals probably bewildered Old Father Miller, but the founder's intentions did not control the evolution of the movement. The irony of the antagonism between Millerites and their opponents is that the supposed deviants actually remained so closely in step with many of their detractors.

The significance of the Millerites for popular religious culture lay not only in what they were or intended to be, however, but also in what they seemed or symbolized. Millerites provided a focal point around which definitions of what was not acceptable evangelicalism could be drawn. It was around the Millerites, in particular, that the stereotype of the premillennialist that would persist until the late twentieth century was sketched out. Premillennialists, as most students of American culture could recite, are so taken with visions of impending doom that they have neither time nor motivation to do anything in this world. Pessimists to their very core, premillennialists remain passive, accept no individual responsibility for present and future needs, and deny that man can do anything for himself or for his miserable, fallen world. In fact, some Millerites could hardly be described as anything but optimists, most Millerite leaders were involved in reform movements, after as well as before their acceptance of Second Adventism, and Miller and Himes were accused of making preparations for the future as often as they were accused of working against proper preparations for the days ahead. But none of these realities could budge the growing conviction of more orthodox evangelicals that they already knew what premillennialists were about, and that they stood for orthodoxy in rejecting the whole pattern.[51]

Evangelicals had a pretty good idea of what they were not in the 1830s and 1840s—not Millerites, also not Mormons, nor Universalists. They spoke less clearly to the question of what they were. Yet the implications and the rhetoric of anti-Millerism can offer a number of clues to the shifts in popular religious culture that were not clear to participants at the time. The dominant changes in nineteenth-century religious life have often been summarized as a process of "secularization." The implication of a rejection of religiousness carried in that term, however, does not completely fit the American case. What is called secularization has been less a loss of religiosity than a shift in the loci of religious experience, authority, and responsibility. In the 1830s and 1840s a new fault line opened up, drawing an ever-firmer distinction between external and internal sources of values and between objective and subjective legitimation. No God "out there" could set the rules and the goals without reference to what man "in here" felt and hoped. In its simplest form, the new set of assumptions is as easy to ridicule as the notion that Christ will drop out of the sky at any moment— why, after all, should God hold off the consummation of his cosmic plan just because man only recently built the first railroads? Or because man might work harder if he believed that he was contributing to an ongoing and divinely blessed linear progress? The new notions of internalized demands and subjective experience were not so simple, however. At its best, this new evangelicalism gave new meaning to the tradition that God created man—if not yet woman—in his image, reconfirmed the necessity of striving constantly toward a balance of purity in heart and energy in action, and established a new basis for social Christianity. If, at its worst, it also fell into a sticky sentimentalism and a tendency to judge means and goals against the worldly standard of American political and social experience, this did not make it utterly irreligious.

The Millerites were—and still are—often blamed for a decline in the membership of some churches and for a general religious malaise in the late 1840s. Historians should perhaps be more wary of laying this kind of unilateral blame. The connection between Millerism and decline in church membership is fuzzy and conjectural at best. The hypothesis that membership decline in denominations coincided with a low incidence of Millerism only demonstrates the pervasiveness of the disillusionment caused by Adventist deviance and disappointment is only one way of reading the evidence.[52] Considering the number of disputes and schisms that broke out in the 1830s and 1840s—those revolving around abolitionism perhaps chief among them—it seems peculiar that Millerism should be singled out as the major cause of disruption within the churches. The outbreak of Adventism and the inability of the churches either to contain its millennial fervor or to prevent the ensuing secessions represented but one example of a larger problem—the inability of the existing denominations to uphold the authority to fulfill the functions that they claimed as their own.

A variety of reasons might be adduced to explain the abdication or forced retreat of the churches. Conflicting demands and opportunities chipped away at the territory covered by traditional religious institutions. The market, the emerging industrial order, the professions, and politics are obvious candidates for chief competitor to the denominations. In addition to these, the dominant religious culture itself might be examined for clues to the cause of its own disarray.

Emerging notions of subjective experience, influence through moral means, and progress initiated by man within history came into conflict with social forms that had gained legitimacy from a different set of assumptions. The power of the clergy and the control of church discipline had flourished along with the assumption that a transcendent order ordained values to be channeled through religious structures. The individualistic and egalitarian implications of evangelicalism had always posed a threat, though often latent, to existing structures of authority. In the 1840s, a flurry of challenges to such structures demonstrated just how tenuous their hold had become. The withdrawal of large numbers of Millerites, among others, highlighted the inability of church discipline to muffle dissent and maintain order within congregations and denominations. The process of laboring with a church member who seemed to be in error, or of bringing that member up for trial within the church, was intended not only to weed out the irredeemable but also to recover the wayward.[53] When Elder Elijah Greenfield, Millerite pastor of the First Baptist Church of Williamson, New York, took at least 25 members out of the church with him, the recovering function of the institution had failed. When Marshall Sherwin of the First Presbyterian Church of Palmyra, New York, not only refused to repent of his absence from services but also denounced the basis of the church as "entirely unscriptural and wrong," the effect was precisely the reverse of a public demonstration of the power and unity of that social institution.[54] Like abolitionists, Millerites voted with their feet as well as with their voices on the question of whether the church still functioned with compelling authority over individuals or with binding force on communities.

Different social forms, it appeared, would have to take up where traditional structures no longer fit the assumptions of the majority. The clergy turned to new bastions of influence and moral force—woman, home, and family—for an alliance that would give them access to new kinds of authority.[55] Because holiness meant active work within the historically progressing providence of God, behavioral norms would be largely defined by the requirements of those institutions that seemed to be forwarding that progress—industries, professions, republican politics. Church and clergy were left to work within the framework set up by others, retaining little more in their own sphere of behavioral demands than the monitoring of the consumption of alcohol.

Not all evangelicals acceded to the changes taking place in the 1830s and 1840s. Some, presumably, held to an ethos associated with Calvinism, premillennialism, straightforward biblical authority, and a transcendent deity. Where were these people to go? The system to which they held had been discredited by association with Millerism. The vociferous anti-Millerites gave the impression that there was no longer room in the churches for those unwilling to accept subjectively derived values, an immanent God, and a progressive, socially derived providence. Little wonder if their fervor waned after 1844. Their successors would regather strength later in the century, but the regrouping would take twenty years and more.

New lines were drawn within American religious culture in the 1830s and 1840s. In retrospect, most critics of Millerism appear to have been lining up the forces of Protestant liberalism. At the time, however, they viewed themselves as defenders of evangelical orthodoxy. Like Millerites, they stood on the traditional cornerstones of new birth, Bible, mission, and millennium. Perhaps the Millerites understood better than their critics, though, how much the "orthodox" had in fact realigned those sturdy stones.

NOTES

1. Biographical material on William Miller is taken from William Miller, *Apology and Defence* (Boston: J. V. Himes, 1845); Sylvester Bliss, *Memoirs of William Miller, Generally Known as a Lecturer on the Prophecies, and the Second Coming of Christ* (Boston: Joshua V. Himes, 1853), chapters 1–5; and Francis D. Nichol, *The Midnight Cry: A Defense of the Character and Conduct of William Miller and the Millerites, Who Mistakenly Believed that the Second Coming of Christ Would Take Place in the Year 1844* (Washington, D.C.: Review and Herald Publishing Association, 1944), chapters 1–4. Whitney Cross said of Millerism that its "most distinctive feature" was "its extreme closeness to orthodoxy." Cross, *The Burned-over District: The Social and Intellectual History of Enthusiastic Religion in Western New York, 1800–1850* (Ithaca, N.Y.: Cornell University Press, 1950), p. 297.

2. Miller's approach drew on the elevation of private judgment and the celebration of the "inductive method" shared by many Americans in the antebellum period. See Nathan O. Hatch, "Sola Scriptura and Novus Ordo Seclorum," in *The Bible in America: Essays in Cultural History*, eds. Hatch and Mark A. Noll (New York: Oxford University Press, 1982), pp. 59–78; George M. Marsden, "Everyone One's Own Interpreter? The Bible, Science and Authority in Mid-Nineteenth-Century America," in *The Bible in America*, eds. Hatch and Noll, pp. 79–100; Theodore Dwight Bozeman, *Protestants in an Age of Science: The Baconian Ideal and Antebellum American Religious Thought* (Chapel Hill: University of North Carolina Press, 1977).

3. This point is also made by David Leslie Rowe in "Thunder and Trumpets: The Millerite Movement and Apocalyptic Thought in Upstate New York, 1800–1845" (Ph.D. dissertation, University of Virginia, 1974), p. 36, recently published under the title

Thunder and Trumpets: Millerites and Dissenting Religion in Upstate New York, 1800–1850 (Chico, Calif.: Scholars Press, 1985). Donal Ward disagrees and argues that there were heated divisions between premillennialists and postmillennialists in Vermont in the early nineteenth century in "Religious Enthusiasm in Vermont, 1761–1847" (Ph.D. dissertation, Notre Dame, 1980), p. 30. In Cross's opinion, "the only difference between premillennialists and postmillennialists was a slight degree of literal-mindedness applied to the prophecies of the Second Coming." Cross, *Burned-over District*, p. 320.

4. Ernest R. Sandeen, "Millennialism," in *The Rise of Adventism: Religion and Society in Mid-Nineteenth-Century America*, ed. Edwin S. Gaustad (New York: Harper and Row, 1974), pp. 108–109.

5. E. B. Crandall to William Miller, November 23, 1837; Daniel Corliss, M.D., and Allen Sprague to Miller, November 25, 1839; Samuel H. Nichols to Miller, February 12, 1840 (unless otherwise specified, all letters are from the *Millerites and Early Adventists Source Collection* (Ann Arbor, Mich.: University Microfilms International, 1978), Section 5, Reels 11–12; *Signs of the Times*, April 15, 1840, pp. 13–14; June 1, 1840, p. 37; March 1, 1841, p. 180; February 15, 1842, p. 172; March 5, 1842, p. 188; June 1, 1842, p. 69; July 13, 1842, p. 114; *Advent Herald*, February 28, 1844, p. 25; *Disciple*, January 1, 1842, p. 15; Hiram Weed to George J. Kaercher, April 25, 1843, Woodruff-Kaercher Papers, Cornell University Department of Manuscripts and University Archives.

6. F. S. Parke to Miller, March 1839; *Signs of the Times*, August 10, 1842, p. 148; February 1, 1843, p. 156; June 28, 1843, p. 132; Richard Carwardine, *Transatlantic Revivalism: Popular Evangelicalism in Britain and America, 1790–1865* (Westport, Conn.: Greenwood Press, 1978), p. 52; Cross, *Burned-over District*, pp. 297–298.

7. Ronald Knox proposed "ultrasupernaturalism" as a synonym for "enthusiasm" in his famous study *Enthusiasm: A Chapter in the History of Religion with Special Reference to the XVII and XVIII Centuries* (New York: Oxford University Press, 1950), p. 2. Hans W. Frei labels one school of biblical criticism "Supernaturalism," with connotations similar to those implied here, in *The Eclipse of Biblical Narrative: A Study in Eighteenth and Nineteenth Century Hermeneutics* (New Haven: Yale University Press, 1974), pp. 86–95. The word "heresy" is used advisedly, and for three primary reasons: rhetorically, because the word emphasizes that Millerite dissent was serious and taken seriously; ironically, because evangelical fear and anger lashed out against a position that was acceptable within their culture just a few years before; and conscientiously, because the word was, in fact, bandied about a good deal by contemporaries. An example of applying the label "heresy" to Millerism can be found in First Baptist Church of Eden, New York, *Records*, March 22, 1845. Reference by a Millerite to his group being labeled "heretics" is in the *Advent Herald* April 10, 1844, p. 78.

8. *Zion's Watchman*, July 25, 1840, p. 117; David T. Arthur, "Adventism," in *Rise of Adventism*, ed. Gaustad, p. 161. See also Anthony Lane to Miller, April 4, 1838, and "Address of the Tabernacle Committee," printed in Silas Hawley, *The Second Advent Doctrine Vindicated: A Sermon Preached at the Dedication of the Tabernacle* (Boston: J. V. Himes, 1843), p. 95.

9. The line of argument chosen by Weeks and Jarvis in these examples was a dangerous one, of course. While denying Miller's conclusions, this approach implicitly favored Miller's method and assumptions. If Miller were incorrect only because he used the biblical numbers poorly, the fact remained that one could find the end through the juggling of numbers. Although Weeks and Jarvis denied this conclusion, their arguments came suspiciously close to naming alternative dates for the final days.

10. *New York Evangelist*, February 22, 1844, p. 30; *Evangelical Magazine and Gospel Advocate*, May 5, 1843, p. 144.

11. Luther Fraseur Dimmick, *The End of the World Not Yet: A Discourse Delivered in the North Church, Newburyport, on the Last Evening of the Year, 1841*, 3rd ed. (Newburyport, Mass.: C. Whipple, 1842), pp. 42–43.

12. A Listener [J. Noble] to Miller, February 26, 1840; *Signs of the Times*, June 7,

1843, p. 106; Norman Cohn included imminence as one of the five defining characteristics of the millenarian vision in *The Pursuit of the Millennium: Revolutionary Millenarians and Mystical Anarchists of the Middle Ages* (New York: Oxford University Press, 1957; rev. ed. 1970), p. 15.

13. *Signs of the Times*, May 11, 1842, p. 44, quoting from a letter to the *Journal of Commerce* on the mistakes of Millerism and the need for increased study of the Scriptures; Dimmick, *End of the World Not Yet*, pp. 13–14.

14. Miller to Truman Hendryx, March 26, 1832.

15. *Methodist Review*, July 1838, p. 342.

16. *Oberlin Evangelist*, July 7, 1841, pp. 110–111.

17. *Christian Reflector*, January 19, 1842 [p. 1]; Charles Grandison Finney, *Lectures on Revivals of Religion*, ed. William G. McLoughlin (Cambridge: Belknap Press of Harvard University Press, 1960).

18. Charles Cole to William Miller, Jr., January 25, 1838.

19. Miller to Truman Hendryx, Oct. 1, 1832; William Miller, *Evidence from Scripture and History of the Second Coming of Christ, about the Year 1843: Exhibited in a Course of Lectures* (Troy, N.Y.: Kemble and Hooper, 1836), p. 222.

20. *Christian Reflector*, November 7, 1844.

21. S. W. Lynd, *The Second Advent of Christ* (Cincinnati: J. B. Wilson, 1843), p. 32.

22. *Signs of the Times*, August 2, 1943, p. 171, quoting from the *Herald of Freedom*.

23. Miller to Truman Hendryx, March 26, 1832: ". . . you must preach *Bible* you must prove all things by *Bible* you must talk *bible*. You must exhort, *bible*, you must pray *Bible*, and Love Bible, and do all in your power to make others Love *Bible* too." Also Miller to Hendryx, October 1, 1832; Miller to J[oseph] and A[nna] Atwood, September 16, 1833; Miller, *Evidence*, p. 222.

24. Miller to Truman Hendryx, November 28, 1834.

25. *Advent Herald*, May 20, 1846, p. 117.

26. Samuel Luckey complained of "the positiveness with which the Millerites assert the coming of Christ in 1843," in *Strictures on Millerism, or the Second Advent Doctrines, as Taught by Its Advocates, and Particularly the System of Measures by which They are Disseminated* (Rochester, N.Y.: R. M. Colton, 1843), p. 18.

27. *Signs of the Times*, May 17, 1843, p. 86.

28. Bliss, *Memoirs*, p. 71.

29. *Signs of the Times*, May 17, 1843, p. 86.

30. *Advent Herald*, April 10, 1844, p. 78.

31. Luckey, *Strictures on Millerism*, pp. 20–24.

32. *Signs of the Times*, May 10, 1843. See also a reprint from *Zion's Herald* in *Signs*, May 15, 1840, and the circular letter of the Fairfield (Conn.) County Baptist Association in *Signs of the Times*, December 20, 1843, p. 149. Similar problems were raised by the "second blessing" and the experience of "perfection" among Methodists, Oberlin perfectionists, and others.

33. Alice L. Hoag, "Millerism," p. 8, in "Essays on Spiritualism and Millerism," Cornell University Department of Manuscripts and University Archives.

34. *New York Evangelist*, March 23, 1843, pp. 94–95, quoting from the *Albany Citizen*.

35. The evolution of this story is traced in Nichol, *Midnight Cry*, pp. 377–378. A reprint of the story and of a retraction from the *New York Observer* appeared in *Signs of the Times*, April 12, 1843, p. 46.

36. *Signs of the Times*, July 12, 1843, p. 150.

37. See, for example, Timothy L. Smith, *Revivalism and Social Reform in Mid-Nineteenth-Century America* (Nashville: Abingdon Press, 1957); Ernest L. Tuveson, *Millennium and Utopia: A Study in the Background of the Idea of Progress* (Berkeley: University of California Press, 1949); Tuveson, *Redeemer Nation: The Idea of America's Millennial Role* (Chicago: University of Chicago Press, 1968).

38. Hawley in *Signs of the Times*, July 12, 1843, p. 150.

39. Ibid. What follows may be taken as an elaboration of Cross's insight that "religious enthusiasm, even as it destroyed itself, built a path . . . toward more modern conceptions of liberal religion . . . ," *Burned-over District*, p. 357.

40. Dimmick, *End of the World Not Yet*, p. 10; Dowling, *Reply to Miller*, p. 35; *Christian Reflector*, April 19, 1843, p. 62; *Christian Reflector*, February 9, 1842, p. [2]; and George Peck, "National Evils and Their Remedy," in George Peck Papers, Syracuse University Archives.

41. The telling example of Henry Clarke Wright is discussed by Lewis Perry in *Childhood, Marriage and Reform: Henry Clarke Wright 1797–1870* (Chicago: University of Chicago Press, 1980), p. 137 and passim; see also the *Liberator*, February 10, 1843, p. 23.

42. Horace Bushnell, *Christian Nurture*, ed. Luther A. Weigle (New Haven, Conn.: Yale University Press, 1967; originally published, 1847), is an early classic statement of this position. See also William G. McLoughlin, "Revivalism," in *Rise of Adventism*, ed. Gaustad, p. 141.

43. Perry, *Childhood, Marriage and Reform*, p. 35.

44. Lynd, *Second Advent*, p. 22.

45. *Liberator*, October 25, 1844, p. 172.

46. *New York Evangelist*, October 16, 1841, p. 165, and June 2, 1842, p. 172.

47. Quoted in the *Advent Herald*, March 13, 1844, p. 45.

48. *Signs of the Times*, July 19, 1843, p. 156, quoting from the *Puritan; Christian Reflector*, January 18, 1844, p. 10.

49. Tuveson, *Redeemer Nation; Christian Reflector*, April 20, 1842, p. [1].

50. *Jubilee Standard*, June 12, 1845, pp. 106–107; Miller to Joseph Atwood, June 28, 1825; First Congregational Church of Rushville, New York, *Records*, and First Presbyterian Church of Palmyra, New York, *Records*, Cornell University Department of Manuscripts and University Archives; *Gospel Standard*, July 18, 1844, p. 10; *Signs of the Times*, January 1, 1845, pp. 165–166; Joshua V. Himes to Miller, January 28, 1845; *Liberator*, February 10, 1843, p. 23; and *Advent Herald*, June 3, 1846, p. 133.

51. Daniel Corliss and Allen Sprague to Miller, November 25, 1839; *Liberator*, October 27, 1843, p. 171; *Evangelical Magazine and Gospel Advocate*, March 13, 1840, p. 87; *Signs of the Times*, May 10, 1843, p. 78. Timothy Weber examines similar contradictions of the stereotype among premillennialists in the late nineteenth century in *Living in the Shadow of the Second Coming: American Premillennialism 1875–1925* (New York: Oxford University Press, 1979).

52. Daniel Dorchester, *Christianity in the United States From the First Settlement Down to the Present Time*, rev. ed. (New York: Hunt and Eaton, 1895; originally published 1887), p. 693; Cross, *Burned-over District*, pp. 355–357; Ward, "Religious Enthusiasm in Vermont," pp. 253–254.

53. Glenn C. Altschuler and Jan M. Saltzgaber, *Revivalism, Social Conscience and Community in the Burned-Over District: The Trial of Rhoda Bement* (Ithaca, N.Y.: Cornell University Press, 1983), pp. 143–169.

54. First Baptist Church of Williamson, New York, *Records*, and First Presbyterian Church of Palmyra, New York, *Records*, Study Center for Early Religious Life in Western New York microfilm collection, Cornell University Department of Manuscripts and University Archives.

55. On this transition see, for example, Ann Douglass, *The Feminization of American Culture* (New York: Avon Books, 1977), and Mary P. Ryan, *Cradle of the Middle Class: The Family in Oneida County, New York, 1790–1865* (Cambridge: Cambridge University Press, 1981).

EIGHT

The Abolitionist-Millerite Connection

RONALD D. GRAYBILL

THE FIERY ABOLITIONIST LEADER William Lloyd Garrison considered Millerites "deluded people" who were victims of an "absurd theory." Still, he had to admit that "a considerable number of worthy abolitionists" as well as "multitudes who were formerly engaged in the various moral enterprises of the age" were carried away by the Advent movement. In Garrison's view, Millerism rendered these erstwhile reformers useless to the abolitionist cause.[1]

But Garrison's attitude toward Millerites was more ambivalent than hostile. Compared with the language he reserved for his perceived enemies, Garrison's comments on the movement could almost be considered sympathetic. After all, he lauded its leaders as sincere and excoriated the hypocrisy of their clerical opponents. The Second Advent was the "keystone in the arch of Christianity," Garrison said, and rightly understood it gave the "death-blow to priestcraft, and all its train of pious impostures." These hypocrites could not abide it, he said, because it "strips them as entirely of all their claims to piety as the scathing winds of winter do the leaves of the forest." True, Garrison found Miller's view "pernicious and untenable," but he was clearly more sympathetic to Millerites than he was to their enemies.[2]

The abolitionist leader's comments on his Adventist counterparts hint at a complex relationship between abolitionists and Millerites. One might expect from a single-minded antebellum reformer such as Garrison his slight of a contemporary millenarian movement that eroded his ranks. Yet a man not known for pulling his punches expressed sympathy as well for a movement with which he took exception. The double side to Garrison's view of the Millerites poses a curious and important puzzle for historians.[3] Precisely what was the relationship between abolitionists and Millerites? Why was there enough of a crossover from the abolitionists to the Millerites to merit Garrison's attention? It is still assumed that millenarians have an antireform cast of mind, that they believe godly people must withdraw and passively await the Judgment.[4] And indeed, abolitionists appear to lose their reform zeal as they convert to Miller-ism. Yet several of the antebellum groups made energetic attempts to perfect this world, or at least their portion of it. The Shakers, the Mormons, and several post-disappointment spin-offs of the Millerites could be cited as evidence of the continuity between otherworldly ideology and this-worldly programs. In the case of the abolitionists and Millerites, a review of their strong individual and ideological ties suggests that they shared much in common.

MILLER'S ABOLITIONISM

Garrison's criticism of Millerite teachings may well have been moderated by his knowledge that so many of the movement's leaders had been active in the cause of immediate abolition and the other reforms of the day. In 1843 he recognized William Miller as one in whom "the cause of temperance, of anti-slavery, of moral reform, of non-resistance," found an "outspoken friend."[5] One example of Miller's outspokenness was his sarcastically humorous response to his friend, Truman Hendryx, when the latter criticized radical abolitionists. "Are you not glad," he asked, "that you are not obliged to love a *Negro* as yourself, in order to fulfill the laws of God?" The Constitution and Bill of Rights guaranteed liberty for white men, Miller pointed out, but was it not fortunate that "God knew what a dilemma we should be placed in, and therefore made [the slaves] black, and so we may beat them, bruise them, sell them, buy them, not teach them, not give them Bibles, not preach to them, hang them, burn them, shoot them, and cut their throats if they should try to get free?" In the same ironic vein, Miller claimed he could not say whether blacks were human; still, he did note that

> they walk on two legs, as we do, they have arms and heads, as we have, they have skulls—but dare you think they have brains my brother as we have? If I thought they had, I should be tempted almost to think they had feelings, and hearts, and souls, like us. And I should begin to think God designed we should love them as ourselves.[6]

But of course, Miller concluded tauntingly, "we must protect the great, benevolent, glorious Colonization Society," and put down the radicals before they "turn the world upside down, and we shall have to walk with our heads *topsy tervy* all the rest of our lives."

There is no record of Miller's active participation in an anti-slavery society, but he nevertheless had a reputation as a reliable and practical abolitionist. Two weeks after the Great Disappointment, a fugitive slave arrived on his doorstep bearing a letter of introduction from a certain Philander Barbour of South Granville, New York, about fifteen miles south of Miller's farm. According to Barbour, the slave's master, accompanied by United States officers, was in hot pursuit. "Not being acquainted with any one in your section that would be more ready to feed the hungry and direct a stranger fleeing to a city of refuge than yourself, I have directed him to you," Barbour said. Miller was to send the man on toward Canada. "You will probably be able to refer him to some abolitionist on his way north," Barbour wrote confidently.[7]

OTHER MILLERITE LEADERS

Joshua V. Himes, Miller's foremost associate from 1840 onward, came with even better credentials as a reformer. Garrison was "intimately acquainted" with Himes. "At a very early period," Garrison said, Himes had "avowed himself an abolitionist, and has been a faithful supporter of the anti-slavery movement."[8] Himes's sympathies were expressed as early as 1833 with a $14 contribution to the New England Anti-Slavery Society.[9]

Himes, like several other Millerites, supported the entire "sisterhood of reforms" then current in New England.[10] He aligned himself with Garrison and stuck with the fiery editor through each new dispute, adopting women's rights, nonresistance, and other of Garrison's causes. Indeed, Himes was one of the organizers of the Non-Resistant Society and served as its first director. Even after joining Miller, Himes remained active in other reform causes. He was a counsellor and contributor to the Massachusetts Anti-Slavery Society until the end of 1842. Only in 1843 did he turn his undivided attention to the Advent movement, and afterward his Chardon Street Chapel remained a popular meeting place for reformers of various stripes.[11]

After the Disappointment, Himes showed that his antislavery principles still burned bright. The famous ex-slave and abolitionist leader Frederick Douglass noted that while attending the convention of the Evangelical Alliance in London in 1846, Himes spoke vigorously in favor of a resolution to refuse to seat slaveholders. The issue was debated for two days in a large committee which included most of the 60-member American delegation. Himes was virtually alone among the Americans, most of whom opposed the antislavery position.[12]

The third most important Millerite leader, Charles Fitch, was well known in abolitionist circles for his tract, *Slaveholding Weighed in the Balance of Truth, and Its Comparative Guilt Illustrated*. In it he showed slavery to be as bad or worse than the liquor traffic, theft, robbery, murder, and treason. "Up my friends," he urged, "and do your duty, to deliver the spoils out of the hands of the oppressor, lest the fire of God's fury kindle ere long upon you."[13] Fitch is better known today as one of Garrison's opponents and as a cosigner of the "Appeal of the Clerical Abolitionists" in 1837. In that statement, he condemned Garrison for his criticisms of clergymen and the Sabbath, and for his harsh, inflammatory language. Nevertheless, Garrison recognized that Fitch too was "well known to the abolitionists of the United States."[14] Thus Garrison recognized the three top Millerite leaders as antislavery men, and noted that two of them, Himes and Miller, also supported other reform causes.

In addition to these most prominent leaders, there were many other Millerite preachers with abolitionist backgrounds. George Storrs, along with Orange

Scott and LeRoy Sunderland, led the fight to capture the Methodist Church for the antislavery cause. It was a bitter and futile struggle for the irrepressible and outspoken Storrs. Conservative bishops persuaded the 1836 General Conference Session in Cincinnati to condemn Storrs for speaking to a local Anti-Slavery Society during the Session. He eventually left the Methodist ministry and communion.[15] Storrs became a minor hero among abolitionists when he was dragged from his knees and arrested in a Northfield, New Hampshire, church as he attempted to prepare for an antislavery lecture.[16] As a Millerite evangelist after 1842, Storrs traveled some five or six thousand miles as he preached his way through Ohio and Indiana.[17] The Seventh-day Adventist descendants of Millerism identify Storrs as the source of their belief in mortalism and annihilationism.[18]

Elon Galusha, who served for many years as chairman of the New York Baptist Missionary Convention, was also a leader of Rochester abolitionists. He chaired the Monroe County Anti-Slavery Society and worked as an agent for the sale of abolitionist publications.[19] Galusha's credentials, as well as his "rich imagination, glowing enthusiasm," and "pure eloquence" lent great respectability to the Millerite movement in New York. Himes was exuberant to learn that Galusha had thrown "the whole weight of his intellect and influence with the Adventists."[20]

Luther Boutelle, one of the leading ministers of the Advent Christian Church, was earlier a cobbler in Groton, Massachusetts, where his home served as a haven for temperance and antislavery reformers. "I was a hot abolitionist and reformer," Boutelle later wrote. "My house was the home of all the stigmatized reformers and free religionists."[21] He was Garrison's host when the latter came to lecture in Groton, escorting him to and from meetings.

Joseph Bates, after a career as a sailor and sea captain, returned to his native Fairhaven, Massachusetts, converted from colonization to immediate abolitionism and helped found the Fairhaven Anti-Slavery Society. In the early 1840s he spent a small fortune preaching and publishing his views on the end of the world and ranks only slightly behind James and Ellen White as a founder of the Seventh-day Adventist Church.[22]

Josiah Litch, one of the editors of the *Signs of the Times*, also shared roots in abolitionism. Lesser-known abolitionists turned Millerites include Henry Jones, Nathaniel Southard, Lorenzo D. Fleming, Nathaniel N. Whiting, and Silas Hawley.[23]

MILLERITE FOLLOWERS

Aside from the Millerite leaders, here and there a follower of William Miller can also be associated with abolitionist sentiments. When Garrison spoke in New Ipswich, New Hampshire, in 1844, a "good Second Advent woman rose . . . saying she felt free to speak in a meeting where William Lloyd Garrison was" and endorsed "every word" he had uttered.[24] Garrison does not identify the woman, but the New Ipswich Millerites were no half-hearted believers. They refused to harvest their potatoes in 1844, confident they would not be around to need them that winter.[25] Elijah G. Greenfield, pastor of the First Baptist Church of Williamson, New York, was at the center of controversies over abolitionism and Millerism, which split his congregation. Greenfield and at least 25 other Adventists split off from the main body. When the pastor returned in 1845 for a church trial, he was criticized both for advocating Millerism and for introducing antislavery petitions during 1843 and 1844.[26] Here then, are at least two Millerites who support antislavery at the height of the Advent movement.

Ezekiel Hale, Jr., a businessman in Haverhill, Massachusetts, is another Millerite follower who also supported abolitionism. Wishing to spend a portion of his wealth in promoting the Advent cause, he parceled out the remainder to his unbelieving children. After the Disappointment, he went to court to recover his property. Testimony from his neighbors showed Hale was well known as a supporter of "ultraisms" such as temperance, antislavery, and Grahamism.[27]

But at its height, Millerism was an intense, consuming, short-lived movement, urgently focused on a single objective: preparing people for the imminent Second Advent of Christ. Naturally, at the peak of the movement, Millerite leaders had little time for other activities. The sketchy evidence available suggests that some individual Millerites continued to support both causes even in 1843 and 1844. But at the height of the movement, few Millerite leaders could be described as being abolitionists—at least not active ones. It is not that Millerites were antireform or passively withdrawn from society. Far from it—they were frenetically active. They were just distracted from social reform movements by an intense religious crusade.

Millerites maintained a bond of sympathy for abolition and other reforms. Garrison anticipated using either Faneuil Hall or the "Miller tabernacle" in Boston for the annual meeting of the American Anti-Slavery Society in 1844.[28] But Millerite papers were almost totally devoid of any articles designed to advance antislavery.

Millerism avoided the controversies over extraneous issues which so fractured abolitionism. It was clearly a one-issue campaign. The erstwhile abolitionist Joseph Bates encountered only the slightest difficulty in preaching the Advent message to both slaves and plantation owners on the Eastern Shore of Maryland in 1843. Aware of Bates's abolitionist background, one planter asked if Bates had come to get his slaves. "Yes," Bates replied with disarming humor, "I have come to get your slaves, and you too."[29] But Bates had left his abolitionist days behind. He had come to get slaves and masters ready for Christ's coming, not to change their earthly stations.

ANGELINA GRIMKÉ WELD'S MILLERISM

To modern sensibilities, abolitionism seems so much more useful, so much more tangible than Millerism. What, then, was Millerism's appeal to abolitionists and other reformers? The question can be answered, in part, by a close look at an individual abolitionist turned Millerite. Perhaps the most famous abolitionist to

SECOND ADVENT

HYMNS;

DESIGNED TO BE USED IN
PRAYER AND

CAMP-MEETINGS.

" In Eighteen Hundred Forty-Three
Will be the year of Jubilee."

BOSTON,
PUBLISHED BY J. V. HIMES.
1842.

23. This small Millerite hymnal, designed for use in camp
meetings, contained only the words of hymns. Courtesy Loma
Linda University Heritage Room.

become a follower of William Miller was Angelina Grimké Weld. Born in a
slaveholding South Carolina family, Angelina and her sister, Sarah, had migrated to Philadelphia, where they converted to Quakerism and adopted abolitionist sentiments. When they took up lecturing at antislavery meetings, their
family background gave them potent arguments against slavery. Soon curious
men began to sit in on their all-women meetings, rousing a storm of criticism
that the Grimkés would be so unladylike as to lecture to "promiscuous" audiences. The Grimkés reacted by adding women's rights to the causes they
supported.[30]

Then Angelina Grimké married Theodore Dwight Weld, a leading abolitionist lecturer, and retired to a farm in New Jersey. In 1843 she had adopted
Millerite beliefs. Gerda Lerner, one of her biographers, said Grimké's Millerism
should be regarded "not so much as an ideological aberration, but as an
emotional response to a profound crisis in Angelina's life." She was, after all,
"anxious and despondent" and thus in a mood which made her receptive to a

"religious fanaticism" from which, in a more active period, her commonsense practicality would have recoiled.[31]

Theodore Dwight Weld's biographer, Robert Abzug, believed Millerism offered Grimké an escape from her "ever more exhausting role in the household," by providing the "discovery, controversy, and intricate reasoning" her powerful intellect craved. It was also clear to Abzug that her interest in Miller's prophecies provided a clandestine weapon against Theodore, whose work in Washington provoked Angelina's jealousy.[32]

Since so many Millerites had abolitionist backgrounds, it would be fair to assume that Millerism seemed to them to be perfectly consistent with "common sense practicality." Psychological factors play a role in any conversion, but there are other explanations of Miller's appeal which lie closer to the surface.

Grimké's letters from early 1843 onward reveal a woman who had been moved by the usual means of Millerite communication. Friends dropped by on a Saturday night to spend a "pleasant" evening discussing the Second Advent and especially George Storrs's lecture which they had recently attended. Grimké had just read a "little book" which gave her "a connected view of the whole subject" and was "the clearest, simplest, and most convincing thing" she had seen.[33] Next, she read Josiah Litch's views concerning the fifth and sixth trumpets of Revelation 9, and found his predictions concerning the fall of the Ottoman Empire "the most startling and convincing evidence that the end of all things is at hand."[34]

Actually, Angelina Grimké was not confining herself to Millerite literature that winter. It was the first time in years she had been able to read much, and yes, she did believe this was helping her to overcome the "crushing sense" of her own inferiority that she had always felt since meeting Weld. He had noticed that for the first time she talked more freely when he was around.[35] He sent her one of John Wesley's tracts, she read it, then explained why she believed Wesley wrong and Finney correct on the subject of human nature.[36]

But Millerism was more than just an intellectual adventure for Angelina. Her letters reveal a woman who knew the Bible thoroughly and took it very seriously. She could discourse on the intricacies of biblical prophecy as ably as any Millerite preacher, and she did so in great detail. For her, biblical prophecy, whether interpreted literally or spiritually, was genuinely predictive. Human beings had a moral obligation to heed what these prophecies were saying: "Do you think," she asked Theodore, "supposing it to be true, that Christ will soon appear in the clouds of heaven and the world be destroyed, that it is a matter of no consequence whether we believe it or not—that altho' God has taken so much pains to point out the time of the great event, we may innocently be ignorant of it?"[37] It would appear then, that one reason why Millerism appealed to abolitionists is because Millerites shared with many abolitionists a similar interest in the Bible's predictions of the millennium.

True, abolitionism tended away from the literalism of William Miller's biblical interpretations. Biblical literalism had proven all too useful in the hands of proslavery ministers who defended slavery from the Old and New Testaments. But although Miller's hermeneutic was, on its face, very literalistic and conservative, he carried it so far as to break with conservative prophetic interpretations of his day. Thus he ended up with a psychologically daring and expansive interpretation which appealed to abolitionists like Angelina Grimké Weld, who knew her Bible well but had little respect for orthodox interpretations.

The abolitionist yearning for personal holiness, purity, and perfection provided Millerism yet another avenue of appeal. Grimké was impressed with the way her anticipation of the Advent caused "great searchings of heart," and "a more earnest desire to know what my spiritual condition really is."[38] Nearly every day an Adventist neighbor, "Dear M. A.," came to visit. Grimké was pleased with the woman's spiritual progress, noting how her study of the Second Advent had helped her come to know "the difference between repenting of sin in view of the consequences and repenting because of its exceeding sinfulness."[39]

Even if the dates were wrong, Grimké said, "the contemplation of the doctrine itself and those connected with it, must produce a good influence on the heart."[40] This, she said, was why she was so anxious Theodore should take more interest in Millerism. It was not, she said, a mere matter of "visions and dates." It was "preeminently practical." "The dates are nothing in comparison to the full realization in the soul of his second coming."[41] She pled with Weld. "Dearest," she said, "all I want you to do is to study *the Bible*" in reference to "these glorious truths." "Shall *one* be taken and the other left to be destroyed with the world of wicked?" she asked her husband. "O my Theodore, let us pray to be made pure and holy as he is."[42]

It has often been noted that abolitionists appealed for a personal conversion very similar to that sought by revivalists. Could it be that many of them were as concerned about their own righteousness as about the sinfulness of slavery and that Millerism offered a sort of ultimate personal purification which abolitionism was unable to deliver?

A striking example of this yearning for perfection is Charles Fitch, who had so antagonized Garrison with his Clerical Appeal. In 1840, Fitch apologized publicly for that episode. Fitch said he had been led to look over his past life and to ask himself what he would think of past feelings and actions "were he to behold Jesus Christ in the clouds of heaven, coming to judge the world." Fitch said he was especially ashamed of the instances where the "ruling motive" of his conduct had been "a desire to please men, for the sake of their good opinion." His "Clerical Appeal" had been thus motivated, Fitch said, and he was confessing this to Garrison because his "conscience and heart" led him to do it and because there was a "judgment seat before me, where I must stand."[43] This kind of meticulous introspective sensitivity had long been an ideal of evangelical religion. In this way, Millerism offered salvation for abolitionists, not just for slaveholders.

Millerism shared with abolitionism a growing mutual antagonism to established churches and clergymen. Garrison said that normally he would have taken the clergy's virulent opposition to Miller as the most compelling proof of the validity of Miller's views.[44] Millerites damned organized religion for its attitude toward millenarianism just as abolitionists damned it for its attitude toward slaves and slaveholders. In 1844, both movements were in a "come-outer" mood, calling for separation from established churches.[45]

The "come-outer" spirit of Millerism, together with Angelina Grimké Weld's own Quaker reliance on the "inner light," helped her reinterpret Miller's message after the Disappointment. She had been, she concluded, only an "intellectual believer" in Miller's prophecies, never able to achieve the "heart faith" she craved. True, it had seemed to her that all the great prophetic periods would expire in 1843 and 1844, but she was not satisfied.[46] As early as March 15, 1843, she had confessed herself "utterly at a loss whether to understand the prophecies literally or spiritually," but she was inclined to the latter. The destruction of the material world was something she did not "realize at all." However, she had felt for some years that a "great and mighty revolution" was at hand and that church organizations were about to be superseded by "the power of religion and the simplicity of the teaching of Jesus and his apostles."[47]

After the Disappointment, this spiritual interpretation clarified. No longer did she expect to see Jesus "in the body with which he ascended." Now she believed his Second Coming was to be "in the hearts of the people." This spiritual advent was to be preceded by a judgment. The "sitting of the Ancient of Days" symbolized the "sitting in judgment of Truth—Eternal Truth, over all human organizations and opinions. Is not that the present state of the world? Who cannot see and feel that we have entered upon a new era. . . . Truth like 'a fiery stream has come forth' and is finding its way into the most sacred recesses of Church and State and is most surely working the overthrow of both."[48]

There never was a time, Angelina believed, when so many were testifying against the "corruptions" of the church and at the same time refusing to form another sect. The era had arrived when "Truth must sit in judgment upon all human organizations—Political, Ecclesiastical, and Social before she can triumph over all error." This, she said, was why judgment is antecedent to the coming of the Son of Man. The sanctuary to be cleansed in the last days was not, as Miller believed, the physical earth, but the hearts of God's people. Therefore, the same work that was going on in the outward world was going on in human hearts. "Yes," she said,

> I fully believe in the downfall of every Earthly throne and the overthrow of every political government—the annihilation of every Ecclesiastical Establishment and the dissolution of every sect and party under the sun . . . but I am calm, hopeful, happy, for I see arising out of their ruins the Everlasting kingdom of God.[49]

So, like the sabbatarian Adventists, Angelina concluded that the present era was an "epoch of judgment" the length of which could not be anticipated. Unlike them, she expected "no sudden revolution" but a "gradual undermining of all things that can be shaken."[50]

THE
ADVENT MESSAGE
TO THE
DAUGHTERS OF ZION.

VOL. I.   BOSTON, MAY, 1844.   NO. I.

AN APPEAL TO THE WOMEN OF OUR BELOVED COUNTRY.

WE have a message of unutterable importance to communicate, and as you value eternal life, we intreat your candid and patient attention. Eighteen hundred years ago our blessed Savior promised his weeping disciples that he would come again; and the angel also told them, at his ascension, that he would in like manner come again, as they had seen him ascend into heaven. He also advised them of different events that should meanwhile transpire, and of certain definite signs, which should immediately precede his return. He assured them, that he would certainly come quickly, and bade them watch continually, and be as servants who wait for their Lord. He also left a command, that when these things should begin to come to pass, his followers should lift up their heads and rejoice, and KNOW that he was near, even at the doors. From diligent and prayerful examination of the prophetic scriptures, and from the confirming signs in our natural, moral, and political heavens, we are solemnly convinced, that the glorious hour of his second Advent is just at hand. We feel that the fearful moment hastens greatly, and that the shadow of his coming glory already enshrouds the dim pageantry of earth. Having this confidence, we intreat you not to turn lightly away from this warning, for our case is urgent, and our errand important. We appeal to the Scriptures alone as authority, and on their naked, simple teachings we rely in perfect confidence. We believe that they are a revelation, and a manifestation of the will of God to man, and we dare not adopt the interpretations of any, however learned or plausible they may be, unless they perfectly harmonize with this revealed will. This word assures us that God will do nothing, but he reveals his secrets unto his servants, the prophets, and that the secret of the Lord is with those who fear him. That we have a sure word of prophecy, unto which we do well to take heed, as unto a light that shineth in a dark place. Also, that he shall send Jesus Christ which before was preached unto you, whom the heavens must receive, until the TIMES of restitution of all things, which God has spoken by the mouths of all his holy prophets, since the world began. Thus we perceive that all the prophets have spoken of the times of restitution, (of Paradise) when Christ is to be revealed. Our Savior directs us to search the Scriptures, and speaking of the state of the world previous to his coming,

VOL. I.   1

24. The first issue of *The Advent Message to the Daughters of Zion*, edited by Clorinda S. Minor and Emily C. Clemons, appeared shortly after the Millerite Disappointment in the spring of 1844. Courtesy Aurora University Library.

Angelina Grimké Weld's Christian anarchy was shared by other Adventists. George Storrs taught that a church was merely a people's coming together "with one accord in one place." Love was its only bond. Any church formed by "man's invention" became "Babylon" the moment it was organized.[51] Views like these were so strong that it was nearly twenty years before the sabbatarian remnant of Millerism would organize into the Seventh-day Adventist Church, and almost that long before the Advent Christian Church was formed.[52] The organizational views of many abolitionists were either transported into Millerism or fully shared by Adventists.

Finally, abolitionists swelled the ranks of Millerites simply because of timing. With the addition of Himes to Miller's camp in 1840, the Advent movement began a period of rapid growth and expansion just as the abolitionist movement was splitting into factions. Miller, like many other committed antislavery men, was disgusted and saddened by the factional squabbles among abolitionists. "They are in trouble, divided, split in two, scattered, and weakened by their uneasy designing and master spirits," he said after attending an antislavery society meeting in New York City in 1840. "The poor slave, has but little chance to be liberated by these two parties. . . . The slaveholder may call in his piquets, he may need no additional guards, his citadel is safe. While the pretended friends of the slave, are expending all their ammunition on each other, the release of the captive will be little thought of." Miller, of course, saw hope only in the coming of Christ. "God can and will release the captive. And to him alone we must look for redress."[53]

Miller was not the only enemy of slavery to conclude that Blacks could look for little help from some of their would-be benefactors in abolitionist organizations. To reformers, sickened and disappointed by factionalism among abolitionists, the Advent movement offered a thriving, growing, unified alternative. Far from seeming impractical, to many of them it seemed to offer a very tangible and dramatic definition for the word "immediate" in "immediate abolition."

Although many Millerites were drawn from reform ranks, and these seem to have maintained their sympathy for abolitionism and other reforms, Millerism as a movement did little to advance the cause of reform. Indeed, the movement distracted many from active labor in reform movements. It is possible, though not yet demonstrable, that many of the thousands of followers of Miller who left the movement after the Disappointment may have resumed reform activities. What we do know is that those leaders who stayed on with their Millerite friends to help found religious denominations were so preoccupied with the mere survival of their movements that they had little time for anything else. Only in the 1860s, after Seventh-day Adventists were formally organized and settled in Michigan did they get back close enough to their reform roots to install health reform as an integral part of the church's mission. Joseph Bates had been a health reformer even before he became an abolitionist, but he failed to push his dietary practices even among his fellow sabbatarian Adventists until the new church was securely established.[54]

Moreover, during the immediate pre-Civil War and War years Adventists couched their apocalypticism in Radical Republican rhetoric and looked upon slavery as the cancer that soon would destroy the American Republic, ushering in the world's end. Their "Radical Republican" eschatology, however, did not prompt political action on the part of Adventists, as the republic seemed doomed and politics futile.[55]

We conclude then, that while Millerism was not hostile to social reform, it was too single-minded to give any great support to abolitionism and other reforms. The appeal of Millerism to antebellum reformers was sufficiently great and sufficiently widespread that Adventist conversions from reform ranks need not be attributed to the individual idiosyncracies. Arriving at the right moment with his biblical millenarianism and moral perfectionism, Miller appealed to values that many reformers held dear. As groups increasingly alienated from established organizations, Millerites and reformers felt a sympathy for each other that also facilitated Adventist conversions.

NOTES

1. William Lloyd Garrison to Elizabeth Pease, April 4, 1843, in Walter M. Merrill, ed., *The Letters of William Lloyd Garrison*, 5 vols. (Cambridge, Mass.: Belknap Press of Harvard University, 1973), *3*: 248; William Lloyd Garrison, "The Second Advent. No. I," *The Liberator*, February 10, 1843, *13*: 23; William Lloyd Garrison to Henry C. Wright, March 1, 1843, in Walter M. Merrill, ed., *The Letters of William Lloyd Garrison*, *3*: 133.

2. Garrison, "The Second Advent. No. I," p. 23.

3. For a review of this problem, see R. Laurence Moore, *Religious Outsiders and the Making of Americans* (New York: Oxford University Press, 1986).

4. Ronald G. Walters, *American Reformers, 1815–1860* (New York: Hill and Wang, 1978), p. 25.

5. Ibid.

6. William Miller to Truman Hendryx, February 25, 1834, quoted in David Rowe, "Thunder and Trumpets: The Millerite Movement and Apocalyptic Thought in Upstate New York, 1800–1845" (Ph.D. dissertation, University of Virginia, 1974), pp. 48–49. As Rowe points out, F. D. Nichol misread this letter in *The Midnight Cry* (Washington, D.C.: Review and Herald Publishing Association, 1944), p. 54.

7. Philander Barbour to William Miller, November 8, 1844, in Vern Carner, ed., *Millerites and Early Adventists*, Microfilm Collection (Ann Arbor, Mich.: University Microfilms, 1977), Sect. 5, Reel 12.

8. Garrison, "The Second Advent. No. I," p. 23.

9. David T. Arthur, "Joshua V. Himes and the Cause of Adventism, 1839–1845" (M. A. thesis, University of Chicago, 1961), p. 10, in Vern Carner, ed., *Millerites and Early Adventists*, Microfilm Collection, Sec. 1, Reel 1.

10. Ronald G. Walters, *American Reformers, 1815–1860*, p. ix.

11. David T. Arthur, "Joshua V. Himes," pp. 11, 15, 17, 36, 39, 41.

12. John W. Blassingame, ed., *The Frederick Douglass Papers*, Series 1: *Speeches, Debates, and Interviews*, 2 vols. (New Haven, Conn.: Yale University Press, 1979), *1*: 421–422.

13. LeRoy Edwin Froom, *The Prophetic Faith of Our Fathers*, 4 vols. (Washington, D.C.: Review and Herald Publishing Association, 1946–1954), 4: 533–534.

14. Charles Fitch and Joseph H. Towne, "Appeal of Clerical Abolitionists, on Anti-Slavery Measures," *Liberator* (August 11, 1837), 7: 130; Fitch and Towne, "Protest of Clerical Abolitionists, No. 2," *The Liberator*, September 8, 1837, 7: 145; Garrison, "The Second Advent. No. I," p. 23.

15. Donald G. Matthews, *Slavery and Methodism: A Chapter in American Morality, 1780–1845* (Princeton, N. J.: Princeton University Press, 1965), pp. 120–121, 127, 133, 138, 141–142, 154, 230.

16. [George Storrs], *Mob, Under Pretense of Law, or, The Arrest and Trial of Rev. George Storrs, at Northfield, N. H.* (Concord, N.H.: Eldridge G. Chase, 1835).

17. Nichol, *The Midnight Cry*, pp. 135, 204–205, 268, 286, 348.

18. Ibid., pp. 205, 300.

19. David Rowe, "Thunder and Trumpets," pp. 115.

20. Ibid.

21. Luther Boutelle, *Sketch of the Life and Religious Experience of Eld. Luther Boutelle* (Boston: Advent Christian Publishing Society, 1891), pp. 21, 24, 25, 33, 36.

22. Joseph Bates, *The Autobiography of Joseph Bates* (Battle Creek, Mich.: Steam Press, 1868), in Carner, ed., *Millerites and Early Adventists*, Sect. 1, Reel 1; Don Neufeld, ed., *The Seventh-day Adventist Encyclopedia* (Washington, D.C.: Review and Herald Publishing Association, 1976), s.v. "Bates, Joseph."

23. Nichol, *The Midnight Cry*, pp. 190–192; LeRoy Edwin Froom, *The Prophetic Faith of Our Fathers*, 4: 529, 632, 633, 639, 671.

24. William Lloyd Garrison to Helen E. Garrison, January 2, 1844, in *The Letters of William Lloyd Garrison*, 3: 248.

25. J .N. Loughborough, *The Rise and Progress of the Seventh-day Adventists* (Battle Creek, Mich.: Review and Herald Publishing Association, 1892), p. 85; Arthur Whitefield Spalding, *Footprints of the Pioneers* (Washington, D.C.: Review and Herald Publishing Association, 1947), pp. 70–72.

26. Records of the First Baptist Church of Williamson, New York, Cornell University, Department of Manuscripts and University Archives.

27. Nichol, *The Midnight Cry*, pp. 213–215.

28. William Lloyd Garrison to George W. Benson, January 15, 1844, in *The Letters of William Lloyd Garrison*, 3: 254.

29. Bates, *Autobiography*, pp. 262, 268–269, 277, 281.

30. Katharine Du Pre Lumpkin, *The Emancipation of Angelina Grimké* (Chapel Hill, N.C.: University of North Carolina Press, 1974), pp. 105–107, 120, 121–122.

31. Gerda Lerner, *The Grimké Sisters from South Carolina: Pioneers for Women's Rights and Abolition* (New York: Schocken Books, 1967), p. 306. I refer to Grimké by her maiden name to avoid confusion with her husband.

32. Robert H. Abzug, *Passionate Liberator: Theodore Dwight Weld and the Dilemma of Reform* (New York: Oxford University Press, 1980), p. 229.

33. Angelina Grimké Weld to Theodore Dwight Weld, Jan. 30, 1843. All of the Angelina Grimké letters cited here are housed at the William L. Clements Library, University of Michigan, Ann Arbor, except that of January 1845, which is in the Library of Congress, Washington, D.C.

34. Angelina Grimké Weld to Theodore Dwight Weld, February 2, 1843.

35. Angelina Grimké Weld to Theodore Dwight Weld, January 30, 1843.

36. Angelina Grimké Weld to Theodore Dwight Weld, March 15, 1843.

37. Angelina Grimké Weld to Theodore Dwight Weld, January 30, 1843.

38. Angelina Grimké Weld to Theodore Dwight Weld, February 2, 1843.

39. Ibid.

40. Angelina Grimké Weld to Theodore Dwight Weld, Monday afternoon, n.d. [1843].

41. Ibid.

42. Ibid.

43. "Letter from Rev. Charles Fitch," *The Liberator*, January 24, 1840, *10*: 35.

44. Garrison, "The Second Advent. No. I," p. 23.

45. Nichol, *The Midnight Cry*, pp. 224–225; Lewis Perry, *Radical Abolitionism: Anarchy and the Government of God in Anti-Slavery Thought* (Ithaca, N.Y.: Cornell University Press, 1973), pp. 92–128.

46. Angelina Grimké Weld to Sarah Grimké, January 1845.

47. Angelina Grimké Weld to Theodore Dwight Weld, March 15 [1843].

48. Angelina Grimké Weld to Sarah Grimké, January 1845.

49. Ibid.

50. Ibid.

51. George Storrs, "Come Out of Her My People," *The Midnight Cry*, February 15, 1844, p. 6.

52. Neufeld, ed., *Seventh-day Adventist Encyclopedia,* s.v. "Organization"; David T. Arthur, "'Come Out of Babylon': A Study of Millerite Separatism and Denominationalism, 1840–1865" (Ph.D. dissertation, University of Rochester, 1970), p. 332.

53. Quoted in David Rowe, "Thunder and Trumpets," p. 185.

54. Ronald L. Numbers, *Prophetess of Health: A Study of Ellen G. White* (New York: Harper & Row, 1976), pp. 79, 81.

55. See Jonathan M. Butler, "Adventism and the American Experience," in Edwin S. Gaustad, ed., *The Rise of Adventism* (New York: Harper & Row, 1974), pp. 173–206.

NINE

"The Wind Sweeping Over the Country"

John Humphrey Noyes and the Rise of Millerism

MICHAEL BARKUN

"THE WIND THAT IS now sweeping over the country is Millerism," John Humphrey Noyes wrote in 1842.[1] Noyes devoted extraordinary attention to Second Adventism, and at the movement's height a polemical flood came from his prolific pen. Noyes viewed the religious claims of others from the audacious perspective of "Perfectionism," a theological position which in his hands entailed the belief that human beings could live a completely sinless life on earth. He insisted that he himself was already perfect, that he could not sin, and that others could attain a similarly advanced spiritual condition. Although his views set him at odds with virtually every religious group in America, the intensity of his concern about Millerism suggests that it touched some deep level of his complex mental life.

Between 1840 and 1845, eighteen articles on Millerism appeared in Noyes's publications *The Witness* and *The Perfectionist*. The centerpiece was a five-part series, "The Second Coming of Christ," in 1842 and 1843 numbers of *The Witness*.[2] Less given than others to ridicule, Noyes nonetheless could scarcely contain his contempt. Millerism was a "popular mania," "delusion," "fanaticism" symptomatic of "a deep craving among the mass of simple minded people." Scarcely less dangerous than Millerism itself was the risk that other misguided or unscrupulous purveyors of error would follow: "Whoever like Miller has impudence enough to seize the helm, can steer the ship into any port he pleases."[3]

At other times, Noyes professed to see a silver lining: "[W]e have reason to rejoice that this delusion makes occasion for many to examine honestly the subject of the Second Coming."[4] In any case, ridicule could not change minds;

only reasoned argument could do that. Miller "must be routed . . . by demonstrating that his calculations about the time [of the Second Coming] are false."[5] To that end, Noyes mobilized all his formidable rhetorical talents. Already active as an anti-Millerite writer, he planned a preaching campaign in New York City for the spring of 1843, but the mysterious throat ailment that began in 1842 forced him to cease all public speaking by the beginning of the following year.[6] Noyes did, however, maintain a stream of anti-Millerite articles and essays, relaxing only in late 1844 when he observed that "the 22nd of October has now passed quietly away; no fiery conflagration has depopulated the earth."[7]

Millerism had eagerly joined itself to a long tradition of millenarian speculation, and Second Adventists approvingly cited and often reprinted the chiliastic tracts of the seventeenth and eighteenth centuries. Like their precursors, they viewed the physical world as a book in which God's message was written. Physical events had only to be "read" in the light of the correct interpretive apparatus. Like popular religion two centuries earlier in England, Millerism "sprang from a coherent view of the world as a moral order reflecting God's purposes."[8]

Noyes too assumed moral coherence, but he was far less prone to place emphasis on portents in the material world. Reading his attacks against Millerism, one is struck less by his disagreement over the dating of the Second Coming than by his distaste for Miller's naïve empiricism, with its political and natural portents and its promised manifestation of Christ on earth. Noyes sought a supramundane reality filled with mysterious energies more powerful than anything in the realm of the senses. Electricity, mesmerism, and later spiritualism provided a knowledge deeper than the old "signs of the times." What was "religious insanity," after all, but a voyage into this realm that had gone off course? The genuinely potent forces might leave physical *traces*—the hypnotic subject's trance behavior, for example—but they themselves were not visible, certainly not in the sense that Miller's descending Christ was visible.

Noyes's penchant for postulating invisible forces was not merely a personal quirk. It was of a piece with attempts through much of the nineteenth century to explain otherwise incomprehensible features of social life by recourse to an unseen reality. These included the fascination with electricity, mesmerism, and spiritualism; conspiracy theories of politics that attributed the world's evil to impenetrable cabals; economic theories and nostrums that purported to tame and explain the invisible forces of the market; and early theories of collective behavior built on concepts of a "crowd mind." Some were more popular in Europe than in America (crowd theories, for example); some preceded others or enjoyed only regional currency. But whatever the pattern of variation, large numbers of individuals found it attractive and reassuring to believe that the prime movers in human affairs could neither be seen nor touched. The very mastery over nature had created a society so complex as to appear uncontrollable by conventional means. Mastery had given way to incomprehension, and incomprehension to anxiety. Miller, by contrast, spoke out of a more confident, perhaps more naïve, past, in which knowledge was still possible through time-tested means. One had only to look carefully at events, Bible in hand, to know the direction in which the world was tending. For others, Noyes among them, the world was no longer so simple; and if appearances deceived, that must be because a more fundamental level of reality underlay them.

However, while many shared this bias for the invisible, there was no consensus on the proper means to discover it. Voyagers in this nineteenth-century "inner space" could not draw on a tradition as venerable as Miller's. Consequently, they were sometimes hailed as pioneers and sometimes stigmatized as profoundly disordered.[9] Thus, although Noyes epitomized the search for a new kind of truth, his was still a risky undertaking, in the absence of clear criteria to separate the innovator from the madman.

What were the origins of Noyes's profound antipathy to Millerism? On the one hand, there seem ample practical and intellectual reasons. Miller was, after all, a competitor, snatching souls from Perfectionism as he had from abolitionism, at a time when Noyes could not afford the losses. Beyond that, Miller attacked a central element in Noyes's theology, the dating of the Second Coming. On the other hand, Miller was far from being the only competitor, and Noyes remained vigilant against Fourierism, Shakerism, and other fashions of

A MILLERITE PREPARING FOR THE 23ᴿᴰ OF APRIL.
"Now let it come! I'm ready!"

25. An anti-Millerite engraving. By permission of the Houghton Library, Harvard University.

the day. The Second Adventists might proselytize with a peculiar vigor but the socioreligious marketplace of the 1840s was a wide-open affair. As far as theology was concerned, Miller was no more at variance with Noyes on the Second Coming than were the conventional Christian churches, a point Noyes implicitly conceded in his numerous attacks on traditional interpretations of Scripture.

This suggests that neither fear of competition nor quarrels over doctrine may be sufficient to explain Noyes's anti-Millerite preoccupation. The source, I shall suggest, lay deeper than either organizational defensiveness or exegetical argument could penetrate, and instead resulted from the striking and ambivalent character of Noyes's psychological experiences long before he had ever heard of Miller. But before developing that claim further, it is imperative that we thoroughly examine the more obvious and accessible explanations.

NOYES AND THE SECOND COMING

While it is not clear precisely how many adherents Noyes lost to Millerism, it is clear that he lost some and that he could ill afford to lose any. Noyes's fragile community, then situated at Putney, Vermont, included less than fifty people. During the climactic years of Millerism (1843–1844), nine adults and five children—more than a third of his followers—withdrew. Some surely went the way of Millerism, for as early as 1842, Noyes observed that "it has found some weathercocks among our nominal brethren."[10] There is no evidence that defections to Millerism were significantly more numerous than those to, say, Fourierism, but although Noyes addressed the Fourierist community-building enterprise, his comments were relatively few and relatively kind.[11] The same may be said of Shakerism, in which he also saw dark theological errors. Why Millerite proselytizing should have been peculiarly vexing is not at all clear. Noyes had plenty of rivals without the Second Adventists. Revenge must have been all the sweeter when, following the Great Disappointment, disillusioned Millerites began appearing on the rolls of the Oneida Community.[12]

Doctrinal disagreement is much less easily disposed of, since it centered on Noyes's idiosyncratic theory of the Second Coming. In the summer of 1833, he came to believe that Christ had appeared to the apostles in A.D. 70, at the time of the Roman destruction of the Jerusalem Temple.[13] He held to this view with extraordinary tenacity: "[If] an angel from heaven, bearing the seal of ten thousand miracles, should establish a religion, which should fail to recognize the truth which blazes on the whole front of the New Testament, viz., that *Jesus Christ came the second time at the destruction of Jerusalem*, I would call him an impostor."[14]

However committed Noyes was to the idea, he recognized that it was neither simple nor problem-free. He first had to deal with the nature of the appearance, insisting that it was an invisible, nonphysical event that might be apprehended by the believers' eyes of faith but by no one else. The visible signs of the times were the events connected with the failure of the Jewish revolt against the Romans, in which, Noyes smugly observed, "millions of the rejecters of Christ and his gospel were slain."[15] Thus he found it essential to distinguish between premonitory signs, which were physical, such as war and "distress of nations," and the Second Advent itself, which was spiritual.

Even after he had made these allowances, Noyes's thesis still produced difficulties. In the first place, he had to account for the sadly flawed character of Christian society after A.D. 70 "[S]omething obviously had gone awry. If a perfection once existed, then why did there follow evil men and corrupt institutions? Noyes answered by saying that when the apostolic church ascended to its spiritual home, it broke its ties with the temporal church which then began its decline."[16] A related and more theologically consequential problem concerned the millennium itself and the fulfillment of biblical prophecies associated with it. Had the millennium already happened? Was it even now in progress? And what of the more dramatic signs of the "last days" which had not occurred in A.D. 70? Clearly, Noyes's reading of the Bible led him to conclusions that seemed at variance with the sadly unredeemed state of the world. He clung to his thesis of an early Second Coming but had difficulty relating it to a consistent theory of the millennium. The result was a troubling doubt about what the millennium meant, and when and how it might happen, and this doubt in turn made him ambivalent and defensive about other, more decisive millennialist views. In particular, he sometimes found it difficult to reject premillennialism with the vigor he wished. It was, as we shall see, tempting to believe that a cosmic day of transformation still lay ahead, if only because of the capacity of such a promise to reconcile one with the imperfections of the present.

Robert Thomas suggests that Noyes *was* a premillennialist, at least in part, for, lacking confidence in human ability to decisively affect history, he placed the Second Coming in the past, thereby relieving himself and his contemporaries of any obligation to bring the millennium about. To the extent that premillennialists linked the beginning of the millennium to Christ's second appearance, Noyes appears to have placed at least one foot in the premillennialist camp. The difficulty, as he himself recognized, was that the events of A.D. 70 had apparently not brought about the desired result.

The millennium was too cherished an idea to give up. As a young man of 20, he later recalled, "My heart was fixed on the Millennium, and I resolved to live or die for it."[17] This commitment, which appears not to have waned appreciably over the next decade and a half (the period that encompassed the rise of Millerism), still had to be reconciled with the argument for a Second Coming already passed. Noyes conceded that "[One] great event is wanting to close the fearful concern, and that is THE DESTRUCTION OF SPIRITUAL JERUSALEM." Lest his view be misunderstood, he hastened to point out that "The Devil . . . still reigns. . . . That great day of the Lord Almighty is yet future." But as he saw it in 1835, its futurity was imminent. Humanity was hurtling toward the destruction of "SPIRITUAL JERUSALEM" with "a rapidity and certainty which no mortal energy can lesson [sic] or foresight can avoid." With all the deterministic passion of a true premillennialist, he concluded: "When that day will fully come, knoweth no man, save the Father only—but looking at prophecy and the movements of his providential hand in waking up the world, we cannot but regard it as near."[18]

This line of argument led Noyes to concede that perhaps the Second Coming of A.D. 70 would be superseded in the future: "We would say once for all, we fully believe a *third* appearance of Christ is approaching, in which the predictions . . . especially of the Old Testament, will be fulfilled."[19] For obvious reasons, when he came several years later to rebut Miller, he chose not to emphasize this point, lest he and Miller appear to be arguing simply about *which* appearance it was going to be. This proved to be a matter of more than numbering systems, since Noyes remained convinced that Christ's return, however counted, was nonphysical and invisible, without Millerism's panoply of theatrical effects.

Noyes's perplexities did not lessen with the passage of time, and he shied away from discussions linking the Second Coming, about which he was certain, with the millennium, about which doubts persisted. Thus in 1840 he wrote to one correspondent:

> I am not fully prepared at this time to enter upon a full discussion of the subject of the millennium *in the Witness*—That subject involves many others of a magnitude that will require very deliberate discussion—In fact—I cannot touch it with any satisfaction—until I am prepared to present and defend a complete view of the whole book of Revelations.[20]

This is a particularly telling admission, since it comes only a few months after Noyes's first published reference to Miller.[21]

Perhaps to rebut Second Adventism more effectively, Noyes found it occasionally useful to assert during the Millerite high tide that not only the Second Coming but the millennium too was past. In this view, the events to come concerned the "release of Satan at expiration of Millennium," for which the signs included the decay of Islam (presumably, the Ottoman Empire's numerous political difficulties); the rise of "pagan" Russia; the "paganization" of Europe as a result of improved communications with Asia; and the corrupting influence of classical antiquity on Western culture. This position, inconsistent though it was with much of the early Noyes, had the advantage of permitting Noyes too to search for "signs of the times" in contemporary culture and politics. In fact, he let the opportunity pass without any extended commentary on portents in the modern world, no doubt because to have done so would have risked opening the logical fissures that have already been pointed out.

Noyes claimed to have gotten the idea of a millennium already past from the writings of George Bush, a biblical scholar at the University of the City of New York, whose work he had read in 1831.[22] That was, one recalls, the year in which he believed the millennium was imminent. Both statements were recorded after the fact and may represent distortions of memory. Alternatively, he may have read Bush in 1831 but only become convinced of the truth of Bush's views later on. But on the face of it, the Noyes of 1831 could not have simultaneously hung on to an imminent millennium while believing it was over.

Noyes may also have chosen not to pursue the matter because in fact Bush's concept of the millennium was as idiosyncratic as Noyes's idea of the Second Coming. For Bush's millennium was only that historic period of the "suppression of paganism within the boundaries of the Roman Empire." There will still be a "latter day of glory," said Bush, but it ought not to be called the "millennium." Bush, like Noyes, took the Second Coming to be an invisible event, and Millerism, consequently, was for him "one of the most baseless of all the extravaganzas of prophetic hallucination."[23] Indeed, Bush admonished Miller in 1844 that "Men of sober and reflecting temperament are revolted by the tone of *absolute assurance* in which yourself and your associates are in the habit of speaking. . . ."[24] Bush and Noyes seem not to have known one another at this time, although by the following year—1845—when Bush had become a major figure in American Swedenborgianism, he and Noyes struck up a correspondence.[25]

Where the Second Coming was concerned, therefore, Noyes possessed a view of rock-hard certainty. But when the Second Coming and the millennium were joined together, as they inevitably had to be, his position became confused. On the one hand, he desired a millenarian theology that would support and be supported by his concept of the Second Coming. On the other hand, he also desperately wished the door of history to remain open to cosmic change. The millennium drew him on with its promise of regeneration, but even as it did so, he drew back in fear that his hard-won conception of the Second Coming would be compromised. Thus he flirted with premillennialism but could never give himself over to it. Miller's plodding and internally consistent logic was therefore an affront both to Noyes's own reconstruction of the history of the early church and to his unfulfilled goal of reconciling this reconstruction with a comprehensive millennial theology.

We might leave matters here, content that the vehemence of Noyes's anti-Millerism had been traced to anxieties about the structure and integrity of his own beliefs. These theological anxieties, it seems to me, still leave the picture incomplete, suggesting as they do that Noyes's detestation of Millerism lay on a wholly intellectual plane. To do so is to avoid a more fundamental arena of conflict, Noyes's own psychic life. For in fact Noyes's uncertainties about the millennium and his anti-Millerite preoccupation may be directly traced to the complexities of a mind periodically at the end of its tether.

THE INNER LIFE OF JOHN HUMPHREY NOYES

At critical points in his life, John Humphrey Noyes feared for his own sanity and was regarded as either insane or nearly so by those closest to him. He explicitly linked these experiences with premillennialism in general and Millerism in particular, a perception made all the more disturbing by the links between Millerism and insanity alleged by both psychiatrists and popular writers. Noyes

wrote eloquently about his troubled mental state, and during and after Millerism sought to explain more generally the relationship between insanity and
religion. His family's anguished watch over his psychological condition is
detailed in the correspondence that passed between them and John and among
themselves.

Any attempt to understand Noyes's psychological crises must begin with
the so-called "New York Experience," a breakdown which occurred during the
spring of 1834.[26] Troubled by Perfectionism's reputation for sexual license,
rebuffed by the New York religious leaders whom he sought to persuade of
Perfectionism's sanctity, Noyes drifted into a dissociative state. Indifferent to
eating or physical comfort, he roamed Manhattan on distracted nocturnal
meanderings:

> Oftentimes, after a day of wearisome labor of mind, and perhaps of body, I would
> retire to my room, hoping for this once to enjoy a night of repose, if not of sleep. But
> suddenly a horror of sleep would come upon me, and a spiritual impulse would
> summon me with an importunity not to be denied, to a night journey in the city.
> When weariness overcame me in these excursions, so that sleep became inevitable, I
> would lie down on a door-stone, or on the steps of the City Hall, or on the benches of
> the battery, and forget myself for a few minutes. In this way most of my sleep for
> three weeks was taken.[27]

Prolonged sleep deprivation can produce dramatic perceptual distortions,
including hallucinations.[28] Unable to sleep, very likely inadequately nourished,
exhausted by his lengthy walks, Noyes in fact had a visionary experience, yet
scarcely the one he expected or desired. Indeed, it was precisely the experience he
had wished to shut out in his theological writings. Described in the *Confessions*
he set down in 1849, it is worth quoting at length:

> I received a baptism of that spirit which has since manifested itself extensively in
> the form of Millerism. My *doctrinal* views had no affinity with Miller's theory of the
> Second Advent. I knew that the first judgment took place immediately after the
> destruction of Jerusalem, and that it was a transaction in the spiritual world. Yet I
> expected a second judgment at the end of the times of the Gentiles, or rather a
> second manifestation of the first judgment, i.e. an extension of it to the visible world.
> The spirit which now came upon me produced an irresistible impression that this
> manifestation was about to take place immediately. It was a terrible moment.
> . . . After several similar crises, the impression left me, and I received in its stead a
> persuasion that the judgment of the world will be a gradual spiritual operation,
> effected by truth and invisible power, without any of the physical machinery which
> alarms the imaginations of most expectants of the great day.[29]

Making due allowance for the fifteen years that elapsed between the event and
its recording, it is evident the experience made a profound impression upon
Noyes, terrified by this sudden cataclysmic vision and neither physically nor
mentally capable of throwing it off. Despite the fact that his account did not

appear until five years after the Millerite "Great Disappointment," the central feature in his perception of the episode was its similarity to Millerism.

Barely able to take care of his daily needs and not always capable of accounting for his activities, Noyes was a source of growing apprehension to his mother and siblings in Putney. His brother Horatio was sent to investigate, John by now having made it back to his previous place of residency, New Haven. Horatio's June 17, 1834, report tried to counteract the lurid rumors that had filtered up to Putney:

> You may be sure that he has been in the Lord's hands, and that he has not been suffered to do anything which shall bring reproach upon the cause of Christ. . . . Had I trusted to stories [I] should have believed him a downright madman. . . . I hope hereafter, you will lay aside all your prejudices and fears about John, and believe him still to possess his right mind.[30]

Horatio's letter did not have its intended calming effect, for the family evidently had independent sources of information, including a no longer extant letter from John. These conflicting reports led Joanna Noyes to observe that "We have reason to suppose . . . that he has been deranged. Judge White has just returned from New York and was told there by S. Houghton and Brooks that John was crazy while there."[31] Elizabeth Noyes added in the same letter: "We hardly know what to think, as you [Horatio] seem to be so confident that all is right with him, while we hear from other quarters that he is deranged and his conduct very strange." Noyes's alternating periods of depression and ecstasy manifested themselves in curious ways. Theodore Weld reported that Noyes insisted that his spirituality made him immune from the effects of alcohol, and by way of demonstration downed rum and raw whiskey together with cayenne pepper. During the same incident, he also ate large quantities of tobacco, and seems not to have been the worse for it. "He afterwards described his exercise as having been most heavenly and extatic [sic]."[32]

The family's apprehensions were certainly not eased by an extraordinary letter John had written to his mother from New York in May. Its imagery suggests saturation in the world of premillennial and adventist symbols. Its breathless syntax bespeaks an agitated state of mind. "We have come," he wrote, "to an interesting crisis," but not of his own psyche so much as of the world teetering on the cataclysmic brink:

> It is like the time when Jerusalem was approaching its predicted destruction. Wars and rumors of wars, famines, pestilences, earthquakes, signs in the sun, moon and stars, universal commotion and universal expectation seem to characterize the aspect of the moral world. Amidst it all for me, I have no fears. Do your hearts fail? It [sic] tell you another coming of the Son of Man is at hand. As the lightening shinest from the east even unto the west, so shall his coming be. . . . Dear Mother, do your hearts fail? If you love God with all your heart Do you keep his commandments? If so, you stand in the evil day.[33]

The litany of signs is almost identical to a list Noyes included in a September 1834 article on the Second Coming of 70 A.D.[34] Was the *third* appearance ("Another coming") now at hand? Had he perhaps sought to bring the "Miller-ite" vision back within the fold of his own adventism by identifying it with a third rather than a second appearance? If so, the theological subtleties were clearly lost on a family more than ever convinced that their firstborn son had taken leave of his reason. Toward the end of the letter, he invoked a metaphor indissolubly linked to mystic experience: "The ocean on which I float is shore-less and bottomless."

When John returned to Putney that summer for a much needed rest, he found himself the object of notoriety: "Rumors of my fantastic performances in New York had preceeded me," he wrote Horatio. Neighbors avoided mention-ing his name to family members to spare them from embarrassment, and Noyes himself was shaken by the cold reception he received from the villagers: "They seem to have entered a combination to avoid conversation with me . . . I am at present living under an embargo."[35]

Noyes's time of tranquility was short-lived. Exactly a year after the New York experience—in the late spring of 1835—he appears to have undergone yet another period of intense turmoil.[36] He visited his sister Joanna, now married and living in New Haven, whose report to the family was filled with foreboding: "He would not reason at all, but denounced everything and everybody. He looked haggard and care-worn, and I felt positive after he left that he was deranged." He spoke of "trials and temptations, like those he experienced in New York," and after he left, Joanna reflected on the link between insanity and religion.

> He seems to be rational now, though I can discover something wild when he speaks about his particular views. The truth of it all is, upon the *subject of religion, he is certainly deranged. It is so.* It is as plain to me as light. His views upon holiness are, I think, rational: that is, if we commit our souls to God's keeping, he will preserve them from *sin*. But he is deranged when he begins to talk about his suffering for the world, and that he is immortal, &c. Do look at it, and see if it is not so: do acknowledge that he is deranged upon these subjects, and likewise when he talks to people in a way to give offense: and do pity him. He is an object of pity.[37]

Had Noyes begun to identify himself with Christ, in which case *he* embodied the "third coming"? Unfortunately, neither Noyes nor anyone else seems to have kept a fuller record of the period on this point. If Joanna was correct, and her brother in fact believed he actually was Christ, then his subsequent attitude toward Millerism makes sense psychologically as well as doctrinally. What distinguished Miller from many millennialist contemporaries was his literalism, his insistence upon understanding biblical prophecies as actual physical events, not as metaphors for spiritual processes. In 1834–1835 Noyes himself inhabited precisely such a world, where, stripped of the defenses of metaphor, he could see a physical Christ descend from the clouds or, alternatively, regard Christ as having come again in him. The Noyes of the 1840s could only draw back in horror as Second Adventism took him back to the troubled visions of 1834–1835.[38]

What may we conclude from these events? First, Noyes was unquestionably regarded as "insane" or "deranged" by those closest to him. Of persons in a position to observe, only his brother Horatio retained confidence in Noyes's sanity. As we shall see, in later years Noyes acknowledged that the sanity issue had been raised. Second, Noyes's alleged derangement was from the outset linked to his religious ideas. Other factors may well have been involved, but during Noyes's periods of "derangement," his agitated mental state was expressed through religious ideas and symbols.[39] Third, the religious ideas and symbols Noyes employed were those of premillennialism and the Second Coming. They were not employed any more consistently during these episodes than in his theological writings, but the physicality of the Advent, which Noyes normally rejected, emerged during periods of psychological stress.

On at least three occasions in later years, Noyes reflected on the relationship between religion and insanity. The first occasion for doing so was the publication in 1840 of a celebrated account of "religious insanity," John Perceval's *A Narrative of the Treatment Experienced by a Gentleman, During a State of Mental Derangement*. Then in 1849, in the *Confessions*, Noyes sought to explain the Second Adventist vision during the New York experience. Finally, in 1852, faced with cases of insanity among followers at both the Oneida Community and Putney, Noyes once more turned to the issue of a link between insanity and religion.[40]

When the second volume of Perceval's *Narrative* appeared in 1840, *The Witness* included both a summary by "H. H. N." (Harriet Holton Noyes) and "Remarks" of a more general character by "The Witness" (presumably John Humphrey). Perceval's story commanded attention on several grounds. In the first place, its author and subject was the son of a British Prime Minister, Spencer Perceval, who had been assassinated in the Houses of Parliament in 1812. The son, an apparent schizophrenic, was institutionalized from late 1830 to early 1834 and employed the *Narrative* to describe his illness from the vantage point of a subsequent spontaneous cure and to expose the inhumanity of asylums. On both counts, the work stands as pioneering. The onset of Perceval's illness was at least in part the result of his involvement in the Irvingite millenarian sect.

Edward Irving's circle included not only Thomas Carlyle, but also John's brother, the younger Spencer Perceval. Convinced of the Second Coming's imminence, the Irvingites looked to charismatic gifts such as glossolalia as premonitory signs. A fortuitous outbreak of speaking in tongues at Port Glasgow, Scotland, in 1830 was taken to be an unmistakable signal that the time was near.[41]

The Port Glasgow events found John Perceval in an already uneasy state. He had been a confirmed millenarian since the late 1820s: "I was . . . strongly persuaded that the time of the end was at hand."[42] Prior to his arrival at Oxford in 1830, he had already had visions "expecting the fulfilment of the Divine prophecies, concerning the end of the world, or the coming of the Lord."

Consequently, he went immediately to Port Glasgow in July 1830 to investigate and at the end of the year underwent a visionary experience which marked the onset of his illness: "Before I rose from my bed, I understood that I was now to proceed through the world *as an angel*, under the immediate guidance of the Lord, to proclaim the tidings of his second coming."[43]

It is not entirely clear that Noyes had actually read the book as opposed to having familiarity with it through another review: "The name of Edward Irving is connected with these 'manifestations' in the review, but the precise relation in which he [Perceval] stood to them does not appear."[44] But Noyes seems to have had at least some familiarity with Irving, and to have recognized the essentially religious nature of Perceval's travail, for he used the occasion to defend psychological risk-taking by religious seekers. The metaphor was again of the explorer adrift on uncharted seas, but now instead of surrendering to a "bottomless and shoreless ocean," "A few learn after a little experience . . . [to] shorten their sail, look well to the helm, slowly and cautiously pick their way through the reefs and quicksands . . . and so land at last on the safe shore of God's unconquerable wisdom." Although poor Perceval had suffered "bewilderment and shipwreck," the experienced voyager must expect dangers and learn to deal with them, even at the risk of madness: "I hold it useless, and worse than useless to attempt to shut out fanaticism and religious insanity, by prohibiting spirituality."[45]

The Noyes of 1840 chose to portray himself as an intrepid spiritual adventurer, the bravura performer whose very audacity permitted him to reach goals in search of which others lost their reason and from whose pursuit most timid souls shrank entirely. By 1849, when he published the *Confessions*, his views had changed. Such questing might not involve insanity at all but rather other mental states which the ignorant could not distinguish from madness. In trying to account for his mental state during the 1834 spiritual crisis in New York City, Noyes insisted that he was in fact sane, appearances to the contrary notwithstanding.

Noyes's explanation for his behavior and his insistence upon his sanity were rooted in a belief that insanity depended upon two necessary conditions, "an external spiritual cause, and a morbid state of the brain to which that cause may attach itself." In the absence of that "morbid state," an outside influence may create behavior and perception that mimic insanity in a sane individual. For Noyes the paradigmatic case of the healthy person subjected to an external mental influence was the hypnotic subject, and he invoked mesmerism to explain that "I was just as insane as impressible subjects of magnetism are—and no more. My mind was sound, but was exposed to external disturbing influences." Since "There is no disease in [the] brain . . . I had the objective, but not the subjective condition of insanity."[46] While Noyes did not move beyond an explanation for his own experience, the clear inference is that observable conduct, no matter how bizarre, is insufficient for a determination of sanity, given the benign and malign influences that may impress themselves upon the sensitive individual's psychic life.

By 1852, faced with two cases of insanity at Oneida and one at Putney, and influenced by subsequent psychiatric literature, Noyes discarded the notion that a physically diseased brain was a major causal factor. The problem was not physical at all but rather resulted from parental neglect, in particular the failure of parents "in respect to subduing the passions, and breaking the will of children while they are young."[47] Without explicitly repudiating his earlier views, he moved to a position perhaps more in keeping with his role as *pater familias* of a growing communal society. Severe mental problems, when they occurred among Putney and Oneida Community members, could now be attributed to events which had taken place long before the sufferers had become affiliated, and since the community took its own child-rearing role with the utmost seriousness, there was no reason to believe such parental errors would be repeated in the new generation.

Having himself come perilously close to a loss of sanity, Noyes was interested as we have seen in similar events in the lives of others and in possible explanations for his own behavior. In this context, it was no small matter that Millerism was widely identified as a cause of insanity, and that what passed for the psychiatric literature of the day accused Millerism of causing breakdowns serious enough to require institutionalization. Noyes took considerable pride in the fact that Perfectionism "has been . . . remarkably free from the reproach of causing insanity," a comment made while discussing the three cases among his own members. Perfectionism was not like revivalism or Millerism, both of which "have been chargeable with exciting weak minds to bewilderment and anarchy, [while] our faith has very rarely been troubled by connection with such disasters."[48] When such disasters occurred, it was doubly important that their causes be identified as something other than religious excitement, in order to preserve both the reputation of Perfectionism and Noyes's own self-conception. Not for him and his were the frenzies of revivalism and the irrationality of Second Adventism. Any association with Millerism thus had the potential for stigmatizing Perfectionists as a group, lumping them in an undifferentiated mass of those prone to religious insanity, and for stigmatizing Noyes, by reopening the issue of his own sanity during the 1830s.

MILLERISM AND INSANITY

The issue had immediate rather than merely speculative significance, for Millerism was widely believed to cause insanity. Recent literature, of which Francis Nichol's book is an example, concentrates on the issue of whether Millerites were in fact more likely than others to be considered insane. To this end, Nichol examined asylum records for Maine, New Hampshire, Vermont, and Massachusetts. He concluded that even if one accepts the rather casual diagnoses of contemporary clinical records, Millerism was implicated in only 39 out of 1,516 cases.[49] In his eagerness to clear Millerism of the taint of insanity, Nichol appears to have seriously distorted the picture. The recent work of Ronald and Janet Numbers, reported in this volume, shows 98 admissions for causes related to Millerism at three asylums in New Hampshire, Massachusetts, and New York.

Their research indicates that breakdowns were not precipitated by disappointed predictions, nor does it show that admitting physicians simplistically equated Second Adventism with mental illness. Rather, the admissions were made on the basis of patients' overt behavior. Millerism itself could not be held reponsible in the majority of cases, which involved chronic mental disorders, except in the indirect sense that some already disordered persons may have self-selected it. But approximately 18 percent of the Millerite cases examined involved acute, short-term illness, for which Millerism might have been a contributing factor.

Whether or not Millerites formed a significant proportion of mental hospital admissions, many contemporaries found the linkage with insanity plausible. If not an orthodoxy, it was at least a widely held view that Millerism was a danger to mental health. An article in the inaugural volume of the *American Journal of Insanity* observed that "The evil results from [Millerism's] recent promulgation are known to all, for we have scarcely seen a newspaper for some months past but contains accounts of suicides and insanity produced by it."[50] This comment is of interest on two counts: In the first place, it speaks volumes concerning the lack of methodological rigor in mid-nineteenth-century psychiatry. Second, it makes clear that reports, rumors, and ideas flowed freely between professional journals and the popular press. Given the latter's tendency to seek the sensational, the reports of alleged Millerite aberrations moved from the front page to psychiatric speculation.[51] The result was to inflate suspicions of Millerism in the minds of both newspaper readers and psychiatrists.

The *Journal's* author concluded that reading Millerite tracts was safe enough, however disreputable they might be, as long as the reader stayed away from meetings and preachers. Notwithstanding the fact that the "Great Disappointment" had already occurred, "the prevalence of the yellow fever or of the cholera has never proved so great a calamity to this country as will the doctrine alluded to."[52] A full nineteen years later, the same journal was still fulminating against religious insanity. Having duly taken note of one asylum administrator's conclusion that religion was rarely implicated in insanity, the anonymous author of an 1864 article deployed his full rhetorical arsenal:

> Have we nothing to fear from the teachings and the measures of fiery zeal and blind fanaticism? In those whirlwinds of passion and frenzied excitement which have too often been gotten up under the sacred name of religion, is there no danger to the timid, the nervous, the sensitive, and especially to those who are hereditarily and constitutionally predisposed to mental derangement?[53]

In short, the linkage between religion and insanity died hard. To trifle with the more *outré* forms of salvation was to place more than one's immortal soul at risk; it was to flirt with insanity, a point Noyes himself had made in his observations about the life of Perceval. Consequently, one can well believe that from Noyes's point of view, the attacks on the sanity of Millerites came too close for comfort, threatening to submerge him as well.

The strength of the association between religion and insanity was the result of two different forces: First, religious excitation fell within a much more comprehensive model of mental illness, making it entirely plausible on grounds independent of doctrinal views to regard any religious ferment as suspect. Second, for almost two centuries prior to Millerism, religious "enthusiasm" had been viewed as a form of irrationality by supporters of more subdued spirituality. Hence, quite apart from developments in early nineteenth-century psychiatry, religionists as well as nonreligionists had grown accustomed to associating religious "excesses" with loss of reason.

By the 1830s American psychiatry believed that the greater the disorder in the environment, the greater the likelihood of madness. Most forms of environmental disorder were secular. We have already seen that Noyes attributed insanity among some of his followers to the failure of parental discipline. In doing so, he was merely repeating the views of Isaac Ray and other pre-Civil War psychiatrists.[54] Similarly pernicious consequences supposedly flowed from social mobility, the economic risks and uncertainties of the marketplace, and the clamor of electoral politics. Indeed, all of antebellum America appeared directed toward undermining the sanity of its citizens by depriving them of an ordered life.[55] Although religious revivalism may have been less important than speculation, status changes, or migration, it did add to the sum total of destabilizing forces. Religion, instead of buffering believers against the shocks of a changing society, introduced new shocks of its own to minds already disoriented and overstimulated. Noyes had some reason for self-congratulation, for communities such as Oneida sought to introduce precisely that order which was perceived as missing in the larger world. Indeed, utopian communities performed many of the same functions as that other novel institution of the period, the asylum.

If Millerism was suspect because of prevailing views in psychiatry, a second and much older intellectual tradition connected religious heterodoxy with irrational behavior. That tradition began with seventeenth-century attacks against "enthusiasm." Defying precise definition, "enthusiasm" became by the 1660s a standard term of derogation directed at opponents of authority and rationality, particularly in religion.[56] Through the balance of the seventeenth century, all of the eighteenth, and the early decades of the nineteenth it carried the more specific meaning of excessively emotional, ecstatic religiosity, of the kind historically encountered among millennialists and revivalists.

The epithet implied more than mere doctrinal deviation. "Enthusiasm" also connoted religious behavior that exceeded the bounds of normality. Those guilty of it were not merely different or heretical; they were quite likely mad.[57] This equation of religious heterodoxy with madness may have resulted, as George Rosen suggests, from the presence of some emotionally disordered individuals within the fringe sects of the English Puritan Commonwealth; or from the difficulty of "distinguish[ing] the godly from the mentally disordered."[58] Alternatively, as Michael Heyd persuasively argues, the concept of "pathological enthusiasm" may have grown out of Galenic theories of an imbalance of the humors.[59] The resolution of the problem is both beyond the bounds of the present discussion and unnecessary to the issue at hand. What remains significant is that unusual religious ideas, particularly millenarian ideas, had been associated with insanity since the late 1600s.

Millerism did not encourage emotional behavior (although some might have unavoidably occurred), and Miller's own temperament was sober and reserved. Nonetheless, there are persuasive circumstantial grounds for believing Millerism caught the residual force of surviving concepts of enthusiasm. Although the word itself had begun to develop the positive associations that now surround it, it had not completely lost its earlier negative charge.[60] Among the subsidiary ideas contained within that pejorative concept was the distrust of rhetoric as "the means by which enthusiast preachers seduced their followers."[61] Overly clever argumentation directed against ecclesiastical authority was thus suspect, even in the absence of ecstatic behavior. Millenarian ideas were particulary singled out as at the very center of enthusiasm.

To the extent that the anti-enthusiast tradition retained some vigor, it reinforced the presumably scientific judgments of psychiatrists; or perhaps planted a seed in psychiatric minds. In any case, opponents of Millerism believed there were ample reasons for doubting the sanity of Second Adventists. Noyes, who had of course also indulged in millenarian rhetoric, might well have thought himself similarly vulnerable to this labeling process. Indeed, we have already seen that friends, neighbors, and family felt he had passed over the line that divided eccentricity from madness. Hence, Noyes had every reason to place as much distance as possible between himself and Miller, lest the religious insanity issue be directed against him and against the Perfectionist movement he aspired to lead.

In short, Millerism created multiple levels of vulnerability for Noyes; he feared the loss of members, he was forced to defend an eschatology that still lacked internal consistency, and—most significantly—his identity as a religious innovator was endangered by psychopathological associations. If Millerism was the road to madness, as so many psychiatrists and journalists believed, Noyes's own reputation was no longer safe. Neither medical practitioners nor the general public could be expected to notice the legitimate differences that distinguished Perfectionism from Second Adventism, or Noyes from Miller. Those differences had to be hammered home, for if they were not, Noyes might find himself cast, like the Millerites, into the category of the deluded and irrational. The dark episodes of the 1830s, when Noyes alternated between sanity and seeming madness, could be all too easily called back in the public tumult over Millerism. Millerism was a theological adversary that had to be defeated on grounds of principle, but it was a far more dangerous psychological enemy. If not dealt with in the most decisive manner, it threatened to expose Noyes to the same public opprobrium he had suffered a decade before.

NOTES

Most of the sources indicated in the notes that follow require no further explanation. However, a word is in order about the "George Wallingford Noyes Papers," referred to in the notes as "GWN." These papers, now in the George Arents Research Library at Syracuse University, take the form of a typescript of correspondence and other documents connected with John Humphrey Noyes and the Oneida Community. George Wallingford Noyes, John Humphrey's nephew, brought this material together as the basis for a history of his uncle's endeavors. It served as the basis for his two books, *The Religious Experience of John Humphrey Noyes* and *John Humphrey Noyes: The Putney Community*.

The books and the papers on which they were based acquire particular significance in that many of the documents reproduced have been lost or destroyed; hence George Wallingford Noyes's versions are the only ones in existence. For many years George Wallingford Noyes's published works were the only sources for these texts, for the typescript was believed destroyed. Now that it has resurfaced, it is possible to compare it with the published texts. Unfortunately for students of Millerism, the typescript is itself incomplete, for voluminous though it is, the years 1841 through 1847 are missing. Since these were crucial years for Second Adventism, the gap is particularly regrettable. Those periods that are covered, however, contain invaluable information on John Humphrey Noyes's intellectual and psychological development.

As indicated, the typescript and the books based upon it purport to reproduce documents the originals of which no longer exist. This raises the question of how reliable are such sources, once or twice removed from the originals. Robert Thomas, with access only to the published versions, concluded they were indeed reliable,

> For when placed alongside independent sources, the letters do have a degree of internal consistency and integrity. In cases where G. W. Noyes's tampering substantially altered the meaning of a letter, one can sometimes find it reprinted in one of the Community periodicals. Through a process of checking and cross-checking documents, one can catch many of G. W. Noyes's alterations and make judgments accordingly.[62]

Now that the published letters can be compared with the typescript, a further check can be made by comparing the typed letters with the published versions.

To the extent that I have made such a comparison, covering only the materials cited here, I support Thomas's conclusion. In most instances, letters moved from the typescript to the books with only minimal changes in spelling and punctuation. In a few cases, letters were more extensively edited by both deletions and paraphrasing, which, while retaining the sense of the "original," sometimes toned down its language. Finally, the typescript contains letters not contained in any form in George Wallingford Noyes's published works, for it was inevitable that some of the vast documentation he collected had to be omitted. In the notes, I have indicated wherever possible the relationship between the text of the typescript and the published version, if any.

Finally, I am pleased to acknowledge the assistance of Mark F. Weimer, rare book librarian of the George Arents Research Library at Syracuse; and the gracious cooperation of Imogen Noyes Stone, who allowed me to use her father's papers.

1. *The Witness* (Putney, Vt.), December 10, 1842, p. 184.

2. *The Witness* published one article on Millerism in 1840, 2 in 1841, 5 in 1842, and 2 in 1843. Its successor, *The Perfectionist*, published 3 in 1843, 4 in 1844, and 1 in 1845.

3. *The Witness* (Putney), December 10, 1842, p. 184. *The Perfectionist* (Putney, Vt.), November 2, 1844, p. 64 (erroneously paginated as 58). *The Witness*, June 6, 1840, p. 152.

4. *The Witness* (Putney), June 6, 1840, p. 152.

5. *The Witness* (Putney), October 9, 1841, p. 47.

6. George Wallingford Noyes, ed., *John Humphrey Noyes: The Putney Community* (Oneida, N.Y., 1931), p. 60. Robert D. Thomas, *The Man Who Would be Perfect: John Humphrey Noyes and the Utopian Impulse* (Philadelphia: University of Pennsylvania Press, 1977), p. 136.

7. *The Perfectionist* (Putney), November 2, 1844, p. 64 (erroneously paginated as 58).

8. Keith V. Thomas, *Religion and the Decline of Magic: Studies in Popular Beliefs in Sixteenth and Seventeenth Century England* (London: Weidenfeld and Nicholson, 1971), p. 91.

9. The subsequent fate of spiritualists in the 1850s is a case in point. R. Laurence Moore, *In Search of White Crows: Spiritualism, Parapsychology, and American Culture* (New York: Oxford University Press, 1977).

10. Noyes, *John Humphrey Noyes*, p. 123. *The Witness* (Putney), December 10, 1842, p. 184.

11. See, for example, *The Perfectionist* (Putney), September 7, 1844, pp. 50–51.

12. "The Oneida Family Register," January 1, 1849, which contains capsule biographies of early members, identifies 8 individuals as former Millerites. Oneida Collection, Syracuse University Library.

13. John Humphrey Noyes, "Religious History—No. 23," *The Perfectionist and Theocratic Watchman* (Putney), March 22, 1845, p. 1.

14. John Humphrey Noyes (Putney, Vt.) to Loren Hollister, March 7, 1840. Emphasis in original. George Wallingford Noyes Papers, Box 1, Oneida Collection, Syracuse University. Referred to below as "GWN."

15. *The Perfectionist* (New Haven, Conn.), September 20, 1834, p. 5.

16. Robert D. Thomas, "The Development of a Utopian Mind: A Psychoanalytic Study of John Humphrey Noyes" (Ph.D. dissertation, State University of New York at Stony Brook, 1973), p. 110.

17. John Humphrey Noyes, *Confessions of John H. Noyes. Part I. Confession of Religion Experience: Including a History of Modern Perfectionism* (Oneida Reserve: Leonard & Co., Printers, 1849), p. 2.

18. *The Perfectionist* (New Haven), August 31, 1835, p. 5. Emphasis in original.

19. *The Perfectionist* (New Haven), March 20, 1835, pp. 30–31.

20. John Humphrey Noyes (Putney, Vt.) to Alexander Wilder, October 31, 1840, GWN, Box 1. Emphasis in original.

21. Noyes's first reference to Miller appears to be in a *Witness* article of June 6, 1840, headed "Miller's Imposture." Although I have found no earlier mention, I would not be surprised if one were located. The gap between the beginning of Miller's career in 1831 and Noyes's first awareness of him almost a decade later may be attributable to the fact that until 1840, Miller's preaching and lecturing were largely confined to the Champlain Valley, immediately adjacent areas of Vermont and New York, and in 1839 the Boston area. Noyes's life revolved largely around southeastern Vermont, Connecticut, and the New York City area.

22. *The Perfectionist* (Putney), May 15, 1843, p. 17.

23. *Hierophant: Or, Monthly Journal of Sacred Symbols and Prophecy* (New York), June 1842, p. 5; August 1842, p. 71. This periodical, edited by Bush, appeared in only 12 numbers, from June 1842 through May 1843.

24. Letter from George Bush to William Miller, reprinted in *Reasons For Rejecting Mr. Miller's Views on the Advent by George Bush, With Mr. Miller's Reply. Also, An Argument from Professor Bush on Prophetic Time* (Boston: Joshua V. Himes, Second Advent Library No. 44, April 15, 1844), p. 9. Emphasis in original.

25. Noyes, *John Humphrey Noyes*, pp. 171–181, contains extracts of their 1845–1846 correspondence.

26. For an account of this episode, see chapter 2 of Thomas, *The Man Who Would Be Perfect*.

27. Noyes, *Confessions*, p. 38.

28. William Sargant, *Battle for the Mind: A Physiology of Conversion and Brain-Washing* (Baltimore, Md.: Penguin, 1961).

29. John Humphrey Noyes, *Confessions*, p. 39. Emphasis in original.

30. Horatio Noyes (New Haven, Conn.) to Mary Noyes, June 17, 1834. GWN, Box 1. This letter appears with only punctuation changes in George Wallingford Noyes, ed., *Religious Experience of John Humphrey Noyes, Founder of the Oneida Community* (New York: Macmillan Co., 1923), pp. 153–154.

31. Noyes family (Putney, Vt.) to Horatio Noyes, June 25, 1834. GWN, Box 1. This letter does not appear in *Religious Experience*.

32. Elizur Wright, Jr., to A. A. Philips, October 29, 1837, quoted in Robert S. Fogarty, "The Oneida Community, 1848–1880: A Study in Conservative Christian Utopianism" (Ph.D. dissertation, University of Denver, 1967), p. 57.

33. John Humphrey Noyes (New York) to his mother. Although the typescript bears the date "May 1835," it is filed with material for June 1834. This, together with the letter's substance and style, argues strongly for an earlier date—May or June 1834. GWN, Box 1. Since the GWN materials are among the last (and lightest) of what were once multiple carbon copies, it is fair to surmise that George Wallingford Noyes corrected the error in date on the original but did not bother to do so on all of the copies.

34. *The Perfectionist* (New Haven), September 20, 1834, p. 5.

35. John Humphrey Noyes (Putney) to Horatio Noyes, July 2, 1834. GWN, Box 1. Excerpts, not including the reference to his own relationships to the villagers, appear in *Religious Experience*, pp. 154–155.

36. For a description of this period, see Thomas, *The Man Who Would Be Perfect*, pp. 77–82.

37. Joanna Noyes Hayes (New Haven) to her family, June 23, 1835. GWN, Box 1. A version of this letter appears in *Religious Experience*, pp. 226–227. The emphasized material does not appear, nor do the references to vicarious suffering and immortality. The paraphrasing has the effect of shifting the subject of the letter to the manner in which Noyes appeared to others and minimizing Joanna's fears.

38. An early commentator on this paper, Robert D. Thomas, provided particularly useful comments on this point.

39. For comprehensive views of Noyes's psychological characteristics, see Thomas, *The Man Who Would Be Perfect*; and Dennis Klass, "Psychohistory and Communal Patterns: John Humphrey Noyes and the Oneida Community," in Frank E. Reynolds and Donald Capps, eds., *The Biographical Process: Studies in the History and Psychology of Religion* (The Hague: Mouton, 1976), pp. 273–296.

40. In 1881, after Noyes had fled to Canada and immediately after the breakup of the Oneida Community, he once again returned to the subject. The occasion was the trial of Charles Guiteau, assassin of President Garfield and a former member of Oneida. Noyes provided a statement to the prosecution in this landmark case in forensic psychiatry. Charles E. Rosenberg, *The Trial of the Assassin Guiteau: Psychiatry and Law in the Gilded Age* (Chicago: University of Chicago Press, 1968), pp. 108–109.

41. Andrew Lansdale Drummond, *Edward Irving and His Circle: Including Some Consideration of the 'Tongues' Movement in the Light of Modern Psychology* (London: James Clarke, 1934 [?]), pp. 133, 135, 142.

42. Gregory Bateson, ed., *Perceval's Narrative: A Patient's Account of his Psychosis 1830–32* (Stanford, Calif.: Stanford University Press, 1961), p. 11.

43. Bateson, *Perceval's Narrative*, pp. 14, 30. Emphasis in original.

44. *The Witness* (Putney), January 30, 1840, p. 107. The two pieces on Perceval are jointly headed "Confessions of a Religious Maniac."

45. *The Witness* (Putney), January 30, 1840, p. 110.

46. Noyes, *Confessions*, pp. 38–39.

47. *The Circular* (Brooklyn, N.Y.), January 4, 1852, p. 34.

48. Ibid.

49. Francis D. Nichol, *The Midnight Cry* (Washington, D.C.: Review and Herald Publishing Association, 1944), p. 495.

50. "Millerism," *American Journal of Insanity*, 1845, 1: 249.

51. Nichol's *Midnight Cry* is filled with descriptions of the anti-Millerite press. An unpublished paper by Jan Kobeski, "The Millerites: An Examination of Press Attitudes Toward the Adventist Movement of the 1840s," documents the same tendencies among the smaller papers of upstate New York. I am indebted to the late Catherine Covert for drawing my attention to Kobeski's paper.

52. "Millerism," p. 250.

53. "Twenty-first Annual Report of the Managers of New York State Lunatic Asylum, for the year 1863," *American Journal of Insanity*, 1864, 21: 250–251.

54. David J. Rothman, *The Discovery of the Asylum: Social Order and Disorder in the New Republic* (Boston: Little, Brown, 1971) pp. 121–122.

55. Rothman, *The Discovery of the Asylum*, pp. 110–119. Rothman's observations point up the link between social conditions and individual psychological functioning. While this paper is primarily concerned with individual behavior, I have addressed the issue of environmental conditions for millennialism in *Disaster and the Millennium* (New Haven, Conn.: Yale University Press, 1974).

56. Michael Heyd, "The Reaction to Enthusiasm in the Seventeenth Century: Towards an Integrative Approach," *Journal of Modern History*, 1981, 53: 258–280.

57. Ibid., p. 279.

58. George Rosen, "Enthusiasm, 'a dark lanthorn of the spirit,'" *Bulletin of the History of Medicine*, 1968, 42: 393–421.

59. Heyd, "Reaction."

60. Susie I. Tucker, *Enthusiasm: A Study in Semantic Change* (Cambridge: Cambridge University Press, 1972), pp. 4, 131–133.

61. Heyd, "Reaction," p. 266.

62. Thomas, *The Man Who Would Be Perfect*, p. xi.

TEN

Had Prophecy Failed?

Contrasting Perspectives of
the Millerites and Shakers

LAWRENCE FOSTER

THE CAREER OF THE midwestern Adventist leader Enoch Jacobs highlights the complex interrelationship between the Millerite and Shaker movements during the 1840s. Serving initially as editor of *The Western Midnight Cry!!!*—a newspaper started in Cincinnati, Ohio, in 1841, with Joshua V. Himes as its publisher—Jacobs tirelessly sought to spread William Miller's message that Christians must repent and prepare for Christ's literal return to earth in 1843. Following the failure of the 1843 predictions and of the prediction of October 1844 as well, Jacobs, like many others who experienced the Great Disappointment, struggled to understand what had gone wrong. The number of exclamation points in the title of *The Western Midnight Cry!* was reduced from three to one, and on February 18, 1845, the newspaper's title was changed to *The Day-Star*, with Jacobs as the sole editor and publisher. The name change reflected a significant change of emphasis: "The day-star must arise *before* the Sun of Righteousness: The Resurrection must take place before Christ can come with '*all* his saints.'"[1]

Jacobs increasingly found himself attracted to the United Society of Believers in Christ's Second Appearing, better-known as Shakers, who were convinced that the Second Coming of Christ's spirit had already taken place in 1770 through the person of their foundress, Ann Lee. Shakers argued that the kingdom of heaven was now literally being realized on earth in their closely knit communities, which shared all things in common like the primitive Christian church and practiced celibacy as a sign of their participation in the resurrected state in which "they neither marry nor are given in marriage." Jacobs opened the columns of *The Day-Star* to spirited letters for and against Shaker claims. An editorial observed: "None should think that the 'Day-Star' is the instrument of a sect or party: it is God's instrument; and God's children ALL have a right to talk through it to each other, and speak aloud the praises of God in the language of Christ."[2]

By May 23, 1846, Jacobs had converted to Shakerism. He began publishing extracts from Shaker doctrinal works, as well as lengthy argumentation on the necessity of celibacy as tangible proof of the overcoming of carnal propensities separating humankind from God. Jacobs repeatedly visited and reported on his visits to the Shaker villages at Whitewater and at Union Village in Ohio. That latter community, near Lebanon, Ohio, was the first and largest Shaker settlement in the Midwest, with some 400 members in the 1840s. Jacobs worked closely with prominent Shaker leaders seeking to convert disaffected Millerites, and he was instrumental in eventually attracting more than 200 persons to Shakerism in the Midwest.[3] In the summer of 1846, Jacobs traveled throughout the northeastern United States on a proselytizing mission. During that time, *The Day-Star* appeared irregularly, with two issues from New York City and one from the Shaker village at Canterbury, New Hampshire, where on September 19, 1846, thirteen hundred copies were issued, the Shakers assisting with typesetting and press work and also contributing $20.00 toward expenses.[4] A large and inconclusive meeting between Millerites and Shakers near Enfield, Connecticut, was thoroughly reported in *The Day-Star*.[5] Following Jacobs's return to Ohio, he and his wife, Electa, and family lived at Union Village, Ohio, publishing *The Day-Star* from that community beginning on November 7, 1846. In all probability, the press used was that of Richard McNemar, an influential figure in the founding of Shaker communities in the Midwest and author of *The Kentucky Revival*, the first published Shaker book.[6] Articles from Union Village increasingly reflected Shaker concerns. Jacobs took vigorous exception to the Millerites who criticized his conversion to Shakerism in a short-lived Adventist publication, *The Day-Dawn*, which was self-consciously modeled on Jacobs's newspaper.[7] Publication of Jacobs's own *The Day-Star* ceased abruptly and without explanation following the issue of July 1, 1847, about the time that Jacobs left the Shakers. A letter from Jacobs published many years later in the Shaker newspaper, *The Manifesto*, in November 1891, showed that he had subsequently been influenced by the Spiritualist movement and that he still retained fond memories of the Shakers.[8]

Enoch Jacobs's curious odyssey raises a host of complex questions. How and to what extent were his experiences representative of those of other Millerites following the Great Disappointment? Why did Shakerism come to have special appeal for some of these distraught Millerites? What was the impact of the sudden infusion of Millerites into the Shaker communities, which had themselves already been suffering great disruption as a result of the "spiritual manifestations" which had begun in 1837? Why did Jacobs, like so many other Millerites who briefly joined the Shakers in the late 1840s, eventually become dissatisfied with the group and move on to continue searching for other, more appealing ways of interpreting his experiences? And from a larger perspective, can the experiences of individuals in these two highly unconventional movements shed light on more general questions of religious development, especially how millenarian movements may be able most effectively to deal with the apparent failure of prophecy?

This article will address these and other questions relating to how millenarian movements handle problems of apparent failure or disconfirmation of their claims. First, I shall analyze Shaker theological beliefs, especially their symbolic understanding of Christ's Second Advent, and raise the question of the degree to which the Shakers by the 1830s and 1840s had found their beliefs confirmed and their social practices satisfying. Second, I shall focus on the reasons that some Millerites joined, and often subsequently left, the Shakers. In conclusion, I shall briefly suggest that the experiences of these Millerites-turned-Shakers may shed light on the eventual success of the Seventh-day Adventist movement, which emerged out of the ashes of the failure of Millerite prophecy.

SHAKER THEOLOGICAL BELIEFS AND
SOCIAL PRACTICES

Both the theological and social aspects of early Shakerism show a remarkable degree of sophistication which would later help account for the appeal of the Shaker movement to disaffected Millerites. Although Shaker and Millerite views of the nature of Christ's Second Advent were initially in sharp opposition, individuals attracted to both groups shared many common dissatisfactions with established religious and social practice. Shaker unorthodoxy and theological liberalism is suggested by the story that Thomas Jefferson was sent a copy of *The Testimony of Christ's Second Appearing* (1808), the first published Shaker doctrinal treatise, and that this free thinker and devotee of "natural religion" pronounced it the best ecclesiastical history he had ever encountered, declaring he had read it through "three times three."[9] Jefferson's letter has not survived and the entire story may well be apocryphal, yet in all probability he would have been impressed by Shaker theology had he read it. The brilliant nineteenth-century free thinker and social reformer Frederick W. Evans was only the most noteworthy of the liberal religious figures who were attracted to Shakerism and rose to prominence within the movement. Such figures were counterbalanced by equally articulate theological conservatives such as Hervey L. Eads, who spent much of the nineteenth century debating Shaker theology with Evans. Within Shakerism, with its emphasis on continuing revelation, there was much room for religious seekers of all varieties.

Looking back, the scholar of American cultural history Constance Rourke notes in her sensitive appreciation "The Shakers" that Shaker theology, breaking with Calvinism, had a remarkably "modern" cast, with its emphasis on secular progress, functionalism, and equality for women. Indeed, she asserts, Shaker views would have been quite appealing to the likes of Thomas Paine.[10] Another scholar of the early Shakers, Stephen Marini, links their appeal following the American Revolution to that of groups such as the Free Will Baptists and

Universalists.[11] And Whitney Cross, dean of scholars of the Burned-over District and enthusiastic religion in western New York State from 1800 to 1850, sees Shakerism throughout this period as "a kind of ultimate among enthusiastic movements." It incorporated many ideas which would become characteristic of the other major enthusiasms of the area and provided a temporal as well as a spiritual refuge for the most earnest seekers who became disturbed by the vagaries of revivalistic religion.[12]

Shaker theology used a spiritualized rather than a literalistic approach to biblical interpretation from a very early date, perhaps from the very beginning of the movement. Three themes are worthy of special emphasis here. First was the call for repentance and confession of sin, specifically the demand that celibacy be practiced as a tangible sign of the realization of the kingdom of heaven on earth. This emphasis grew primarily out of the traumatic sexual experiences of Ann Lee, an illiterate but highly intelligent factory worker from Manchester, England, who eventually would bring the Shakers to America and prepare the foundations for the group's subsequent expansion in the United States. During nine turbulent years in England following her marriage in 1761, Lee bore four children, all of whom died in infancy or early childhood. Her last delivery was exceptionally difficult, and for hours afterwards she lay near death. In 1770 following a powerful visionary experience in Manchester, Lee concluded that lustful sexual intercourse was the original sin in the Garden of Eden, the specific act of disobedience committed by Adam and Eve which had resulted in the fall of man and the entry of sin into the world. Only by giving up all carnal propensities and devoting oneself wholly to God could humankind ultimately achieve salvation.[13]

Later Shaker theological writers, such as Calvin Green and Seth Y. Wells in *A Summary View of the Millennial Church* (1823), greatly elaborated on this symbolic rather than literal interpretation of the Garden of Eden story. They declared that although disobedience to a specific command of God was the *cause* of man's fall, the specific *act* of disobedience was one of carnal intercourse engaged in out of its proper time and season. The specific curse pronounced upon the woman, sorrow in her conception and childbearing, was a response to sexual transgression.

> This same curse has been more or less felt by the fallen daughters of Eve to this day. . . . Thus the woman is not only subjected to the pains and sorrows of childbirth, but even in her conception, she becomes subject to the libidinous passions of her husband. . . . This slavish subjection is often carried to such a shocking extent, that many females have suffered an unnatural and premature death, in consequence of the unseasonable and excessive indulgence of this passion in the man. Thousands there are, no doubt, who are able to bear sorrowful testimony to the truth of this remark.[14]

A second theme in Shaker theology related to the role of Ann Lee and the nature of the millennium. In her vision in Manchester in 1770, Ann Lee not only became convinced that lustful carnal intercourse was the root of all evil but she also felt herself infused by the spirit of Christ and became convinced that she had a special calling to spread her message to the world. Later Shaker theological writers argued that at this time Ann Lee had been infused by God's spirit in the same way that Jesus had previously been infused by God's spirit. Ann Lee was, therefore, Christ's Second Appearing—using the term "Christ" not to refer to the man Jesus but rather the Divine spirit which had similarly animated Jesus. With this second coming of Christ's spirit to earth, realization of the millennium, the kingdom of heaven on earth, was now underway. Christ's Second Advent had not occurred instantly in literal "clouds of glory," as so many expected it would, but was rather "gradual and progressive like the rising of the Sun." The first coming had been through a male; the second, in order to maintain balance, was through a female. Reflected in this notion of restoring a true balance between the sexes was the Shaker rejection of the Trinity, which they took to be an exclusively male conception of God. Instead, the Shakers argued that God, like the whole of creation, was dual, a combination of male and female elements harmoniously related to each other.[15]

The extent to which this complex theology was developed and articulated by Ann Lee and her followers prior to her death in 1784 is open to question. Available evidence, however, suggests that much of this theology had indeed become established, at least in embryonic form, while Lee was still alive. In the first published apostate attack on the Shakers, written in 1780, Valentine Rathbun notes: "Some of them say, that the woman called the mother [Ann Lee], has the fulness of the God Head, bodily dwelling in her, and that she is the queen of heaven, Christ's wife: And that all God's elect must be born through her; yea, that Christ through her is born the second time."[16] Whatever Ann Lee herself may have believed, her followers came to express their love and affection for her by viewing her as a distinctive embodiment of the Divine spirit in human history.

A third element in Shaker theology was their restorationist effort to return to the spirit of early Christianity, the "primitive Christian church," in which believers truly loved each other and held "all things common," sharing not only their spiritual commitment but all aspects of life. As in their dealings with other issues, the Shakers did not slavishly attempt simply to copy the specific forms which had been used by early Christians. Instead, believing that a progressive revelation and elaboration of truth was going on in their own as well as in biblical days, they sought to infuse the spirit of early Christianity into new forms appropriate for their time. All aspects of life would ultimately come to form a unified spiritual and temporal whole within a distinctive community devoting itself, like a monastery, to the service of God. Shaker success in linking spiritual and temporal life would ultimately prove a key factor in their appeal to dissatisfied individuals seeking a secure spiritual home which would free them from the emotional roller coaster of revivalistic religion.[17]

Although Shaker restorationism was present from the very beginning of the movement, the precise forms that Shaker communal life would take did not become established until after Ann Lee's death. The first "gathered" Shaker community was established in 1787 at New Lebanon, New York, and by the close of the 1790s, eleven communal centers, each composed of numerous smaller "families" of thirty to ninety individuals, had been established in New York State and in New England and were thriving with sixteen hundred members.[18] A distinctive dual governmental organization, with parallel and equal leadership roles for both men and women at all levels of the group, was institutionalized. All possessions except the most personal were held in common, and the group attempted continually to focus its attention and loyalty on God, both through frequent religious services and through daily living. As early as 1803, two Shaker communities were sufficiently well established that they could give away thousands of dollars of specie, livestock, and produce to help feed the starving poor who were suffering from cholera in New York City.[19] A second wave of expansion in the Midwest, growing out of the Kentucky Revival of the early 1800s, and a lesser revival in 1827, brought the Shakers to eighteen communal centers across New England, New York, and the Midwest, with more than four thousand members by 1830, the date at which the Shakers felt they had reached the peak of their spiritual and temporal strength.[20]

Visitors to Shaker communities during the period were struck by the order, serenity, and simplicity of Shaker life, and the impressive degree of fellow feeling which was manifested. One observer noted: "The people are like their village . . . soft in speech, demure in bearing, gentle in face; a people seeming to be at peace not only with themselves, but with nature and with heaven."[21] John Humphrey Noyes, founder of the Oneida Community and commentator on the nineteenth-century communitarian movements, was another individual who found much of Shaker spiritual and temporal life appealing. He praised the Shakers for providing the "specie basis" which counteracted the failures of numerous other experimenters of the period, proving that a thoroughgoing cooperative and communistic system was not simply an impractical pipe dream but a form of organization that could successfully be established throughout the world.[22]

In summary, the Shakers had numerous strengths, both theologically and socially. Theologically, the Shakers began with a sophisticated and largely spiritualized understanding of the basis for their movement, which could easily be modified to deal with changing circumstances. Socially, the Shakers had achieved recognized excellence in communal living, and even their critics were forced to admit that the fruits of Shaker spirituality appeared to be good. Although celibacy and communal living were demanding practices, they also called forth a high degree of commitment which initially strengthened the group. The Shakers might have been expected to look toward the future with confidence.

Yet by the late 1830s, the Shakers clearly were experiencing a decline. In 1837, exactly fifty years after the formal gathering of the first Shaker community in 1787, most of the believers who had known Ann Lee and the other early leaders personally had died or grown old and feeble. A serious gap existed between the old and young in many communities. Discipline was becoming lax. Curious visitors would come in to stare with uncomprehending amusement at the strange Shaker worship services. The leadership had a sense that they were gradually and ever-so-subtly beginning to lose control over their communities. Even though Shaker theological beliefs were remarkably flexible, the loss of spiritual dynamism in the group was calling into question whether the Shakers would be able to continue to see themselves as key movers in setting up the kingdom of heaven on earth.[23]

In response to the growing Shaker internal tensions and loss of nerve— which coincided with the Panic of 1837 and ensuing depression in the outer world—a remarkable decade of "spiritual manifestations" began among the Shakers in 1837 and rapidly spread throughout all the Shaker communities. The extraordinary revivalistic effusions included everything from deep trance and possession phenomena to speaking in tongues, ecstatic dancing, and thousands of reports of messages supposedly coming from deceased Shaker leaders and others. The details of this upwelling of fervor and its impact on the group have been discussed elsewhere and need not be recounted here.[24] Suffice it to note that the manifestations helped to revitalize the spiritual commitment of some believ- ers, but they also provided an opportunity for others—especially young female mediums—to challenge the authority of Shaker leadership. Many Shaker lead- ers initially were cautiously supportive of the phenomena, seeing them as a means of strengthening the group by encouraging young Shakers and other flagging believers to undergo a powerful direct experience of the truth of the Shaker message. Eventually, however, the anarchic potential implicit in indi- vidual revelation coming from all members of the group forced the leadership to restrict the "spiritual manifestations" and reassert full control over the societies.[25]

The dramatic Shaker spiritual phenomena peaked at approximately the same time during the early 1840s when Millerite tensions were also beginning to rise to a crescendo. By the time that the Millerite Great Disappointment took place in October 1844, the Shakers had largely reestablished order in their communities and were able to supply a seemingly secure and appealing alterna- tive for some Millerites who were seeking further light to help them understand their difficult experiences. In curious and very different ways, both groups during this period were struggling to come to terms with an apparent failure of prophecy. Alert Shakers could sense that their communities, the visible sign of Christ's second appearance on earth, were beginning to experience a temporal decline, while dedicated Millerites were painfully aware that Christ had not returned to earth a second time when they had expected him.

MILLERITE RELATIONS WITH THE SHAKERS

The reasons why some Millerites became converted to Shakerism and why many of those same converts eventually left the movement can clearly be seen by looking at the heated argumentation that took place in the pages of The Day-Star between 1845 and 1847. The final failure of the Millerite prediction of the specific date for Christ's literal Second Coming was emotionally shattering

26. In 1848 William Miller donated land for a small chapel to be built a short distance to the west of his farmhouse. Here he worshiped with other Adventists in the area. Courtesy James R. Nix.

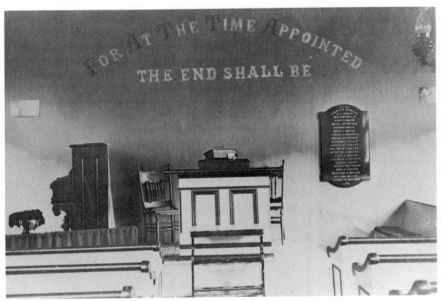

27. The interior of Miller's chapel retains much of its original appearance, including the text from Daniel 8:19, which Miller so often cited. Courtesy James R. Nix.

to many in the movement. Shock, grief, and perplexity were widespread. De-rided by outsiders and unsure themselves of what had gone wrong, Second Advent believers desperately sought to salvage something out of the commit-ment which they had so sincerely devoted to the cause. Some individuals fell apart emotionally, at least for a time, due to the "tribulations deep" which they experienced, or else became completely cynical about all religion and morality. Some continued, though in ever-decreasing numbers and with less and less enthusiasm or success, to set new dates for Christ's Second Advent, each of which eventually would prove false. And some returned to orthodoxy.[26]

But for those who had been thoroughly convinced, a return to orthodoxy offered no solution. Rather than "go back," they felt that they must "go on" to a new and fuller understanding of God's will and plan for their lives. The Shakers had much to offer these more committed believers. In the first place, the Shakers, too, were devout Second Adventists who, it seemed, had already gone through many of the same thought processes that disappointed Millerites were now experiencing. Enoch Jacobs spoke approvingly of how the Shakers, unlike so many others, took his Second Advent concerns seriously. He was astonished to discover that Shaker accounts going back to the Kentucky Revival of the early 1800s were almost uncanny in the degree to which they seemed to illustrate emotional and thought processes which he was experiencing, as though for the first time, many years later.[27] Jacobs was impressed to discover that a Shaker poem composed in 1807 or 1808, "The Midnight Cry," could speak so clearly to his present condition.[28] Articulate Shaker leaders worked with him as an individual, encouraging him to "go on" to develop a deeper spiritual insight. Given these circumstances, Jacobs was at least open to considering that the Shakers might have something to teach him.

The most appealing aspect of Shakerism for Jacobs and other Millerites like him was not so much theological as social. The Shakers really seemed to be living their faith successfully, unlike so many Millerites. Even Millerites who were most critical of the Shakers in the columns of *The Day-Star* could not restrain their grudging admiration for the well-ordered, loving communities that the Shakers appeared to have created.[29] Jacobs commented how impressed he was by the Shakers' stress on works, not on mere talk. Though Jacobs initially had difficulty accepting the Shaker contention that their organization was the true representative of the "body" of Christ on earth, he noted that "the spirit of the Shakers is much more like Christ, than the spirit that opposes them."[30] If the test by which one was to know truth was by its fruits, then the Shakers scored high marks, especially for those individuals who had been so badly burned by the revival fires and were seeking true religious security.

Henry B. Bear, a Millerite who joined the Shakers and wrote a reflective account of his Advent experience, exhorted his brethren: "O come and be gathered . . . I know there can be no happiness in being thus scattered."[31] Even more eloquent was Enoch Jacobs's peroration:

O what an ocean of contradictory theories is that upon which the multitudes have been floating for the last 18 months. Do you not long for rest from these conflicting elements? Do you want to find a place where Advent *work* takes the place of Advent *talk*,—where "I" is no longer the prominent *idea* in any theory—where the purity of wives and husbands is the purity of heaven, and where your little children are protected from the poisonous influence of the world.[32]

The Shaker symbolic rather than literal interpretation of Christ's Second Advent was in sharp opposition to Millerite literalism, yet a symbolic approach appeared much more appealing following the Great Disappointment. Shaker doctrinal works going back to *The Testimony of Christ's Second Appearing* in 1808 presented an extremely persuasive case for seeing Christ's Second Advent as an inner not an external phenomenon. In the wake of Christ's failure to make a literal return as they had anticipated, Millerites searching the Scriptures for guidance could come to the conclusion that the error had been in their *own* understanding and not in the Lord's word.

Enoch Jacobs again articulated the Shaker alternative to Millerite literalism:

> Have you found salvation? It was that for which we looked in 1843, and in the autumn of 1844. On the 10th day of the 7th month of the last named year, we were all placed in a situation to receive it, if it had come in *our way*. George Storrs told me that he felt just as completely dead to the world as though he had been laid in his coffin—buried under ground and waiting for a resurrection. This was the feeling of thousands. It was mine. Earthly ties were as completely sundered, for the time being, as though they had never been known. Thus we waited, but Salvation did not come: We thought the fault was all without—sad mistake!! It was *within*. This out of doors salvation has always been a precarious thing.[33]

And a stanza from a poem by the Shaker Charles Main also made the same point:

> So stand no longer waiting, ye men of Galilee,
> Into the literal heavens, your Savior there to see;
> But listen to his teaching, and cleanse your soul from sin,
> The everlasting kingdom must be set up within.[34]

There were problems, of course, with the specifics of Shaker adventist theology. Why, for example, should Christ's Second Advent have been through a woman? And, even if one were to accept such a possibility, why should one conclude that Ann Lee was that woman? Yet in the face of great need for a new understanding of their experience, even the unorthodoxy of Shaker theology was not an insurmountable stumbling block to devout Millerites who found the Shakers otherwise attractive.[35]

The great stumbling block, instead, was celibacy. This, not Shaker theology per se, had always been the ultimate limiting factor in the growth of the group. Not only did celibacy make Shakerism entirely dependent upon a continuing supply of converts from the outer world for its survival and growth, but celibacy was also a powerful test of whether the dedication of new converts was sufficiently great that they were prepared to give up "all" for Christ. By demanding an extreme degree of loyalty and the severing of normal earthly relationships, Shaker celibacy could have considerable appeal to the most devoted believers in the great revivals who sought to commit their lives wholly to God without any carnal distractions. Millerites who had been eagerly awaiting Christ's Second Advent, living with husbands or wives, following St. Paul's advice, as though they had none, could understand the need for such sacrifice, at least for a time.[36]

Yet when Christ did not literally appear in clouds of glory in 1844, even devout Millerites must have reassessed the desirability of continued celibacy. As a lifelong practice rather than a prelude to eternal glory, the demands must have seemed excessive to most. Enoch Jacobs himself struggled with his impulses and with those of his wife, who initially opposed Shakerism because of that demand.[37] Again and again, Jacobs emphasized how difficult the commitment to celibacy was:

> I now ask if there is one Advent believer in the land, who would not gladly share the peaceful home they [the Shakers] enjoy, were it not for the cross [celibacy]? Excuse after excuse is brought forward, while the real one is hidden. You wish to reserve the privilege of gratifying the lusts of the flesh, which you know you cannot do under any circumstances, in the dispensation in which we live, appealing to God that you do it for his glory.[38]

Some Millerite converts to Shakerism accepted the Shaker celibate cross permanently. Henry B. Bear and his family, for example, remained committed members of the group throughout the remainder of their lives. Yet far more Millerite converts to Shakerism appear to have "turned off" from the movement than remained. Although Shaker membership figures still have not been completely analyzed, the work done to date is suggestive. The membership records of the New Lebanon Second Family between 1830 and the dissolution of the community in 1896 show, for example, that only slightly more than 10 percent of all converts during the entire period remained in that community for the rest of their lives.[39] The percentage of converts who stayed faithful dropped precipitously in the 1830s and 1840s.[40] The fluidity of membership was even greater in the Sodus Bay, New York, community from 1826 to 1838, where more than 50 percent of the group changed in some years.[41] While we do not yet know the reasons that Millerites who joined the Shakers in the 1840s often subsequently failed to stay, celibacy must have been an important factor. The story is that Enoch Jacobs himself left the Shakers declaring that he would "rather go to hell with Electa his wife than live among the Shakers without her."[42]

If some Millerites were influenced for a time by Shakerism, then how, correspondingly, were Shakers influenced by Millerites? Only a few hypotheses can be raised here. The impact of significant numbers of Millerite converts joining some Shaker communities, particularly in the Midwest, and then subsequently leaving the group must have been considerable. In the first case, the

Shakers surely were enthusiastic at the infusion of new converts and may well have modified the emphasis of their group in order to retain the Millerites. In the extreme case of the Shaker village at Whitewater, Ohio, in 1845, for example, 80 out of a total of 144 members were former Millerites, and their influence on the direction of the group must have been considerable.[43] At Union Village, Ohio, the largest and one of the most internally troubled Shaker communities during the 1830s and 1840s, thirty Millerites were added to one family alone in the course of six months.[44] Even if no direct changes in Shaker theology or practice were made, such an infusion of converts must have had an impact on what aspects of Shakerism were emphasized at the time.

Direct Millerite influence on the Shakers is difficult to establish, based on available evidence, but experimentation with new forms of ritual may have been one activity stimulated by the Millerite influx. One of the most colorful of the new forms of group worship which the Shakers introduced during the 1840s, for example, was called the "Midnight Cry." A platoon of Shaker mediums—six male and six female, with two elders in the lead carrying lighted lamps in their right hands—marched through all the community buildings at midnight every night for a period of two weeks. "Every medium wore upon the right wrist, a scrap of scarlet flannel, some two and one half inches wide, and attached to this a written inscription as follows—'War hath been declared by the God of heaven, against all sin, and with the help of the Saints on earth, it shall be slain.'"[45] These activities were interpreted as the actualization of the "searching as with candles" foretold at the beginning of the manifestations. At midnight on one of the nights, the brothers and sisters were awakened with singing:

> Awake from your slumbers, for the Lord of Hosts
>   is going through the land,
> He will sweep, he will clean his holy sanctuary.
> Search ye your Camps, yea read and understand
> For the Lord of Hosts holds the Lamps in his hand.[46]

All the believers dressed quickly and hurried out to join in the marching and singing, before repairing to the meeting house for an hour of active worship. "This strange alarm had a wonderful effect on the minds of those thus suddenly aroused."[47]

If a new spirit and enthusiasm was imparted to Shakerism by the Millerite influx, then the subsequent departure of many of those same Millerite converts a few years to a decade later must have undercut Shaker morale, contributing to the deep pessimism apparent in so much of the Shaker writings of the 1850s and 1860s. While difficulty in retaining converts can be traced to the decade of the 1830s, before the Millerite infusion, the length of time that the Shakers were able to keep their converts became progressively shorter with individuals who entered during the 1840s, 1850s, and 1860s. Thoughtful Shakers must have wondered if their own efforts had also "failed," not theologically but socially.

Ultimately the most appealing answer to the apparent failure of Millerite prophecy of the 1840s was provided not by the spiritualized Second Advent beliefs and practices of the Shakers, but by the beliefs and practices introduced by Ellen G. White and others, who argued that, on October 22, 1844, Christ had entered the most holy compartment of the heavenly sanctuary to begin the "investigative judgment" preliminary to the Second Coming. In effect, belief in a heavenly event which could not immediately be confirmed or disconfirmed was substituted for Millerite belief in an earthly event which had not occurred as anticipated. On the foundation of this new belief, as well as other distinctive beliefs and practices, would rise the Seventh-day Adventist movement, a classic example of a successful group which developed out of the ashes of an apparently failed prophecy.[48]

NOTES

1. *The Day-Star*, February 18, 1845, 5: 3. For bibliographical details on *The Western Midnight Cry* and *The Day-Star*, see Mary L. Richmond, *Shaker Literature: A Bibliography*, 2 vols. (Hanover, N.H.: University Press of New England, 1977), 1: 69. Although Jacobs's newspaper was published in thirteen volumes between 1841 and July 1, 1847, the version available on microfiche at the Western Reserve Historical Society in Cleveland, Ohio, and at the Library of Congress in Washington, D.C., begins with volume 2, number 1, on December 9, 1843, and appears to be complete thereafter. The interpretation of the Shakers presented throughout this paper is an outgrowth of the work reported in Lawrence Foster, *Religion and Sexuality: Three American Communal Experiments of the Nineteenth Century* (New York: Oxford University Press, 1981), and reprinted in a paperbound version, with identical pagination, as *Religion and Sexuality: The Shakers, the Mormons, and the Oneida Community* (Urbana: University of Illinois Press, 1984), pp. 21–71, 226–247.

2. *The Day-Star*, May 9, 1846, 10: 44.

3. Richmond, *Shaker Literature*, 1: 69. Shaker membership figures are often fuzzy, but there is no question that numerous Millerites were attracted, for varying periods of time, to the Shakers.

4. Ibid., p. 69.

5. A detailed summary of the proceedings at Enfield was provided in *The Day-Star* on August 25, 1846, and in subsequent issues.

6. John P. MacLean, *Sketch of the Life and Labors of Richard McNemar* (Franklin, Ohio: Franklin Chronicle, 1905), p. 61n.

7. *The Day-Star*, August 8, 1846, 11: 18.

8. *The Manifesto*, November 1891, 21: 250–251, prints Jacobs's letter to Elder Hervey L. Eads and Elder Henry C. Blinn's favorable comment.

9. Benjamin Seth Youngs's *The Testimony of Christ's Second Appearing* was first printed at Lebanon, Ohio, by John McClean in 1808. For the Jefferson story, see John P. MacLean, *A Bibliography of Shaker Literature* (Columbus, Ohio: F. J. Heer, 1905), p. 6.

10. Rourke's fine essay "The Shakers" appeared in her *The Roots of American Culture and Other Essays*, ed. Van Wyck Brooks (New York: Harcourt Brace, 1942), pp. 195–237.

11. Stephen A. Marini, *Radical Sects of Revolutionary New England* (Cambridge, Mass.: Harvard University Press, 1982).

12. Whitney R. Cross, *The Burned-over District: The Social and Intellectual History of Enthusiastic Religion in Western New York, 1800–1850* (New York: Harper & Row,

1965; originally published by Cornell University Press in 1950), p. 32. One reason for Cross's great appeal to scholars is that at one point or another through his book he refers to virtually every one of the many groups that he analyzes as the key to understanding the Burned-over District. As only a few examples, if the Shakers are "a kind of ultimate among enthusiastic movements," the Millerites are, quoting Ludlum, "the summation of all the reforms of the age," p. 317, and Noyes's Oneida Community is "veritably the keystone in the arch of Burned-over District history, demonstrating the connection between enthusiasms of the right and those of the left," p. 333. Scholars who must justify their work by pointing to the centrality of the particular group they have chosen to understanding an age can use Cross to give credibility to the study of almost any group in the Burned-over District.

Among the most insightful of the discussions of Shakerism as a refuge from the vagaries of revivalism, see Stow Persons, "Christian Communitarianism in America," in *Socialism and American Life*, eds. Donald Drew Egbert and Stow Persons, 2 vols. (Princeton, N.J.: Princeton University Press, 1952), 1: 127–151.

13. For the most authoritative primary source on Ann Lee's life, see the rare *Testimonies of the Life, Character, Revelations, and Doctrines of Our Ever Blessed Mother Ann Lee and the Elders with Her* (Hancock, Mass.: J. Talcott and J. Deming, Junrs., 1816). Also see the treatments in Calvin Green and Seth Y. Wells, *A Summary View of the Millennial Church or United Society of Believers (Commonly Called Shakers)* (Albany, N.Y.: Packard and Van Benthuysen, 1823), and Edward Deming Andrews, *The People Called Shakers*, new enl. ed. (New York: Dover, 1963). The treatment of the Shakers given here is condensed from Foster, *Religion and Sexuality*, pp. 21–71.

14. Green and Wells, *Millennial Church*, pp. 132–133.

15. See Youngs, *Testimony of Christ's Second Appearing*, and Green and Wells, *Millennial Church*. A revealing secondary analysis of Shaker theology is Rourke, "The Shakers." Normative Shaker christological beliefs of the early nineteenth century are succinctly presented in the following affirmation: "Christ first appeared in Jesus of Nazareth, by which he was constituted the head of the new spiritual creation of God. ... [The human tabernacle of Ann Lee] was a chosen vessel, occupied as an instrument, by the spirit of Christ, the Lord from Heaven, in which the second appearance of that Divine spirit was ushered into the world." Green and Wells, *Millennial Church*, pp. 216, 219.

16. Valentine Rathbun, *An Account of the Matter, Form, and Manner of a New and Strange Religion* (Providence, R.I.: Bennett Wheeler, 1781). Rathbun dated his account December 5, 1780.

17. See Persons, "Christian Communitarianism in America," and Cross, *Burned-over District*.

18. "Introduction to Records of Sacred Communications" (New Lebanon, N.Y.: ca. 1843), p. 10. This is a manuscript in the Western Reserve Historical Society Library in Cleveland, Ohio, which provides the best contemporary Shaker analysis of the factors which led to the unusual outbreak of "spiritual manifestation" which began in 1837. It also provides a brief summary of earlier Shaker membership growth.

19. Thomas Brown, *An Account of the People Called Shakers* (Troy, N.Y.: Parker and Bliss, 1812), p. 343.

20. "Introduction to Records of Sacred Communications," p. 10.

21. William Hepworth Dixon, *New America*, 6th ed., 2 vols. (London: Hurst and Blackett, 1867), 2: 86.

22. John Humphrey Noyes, *History of American Socialisms* (Philadelphia: J. B. Lippincott, 1870), p. 670.

23. "Introduction to Records of Sacred Communications."

24. An overview of the phenomena is provided in Foster, *Religion and Sexuality*, pp. 62–71. Also see Lawrence Foster, "Shaker Spiritualism and Salem Witchcraft: Social Perspectives on Trance and Possession Phenomena" (paper presented at the annual

meeting of the National Historic Communal Societies Association in New Harmony, Indiana, on October 15, 1983).

25. One of the most disruptive phenomena occurred, for example, in 1839 when three leading Shakers, including the venerable Richard McNemar, a key figure in the founding of the midwestern Shaker communities, were expelled from the Union Village, Ohio, community at the behest of a young medium. Only belatedly were McNemar and his associates reinstated by a directive from the central office at New Lebanon, New York. Following this episode, rules began to be formulated to test the validity of spiritual communications.

26. For a summary of reactions, see Cross, *Burned-over District*, pp. 307–321, and David T. Arthur, "Millerism," in *The Rise of Adventism: Religion and Society in Mid-Nineteenth-Century America*, ed. Edwin S. Gaustad (New York: Harper & Row, 1974), pp. 154–172.

27. Jacobs prints extracts from a letter of John Dunlavy to Barton W. Stone in 1805 during the Kentucky Revival, *The Day-Star*, June 13, 1846, *11*: 6–9.

28. Ibid., May 23, 1846, *10*: 56.

29. See O. L. Crosier's "Visit to the Shakers," printed in its entirety, ibid., August 8, 1846, *11*: 18–19.

30. Ibid., May 9, 1846, *10*: 44.

31. Letter of April 24, 1846, from Henry B. Bear, ibid., May 9, 1846, *10*: 44. Bear's pamphlet, *Henry B. Bear's Advent Experience* (Whitewater, Ohio, n.d.), reprinted in the appendix to this volume, is one of the finest summations of the emotional and intellectual processes through which a thoughtful Millerite went during the 1840s.

32. *The Day-Star*, May 23, 1846, *10*: 51.

33. Ibid., June 13, 1846, *11*: 9.

34. Ibid., June 13, 1846, *11*: 5.

35. Numerous discussions by Enoch Jacobs show that Shaker theology was sometimes difficult to justify to Millerites, but Jacobs continually stressed the importance of considering the whole achievement of the Shakers rather than individual bits of theology in isolation.

36. For example, see the letter from Sister E. S. Willard approving of celibacy prior to Christ's Second Advent, ibid., May 9, 1846, *10*: 42.

37. Ibid., May 9, 1846, *10*: 42.

38. Ibid., June 13, 1846, *11*: 12.

39. See the analysis in Foster, *Religion and Sexuality*, pp. 54–58. Approximately 20 percent of converts either remained in the Second Family or transferred to another Shaker group.

40. Ibid., p. 56. Further analysis would be necessary to determine how many of the individuals who left the Shakers after joining in the late 1840s were former Millerites, but it seems certain that a significant proportion had been associated with the Millerite movement.

41. Ibid., pp. 56–58.

42. MacLean, *Bibliography of Shaker Literature*, pp. 19–20.

43. *The Day-Star*, August 8, 1846, *11*: 18.

44. Ibid., November 7, 1846, *11*: 36.

45. Henry C. Blinn, *The Manifestation of Spiritualism Among the Shakers, 1837–1847* (East Canterbury, N.H., 1899), p. 49.

46. Andrews, *People Called Shakers*, pp. 160–161.

47. Anna White and Leila S. Taylor, *Shakerism: Its Meaning and Message* (Columbus, Ohio: Fred J. Heer, 1904), p. 235.

48. For a provocative analysis of the transformation of the Adventist movement after the Great Disappointment, see Jonathan M. Butler, "Adventism and the American Experience," in *The Rise of Adventism*, ed. Gaustad, pp. 173–206. Discussions of the

early development of Adventist sanctuary theology are found in LeRoy Edwin Froom, *The Prophetic Faith of our Fathers: The Historical Development of Prophetic Interpretation*, 4 vols. (Washington, D.C.: Review and Herald, 1954) 4: 877–905; M. Ellsworth Olsen, *A History of the Origin and Progress of the Seventh-day Adventists* (Washington, D.C.: Review and Herald, 1925), pp. 177–197; and Ingemar Lindén, *The Last Trump: An Historico-Genetical Study of Some Important Chapters in the Making and Development of the Seventh-day Adventist Church* (Frankfurt-am-Main: Peter Lang, 1978), pp. 129–131.

One of the best theoretical discussions of the larger issue of how groups adapt to an apparently failed prophecy is provided in J. Gordon Melton's "What Really Happens When Prophecy Fails?" (paper presented at the Conference on American Millennialism held at the Unification Theological Seminary, Barrytown, New York, October 24–26, 1980). Melton criticizes the approach adopted in the classic study by Leon Festinger, Henry W. Riecken, and Stanley Schachter, *When Prophecy Fails: A Social and Psychological Study of a Modern Group that Predicted the Destruction of the World* (New York: Harper & Row, 1964; originally published by the University of Minnesota Press in 1956). Melton argues that millenarian groups are not primarily organized around the prediction of some future event. Instead, prediction in a well-organized millenarian movement is only one of many important elements in the group's belief system. When a specific prophecy does not occur, millenarian movements typically reinterpret or "spiritualize" the prediction. It is decided that "the prophecy was not incorrect, the group merely misunderstood it. The group understood it in a material earthly manner. Its truth comes as a spiritual, invisible (except to the eye of faith) level. Thus from the original prophesied event, the believers create an 'invisible,' 'spiritual' and more importantly unfalsifiable event." (p. 5) An incisive analysis of the development of early Christianity from a similar perspective is found in John G. Gager, *Kingdom and Community: The Social World of Early Christianity* (Englewood Cliffs, N.J.: Prentice-Hall, 1975).

ELEVEN

The Making of a New Order

Millerism and the Origins of Seventh-day Adventism

JONATHAN M. BUTLER

IN HIS COMPARATIVE ANALYSIS of numerous millennial movements, anthropologist Kenelm Burridge construes a formula for cultural change from "old rules" to "no rules" to "new rules."[1] The first phase of these movements invariably involves a period of social unrest. Society deviates from the "old rules" as old formulas fail and institutions malfunction. People flout the political, religious, and social establishments with seemingly unpatriotic, blasphemous, and antisocial acts. In the next phase, society hangs between the old order and the new in an interim period in which neither the old standards nor the new hold sway. In these stressful and confusing, exciting and invigorating times, millennial movements often materialize in search of a new society. Burridge defines them as new cultures or social orders coming into being. Rather than "oddities" or "diseases in the body social," they involve "the adoption of new assumptions, a new redemptive process, a new political-economic framework, a new mode of measuring the man, a new integrity, a new community: in short, a new man."[2] The prophet emerges to organize the new assumptions and articulate them. Transcending the hazardous interlude of no rules, he wrings order out of anomy. In the third and final phase, the "new rules" solidify as the new culture takes shape, which in time may represent the old rules and old order for a future prophetic movement. Millenarians cannot last *as millenarians*. They endure only as they scuttle or transform their millenarian outlook. "To ask whether particular activities have 'succeeded' or 'failed' in attaining their objectives is, however, the wrong question," according to Burridge. The issue is not whether the bullets turned into water or the cargo arrived or the Second Coming occurred but whether the group produced "a satisfactory measure of the nature of man. In this sense," he says, "all millenarian activities succeed."[3]

American history may be interpreted as a series of cultural awakenings analogous to what the anthropologist describes. The Second Great Awakening, which ignited a series of conflagrations between the 1790s and 1860, was perhaps the central, pivotal event in shaping the American, the new man.[4] In applying the Burridge model to this culturally transformative period, one historian suggests that the Federalist era represented the old rules, that the era of Romantic revivalism and "freedom's ferment" marked the time of no rules, and that post-Civil War corporate capitalism provided the new rules.[5] In the evanescent, highly creative interim, the new religions of Mormonism, Shakerism, and Oneida Perfectionism flowered, as did the social movements for temperance, abolition, feminism, peace, and dietary reform.[6] Inevitably, however, the intensity of the era spent itself and a move from no rules to new rules ensued. John Higham dubs this move a transition from "boundlessness to consolidation." And he argues that the change happened in a single, critical decade. "In the United States, as well as England and much of Europe," he observes, "the 1850's witnessed a subsidence of the radical hopes and reactionary fears of the early nineteenth century and the formation of a more stable, more disciplined, less adventurous culture." Americans passed from freedom to control, from movement to stability, from diversity to uniformity, from diffusion to concentration, from spontaneity to order.[7]

The dramatic cultural transformation of mid-nineteenth-century America provided the macrocosm in which Millerism evolved into Seventh-day Adventism, the most significant institutional legacy of the Millerite movement. Like every other millenarian movement, Millerism met with obvious failure, and yet out of this failure eventually emerged another of the American sectarian success stories. How did the single-minded otherworldliness of 1844 Millerism develop, by the 1860s, into a durable, complex, and established Adventist sect with wide-ranging interests that included sabbatarianism, temperance, medicine, education, and religious liberty? In analyzing the shift from Millerism to Seventh-day Adventism, the historian gains fresh, if unconventional, access to the inner core of a profound transition in mid-nineteenth-century American culture. The colorful and spectacular boundlessness of millenarian beginnings generally has attracted more scholarly attention than the later quietistic and consolidated stage of these movements. This circumstance has left unexplored many of the more intriguing questions as to how millenarians transcend their origins.[8] The purpose of this study is to determine, then, not only the ways in which Millerism imbibed of antebellum American boundlessness and freedom, movement, diversity, and spontaneity, but to document the means by which Millerism successfully established itself, in Seventh-day Adventism, as an expression of late-nineteenth-century consolidation and control, stability, uniformity, and order.

MILLERITE BOUNDLESSNESS

Following the War of 1812, the new sense of national security, the vast widening of horizons geographically, technologically, and culturally, the emotional energy of evangelical Christianity, and the intellectual rationale of an imported Romanticism all proved conducive to an antebellum American assault on limits. Millerism, as much as any other social or religious movement of the time, reflected the boundlessness that resulted. As the boundaries of status eroded as a result of the egalitarian celebration of the common folk, the diffident Miller personified the self-made Jacksonian man. A theological rustic, proudly equipped with nothing more than the ordinary Bible and *Cruden's Concordance*, Miller attracted a diverse, popular movement of both the rabble and the respectable, much as Jackson had done for politics.[9] When the limits of history yielded to a historyless dedication to the future, Miller transmuted history into eschatology, seeing the past as apostasy and the future as apocalypse. When the limits of reason receded before the infinite possibilities of intuitive knowledge, Miller's methodology unlocked the symbolic, typological meanings of the Scripture. While his appeal to prophecy as "evidence" echoed the earliest, conservative Enlightenment thinkers, Miller's lush, intricate expositions on biblical prophecy relied as much on the poetic intuitions of a Romantic mind. When the limits of human nature expanded with the ecstatic promise of liberation from sin and social wrong, Millerites, despite the Old School Calvinist sympathies of Father Miller, scaled the heights of "holiness" in pietistic preparation for the Second Advent; their cosmic determinism did not impede individualistic perfectionism. And just when a static view of nature gave way to a new, dynamic world view marked by vitality and endless growth, Millerites saw in the dazzling Shower of Stars and Great Comet, the ominous Dark Day, and other extraordinary natural phenomena portents of the world's end. If Newton's cosmic machine might in theory last forever, Millerites knew from the signs of their own times that in historical fact it would not.[10]

Millerism provides, then, as much a characterization of Jacksonian America as a caricature of it. It proved a child of its times, albeit a willful child, in regard to four prominent aspects of antebellum American boundlessness: first, the millennialism that broke down past barriers to the kingdom; second, the perfectionism that pursued unlimited potential in an era of eschatological expectancy; third, the voluntaryism which disregarded denominational boundaries in quest of common goals; and fourth, the revivalism which provided the means to these unprecedented ends. But while each of these four impulses of the era inspired Millerism, the revivals of the Second Awakening had begun to wind down by the time Millerism appeared. Even before the financial crisis of 1837, revivalists sensed that a mysterious calm had emptied their once-full sails.[11] Though seeking to extend the awakening, Millerism wound up finally expending the energy of the awakening.

Of the four impulses of antebellum America that prompted Millerism, millennialism proved obviously of primary importance. The millennium produced in the new Republic a sense of hope and progress which masked a deep anxiety and insecurity. The buoyant optimism and expansiveness knew a darker side. While distinctions between reformism and revolutionism, gradualism and immediatism, postmillennialism and premillennialism remain instructive for understanding the nation between the War of 1812 and the Civil War, these contrasting perspectives enjoyed compatibility in this period.[12] Both the evangelist Charles Finney and the prophetic lecturer William Miller looked eagerly for something of eschatological importance to happen in their immediate future. Thus Finney, who once had predicted the inauguration of his version of the millennium within three years, could hardly snub Miller for the apocalyptist's short timetable. In fact, Finney's criticism of him involved the nature of his millennium, not the nearness of it.[13] By projecting an end to the world "about 1843," Miller posed the "logical absolute" of contemporary millennialism, or a "sensational variant" of the views other Protestants then preached.[14] He sought to reheat revival embers with the specificity of his prediction. While his efforts rekindled the revivals for a time, his ill-conceived tactic ultimately doused its flames. Though Edward Irving provoked a far worse scandal for British dispensationalism than Miller did for American premillennialism, Miller remains one of those tragic figures whose notoriety prompted precisely the opposite effect he had wanted. All future American millenarians would live in the shadow of his Great Disappointment.

Perfectionism resulted from the millennial impulse that the world's last days called for the total eradication of evil. An era which expected judgment of the wicked and triumph of the righteous recoiled from compromise with sin. The strident, sweeping crusades for total abstinence, abolition of slavery, women's rights, peace, and hygiene showed little tolerance for political expediency. Immediatism had replaced gradualism, just as comprehensive rather than partial answers energized Romantic reforms. While Jacksonian Democrats sought to diffuse power and expand the spatial boundaries of freedom, Whig reformers meant to cleanse and to purify people's relations with one another by assaulting the bonds of sin, ignorance, and vice. This same reformist sociology, perfectionist and immediatist, Romantic and Whig, produced Millerism.

Given the lateness of the hour and the failure of earlier efforts to transform society, however, Millerism possessed an even deeper cynicism for the political solution, insofar as that was possible in these times, and certainly no patience at all with the partial solution. Shunning social, political, and ecclesiastical means to the millennium, Millerites made whatever perfection might be attained in their wicked world purely an individual matter. Consequently, they attracted numerous "holiness" types. Just when the later Finney was developing his holiness theology, they provided a mass movement highlighted by perfectionist impulses. They met long-standing financial and moral obligations. They cleansed body and soul. They prepared for the end. But the weight of millennial expectation proved crushingly burdensome to some of them, and their individualism turned idiosyncratic and neurotic. Millerite leader John Starkweather, for example, a product of Andover Seminary, sought the "second blessing" through bodily sensation, waved a green bough over his audience to discern the saved from the damned, and implored the people to discard as worldly ornaments everything from breast pins to false teeth. Although he was finally removed from Millerite headquarters as a fanatic, he was hardly alone in his extremism. The hardheaded independence of Millerites was not easily disciplined by a handful of Millerite leaders.[15]

Voluntaryism offered the practical means to millennial perfection. In the open market of disestablishment, voluntary associations for home and foreign missions, Bible and tract distribution, Sunday School, temperance, education, and antislavery sold themselves by way of persuasion rather than coercion. Expansively ecumenical, they minimized the boundaries of faith and order in pursuit of the life and work of Christendom.[16] At the outset, Millerites might have been taken for one among the many of these voluntary associations. They eschewed sectarianism for an interdenominationalism through which they remained, for the most part, Methodists, Baptists, Presbyterians, and "Christians" (that is, members of the Christian Connection). And in an era of the multi-reformer, they recruited antislavery, temperance, and education advocates. Miller himself had been a radical abolitionist. His promoter and the pastor of Boston's Chardon Street Chapel, Joshua V. Himes, a friend of William Lloyd Garrison, had sponsored abolition, nonresistance, and other reform causes. Joseph Bates, erstwhile sea captain, had helped to organize a local temperance society as early as 1827 and an antislavery society in the mid-1830s before becoming a Millerite. Henry Jones, who joined Himes in publishing *Signs of the Times*, had been a temperance lecturer. The prominent New Yorker Elon Galusha and the Harvard-educated Henry Dana Ward had been abolitionists before they were Millerites.[17]

Miller viewed the benevolent reforms as forerunners of his own movement, while Bates saw Millerism as the "fountainhead" from which effective moral reform flowed.[18] Both Miller and Bates proved to be, however, the exception rather than the rule among the Millerites. Their magnanimity toward the evangelical empire was rarely shared by fellow believers. The faltering enthusiasm for reform activity among evangelicals had become, for Millerites, a profound ennui. Accordingly, they looked to the Second Coming not to reward reform success but to erase its dismal failures. Almost without exception, they abandoned the evangelical crusades as Millerism absorbed their reform spirit. Enlistment in Millerism was not at all voluntary in the sense of optional, but it was mandatory for eternal life. The voluntary associations had proved impractical or wrongheaded, and were now rendered unnecessary by the impending apocalypse. With this more exclusive self-definition, Millerites were far nearer sectarianism than when they first believed.

The engine of revivalism, which powered the antebellum benevolent empire, seemed low on fuel when Millerism appeared on the scene in the late 1830s. The flagging of such an awakening was perhaps less a mark of defeat than of victory, as the many that had been converted left fewer who needed conversion. Moreover, Finney's "new measures," by which he stirred revival fervor, probably had lost impact as they lost novelty. Millerism partook of the Second Awakening ethos in an attempt to sustain it. Prophetic lecturers not only predicted the end of the world as apocalyptists but called people to Christ as evangelists. They counted not only those who adopted faith in Christ's "soon

28. The earliest prophetic chart produced by a Saturday-keeping Adventist resembled in many ways the famous 1843 Millerite chart. Designed by Samuel Rhodes, an early minister of that persuasion, it was published by another believer, Otis Nichols, of Dorchester, Massachusetts. Courtesy Loma Linda University Heritage Room.

appearing in the clouds of heaven" but "converts to Christ" who turned grog shops into meetinghouses, shut down gambling halls and testified of changed hearts.[19] They drew upon Finneyite measures such as the itineracy of lecturers and their direct, unaffected speaking style, the protracted and informal, open-air, mass meetings, the hymnody (innovative enough that Ralph Waldo Emerson believed there could be no history of New England without reference to Millerite hymns), and the prominence of women speakers.

In order to reawaken the Second Awakening, however, Millerites needed newer measures. Primary among these was their prophetic chronology. They defended the approximation of the world's end "about 1843" on scriptural grounds (the Lord had said only the day or the hour was in doubt, not the year) and on a sociological basis (preaching "the time" raised audiences and brought "results").[20] In addition, history delivered another Millerite measure, as prophecy involved more hindsight than foresight. At numerous historic dates from the rebuilding of the Jerusalem wall in 457 B.C. to the "wounding" of the Papacy in A.D. 1798, Miller set piles to underpin an overarching 2,300-year prophecy; the more piles the sturdier his support for biblical prophecy. Furthermore, prophetic astronomy served to impress Millerite audiences as "New England, being the most pious portion of the earth," according to one *Signs of the Times* editorial, "would naturally be the theatre of the darkening of the sun and moon, and the falling of the stars."[21] Still another Millerite measure, as impressive as any, was the lithographic, pictorial chart of apocalyptic symbolism that John Greenleaf Whittier, as an observant spectator at a Millerite camp meeting, said represented "Oriental types, figures, and mystic symbols, translated into staring Yankee realities, and exhibited like the beasts of a travelling menagerie."[22] Finally, the Great Tent, in an era when Finney competed for audiences with the circus, loomed large and spectacular against the skyline. Its 55-foot center pole, circumference of over 300 feet, and three to four thousand seating capacity typified Millerism as a millenarian sensation both too popular to contain in modest meetinghouses and too marginal to be tolerated there.

The Millerite attempt to revive a dispirited Second Awakening met, in time, with its own disappointments. If in 1840, Millerites hoped to serve as the Second Awakening's avant-garde whose newest measures might invoke the millennium, their millenarian failures in the spring of 1844 escalated the novelty to eccentricity, the avant-gardism to affectation. When Finney's earlier renovations had fallen short of the millennium and Miller's later revisions on them likewise were frustrated, novelty inflated to triviality.[23] Millerite time-setting charted this process. Until 1842, Millerites had inspired an apocalypticism that lacked specificity as to the time of the world's end. Resistance to a precise prediction had characterized Miller's career and even more adamantly that of his esteemed associate Henry Dana Ward. In May of 1842, however, the Boston Second Advent Conference placed the issue of a definite time at the top of its agenda and there, in the view of one historian, Adventism was transformed into Millerism.[24] Based on a Jewish calendar, the year 1843 prompted two popular dates for Christ's return, on March 21 and April 3, 1844. As the passing of these dates caused the "first disappointment," Millerites only sharpened and intensified their millenarianism. The so-called "seventh-month" faction, made up of youthful, under-educated "radicals," usurped or bypassed Millerite leadership, and by August predicted the Second Advent on October 22, 1844.[25]

In the late summer of 1844 these Millerites enjoyed as purely millenarian an expectatation of the world's end as any movement in American history. Their expectation predisposed them to the powerful outpouring of charismatic prophesyings, tongues, healings, and other "signs and wonders," which fulfilled the biblical promise for the "last days." Moreover, an increased stridency within the movement, in the face of public scoffing and ridicule, led them to the usual millenarian come-outerism, in which they decried the decadent and corrupt old order as they longed for the breaking in of a splendid and everlasting new order. Here the transitional moments between old order and new marked Millerites with ostensibly bizarre and unrealistic behavior. And with their backs turned on the world, they embraced each other in warm outbursts of communal emotion. Their gatherings convulsed with shouts, praises, weeping and "melting seasons of prayer." As late as September, Miller had been a dubious onlooker of much of this radical millenarianism. Basically moderate and rational by temperament, he not only disliked time-setting but reconciled himself neither to the charismatic aspects of the seventh-month Millerites nor to their come-outerism. In early October, however, he finally succumbed to their pleas for his endorsement by allowing that "if the Lord does not come in the next three weeks I will be twice as disappointed as I was in the Spring." He exclaimed, "I see a glory in the seventh month which I never saw before. . . . I am almost home. Glory! Glory!! Glory!!!"[26]

Miller's three exclamations of "Glory!" borrowed a familiar idiom from the Shouting Methodists who, along with Baptists, Presbyterians, and Christians conditioned Millerites for ecstasy and enthusiasm.[27] While Millerite leaders largely opposed charismatic phenomena, their inability to dampen the spirits of the rank and file betrayed itself in the fact that outsiders commonly criticized Millerites for such "fanaticism" as healings, speaking in tongues, visions, and prophesyings. One Millerite visionary, for example, John T. Mathews, saw himself as the "promised comforter."[28] Notably, several Millerite women received press coverage for their visions.[29] Both historians and anthropologists have noted the predominance of women in new prophetic movements and the disproportionately large number of female visionaries. Literally speaking, the "new man" frequently has been a new woman. Of course, women have endured sustained and systematic social disenfranchisement, and have gained much from a dissolution of the old rules and old structures and a new way of measuring "man" which allows for novelty, spontaneity, egalitarianism, and ecstasy.[30] Millerites lifted up one familiar passage in Joel 2, which promised that not only their sons but their daughters would prophesy. Moreover, their Second Awakening prelude had featured women, and the Christian Connection background of many of them further encouraged women in careers as Adventist preachers, typically accompanied on their circuits by a husband or father. After her marriage to James White, himself from the Christian Connection, Ellen

Gould Harmon, a frail, impressionable teenager, would emerge as the Seventh-day Adventist visionary. Though only one among numerous, anonymous seventh-month mediums, Ellen would eventually earn a place as the prophet-foundress of a major American sect.[31]

This latter-day Pentecost placed a divine sanction on the seventh-month movement which both emboldened it to decry an unsavory old order and aroused it to seek a new spiritual order. Orestes Brownson saw the kind of come-outerism that seized Millerism as an effort to "resist the existing order, to abjure its laws, and to attempt to introduce an entirely new order." He suggested that such radicalism represented nothing less than "the common faith of the country pushed to its last consequences."[32] Especially in 1843 and 1844, Millerites were scoffed, lampooned, ridiculed, and ostracized. Hooligans released greased pigs in their camp meeting crowds and collapsed tents on them. More ominously, threats to person and property along with actual violence victimized the Adventists as they had abolitionists and Mormons.[33] Far from demoralizing them, however, the opprobrium and persecution only legitimated them as God's remnant. Indeed, they so welcomed the oppressed role as to be suspected of inviting it upon themselves. The later the hour the more aggressively they attacked the churches and the clergy in a spirit sociologically indistinguishable from the come-outerism of abolitionists and feminists.[34] In addition to the usual aversion to Catholics and Unitarians, they eventually dismissed all evangelical Protestants as "Babylon." In his pamphlet of 1843 entitled "Come Out of Her, My People," Charles Fitch lifted the animosity to the level of doctrine by stating, "If you are a Christian, *come out of Babylon*. If you intend to be found a Christian when Christ appears, *come out of Babylon*, and come out *Now*. . . ."[35] Not only the religious but the material foundations of society seemed corrupt to Millerites, as they particularly lambasted, in Jacksonian fashion, crassly monopolistic wealth.[36]

Flaunting their alienation from the old older, many threw themselves into an excitedly extravagant no-rules state. Status-labeling fashions were discarded, reportedly, for nudity. Acquisitive materialism gave way to a "no work" doctrine that left crops unharvested. Class-consciousness was abandoned for the bizarre practice of crawling on all fours through the streets to become as little children for the kingdom. The inhibitions of Victorian society were relieved by "holy kissing" and "promiscuous" foot-washing. The limitations of bourgeois family life were exchanged for boundless sexual license and gluttony was replaced by self-starvation. Accordingly, Joshua Himes, Miller's agent and promoter, disparaged the seventh-month Millerites who "live in continual association in exciting, and social meetings," degenerating into "fleshly and selfish passions."[37]

Despite such an uncharitable appraisal of this millenarian limbo, as old a parody as first-century criticism of Christian millenarians, Millerites enjoyed a profound sense of community in this period. They sacrificed careers and all material goods to the cause, shared possessions among themselves in a primitive Christian communalism, lost family and friends in exchange for their warm, vital kinship, and occasionally suffered the heroic loss of life for their efforts. This sense of community led one of their number to ask, "Who can look at the bands of believers in the Lord's speedy return, scattered through the land, and not be reminded of the days when no man said that anything was his own, but they had all things in common? Love was the bond of union then, and blessed be the name of the Lord, he is a people now, organized under the very same creed."[38] "Brothers" and "sisters," celebrating the humble, egalitarian sense of community, restored as informal sacraments the early Christian foot-washing and "holy kiss."[39] If the Millerites were to survive and transcend these times, it would be by drawing upon the deeply satisfying spiritual resources of a community which had cost them so much of this world, but had earned them so much of the "other world."[40]

SEVENTH-DAY ADVENTIST CONSOLIDATION

Just as many aspects of antebellum American life became a permanent part of the national character and have surfaced in unsettling and stimulating ways throughout American history, Millerism contributed to the Seventh-day Adventist identity and has sustained an impact throughout Adventist history. For Adventism as a whole, as for the nation, the movement from diffusion to concentration, from spontaneity to order has been less a steady, uninterrupted flow in one direction than an ebb and flow between boundlessness and consolidation. Nevertheless, the shift from Millerism to Seventh-day Adventism represented as marked a transformation as had been experienced by American culture in the same period. Despite important continuity with Millerism, Adventism emphatically distanced itself from its millenarian origins. It remains for us to determine the nature of this development.

In accounting for the metamorphosis of Millerism into Seventh-day Adventism, it should be pointed out, at the outset, that this was hardly an inexorable process. Notwithstanding the occasional spectacular successes of resilient religious groups that have overcome millenarian beginnings, most notably Christianity itself, nothing proves more ephemeral than millenarian movements.[41] For the handful of Adventists following October 22, 1844, who hoped to build upon their Millerite experience rather than to abandon it, the prospects were at best uncertain. The key to transforming an effervescent apocalypticism into an established, complex religious system includes, above all, an elongation of the eschatological timetable. As long as a group sustains short-term, specific predictions of the end it remains volatile. With each passing of a prophetic date, conversions vaporize into apostasies, the promised harvest results in crop failure. The sooner the group can shed its short-term millenarianism, the sooner it can accommodate to the practical business of living life in the world.

The morning after October 22, 1844, marked the Great Disappointment for Millerites. The scroll the angel commanded them to eat in Revelation 10 had been sweet as honey in the mouth but bitter in the stomach. But despite their disillusionment, many Adventists continued to set times for the next seven years. Some earmarked the end for October 23 at 6:00 P.M., others for October 24. There were high expectations for exactly a year after the Great Disappointment on October 22, 1845, with 1846, 1847, and the seven-year point of 1851 also heating up the millenarianism.[42] What is so remarkable about post-disappointment Adventism, however, is not that it persisted in setting times, but that it did so for such a relatively brief period. Mormons, on the contrary, maintained a form of millenarian expectancy throughout much of the nineteenth century, and Jehovah's Witnesses looked for a series of end-time dates for about a half century. Consequently, both movements prolonged the period of ideological and institutional instability.[43] The fact that Seventh-day Adventists accomplished the transition to a largely stable, uniform organization more rapidly than either Mormons or Jehovah's Witnesses should be attributed to their more abbreviated millenarian phase.

Sociologist Bryan Wilson provides a typology of sectarian responses to the world which helps explain the Millerite-Seventh-day Adventist development. Among his seven sect types, Wilson's "revolutionist" and "conversionist" types seem most relevant to Adventism. In the revolutionist response, because of evil

> only the destruction of the world, of the natural, but more specifically of the social, order, will suffice to save men. This process of destruction must be supernaturally wrought, for men lack the power if not to destroy the world then certainly to re-create it.... In this case men may not claim to be saved now but do claim that they will *very soon* be saved: salvation is imminent. No subjective reorientation will affect the state of the world: its objective condition must be recognized.

For conversionists:

> The world is corrupt because men are corrupt: if men can be changed then the world will be changed. Salvation is seen not as available through objective agencies but only by a profoundly felt, supernaturally wrought transformation of the self. ... What men must do to be saved is to undergo emotional transformation—a conversion experience.... [This response] is not concerned simply with recruitment to a movement, but with the acquisition of the change of heart.[44]

For Wilson, these responses to the world represent hypothetical or pure types. Actual sects may adopt one or more approaches at any time, or may move from one response to another with the passage of time. Mutation of response may occur, for example, when events such as the failure of prophecy force the reappraisal of doctrine. Among the various kinds of sects, the conversionist type is most likely to undergo a process of denominationalization whereby it sloughs off specific sectarian characteristics and accommodates to the world.

Millerism blossomed in early-nineteenth-century America when evangelical Protestantism exhibited powerful conversionist impulses. As we have seen, the Millerites diverged from evangelicals by defining themselves along revolutionist-adventist lines, but conversionist elements of their own left the revolutionist response impure. Though Wilson does not class it as conversionist, he notes that Adventism has shown more of a denominational development than other separatist bodies which emphasize the Advent.[45] In fact, we shall see that Adventists drew upon their conversionist component in overcoming the failed prophecy of 1844 and establishing themselves on a permanent basis.

Suggesting ideological and institutional factors that have moved the group toward denominationalism, Wilson touches on the contours of Seventh-day Adventist stability, order, and consolidation. These include: First, the movement did not emerge simply as a separate Adventist body, but rather in disappointment about the Advent and after the reformulation of ideas; second, from the beginning, its millenarianism was one among several concerns, as the group not only preached the Advent but the conditions for it; third, these conditions were validated by divine inspiration, whereby the group acquired an independent source of inspiration, apart from the Scriptures, which might prompt development away from strict revolutionism; fourth, the movement established a professional ministry which opened the way to other specialized agencies that all disengaged it from more egalitarian origins; fifth, the accretion of concerns for education, diet, medical care, religious liberty, and sabbatarianism further advanced its denominationalization both ideologically and institutionally.[46]

For the remainder of the study, we shall trace ways in which Seventh-day Adventism, the product of Millerite boundlessness, achieved consolidation through the development of its doctrine and structure. Doctrinally, formulating Adventist eschatology, seventh-day sabbatarianism, and the prophetic gift (termed the "Spirit of prophecy") manifested this stablizing process. Institutionally, organizing the church, professionalizing the ministry, establishing the publication and the educational and medical programs all contributed to this solidification.

Most Millerites believed that the prediction of October 22, 1844, had involved a prophetic miscalculation. But the small fraction of their number who would become Seventh-day Adventists embraced the idea of Hiram Edson, an upstate New York farmer, that only the event, not the date, had been misinterpreted. Drawing upon their typological reading of the biblical sanctuary, these Adventists believed that on the fateful tenth day of the seventh month Christ, the "High Priest," had not come to earth but had moved from the holy to the most holy place in a heavenly sanctuary. The "cleansing of the sanctuary" had not referred to Christ's Second Coming but rather to the investigation of the sins of God's people in preparation for the end of the world.[47] With their doctrine of the sanctuary, not only had Adventists rationalized the delayed Advent but had erected a framework in which to stabilize and order life while awaiting the end.

By the 1840s, Americans had gained release from religious and cultural confinements which had bound them to a fixed place in God's cosmos and the social order. But as the external ties relaxed, the internal ties of conscience firmed their grip. The loss of religious and social limits had fostered an exceptionally strict moral code. In the transition from Puritanism to Victorianism, from piety to moralism, the individual came to bear the inordinate moral weight of character building.[48] Within this larger cultural context, Adventists found their "new mode of measuring the man," their "new integrity" in the sanctuary doctrine. The Puritanical emphasis on the Old Testament as a model of life and the sense of chosenness, the Wesleyan drive for sanctification and perfection, the stress on the law to the point of a Pelagian legalism all surfaced in their understanding of the sanctuary.

In a statement that implied a lengthening of the eschatological timetable, the Adventist visionary, Ellen White, linked the delay of the Advent to the need for morally improving God's people. "I saw that this message would not accomplish its work in a few short months," she wrote in 1859 to a second generation of Adventists. "It is designed to arouse the people of God, to discover them their backslidings, and to lead to zealous repentance, that they may be favored in the presence of Jesus, and be fitted for the loud cry of the third angel. . . ." She added, "If the message had been of as short duration as many of us supposed, there would have been no time for them to develop character."[49] With this jeremiad, the prophetess had ceased blaming the unfaithfulness of Catholics and Protestants for the delay of Christ's coming and turned on Adventists themselves. In this way Adventists were flung, in Perry Miller's phrase for the Puritans, onto a "wrack of introspection." Searching their own shortcomings in the shadow of Christ's heavenly "investigative judgment," Adventists had reduced the history of the world to a spiritual autobiography. Christ would not come until they had measured up to the new moral demands.

For a few years after the disappointment, the Seventh-day Adventist outgrowth of the seventh-month movement believed that only those who had accepted Millerism now could prepare themselves for the end. Early in 1845, two Adventist editors, Apollos Hale and Joseph Turner, convinced these Adventists that human destiny had been decided. The "door of mercy" had shut on all those that had spurned the Millerite "Midnight Cry." While harsh on nonbelievers, this "shut-door" doctrine confirmed the faith of believers that had bent but not broken in late 1844. The corollary of their faith in the meaning of October 22 confirmed the faithlessness of a scoffing world. God's presence in their movement could not have seemed so real, so palpable had the Scriptures spun them a fable, had their experience been a folly, had their detractors been correct. Adventists clung to their Millerite calculations based on more than muleheaded Yankee stubbornness or pride; Adventism had nurtured a powerfully moving experience which reinforced faith at a far deeper level than that of numerical certitude. Their community of fellow believers as much as their common belief encouraged them to hold fast.[50]

Between 1844 and 1851 or 1852, Adventists sustained their shut-door era in which they disavowed all evangelism, after the manner of antimission Baptists. Whatever community support they rallied in their post-disappointment period came from within their group as it then stood, not by adding to their number. Their moratorium on evangelism allowed Adventists a time in which to retrench and rebuild. But with the further delay of the Advent, and with the

unforseen influx of converts who had not come by way of Millerism, the shut
door creaked open as Adventists hesitatingly embarked on missionary expansion. Prompted by revolutionist and conversionist impulses, Adventists believed
God, in His mercy, had delayed the Advent to give them more time to save souls
for His coming. The missionary expansion could not have occurred without the
broadening and deepening of an institutional base, as we shall see shortly, which
further consolidated Adventism. At the same time, missionary outreach continued to expose Adventism to the boundlessness of the frontier, from western
New York to southern Michigan, from the Midwest to the Far West to Australia, and then much later to that perpetual study in instability, diversity, and
diffusion, the Third World.[51]

The doctrinal development which did the most to define Seventh-day
Adventism—to set the boundaries between it and other religious groups—was
seventh-day sabbatarianism. In 1846, Joseph Bates urged the practice on Adventists. Though a legacy of Seventh Day Baptists, the belief found somewhat
new expression within the context of Adventism's eschatological system. For
Adventists, sabbatarianism was imbued with pivotal significance; the Old
Testament law had been restored, and a symbol which looked backward to
creation projected forward as well to the new creation. The sabbath evoked
nothing less than the "new law" or the "new redemptive process" toward which
these millenarians moved. By way of seventh-day sabbath observance Adventists sought to attain that "new integrity," that "new mode of measuring the
man," indeed that "new man" capable of standing without sin at the Last Day.[52]
Burridge suggests that "if the new rules are merely a slight qualification on the
old rules they hardly deserve a millenarian frame. This demands a new beginning, a new whole-status with appropriate rules which transcends the old."[53]
Nothing contributed more to the Adventist identity on a week-by-week basis
than the casuistry of seventh-day sabbatarianism, the matter of when and how
the day should be observed. But this observance in itself would not have been
enough of an innovation to warrant a new culture-in-the-making. Evangelical
Sunday keepers themselves hoped for strict sabbath reform, which reflected the
practice if not the occasion of seventh-day keepers. The "new rule" of seventh-
day sabbatarianism established boundaries between Adventists and non-
Adventists at numerous fundamental points: Adventists from Catholics, whom
they blamed for changing the day of worship from Saturday to Sunday; Adventists from Protestants, whom they saw seeking "blue law" legislation on behalf
of Sunday observance; Adventists and trade unionists, who "conspired" with
Catholics and Protestants for Sunday laws to shorten the work week; Adventists
and evolutionists, who destroyed the literal creation week for which the Sabbath
served as a memorial.[54]

Late in 1844, Ellen Harmon began having visions which validated the
sanctuary, shut-door, and sabbath doctrines. Her hometown of Portland,
Maine, had been notorious for the "continual introduction of *visionary non-
sense*" and nothing proved more spontaneous and boundless than charisma. In
large camp-meeting crowds or in small meetings in houses or barns, the "gift of

prophecy" poured itself out plentifully. Not only was it no respecter of persons, as women along with men received the Spirit, but it seemed to overflow all confinements. Shouts from the "slain" were heard everywhere as were sighs from swooners. Ellen might have faded into this inchoate charismatic background and entirely disappeared had not James White married her, in August of 1846, and served not only as her husband and protector, but her promoter and publisher. She the visionary, exhorter, and counselor and he the organizer and entrepreneur combined in the "first family" of Adventism both boundlessness and consolidation, as together they traversed the hazardous period of "no rules" and established "new rules."

While the Adventist brethren functioned as the theologians, biblical exegetes, and organization men, the prophetess evoked an intuitive, Romantic "gift of prophecy" which exerted more of a vicarious influence than direct, organizational power. In something of a "sex-war" between husband and wife, James declared, as early as 1851, that in order to be effective the "gifts" must be held within limits by a guardian, rather than run wild. For a four-year period, in fact, he excluded Ellen's trance writing from the *Adventist Review and Sabbath Herald*, the Adventist organ. The heavy hand of James as organization man could not hold down the irrepressible spirit of the visionary, however, and by the mid-1850s, Ellen had asserted herself again. But Adventism had channeled its exuberant charismatic origins through a single conduit.[55]

As improbable a source as the doctrine of conditional mortality further illustrated the Adventist shift from disorderly enthusiasm to an ordered rationalism. This doctrine of soul-sleep, introduced to Adventists by the Millerite George Storrs, represented not only the anti-Calvinist rejection of eternal punishment (part of the "old rules") but an effort to obliterate Spiritualism (an outgrowth of the "no rules" era). James White had noted the "startling fact" that the period after 1844 saw "the rise of foul spirits." J. N. Andrews, Adventist intellectual and writer, concurred that "an innumerable host of demons are spreading themselves over the whole country, flooding the churches and religious bodies of the land to a very great extent."[56] The encroachment of female spiritualist mediums sociologically identical to Mrs. White (her "counterfeit" in Adventist terms) aroused the visionary's severest criticism. The doctrine of soul-sleep therefore sought to silence the cacophonic voices of the spirit world by disclaiming their existence.[57]

Turning from the doctrinal to the institutional transformation from boundlessness to consolidation, we find that Adventists, along with Americans in general at this time, struggled to impose social control on an undisciplined culture rampant with individualism. The 1850s were less the times for prophets and reformers than for planners and organizers. The millennial enthusiasm that sparked the reforms of the preceding era gave way to regulated, systemized, professional reformism. In 1859, Ellen White reflected the times by commenting that "God is well pleased with the efforts of his people in trying to move with system and order in his work. I saw that there should be order in the church of God, and arrangement in regard to carrying forward successfully the last great message of mercy to the world." Two years later she suggested that "some have feared that our churches would become Babylon if they should organize [but] unless the churches are so organized that they can carry out and enforce order, they have nothing to hope for in the future."[58]

By 1859, Sabbath-keeping Adventists had passed from the anticlericalism of Millerism to the ordination of clergy. The practical problems of providing for the ministry were met with a program of "systematic benevolence" which would be replaced in time by tithing members. The Adventists grew from a "scattered flock" of 200 members in 1850 to a membership of 3,500 at their formal organization in 1863. By then there were 22 ordained ministers and 125 churches. The organization of the church resulted from the pragmatic need to incorporate the publishing enterprise. The free-spirited self-publishing of Millerite periodicals had centralized in Adventism in the single denominational press which began editing the *Second Advent Review and Sabbath Herald* in 1850. By the fall of 1860, James White, the publisher, urged incorporation so that the church rather than a private party might own the press. There was the chance, he argued, that the publishing house or a meetinghouse might revert to a winery. This called for a legal organization of the church which was done under the name "Seventh-day Adventist." The history of Adventism had been a matter of "publish or perish" since Mrs. White envisioned "a little paper" that would cast its "streams of light" throughout the world.[59] Such lofty spiritual vision, however, had led to the practical consideration of organization. As far as ecclesiastical bureaucracy was concerned, in the beginning was the word.

If publishing instigated organization, entry into medicine exerted as profound an impact on the nature of that organization as anything in Adventism. From the healings of Millerism, Adventism grew to establish a vast network of sanitariums and hospitals throughout the world. This development began in 1866, in the wake of an epidemic of illness among church leaders and Mrs. White's discovery of "water cure" and vegetarianism. Adventists built the Western Health Reform Institute in that year and began publishing the *Health Reformer*, a monthly magazine. Adventism would make still another leap, in the distant future of the twentieth century, from counter-establishment health reform to establishment medicine. This shift led, first, to a reorganized medical school, then to the accreditation of colleges to feed the medical school, then to professional seminary education to keep the ministry apace with medicine. And this general upgrading of education and professionalism was accompanied by a social and economic upward mobility in Adventism at large. The blend of material and spiritual impulses which characterized mid-Victorianism played itself out in the movement, as Adventists came a long way, and rather quickly, from the sacrificial Millerites.[60]

Both for American culture and for its Adventist subculture, institutional consolidation has evolved steadily. Yet spiritually it has never satisfied. Indeed, sociologists inform us that nothing proves more inimical to sectarian fervor than bureaucracy. Thus a new generation rebels against the closed, claustrophobic system by invoking the open, spontaneous spirit of boundlessness. The new rules of one era become the old rules of the next and millenarian transformation begins again. If Adventist developments were viewed as stages of life, Millerism provided a creative, if quixotic, adolescence that a more mature, stable sect outgrew but still recalled with nostalgia. In fact, Adventists periodically have precipitated a form of "mid-life crisis" by seeking, usually without lasting success, to recover their millenarian adolescence. Throughout the nineteenth century, Adventist "revivalists" were measured for spiritual authenticity against the Millerite revival. The prophetess White, who remembered 1844 as "the happiest year of my life," felt that the pioneering generation of the Millerite experience deserved to be venerated in regard to doctrinal and institutional matters by latecomers of shallower memory in the movement.[61] Yet despite such wistfulness for a lost past, Adventist development has benefited both from periods of movement, spontaneity, and disorder, and from those of stability and structure. Only through consolidation has Adventism continued to exist, but only the spirit of boundlessness has made that existence worthwhile.

NOTES

This essay appeared in a shorter and somewhat different form in "From Millerism to Seventh-day Adventism: 'Boundlessness to Consolidation,'" *Church History* 55 (March, 1986).

1. *New Heaven, New Earth: A Study of Millenarian Activities* (New York: Shocken Books, 1969),. esp. pp. 105–116.
2. Ibid., p. 13.
3. Ibid., p. 112.
4. For his notable interpretive study of American awakenings as "revitalization movements," see William G. McLoughlin, *Revivals, Awakenings, and Reform: An Essay on Religion and Social Change in America, 1607–1977* (Chicago: University of Chicago Press, 1978).
5. Klaus J. Hansen makes this application in *Mormonism and the American Experience* (Chicago: University of Chicago Press, 1981), pp. 48–50.
6. For the use of anthropological perspectives in the comparative study of Mormonism, Shakerism, and Oneida Perfectionism, see Lawrence Foster, *Religion and Sexuality: Three American Communal Experiments of the Nineteenth Century* (New York: Oxford University Press, 1981).
7. *From Boundlessness to Consolidation: The Transformation of American Culture, 1848–1860* (Ann Arbor, Mich.: William L. Clements Library, 1969), passim. For other characterizations of Victorianism as a transitional age, see Daniel Walker Howe, "Victorian Culture in America," in Daniel Walker Howe, ed., *Victorian America* (Philadelphia: University of Pennsylvania Press, 1976), pp. 3–28; George Frederickson, *The Inner Civil War* (New York: Harper & Row, 1965); for a single illustration of a changing Victorian, see William G. McLoughlin, *The Meaning of Henry Ward Beecher: An Essay on the Shifting Values of Mid-Victorian America, 1840–1870* (New York: Alfred A. Knopf, 1970); for a superb analysis of Victorian change in Britain, see Walter Houghton, *The Victorian Frame of Mind* (New Haven, Conn.: Yale University Press, 1957).
8. George Shepperson raises a similar point in "The Comparative Study of Millenar-

ian Movements," in Sylvia L. Thrupp, ed., *Millennial Dreams in Action: Studies in Revolutionary Religious Movements* (New York: Schocken Books, 1970), pp. 44–52.

9. For the best study of Millerism and its relation to popular culture, see David L. Rowe, *Thunder and Trumpets: Millerites and Dissenting Religion in Upstate New York, 1800–1850* (Chico, Calif.: Scholars Press, 1985).

10. Ibid., pp. 56–62. Perry Miller discusses Newton's cosmology in *Errand Into the Wilderness* (Cambridge, Mass.: Harvard University Press, 1956), pp. 217–239.

11. Perry Miller, *The Life of the Mind in America: From the Revolution to the Civil War* (New York: Harcourt, Brace and World, 1965), pp. 73ff.

12. The more complex reading of Jacksonianism may be found in Marvin Meyers, *Jacksonian Persuasion: Politics and Belief* (New York: Random House, 1960); and Daniel J. Boorstin, *The Americans: The National Experience* (New York: Random House, 1965).

13. Chalres G. Finney, *Memoirs of Rev. Charles G. Finney* (New York: A. S. Barnes, 1876), pp. 370ff.

14. Whitney R. Cross, *The Burned-over District: The Social and Intellectual History of Enthusiastic Religion in Western New York, 1800–1850* (New York: Harper & Row, 1965), p. 320; Timothy L. Smith, *Revivalism and Social Reform: American Protestantism on the Eve of the Civil War* (New York: Harper & Row, 1965), p. 228.

15. Everett N. Dick offers the best discussion of fanaticism in the movement in "The Adventist Crisis of 1843–1844" (Ph.D. dissertation, University of Wisconsin, 1930).

16. Sidney Mead, *The Lively Experiment: The Shaping of Christianity in America* (New York: Harper & Row, 1963), pp. 113–121.

17. Francis D. Nichol, *The Midnight Cry: A Defense of the Character and Conduct of William Miller and the Millerites, Who Mistakenly Believed that the Second Coming of Christ Would Take Place in the Year 1844* (Washington, D.C.: Review and Herald Publishing Association, 1944), pp. 174–185.

18. On Miller, see P. Gerard Damsteegt, *Foundations of the Seventh-day Adventist Message and Mission* (Grand Rapids, Mich.: William B. Eerdmans, 1977), p. 42; for Bates's comment, see Joseph Bates, *The Autobiography of Joseph Bates* (Battle Creek, Mich.: Seventh-day Adventist Publishing Association, 1868), p. 262.

19. Isaac C. Wellcome, *History of the Second Advent Message and Mission, Doctrine and People* (Yarmouth, Maine: Isaac C. Wellcome, 1874), p. 87.

20. Damsteegt, *Foundations of the Seventh-day Adventist Message and Mission*, p. 37.

21. Ibid, p. 53.

22. For the complete essay on his visit to a Millerite camp meeting, see "Father Miller," in *The Writings of John Greenleaf Whittier*, Riverside ed., *Prose Works* (Boston: Houghton, Mifflin & Co., 1889), 5: 419–427; reprinted as "The World's End," in *Adventist Heritage*, July, 1974, 1: 14–17.

23. I borrow this point, for my own somewhat different purposes, from a comment by Jonathan Miller in Frank Kermode, *The Sense of an Ending: Studies in the Theory of Fiction* (London: Oxford University Press, 1967), p. 121.

24. David T. Arthur, "Come Out of Babylon: A Study of Millerite Separatism and Denominationalism" (Ph.D. dissertation, University of Rochester, 1970), pp. 31–33.

25. See David T. Arthur, "After the Great Disappointment: To Albany and Beyond," *Adventist Heritage*, January, 1974, 1: 5–10, 58.

26. Cited in Rowe, *Thunder and Trumpets*, p. 136.

27. Winthrop Hudson describes Shouting Methodist enthusiasm in his "Shouting Methodists," *Encounter*, Winter, 1968, 19: 73–84.

28. Rowe, *Thunder and Trumpets*, p. 65.

29. Frederick G. Hoyt enumerates the Millerite women visionaries in "The Millerite Movement in Maine: Cradle of Seventh-day Adventism" (presidential address to the Association of Western Adventist Historians, Angwin, Calif., April, 1982), p. 8.

30. For a social anthropologist's comment on the relation of women to ecstasy, consult I. M. Lewis, *Ecstatic Religion: An Anthropological Study of Spirit Possession and Shamanism* (Baltimore: Penguin Books, 1971). Ronald A. Knox finds corroboration for Lewis's findings in Christian history in his *Enthusiasm: A Chapter in the History of Religion, with Special Reference to the XVII and XVIII Centuries* (Oxford: Clarendon Press, 1951).

31. On the place of women in early-nineteenth-century evangelicalism, see Nancy F. Cott, *The Bonds of Womanhood: "Woman's Sphere" in New England, 1780–1835* (New Haven: Yale University Press, 1977); and Kathryn Kish Sklar, *Catherine Beecher: A Study in American Domesticity* (New Haven: Yale University Press, 1973).

32. Cited in Rowe, *Thunder and Trumpets*, p. 112. For the come-outer story in Millerism, see David Arthur, "Come Out of Babylon," and his "Millerism" in Edwin S. Gaustad, ed., *The Rise of Adventism: Religion and Society in Mid-Nineteenth Century America* (New York: Harper & Row, 1974), pp. 154–172.

33. For mobocracy in relation to abolitionists, see Leonard L. Richards, *Gentlemen of Property and Standing: Anti-Abolition Mobs in Jacksonian America* (London: Oxford University Press, 1970); Everett Dick reviews the assaults on Millerites in "Advent Camp Meetings of the 1840s," *Adventist Heritage*, Winter, 1977, 4: 3–10.

34. Lewis Perry relates the come-outer spirit of abolitionism in *Radical Abolitionism: Anarchy and the Government of God in Antislavery Thought* (Ithaca, N.Y.: Cornell University Press, 1973); the rise of feminism is tied to abolitionism in Aileen S. Kraditor, *Means and Ends in American Abolitionism: Garrison and His Critics on Strategy and Tactics, 1834–1850* (New York: Pantheon Books, 1969).

35. Cited by David Arthur in *The Rise of Adventism*, p. 167.

36. Rowe, *Thunder and Trumpets*, pp. 75–76.

37. Ibid., p. 147.

38. Ibid., p. 113. For an illuminating anthropological discussion of this compelling sense of community or in his term "communitas," see Victor W. Turner, *The Ritual Process: Structure and Anti-Structure* (Chicago: Aldine, 1969); Lawrence Foster skillfully appropriates Turner's theoretical framework in *Religion and Sexuality*.

39. See Ron Graybill, "Foot Washing and Fanatics," *Insight*, January 2, 1973, 4: 9–13.

40. John Gager explains the survival of Christianity beyond its millenarian origins in these terms in his *Kingdom and Community: The Social World of Early Christianity* (Englewood Cliffs, N.J.: Prentice-Hall, 1975); Gager relies for his explanation on Leon Festinger, Henry W. Riecken, and Stanley Schachter, *When Prophecy Fails: A Social and Psychological Study of a Modern Group that Predicted the Destruction of the World* (New York: Harper & Row, 1964).

41. See Gager, *Kingdom and Community*.

42. Ronald L. Numbers, *Prophetess of Health: A Study of Ellen G. White* (New York: Harper & Row, 1976), pp. 26–27.

43. See Joseph F. Zygmunt, "Prophetic Failure and Chiliastic Identity: The Case of Jehovah's Witnesses," *American Journal of Sociology*, May, 1970, 75: 926–948; on Mormonism, see Jan Shipps's chapter, "The Millennial Vision Transformed," in her *Mormonism: The Story of a New Religious Tradition* (Urbana: University of Illinois Press, 1985), pp. 131–145.

44. *Magic and the Millennium: A Sociological Study of Religious Movements of Protest Among Tribal and Third-World Peoples* (New York: Harper & Row, 1973), pp. 22–26.

45. See his "Sect or Denomination: Can Adventism Maintain Its Identity?" *Spectrum*, Spring, 1975, 7: 34–43.

46. Ibid., p. 39.

47. On the Adventist sanctuary doctrine, see Roy Adams, *The Sanctuary Doctrine:*

Three Approaches in the Seventh-day Adventist Church, Doctrinal series, vol. 1 (Berrien Springs, Mich.: Andrews University Press, 1981).

48. See Joseph Haroutunian, *Piety vs. Moralism* (New York: Henry Holt & Co., 1932); on Victorians as character builders, see Daniel Walker Howe, ed., *Victorian America*, pp. 21–23.

49. *Testimonies for the Church*, 9 vols. (Mountain View, Calif., n.d.), *1*: 186; see also Ellen G. White, *The Great Controversy Between Christ and Satan* (Mountain View, Calif.: Pacific Press Publishing Association, 1911), pp. 479–491.

50. On the shut door, see Numbers, *Prophetess of Health*, pp. 14–17; for an alternative view, see Damsteegt, *Foundations of the Seventh-day Adventist Message and Mission*, passim.

51. Roy Branson provides an excellent historical and theological discussion of the move from Millerite to Seventh-day Adventist eschatology in "Adventists Between the Times: The Shift in the Church's Eschatology," *Spectrum*, September 1976, *8*: 15–26.

52. See Raymond Cottrell, "The Sabbath in the New World," in Kenneth Strand, ed., *The Sabbath in Scripture and History* (Washington, D.C.: Review and Herald Publishing Association, 1982), pp. 244–263.

53. Burridge, *New Heaven, New Earth*, p. 169.

54. See Jonathan Butler and Ronald Numbers, "The Seventh-day Adventists," in Mircea Eliade, ed., *The Encyclopedia of Religion* (New York: Macmillan, 1986).

55. The best scholarly introduction to Ellen White is Ronald Numbers, *Prophetess of Health*. See also Ronald Graybill, "The Power of Prophecy: Ellen G. White and the Women Religious Founders of the Nineteenth Century" (Ph.D. dissertation, Johns Hopkins University, 1983).

56. Cited in Damsteegt, *Foundations of the Seventh-day Adventist Message and Mission*, p. 183.

57. For her comment on spiritualism, see White, *The Great Controversy*, pp. 551–562.

58. Cited in Branson, "Adventists Between the Times," p. 21.

59. For a discussion of Adventist organization, see the best narrative text on Adventist history, Richard Schwarz, *Light Bearers to the Remnant* (Mountain View, Calif.: Pacific Press Publishing Association, 1979), pp. 86–103.

60. On Adventists and health, see Numbers, *Prophetess of Health*; also, Richard Schwarz, *John Harvey Kellogg, M.D.* (Nashville, Tenn.: Southern Publishing Association, 1970).

61. *Testimonies for the Church*, *1*: 54. For Ellen White's appeal to tradition in late-nineteenth-century Adventism, see Ron Graybill, "Ellen White's Role in the Resolution of Doctrinal Conflicts in Adventist History" (duplicated, Washington, D.C., 1980).

Appendix

The Disappointment Remembered

The Recollections of Luther Boutelle,
Hiram Edson, and Henry B. Bear

LUTHER BOUTELLE, a Millerite lecturer from Groton, Massachusetts, later became a leader of the Advent Christian Church, a denomination that emerged from the main body of ex-Millerites. The following account from his auto-biography, *Sketch of the Life and Religious Experience of Eld. Luther Boutelle* (Boston: Advent Christian Publication Society, 1891), pp. 62–72, describes his activities and emotions in 1844.

As WE ENTERED UPON the year 1844, the interest, instead of decreasing, kept up; and during the summer the number of Campmeetings, Grovemeetings and Conferences increased, and the workers in the Lord's vineyard had all that they could do.

In the early part of the summer our attention was directed to the fall as the time for the Lord to come, according to the types in the Old Testament, which began to be studied and preached. By July there was such a concentration of thought among the strong ones on time, that it was called "the midnight cry." Thus a new impetus was created, and the work of holding meetings and preaching was increased. As we fell, one after another, into the current belief that the fall would witness the coming of our Lord, it became in faith a certainty—we believed it with our whole souls. Thus the cry, "Behold, the bridegroom cometh!" was, by the "time argument," made to end in the fall of 1844, Jewish time, tenth day of the seventh month, supposed to be Oct. 20, 21, or 22. This brought us to a definite time, and in coming up to it, the works of Adventists demonstrated their faith and honesty, not to be questioned. As they moved on with the point of time before them, all grew more enthusiastic. Crops were left unharvested, their owners expecting never to want what they had raised. Men paid up their debts. Many sold their property to help others to pay their debts, who could not have done it themselves. Beef cattle were slaughtered and distributed among the poor. At no time since "the day of pentecost was fully come" had there been the like—a day when that pentecost was so completely duplicated as in 1844, when Adventism prevailed and reigned.

There was a great stir and talk, in many places, about putting the Millerites under guardianship. But this did not cause any to go back on their faith. They were firm and held fast, believing they should speak and act. Thus they were known by their fruits. There was some fanaticism, but the body of Adventists were sober, honest, a holy people, with strong faith and ready to meet their Lord—to see the King in his beauty. As the time to which all looked drew near, the Bible was studied even more, and a fuller consecration made. There was a harmony that made us a unit at this time, and the representatives of Adventism and the flock were all one.

THE GREAT DISAPPOINTMENT

The *Advent Herald*, the *Midnight Cry*, and other Advent papers, periodicals, pamphlets, tracts, leaflets, voicing the coming glory, were scattered broadcast and everywhere, like autumn leaves in the forest. Every house was visited by them. They were angels of mercy sent in love for the salvation of men. Everything now began to converge to a point. October was the closing time of probation! the judgment and rewards! A mighty effort through the Spirit and the word preached was made to bring sinners to repentance, and to have the wandering return. All were awake to this great end—salvation. The tenth day of the seventh month drew nigh. With joy all the ready ones anticipated the day. Solemn, however, were the last gatherings. Those of a family who were ready to meet the Lord, expecting an eternal separation from those who were not ready. Husbands and wives, parents and children, brothers and sisters separated, and that forever! The leading preachers of Adventism had all endorsed the tenth day of the seventh month as the time when the Lord should be expected. On Oct. 6, Mr. Miller accepted the argument as true, and wrote an endorsement to it.

Geo. Storrs, Sept. 24, 1844, in the *Bible Examiner* said, "I take my pen with feelings such as I never had before. Beyond a doubt in my mind the tenth day of the seventh month will witness the revelation of our Lord Jesus Christ from heaven."

The *Voice of Truth*, of Oct. 2, stated that Elders Marsh, Galusha, Peavy and others had endorsed it.

In closing the *Advent Herald* office on the 16th of October, an immense edition of that paper was issued for free distribution in all parts of the land. This was considered the last edition ever to be published.

We now give an extract from Bro. S. Bliss. He wrote, "The time immediately preceding the 22nd of October was one of great calmness of mind and pleasurable expectation on the part of those who regarded the point of time with interest. There was a nearness of approach to God, and a sacredness of communion with him, to which those who experienced it will ever recur with pleasure. During the last ten days secular business was, for the most part, suspended, and those who looked for the advent gave themselves to the work of preparation for the event as they would for death, were they on a bed of sickness, expecting soon to close their eyes on earthly scenes forever."—*History of the Second Advent Message*.

These quotations harmonize with what I knew to be at the time. Such a concentration of thought; such a oneness of faith was never before witnessed; certainly not in modern times. All that did speak spoke the same things. Solemn, yet joyful. Jesus coming! we to meet him! Meetings everywhere were being held. Confessions made, wrongs righted; sinners inquiring what they should do to be saved. Those who were not with us were mightily effected [*sic*]. Some were exceedingly frightened with awful forebodings.

But the 22nd of October passed, making unspeakably sad the faithful and longing ones; but causing the unbelieving and wicked to rejoice. All was still. No *Advent Herald*; no meetings as formerly. Everyone felt lonely, with hardly a desire to speak to anyone. Still in the cold world! No deliverance—the Lord not come! No words can express the feelings of disappointment of a true Adventist then. Those only who experienced it can enter into the subject as it was. It was a humiliating thing, and we all felt it alike. All were silent, save to inquire, "Where are we?" and "What next?" All were housed and searching their Bibles to learn what to do. In some few places they soon began to come together to watch for some development of light, relative to our disappointment.

Not quite content with being housed, after such stirring times, I went to Boston. Found the *Advent Herald* office closed, and all still. I next went to New Bedford. Found the brethren in a confused state. Had a few meetings; comforted those who came as best I could, telling them to hold fast, for I believed there would be a good come out of this matter. Returning from New Bedford to Boston, I found the office of our *Herald* open, and Bro. Bliss there. He said he had hardly been from his house since the time passed. He inquired if there were any meetings being held. I told him there was to be one in the city that evening, and that in other places they were coming together to comfort one another. Some fanaticism was seen, but the many were sober watchers for their Lord.

I learned of a company that had come together to stay until the Lord came. I felt like visiting them. Accordingly I took a carriage ride to the place. I found about seventy believers in a large house, living there and having meetings daily. They had put all their money in a milk-pan, and when they paid for anything they took the money from the pan. All was common stock. We held a meeting with them and advised them as best we could to keep the faith and separate, and see to their individual interests, and those of their families, which advice they kindly took, and very soon separated, going each to his or her calling.

After a time in looking over the way the Lord had led us, and bearing the reproach in consequence of our failure, we found there was to be a disappointment in the fulfillment of the parable. The words of Jesus were, "While the bridegroom tarried, they all slumbered and slept." From the first of our experience as Adventists, we believed we were fulfilling the parable by going forth to meet the Lord in our faith and preaching of his coming, but we did not see that the Bridegroom—the Lord—would not come when we expected him. But it was not long after our disappointment before the light began to break in upon us, and we saw there was to be a waiting time, a midnight before the Lord would come. Turning to Rev., tenth chapter, we saw that after the "little book" was eaten, and sweet in the mouth, there was a bitterness to be experienced. Our disappointment was bitter, and it was by eating the word of God, or the little book. Since that time a new inspiration has been given us, and we have done even more than we did before our disappointment; for the little book was to "prophesy again before many peoples, and nations, and tongues, and kings." Thus the word of God is fulfilled by us, and we can still repeat:

> In eighteen hundred forty-four,
> We thought the curse would be no more.
> The things of earth we left behind,
> To meet the Saviour of mankind.
> With many we took the parting hand,
> Till meeting in a better land.
> The day passed by—no tongue can tell
> The gloom that on the faithful fell.
> That what it meant they hardly knew
> But to their Lord they quickly flew.
> They searched the Word, and not in vain,
> For comfort there they did obtain.
> They found "the bridge" they had passed o'er;
> Then they rejoiced and grieved no more.
> Their faith was firm in that blest Book,
> And still for Jesus they did look.

RESUMING THE WORK WITH GOOD COURAGE

And now a new era was begun. These divine utterances were heard with such distinctness that it was easy to believe them; and with a zeal equal to our former one, we took hold of the work now given us to do. We found that the truth was not to be all learned at once. Thus we came into the tarrying time. This helped us to bear our disappointment, and put our feet on solid land. Prophecy again rang in our ears, and we were now on the wing again, and the world found Millerism, which they buried, still alive. So while the Bridegroom tarried, meat in due season was to be given. With the assurance of light and divine help we quickened our pace in itinerating, and soon found the whole body was breathing more freely. We as a people righted up, and the sound of rejoicing was heard. The scattered Advent body was gathered again, and commenced anew their work of love.

In Jan. 1845, the *Advent Herald* appeared again in the field, acknowledging our disappointment, but urging the necessity of keeping the signs of the Lord's soon coming before the people. Thus encouraged, our meetings, Conferences and Campmeetings were resumed with the former interest, while the way opened wonderfully before us for missionary work, scattering the light of the gospel in all directions. We now had calls as many as we could attend to.

HIRAM EDSON, a Millerite farmer from Port Gibson, New York, after 1844 joined the small group of sabbatarians who formed the Seventh-day Adventist Church. The following recollection, from an undated manuscript fragment in the possession of the Heritage Room, Andrews University Library, begins with the evidence that convinced him of the truth of Millerism and ends in mid-sentence in a discussion of the seventh-day Sabbath.

I BEGAN TO MUSE on this wise; If all this is the fruit of the new doctrine, the evidence is clear that it is from heaven; for it is written, "by their fruits ye shall know them." "A corrupt tree cannot bring forth good fruit;" And thus this question was settled with me.

In this incident of my experience I also learned an additional lesson, namely, that God was ready and willing to hear and answer prayer for the sick, and to stretch forth his hand to heal and raise them up, and restore them to health. Since which time, I have shared in, and witnessed many incidents of like character.

The next morning the physician came to visit his patient, and to his great astonishment met him out of doors walking up and down the lane, praising God with a loud voice. He gazed and listened with wonder and astonishment at the narration of what God had wrought. Pale, and trembling he returned home, relating what he had seen and heard, his residence being but a few doors from the church where the lectures were given.

When Monday evening came [both?] our [families?] went to the prayer meeting, appointed the night before at the close of the lectures. The meeting house, though large, was filled to overflowing as it had been during the lectures. It was judged best to have a short sermon, and then a season for testimonies. The brother who had been healed, and myself, bore our testimonies: what God had wrought for us; which had its influence on the minds of the congregation. Before the close of the meeting, our preacher very hesitatingly gave a faint invitation, that, if there were any in the congregation who felt like seeking the Lord, and desired prayer for them, if they would make it manifest by rising on their feet we would engage in prayer for them; when some eighty at once arose, without being urged. And thus I saw literally fulfilled, what was presented before me the night before, when in prayer before the manger. But the voice which said, "Go talk the truth to your neighbors, and fellow men," and my promise to do so, was lost sight of, and did not come into mind.

I was endeavoring to walk carefully before the Lord. I did not want to loose [sic] the victory, the liberty, and freedom I had been sharing. But notwithstanding all my efforts darkness was stealing over me; the heavens became as brass, and I could find no answer from God—I knew not why, until I sought the Lord in persevering secret prayer, and, in earnest, to know what intervened and hid his face from me. At length while in prayer in the forest my mind was carried back to the voice which said, "Go talk the truth to your neighbors," which I had promised to do, and that I could not share the light of his countenance, or freedom of his spirit, until I lifted that cross and discharged that duty. This seemed the heaviest cross which had ever been presented for me to lift. It seemed more than I could consent to do; but no relief came, till, at length, I consented to make the effort. And not until I reached the third family did much victory or freedom return to me, but here the cloud seemed to break, and old and young, the greyheaded and youth, were melted to tears; expressing their desire for saving grace. As I moved forward in this work day times; and attending the evening meetings; for they were protracted, until it was claimed that between three and four hundred professed conversion, the cross grew lighter, or, my strength increased in bearing it. There was one family I had passed several times without calling on them. The head of the family was dissipated, and I thought it would be but casting pearls before swine; so I passed them by.

After laboring as above, night and day, I became worn and felt I needed rest. I decided not to attend meeting that evening, also, not to make any more calls but go directly home and obtain rest. On passing the above named house I was stopped in the road opposite the house, by some unseen power, and could not make progress. I know not what was the cause, and began to ponder whether it was duty to enter the house. While thus waiting a shadowy form in human shape stood before me, and led toward the house, at which I said, Can there be duty to call here? The form repeated the lead toward the house twice, or thrice, and I followed, gathering assuredly that the Lord's angel was accompanying me and leading me in the way I should go. I entered the house, was received kindly, had a free time talking and praying with them, learnd that they were backsliders, and were desiring to return unto the Lord. The above revival and ingathering of souls, being the result and legitimate fruit of the above lectures, was additional evidence that this new doctrine was from heaven; for it is a good tree that brings forth good fruit. "A corrupt tree cannot bring forth good fruit."

During what is called the seventh month movement, in 1844, myself and several other Brn. were engaged in circulating publications on the coming of Christ, day times, and holding meetings at my own private house evenings. As we were about to commence our evening meeting on one occasion, a two horse waggon load of entire strangers came; and after preparing seats for them we commenced our meeting by singing, "Here o'er the earth as a stranger I roam, Here is no rest, is no rest." It was sung with the spirit and with the understanding, and the spirit which accompanied the singing gave to it a keen edge, and before the hymn was sung through, the entire company of strangers were so deeply convicted that rather than bear the reproach of being convicted, or converted at a Millerite meeting, they all started to leave the house. One man and his wife succeeded in getting out of doors; but the third one fell upon the threshhold; the fourth, the fifth, and so on, till the most of the company were thus slain by the power of God. And such agonizing cries and pleading for mercy, is not often witnessed. Some thirteen, or more, were converted before the meeting closed. The man and his wife who left the house labored hard to persuade the rest of their company to leave at once for home; but not succeeding, and rather than remain through the meeting they went home on foot in a dark night, a distance of five, or six miles, carrying a child a year old. But this was not their heaviest burden. Their conviction was too deep to be easily shaken off; they were back again at the next evening meeting found pardon, and peace in believing. And, "so, mightily grew to word of God and prevailed."

Passing over other like manifestations of the power of God, we glance at our disappointment at the tenth of the seventh month, 1844. Having the true cry, Behold the Bridegroom cometh, on the tenth day of the seventh month, and, having been early taught by modern orthodoxy that the coming of the Bridegroom to the marriage would be fulfilled in the personal second advent of Christ to this earth, (which was a mistaken idea) we confidently expected to see Jesus Christ and all the holy angels with him; and that his voice would call up Abraham, Isaac, and Jacob, and all the ancient worthies, and near and dear friends which had been torn from us by death, and that our trials and sufferings with our earthly pilgrimage would close, and we should be caught up to meet our coming Lord to be forever with him to inhabit the bright golden mansions in the golden home city, prepared for the redeemed. Our expectations were raised high, and thus we looked for our coming Lord until the clock tolled 12 at midnight. The day had then passed and our disappointment became a certainty. Our fondest hopes and expectations were blasted, and such a spirit of weeping came over us as I never experienced before. It seemed that the loss of all earthly friends could have been no comparison. We wept, and wept, till the day dawn.

I mused in my own heart, saying, My advent experience has been the richest and brightest of all my christian experience. If this had proved a failure, what was the rest of my christian experience worth? Has the Bible proved a failure? Is there no God—no heaven—no golden home city—no paradise? Is all this but a cunningly devised fable? Is there no reality to our fondest hopes and expectation of these things? And thus we had something to grieve and weep over, if all our fond hopes were lost. And as I said, we wept till the day dawn.

A second glance over past experience, and the lessons learned, and how when brought into strait places where light and help was needed by seeking the Lord he had answered by a voice and other ways, I began to feel there might be light and help for us in our present distress. I said to some of my brethren, Let us go to the barn. We entered the granary, shut the doors about us and bowed before the Lord. We prayed earnestly; for we felt our necessity. We continued in earnest prayer until the witness of the Spirit was given that our prayer was accepted, and that light should be given, our disappointment be explained, and made clear and satisfactory.

After breakfast I said to one of my brethren, "Let us go and see, and encourage some of our brn." We started, and while passing through a large field I was stopped about midway of the field. Heaven seemed open to my view, and I saw distinctly, and clearly, that instead of our High Priest coming out of the Most Holy of the heavenly sanctuary to come to this earth on the tenth day of the seventh month, at the end of the 2300 days, that he for the first time entered on that day the second apartment of that sanctuary; and that he had a work to perform in the Most Holy before coming to this earth. That he came to the marriage at that time; in other words, to the Ancient of days, to receive a kingdom, dominion, and glory; and we must wait for his return *from the wedding*; and my mind was directed to the tenth ch. of Rev. where I could see the vision had spoken and did not lie; the seventh angel had began [*sic*] to sound; we had eaten the littl [*sic*] book; it had been sweet in our mouth, and it had now become bitter in our belly, embittering our whole being. That we must prophesy again, etc., and that when the seventh angel began to sound, the temple of God was opened in heaven, and there was seen in his temple the ark of his testament, etc.

While I was thus standing in the midst of the field, my comrade passed on almost beyond speaking distance before missing me. He inquired, "Why I was stopping so long?" I replied, "The Lord was answering our morning prayer; by giving light with regard to our disappointment." I talked these things to my brethren.

In those days I was closely associated with O. R. L. Crosier; and Dr. F. B. Hahn, Crosier making his home with me a portion of the time. He examined the Bible on the subject of the sanctuary. F. B. Hahn and myself, was connected with Crosier in the publication of the paper called, "The Day-Dawn." Br. Hahn and myself, held a consultation with regard to the propriety of sending out the light on the subject of the sanctuary. We decided it was just what the scattered remnant needed; for it would explain our disappointment, and set the brethren on the right track. We agreed to share the expense between us, and said to Crosier, "Write out the subject of the sanctuary. Get out another number of the Day Dawn, and we will try to meet the expense." He did so, and the Day Dawn was sent out bearing the light on the sanctuary subject. It fell into the hands of Elders James White, and Joseph Bates, who readily endorsed the view; and it was shown in vision to be light for the remnant. This number of the Day Dawn opened a communication between us and these Eastern brethren. We appointed a conference of the scattered brethren to be held at my house, and invited these our Eastern brethren to meet with us. Br. W. made the effort to come; but his way was hedged up. Father Bates came on. His light was the seventh-day Sabbath.

From my understanding of the opening of the tabernacle of the *testimony* in heaven, and the seeing of the ark of his testimony, and a few lines I had seen from the pen of T. M. Preble, I had been looking at the subject of the seventh-day Sabbath and talking it to my Brn. I had said to them, "If we abide by . . .

HENRY B. BEAR, a little-known Millerite convert from Lancaster County, Pennsylvania, left the Millerite movement to join the Shakers. The following is the complete text of a printed pamphlet, *Henry B. Bear's Advent Experiences* (Whitewater, Ohio, n.d.), found by Lawrence Foster.

IN THE EARLY PART of the year 1843, then living in the town of Hempfield, county of Lancaster and State of Pennsylvania, there was loaned to me one volume of Miller's lectures on Christ's second coming, which, it stated, would take place during the very year upon which we had then entered. I read the lectures carefully at first, and later prayerfully. Miller's manner of reasoning; his explanation of the prophecies, and the starting point he gave to them, appeared to me so correct that they caused convictions to grow up in my mind that he was correct in his views. These convictions were much strengthened by the determined opposition of the professed disciples of Christ. My reasoning led me to inquire, did they love Christ as they professed? If so, all prophecies and evidences that looked toward a promise of his coming, they would, undoubtedly, very eagerly accept as evidence of such a promise, and a much desired glorified event, in which they had the promise of being glorified with their Redeemer. But not so; the professed church opposed it with all their power: they searched the scriptures, and hunted up all the evidence they could find to refute the prophecies favorable to his coming, thereby showing that they did not love His appearing; and this corresponded with the sayings of Christ: "When the son of man cometh, shall he find faith on the earth." Again, "There shall be scoffers in the last days, saying, where is the promise of His coming?" The behavior of the church convinced me that she was just in such a state as was prophesied she would be at the second appearing of Christ. She was not prepared and looking for such an event, any more than was I—a non-professor. I concluded to heed Miller's admonition to get ready, and if it did come, we would be prepared for it. I accordingly set about the work, being under very deep convictions that the history of my life would not stand the fiery trial of such an event as the second coming of Christ, to judge the world in righteousness. Therefore, according to the teachings of a blind church, I sought the remission of my sins through prayer and faith in a redeemer, and by perseverance in prayer, exercise of faith and sincere promises, it had the desired effect, so far as to remove my condemnation for the time being: which change of feeling I accepted as the forgiveness of my sins according to the aforesaid teaching. Whatever the error in teaching, prayer for and accepting the change as the remission of sins, it was a very great blessing in believing my sins were forgiven and that I was in a justified condition. Now I could live, hope and work, in fulfillment of my promise to God, in covenanting for the remission of my sins, which covenant I kept faithfully, and this caused me to be led to the judgement seat, where God has placed His name for the remission of sins.

At my conversion (so called) I had a very bright and sudden change of feeling, by which I was instantly relieved from the burden of my sins. My heart had felt throughout the day as heavy as a stone, but now became as light as a feather and my joy was full. Involuntarily I cried out with all my might, and thought if I could make all the world hear, I would; my love was so strong for all the human family at the time. For about a week everything appeared to me different, as if it were new. By and by this wore off, and I went through the different changes of cloudiness and sunshine, according to the experience of the professed Christians; sometimes hope strong, then again in doubt as to being in a safe condition.

Previous to my conversion I was in the liquor business, rectifying and redistilling liquors and manufacturing vinegar, etc. As the liquor business appeared to be inconsistent with my faith—particularly faith in the immediate coming of Christ—I thought it my duty to wind up that business. I had considerable of a stock of old liquor on hand, which, in order to wind up the business, I shipped to market and sold at wholesale for one-third its home value.

I was, by my conversion, a Millerite. Consequently, I was more interested in that doctrine than any other, and would preach it to others; this course, however, and that of others preaching against the advent doctrine, eventually brought about the difficulties hereinafter mentioned. The subject of baptism and uniting with a church coming up, and there being a church in our neighborhood called by its members "The Church of God," (and by others "Winebrennarians") who were quite favorable to the advent cause, admitting the Millerite lectures into their churches, and preaching it much themselves: and who baptized by immersion, (which baptism was according to my faith) I was baptized by them and joined their church. But eventually the preachers of this church turned more and more against the advent cause, until I felt that I was in reality both building up and pulling down the same cause—an inconsistency. We lived in a large house on the railroad; part of it was occupied as a dwelling and part for a warehouse and other purposes. There was ample room for holding meetings. At an appointment for preaching at our house one night, there was present a preacher of the church, and also an advent lecturer, who had become so separated and opposed in their views that I was obliged to take sides with one or the other: consequently I told the Winebrennarian how I felt on this subject, and that I was obliged to withdraw from them, as I could not support those who were pulling down what I was trying to build up. When the meeting commenced, the Winebrennarian spoke in reference to this difficulty, then wiped the dust off of his boots against us Millerites and invited the "People of God" to meet with him at another house not far off. So the Winebrennarians and the Millerites separated so far as we and our house were concerned. As stated before, being a Millerite, I of course made the study of prophecy, in relation to the coming of Christ, a labor, and I became strong in the faith of Christ's second coming at the time prophesied of in the scriptures, which, according to our calculations, ended in 1843. We afterward discovered that just such part of the year in which the prophecies started as had passed before their commencement, just so far would the time run over into the year 1844 to fulfill the full length of time in years. This brought the tarrying of the bridegroom and virgins, mentioned in Matt. 25th chap.: "And at midnight there was a cry made, behold the bridegroom cometh: go ye out to meet him." This cry the Millerites made on the 10th day of the seventh month, 1844. And on this day we thought would be ushered in the great year of jubilee of jubilees; when all the bondsmen of this world would be set free. Thus at last was the time definitely set for the expected event. This midnight cry brought another trial of my faith. It was preached to be necessary to have an undoubted faith in this particular time. I began to labor for it, and labored until I obtained it. In this labor I went through another conversion, which was my second—a change like unto the first. Here was a requirement to carry out in works, an undoubted faith, which I did.

It will be necessary here, to bring in my former companion in life, Julia Ann, as she acted a conspicuous part in this experience from this time out, although she was in this work with me from the beginning. At this time we received convictions that to live consistently with our faith in the Lord's coming on a particular day, we should work as having no doubts upon the subject. "Faith without works is dead." We were convicted that it was our duty to go to our relatives and tell them of our faith, that the Lord was coming on such a day; that this world would burn up, and all not prepared to meet him in peace would be burned up with it. Julia Ann received convictions that she ought to go without a bonnet, which conviction was produced by observing Isa. 3d chap. 18 to 23. We started, she without a bonnet. We went to her relatives first, some of them of the higher class of society. Some manifested considerable contempt for our weakness and insanity; others pitied us as poor deluded beings and again others trembled, fearing these things might come to pass. We passed around among the most of our relatives, doing as we thought, this duty, and returned home.

I next received convictions that I ought to go see those indebted to me, as I had been doing considerable business on the credit system. I presented my accounts; if they were paid, well, and if not, I told them I would square their accounts, as I believed the Lord would come by such a time which would settle up all accounts between creditor and debtor. Those who accepted of this offer I never asked afterward for pay, but those who did not (some would not) I had no hesitancy in asking for a settlement after our time passed by. The money I got I made use of in distributing advent publications, paying debts for the poor in the advent faith, as they had by this time quit work. Some had debts and the people would say that they had no right to quit work while being in debt, which was true. Therefore I paid their debts for them. I had some things for sale; when any person came to buy, I would let them have these articles. When they wanted to pay for them I would not receive it, telling them that the world was coming to an end by such a time, and I needed no money as it would do me no good. Of course they sometimes stared at me, astonished.

We had a little girl living with us. One Sabbath day the girl was out on the porch, (the house being close to the public road,) and some person riding by told her to go in the house and tell me to get up on the chimney top; signifying, of course, to be ready when "the Lord would descend with a shout and the trumpet of God."

As the 10th day of the seventh month (September) drew nigh we endeavored to get ready for the expected event. I got rid of all my money except eighty dollars; this I laid on the table, in our house; locked up the house, and gave the key to our neighbor, (a tenant in my father's house, near by,) to give to some of my folks. We now left, as we believed, never to return to that house: and went to one of the advent believers about three miles distant, where all the Millerites had agreed to meet and await the coming of the Lord within twenty-four hours, (so we believed.) However, shortly previous to this, there had been a question raised as to whether we had the correct time in regard to the tenth day of the seventh month being in September, or whether it was not in October. It appeared, the different jews, differed one month as to this time, some of them holding to September, and others to October. This circumstance rather shook my faith as to the day we had set in September being the correct one. My idea then was, that if the time was not correct as to September, it would be the more certain to come in October, this view of a month's delay seemed to me, would literally fulfill the scriptures, as regarding the tarrying of the bridegroom, a time for scoffers to be mocking, and saying, "Where is the promise of his coming?" etc. However, we looked anxiously and prayed, that our Redeemer should come, having sincerely relied upon the scriptures, and trusted confidently in the correctness of the prophecies, and the teaching of the spirit in relation to the same, therefore I could not bear the idea of a failure.

That the wicked should triumph and rejoice over us in our failure to realize what we so honestly believed and confidently predicted, was more than I felt to wish them the privilege of enjoying. Nevertheless they did have it. We looked in vain—we were disappointed. The scoffers had their day, and we had to bear it in humiliation.

We had concluded that if the event did not take place in September, to await the time in October, and not return home. In a day or two after our expected time passed by, we were invited by one of our neighbors to return home with him for company until October. In about a week after, my father and Julia Ann's uncle came to see us, and prevailed on us to return home, and see to our things, which we did. As we had not expected to live in this state of things beyond September, we made no provision for living beyond it; therefore, on returning home we found our store of eatables rather small. Our friends thought it best not to give us our money just then. I suppose they thought we ought to suffer some for our foolishness. We lived a little scantily a few days, but in a short time after they gave us our money, and were kind to help us again, as to making a living.

Some time after we had a prayer meeting, and at this time a gang came to stone and egg our house. They threw the eggs against the house and on the porch of the second story. Those eggs, Julia Ann left as a sign of persecution. She never washed them off while we lived in the house. This affair was instigated by some of our relatives, so we were informed afterwards.

We concluded to move to the west, and began to make arrangements accordingly by converting what property we had left into money. I was owner of one-half the house we lived in, and had some outstanding accounts, which I considered I was justifiable in collecting: such as were not accepted as presents, as previously stated. I was also owner of one-half of a warehouse in Columbia, Penn., which I could not bring into market at that time, but I got together ten or twelve hundred dollars, and several hundred dollars' worth of dry goods which I had previously received in a trade. Our bedding and some of our furniture we boxed up, and with it, we started for the west. We went on the canal; there was at that time no railroad finished through to Pittsburgh. We put all our blankets into a bundle and lost them in Cincinnati, I think the drayman stole them. We stored the goods in Cincinnati, and left on the Dayton canal for Miamisburg, ten miles south of Dayton, where I had a sister living. There we rented two rooms in the house of a distant relative. This family was very kind. I then returned to Cincinnati and got our goods and we commenced housekeeping again.

My intention was, before we left Pennsylvania, to manufacture alcohol from whisky for a business, and for that purpose I brought distilling apparatus with me. I went to Dayton to see whether there would be an opening there for this business. Being desirous to see some adventists, and knowing that people were very much in the habit of not giving such information to inquirers, I walked the pavement up and down through the market place, and viewed the people, to see some person I could trust to ask. I always prayed for guidance in such undertakings. The habit I have not left off yet; I met one whom I thought a candid, honest person; I asked him if he could tell me where I could find some adventists. He showed me the house where one resided close by—a very nice man with whom I had a very pleasant conversation on the advent question.

I could see nothing very encouraging in regard to my intended business in Dayton, so I returned home again. I then went to Cincinnati, but saw nothing that looked favorable there.

We desired to go to some neighborhood in which there were some adventists living and having learned that there were a number of them living in the neighborhood of Indianapolis, Ind., I concluded to go out there and see if I could find something to suit us.

There was an adventist living about one day's journey on the road to Indianapolis; I aimed to make that my point to stay the first night. He, by the way, was a perpetual motionist, about as much that as an adventist. When I got to his house, I was kindly received, but he said: "If you had not come this day, I would have finished my machine." Rather a sad misfortune to this world, as it has not got the machine perfected to this day.

We moved on a farm in Union county, Ind., the latter part of June, 1845, and things moved along smoothly for some months. We had very kind and clever neighbors. We said nothing, or very little, about our faith, which, however, never faltered as to the time of Christ's coming being near at hand. There were but a few advent believers in this neighborhood; one a preacher, living in Liberty, and John Creek, at whose home I had stayed two nights. We continued to take the advent papers to keep up with the progress of the movings of the spirit. The *Day Star*, edited by Enoch Jacobs in Cincinnati, seemed at this time to take the lead in bringing forward the most advanced ideas of the advent movement. In the fall a new light began to be advocated, that the promised kingdom which we were looking for was not a literal kingdom, but a spiritual one; that it comes not by outward observation; that it is within and already set up. This was a new idea to me, and I began to search the scriptures to see what I could find about this spiritual kingdom. The following scriptures were fastened in my mind: "Take no thought, saying, what shall we eat, or what shall we drink? or wherewithal shall we be clothed? But seek ye first the kingdom of God and his righteousness, and all things shall be added unto you." "The kingdom of God is like unto a treasure hid in a field: the which, when a man hath found, he hideth, and for joy thereof, goeth and selleth all that he hath, and buyeth that field." "Sell that thou hast and give to the poor, and thou shalt have a treasure in heaven, etc." Here I found there was some more work to be done—more sacrifices to be made. I had gotten a piece of land again, and here was a call to sell it and give it to the poor. I dare not make the excuse that I must first prove it; the call was "sell that thou hast and give to the poor." What, sell all and have nothing? The answer was, "there are many people that have nothing. You have hands; you can go to work and make a living." I thought again: when I sell my land, stock, grain, etc., and give it to the poor, that, I suppose, will suffice. The answer, "sell all thou hast." I thought again, we have beds which we need to sleep in. The answer again, "sell all thou hast." We certainly cannot do without a stove to cook with and dishes to eat out of. The answer again, "sell all thou hast." Well, this seemed a very tight place to be in: no home to live in, no bed to sleep on, no stove to cook with, no dishes to eat out of, nor anything to put in them, and no Savior to come to day, tomorrow or the day after that I know of. A kingdom, it is said, is set up, but where. Is it in America, Europe, Africa or Asia? When will I get there, or how can I find it? There is no person I know that can direct me thither, nor do I know that there is one set up on the earth at all. How can I know? I thought I had the evidence in the scriptures, and also the witness of the spirit within myself that Christ would come in 1843, but as He failed to come then, I was again positive it would take place in 1844. I had trusted in the prophecies and been disappointed. Now again I may perhaps labor myself into a faith that the kingdom of God is set up on earth; sell all I have, go out in search of it, not knowing where to go, and no one to direct, be at last disappoint, and a fool sure enough. On the other hand, can I bear the idea of stopping now, and coming short of the kingdom after having gone through so much, trusting my all in the scriptures and in God. I cannot bear this idea. In this case I would have acted the fool indeed, having lost my substance, my character, my friends, my all. And next, must my confidence in the scriptures and in God himself fail. Then, where am I? Yet, this must be the inevitable result in case of a failure, either now or hereafter. These were my thoughts, and they were very serious ones to me. If when trusting in the scriptures, and praying to God to enlighten, guide and direct me, and I obeying my convictions honestly and faithfully, be deceived and go astray, how could I trust any such being thereafter? I could not.

But then, I must trust him to the end. I had not come to a stopping place since the start, and have not been lost or really in the dark so as to be discouraged. And now I have light and convictions of duty which I must obey, else the fault will be mine for not obeying while seeing and being urged on to duty. Thus, many were my thoughts and convictions during 5 or 6 days. But at last I resolved to obey my convictions, sell all, give to the poor, and go out to seek the kingdom of God: but where, I knew not. When I had made the decision, I was blessed exceedingly. This was to me another (the third) conversion; and if laughing a week, almost constantly, is any sign of happiness, then was I happy. I think that was the happiest week in my life. I had no more fears, no doubts, as to the kingdom being set up or that I would be led to it. Nor had I any concern or care about anything. I felt so certain that our deliverance was near at hand. I thought I had got into an experience—a church where half hearted hypocrites could not enter. In this opinion I found out afterwards that I was mistaken.

When I made known that I would sell our farm, and the reasons for doing so became known, the people again considered me crazy. Our nearest neighbor wanted to buy a farm. His son for whom a farm was to be bought came to our house one morning. I told him I would sell them our farm. He said they would not buy from a crazy person. I then advertised the farm and personal property to sell at public sale. It was to be put up, and if it did not go above the price agreed upon, he was to have it at that: but, if it went above he was to get one half of the advance. This man got the farm according to our agreement. When we commenced selling the personal property, some of the people made an attempt to stop the sale. They accused the previously mentioned advent preacher, that it was through his influence I was selling out, that we would come to want, and that it was his duty to persuade me to stop the sale. But he said that he had nothing to do with it; that I acted upon my own faith, and I alone was responsible for what I did, and he would not interfere, consequently the sale went on, and the property sold at fair prices. At this time we heard that the adventists were gathering in Cincinnati, consequently we concluded to go to the city and await further inspiration.

Arriving in Cincinnati we went to a house where the adventists were in the habit of meeting. There were quite a number there at the time, and among them were three Shakers, Elder Philip Antis, Elder Joseph B. Agnew and Ezra Sherman, of Whitewater Village. When I saw the Shakers I thought they were Quakers in the advent faith. Elder Philip asked me if I was one of the little flock. I said I hoped so. I soon afterwards learned who they were, and also that some of the adventists had been to Whitewater Village. Consequently Shakerism was considerably discussed. I listened very attentively to what was said, for and against it. My suspicion was considerably awakened about the Shakers, thinking they might be deceivers. As I had quite lately so great a labor and struggle to free myself entirely from the world, I meant to be very cautious not to receive back again that which I had been called upon to forsake; and, this appeared to me, would be the case in uniting with the Shakers, as they had houses and lands, etc., the very same things I was called upon to forsake.

Learning that Enoch Jacobs had gone down the river to Madison, I was very anxious to see him. Consequently I started down to the steamboat landing to take a passage for Madison. Just as I got to the landing near the boat, my previously faith-quieted tooth began to ache severely. I stopped at once, thinking, what does this mean? Inspiration came saying, "you must not go after Enoch Jacobs." My reply was, "if this be a true warning, my prayer is that my tooth may not quit aching before the boat leaves; in that case I will not go; but if it quits aching previous to the leaving of the boat, then it shall be a sign that I should go.["] I waited to see the result. The tooth ached, the boat started, and I returned back. Whether this was the end of my immortality faith of the natural body, I can not now state positively, but think I was convinced of that error after uniting with the Shakers. In the evening there was a meeting at the house and we remained. Elder Philip Antis spoke some. I noticed in his remarks he encouraged the adventists to "go on." The words "go on" struck me particularly as being different from anything I had heard in my experience from those outside of our faith. The cry was "come back, you are going astray, you are going crazy, etc." The words "go on" impressed me with this idea: Here is a person that speaks as though he comprehends our whereabouts, and understands our path ahead. The meeting over I went to bed thinking. About midnight I awoke, and the following scriptures came into my mind, "By this shall all men know, that ye are my disciples, if ye have love one for another." My mind was called to the Shakers: to compare their love with that of the adventists. The principle of a united consecration convinced me of their superior love, for while the Shakers lived in common in their houses, the adventists were living, some in fine houses, and others in poor rented hovels. Some could, and would, ride in fine carriages, while others had to walk. In view of these facts I had concluded that the manifest love of the Shakers condemned that of the adventists. Again, Isa. 3, 18 to 23, "In that day I will take away the bravery of their tinkling ornaments, the ornaments about their feet and legs. Their chains, and the bracelets, and the mufflers, the head bands, the tablets and earrings, the wimples, and the crisping-pins," etc. Here again I had to acknowledge that those ornaments were more or less among the adventists. My attention was again called to the Shakers, and was shown that there those things would be taken away. In this way I was, before day, almost persuaded that the Shakers were in possession of the kingdom we were looking for and which had cost us so much tribulation.

There was a general feeling among the adventists that they were going up to the Shakers to take possession of the kingdom. Quoting the scriptures: "Fear not, little flock; it is the Father's good pleasure to give you the kingdom." As though God had prepared through the Shakers a kingdom expressly for us, and would deliver it up to the adventists wholesale. It was a very common saying we are going up to take "Ai." But I got strong suspicions by this time that the taking would be in the other direction; that the captives would be out of the ranks of the adventists. At this time there was an appointment made to hold a convention at Whitewater Village on Thursday of the following week by the Adventists and Shakers. However, I, in company with a few others, left Cincinnati on Saturday and arrived at Whitewater Village on Sabbath morning, previous to the convention. Julia Ann remained in the city until the following Wednesday to attend to some duties. We were admitted into meeting on Sabbath. I was much affected in meeting; it appeared to me a very solemn mode of worship. I read some, and was considerably convinced that the Shakers had the truth. There seemed to be some difficulty in my way to unite; that was, I knew my former experience was correct, that I was led by God. I could not see but that by uniting with the Shakers I would be throwing away my experience—denying it—and that I could not do. But on Monday morning I went up into the woodshed loft and communed with God on this wise: "I have come this far, (thou hast led me,) and I have obeyed thee to the forsaking of all, and going out to seek the kingdom of God. It is asserted that this is it; if so, grant me to see it, and I will obey." After this I went into the house, in the room where I stayed. Elder Joseph B. Agnew came in. We entered into conversation about the faith. There had not been much said before he asked me whether I had thought anything about the confessions of sins to man? I answered, that it was a subject new to me, that I knew that the Catholics confessed sins but that I had no faith in such confessions. I said further that I had read some upon the subject in a small pamphlet ("Exposition"), and I found there was more evidence in favor than I was aware of. But just here there was another convincing evidence presented itself to me.

All my sins rolled back upon my conscience, which I had thought were forgiven me, in my first conversion, three years previous. I began to think what does this mean: there must be something wrong about my conscience. What caused these convictions? The answer: speaking with this man about the confession of sins, brought them all back with the full weight of condemnation, therefore they could not have been forgiven, and I received convictions at once that I ought to confess them. According to the promise I had just made to God in my prayer, that I would obey the light given me, I dared not delay obedience to convictions; I therefore said to Elder Joseph, there can be no harm in confessing my sins, I would do so, and went with him to his room, and made an honest confession of all my sins that I could think of at the time. I think I was not as long about coming to the conclusion to make my confession, from the time Elder Joseph and I commenced talking about it, as I have been penning the relation of it. Nor was the idea of being a Shaker included in the above decision; I only thought to obey the light as fast as it was made known to me, according to my promise. But no sooner had I made my opening, than all was plain, and as clear as day. I had no more trouble in harmonizing my experience with entering into the kingdom of God. It was all beautiful and harmonious. I could literally see the circuitious [sic] road; I came along the winding mountain, ascending from the plain below up to the top of the mountain, and entering in at the arched gate into the everlasting plain above—the kingdom of God. I now felt that the most dangerous part of my journey was over.

And here I wish to say that the greatest blessing, help and encouragement I had in the aforesaid dangerous journey, was that Julia Ann, was always ready and willing to obey any increase of light, no matter how great the sacrifice required, or what tribulation obedience to such light would lead us into. I do not know that she ever expressed a fear or doubt in relation to any move or sacrifice I felt called upon to make, and always appeared to be glad for any call to go forward, and never hesitated for fear of consequences. When she came to Whitewater Village three or four days after I had come, I told her that I had confessed my sins, that this was undoubtedly the kingdom we had gone out to seek. She received the news with gladness and said, "This is too good news, I expected we would have much more trouble and tribulation before we would find a resting place." She had no hesitancy in making the decision to enter into the inheritance.

By Thursday, the appointed time for the convention, many adventists had arrived; I suppose not far short of a hundred. The believers and adventists assembled in the meeting house; the believers sat in order, and some of the elders spoke to the assembly, but of what I do not now remember. Afterwards the adventists argued the question of Shakerism among themselves, pro. and con., until they all took sides, either for or against it, and then they separated; some were wise virgins, and had oil in their lamps, and entered in, while the other foolish virgins went to buy more oil. In the evening of the same day we had a meeting, in which Enoch Jacobs spoke, and said, in his remarks, that if he thought that he had the least spark of pride in him, he would get right down on the floor and roll over; the remark caused me to think, "have I any pride remaining in me?" "How would I like to roll on the floor before all these people?" My feelings soon convinced me of pride within, and I received convictions that I ought to get down on the floor and roll: I took resolution and did so. The Shakers present followed suit immediately, and then many of the adventists. Consequently it began to work on Enoch Jacobs, and he got down at last, but his awkward, still unnatural movements, convinced me that he had some pride left, if they did not convince himself.

In the beginning of my Shaker life I said, to some of the old believers, that I thought I had passed over the most difficult and dangerous part of the road, that my hardest trials were over. They thought not. But now, in twenty-seven years' experience of Shaker life, I have not had any thing like as hard, difficult and dangerous trials as I had in my former experience. I have often said, "not for all the world would I have missed going through my advent experience; nor for all the world would I want to go through it again.["] Although in the advent my confidence was strong, my faith undoubted the greater part of the time, yet it was not always so. At times I was exceedingly happy, but, after all, it was faith and hope: whereas in the present work, it is knowledge and sight, not faith and hope. St. Paul said in Romans, 8, 24–25. "Hope that is seen, is not hope: for what a man seeth, why doth he hope for? But if we hope for what we see not, (as did we) then do we with patience wait for it;" as also did we wait, but now as we have waited, seen and received, faith and hope is changed into sight, and knowledge. In my former experience I had to act upon belief only, but now upon knowledge and in obedience to direct counsel from a visable [sic] lead. Here no evil spirits can come, believers to deceive; therefore it is much less difficult to obey, because certain.

Contributors

ERIC ANDERSON (Ph.D., University of Chicago, 1978) is Professor and Chairman, Department of History, Pacific Union College, Angwin, California. A specialist in Afro-American history, he is the author of *Race and Politics in North Carolina, 1872–1901: The Black Second* (Baton Rouge: Louisiana State University Press, 1981) and a contributor to Howard Rabinowitz, ed., *Southern Black Leaders of the Reconstruction Era* (Urbana: University of Illinois Press, 1982). With Alfred A. Moss, Jr., he is currently writing a history of philanthropy and black education, 1880–1954, for which they received a Ford Foundation Research Fellowship.

DAVID T. ARTHUR (Ph.D., University of Rochester, 1970) is Professor of History at Aurora University, Aurora, Illinois, where from 1974 to 1982 he served as Academic Dean. A former Danforth Fellow, he wrote a doctoral dissertation titled " 'Come out of Babylon': A Study of Millerite Separatism and Denominationalism, 1840–1865." He is the author of "Millerism" in Edwin S. Gaustad, ed., *The Rise of Adventism* (New York: Harper & Row, 1974), and of "After the Great Disappointment: To Albany and Beyond," *Adventist Heritage* (January, 1974).

MICHAEL BARKUN (Ph.D., Northwestern University, 1965) is Professor of Political Science at Syracuse University, where he has taught since 1965. He is a recipient of fellowships from the Ford Foundation and the National Endowment for the Humanities and has served on the council of the International Society for the Comparative Study of Civilizations. His numerous publications include *Law without Sanctions: Order in Primitive Societies and the World Community* (New Haven: Yale University Press, 1968); *Disaster and the Millennium* (New Haven: Yale University Press, 1974), which appeared in a Japanese translation in 1985 and in an American paperback edition (Syracuse University Press) in 1986; and *Crucible of the Millennium: The Burned-Over District of New York in the 1840s* (Syracuse, N.Y.: Syracuse University Press, 1986), which explores Millerism and utopian communities in upstate New York.

LOUIS BILLINGTON (M.A., University of Bristol, 1966) is Chairperson of the American Studies Programme at the University of Hull, where he has been a lecturer since 1967. He is the author of many papers on nineteenth-century British and American religious history and social reform, as well as a forthcoming book on *Popular Evangelicalism in Britain and North America, 1730–1850*

(London: Methuen), which includes a discussion of Millerism. His current research, on the roles of women preachers in early-nineteenth-century New England, has resulted in an article on " 'Female Laborers in the Church': Women Preachers in the Northeastern United States, 1790–1840," *Journal of American Studies* (December, 1985).

JONATHAN M. BUTLER (Ph.D., University of Chicago, 1975) is a Visiting Scholar in the Department of History, University of California, Riverside. He formerly taught in the Department of History and Political Science at Loma Linda University, where for a decade he served as editor of *Adventist Heritage: A Journal of Adventist History*. His writings on millenarianism include "Adventism and the American Experience," in Edwin S. Gaustad, ed., *The Rise of Adventism* (New York: Harper & Row, 1974); and "From Millerism to Seventh-day Adventism: 'Boundlessness to Consolidation,' " *Church History* (March, 1986). He is currently completing a book tentatively titled *Ellen G. White and Victorian America: A Study of Prophecy, Culture, and Social Change*, for which he received a fellowship from the National Endowment for the Humanities.

RUTH ALDEN DOAN (Ph.D., University of North Carolina at Chapel Hill, 1984) is Assistant Professor of History at Hollins College, Roanoke, Virginia, where she teaches American history. She is the author of *The Miller Heresy, Millennialism, and American Culture* (Philadelphia: Temple University Press, 1987).

LAWRENCE FOSTER (Ph.D., University of Chicago, 1976) is an Associate Professor in the School of Social Sciences at the Georgia Institute of Technology in Atlanta, where he has taught since 1977. A former Woodrow Wilson and Ford Foundation fellow, he has written extensively on American social and religious history. His book *Religion and Sexuality* (New York: Oxford University Press, 1981; paperback edition, University of Illinois Press, 1984) is a comparative study of the Shakers, the Mormons, and the Oneida Community that won the Mormon History Association award for "best book of the year in Mormon history." His second book, now nearing completion, is entitled *Women, the Family, and Alternative Lifestyles in America: Essays on the Shakers, the Mormons, and the Oneida Community*. During 1981–1982 he held a fellowship from the National Endowment for the Humanities to begin research for a book on Antioch College and innovation in American higher education, tentatively entitled *Antioch—The Unfinished Revolution*. In 1985–1986 he served as a Visiting Fulbright Professor of American History at the University of Sydney in Australia and at the University of Auckland in New Zealand.

RONALD D. GRAYBILL (Ph.D., Johns Hopkins University, 1983) is Assistant Professor of History, Loma Linda University. Formerly Associate Director of the Ellen G. White Estate, he is the author of *Ellen G. White and Church Race*

Relations (Washington, D.C.: Review and Herald Publishing Association, 1970); *Mission to Black America: The Story of J. Edson White and the Riverboat Morning Star* (Mountain View, Calif.: Pacific Press, 1971); and an unpublished dissertation on "The Power of Prophecy: Ellen G. White and the Women Religious Founders of the Nineteenth Century." He is currently working on an interpretive biography of White.

WAYNE R. JUDD (M.A., Andrews University, 1965; B.D. Andrews University, 1966) is Vice President for College Advancement at Columbia Union College in Takoma Park, Maryland. From 1975 to 1984 he taught history and religion at Pacific Union College. A prolific writer of popular books and articles, he has studied American religious history at the Graduate Theological Union in Berkeley, California.

JAMES R. NIX (M.Div., Andrews University, 1972; MSLS, University of Southern California, 1975) is Chairman of the Department of Archives and Special Collections, Loma Linda University Libraries. From 1975 to 1980 he served as Managing Editor of *Adventist Heritage: A Journal of Adventist History*. His current activities include the preparation of a comprehensive descriptive bibliography of Ellen G. White imprints in English, 1846–1917.

JANET S. NUMBERS (Ph.D., University of Wisconsin-Madison, 1983) is a clinical psychologist on the staff of the Dean Medical Center in Madison, Wisconsin. From 1983 to 1985 she was a postdoctoral fellow at the Menninger Foundation in Topeka, Kansas. In addition to several articles in psychology, she has written (with Ronald L. Numbers) "Science in the Old South: A Reappraisal," *Journal of Southern History* (May, 1982); and "The Psychological World of Ellen White," *Spectrum* (August, 1983).

RONALD L. NUMBERS (Ph.D., University of California, Berkeley, 1969) is Professor of the History of Medicine and the History of Science at the University of Wisconsin-Madison. Formerly on the faculties of Andrews University and Loma Linda University, he was the founding editor of *Adventist Heritage: A Journal of Adventist History*. He has written or edited numerous books, including *Prophetess of Health: A Study of Ellen G. White* (New York: Harper & Row, 1976); and, with David C. Lindberg, *God and Nature: Historical Essays on the Encounter between Christianity and Science* (Berkeley and Los Angeles: University of California Press, 1986). He is currently completing a history of creationism in the twentieth century, for which he received awards from the John Simon Guggenheim Memorial Foundation and the National Science Foundation.

DAVID L. ROWE (Ph.D., University of Virginia, 1974) is Assistant Professor of History at Middle Tennesee State University in Murfreesboro, where he has taught American history and historic preservation since 1981. Prior to that time he served as Executive Director of Landmarks Association of Central New York, Inc., in Syracuse, New York. In addition to the book *Thunder and Trumpets: Millerites and Religious Dissent in Upstate New York, 1800–1850* (Chico, Calif.: Scholars Press, 1985), he has written several articles on Millerite history. He is currently working on a cultural biography of William Miller.

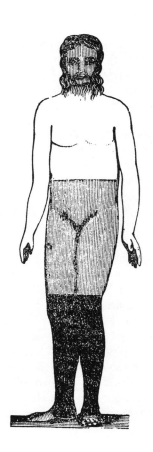

Index